Cavendish
Publishing
Limited

CIVIL LIBERTIES

TITLES IN THE SERIES

Cavendish
Publishing
Limited

CIVIL LIBERTIES

Helen Fenwick, BA, LLB
Lecturer in Law
University of Durham

First published in Great Britain 1996 by Cavendish Publishing Limited, The Glass House, Wharton Street, London WC1X 9PX

Telephone: 0171-278 8000 Facsimile: 0171-278 8080

British Library Cataloguing in Publication Data. A catalogue record for this book is available from the British Library.

ISBN 1 85941 165 7

Cover photograph by Jerome Yeats

Printed and bound in Great Britain

Preface

This book is intended for the student studying law at degree level or on the Common Professional Examination course. It will also be helpful to students who are taking some courses in law as part of their course or as an option. Apart from students taking a course in civil liberties, it will be helpful for those taking constitutional law or public law. Subjects such as public order, police powers, and the Bill of Rights question often form a large part of such courses but are sometimes not treated in sufficient detail, or in a very accessible manner, in constitutional law textbooks.

This book is intended to be used as lecture notes and the margins of the pages can be used by the student to add further material. A summary together with key cases is presented at the end of each topic on sheets which can be removed for ease of revision. The book is based on my textbook on civil liberties which provides a more extensive coverage of the topics, coupled with a greater emphasis on critical opinion.

The topics chosen reflect those generally found on civil liberties courses. However, civil liberties, perhaps more than any other subject, is rapidly developing and this book seeks to concentrate on those areas which are of particular interest at the present time. These include: moves towards freedom of information, the curtailment of the right to silence and the extension of police powers under the Criminal Justice and Public Order Act 1994. The position of the UK – as almost the only democracy without a Bill of Rights or a Freedom of Information Act – is arguably coming to seem untenable, and this is reflected in the growing acceptance of the influence of the European Convention on Human Rights. Therefore this book emphasises the significance of the Convention.

The law is stated as at 10 February 1996.

Helen Fenwick
February 1996

Contents

Table of Cases

Table of Statutes

Chapter 1

Civil Rights and Civil Liberties

This book is intended to provide an analysis of the legal protection given to civil liberties in the UK. The term 'civil liberties' is the name used to denote the areas of freedom which correspond with the broad class of rights generally known as civil and political rights. In many western democracies the rights of citizens are enshrined in a constitutional document sometimes known as a Bill or Charter of Rights. As part of constitutional law these rights of citizens are protected because constitutional law comes highest in the hierarchy of laws in two senses: firstly, it cannot be changed as easily as other laws, and secondly, it constrains other laws – if they conflict with it they will to that extent be repealed. The UK, however, has no Bill of Rights in the modern sense and therefore in order to discover which freedoms are protected and the extent of that protection, it is necessary to examine the common law, statutes and the influence of Treaties to which the UK is a party, especially the European Convention on Human Rights. Certain particular characteristics of the UK constitution determine the means of protecting civil liberties in the UK. The doctrine of the supremacy of Parliament means that constitutional law can be changed in the ordinary way – by Act of Parliament. Thus Parliament has the power to abridge freedoms which in other countries are seen as fundamental rights. It follows from this that all parts of the law are equal – there is no hierarchy of laws and therefore constitutional law cannot constrain other laws. Further, there is no judicial review of Acts of Parliament: a judge cannot declare a statutory provision invalid because it conflicts with a fundamental right. So, for example, if a statute is passed containing a provision which constrains freedom of speech, a judge must merely apply it, whereas in a country with a Bill of Rights the law would be struck down as unconstitutional. However, there is a constraint on this process: if the judge considers that the provision in question is ambiguous he or she may interpret it in such a way that freedom of speech is maintained, either by relying on the common law doctrine of respect for fundamental rights or on the European Convention on Human Rights (see Chapter 3).

Thus, in general, civil liberties in the UK are in a more precarious position than in other countries (although this does not necessarily mean that they are always less well protected:

1.1   Introduction

sometimes Bills of Rights give only theoretical protection to freedom: see Chapter 11). Civil liberties are residual, not entrenched as in other countries: they are the residue of freedom left behind after the legal restrictions have been defined. Civil liberties may be seen as areas of freedom of action surrounded by legal constraints which press upon them; sometimes such constraints encroach more, sometimes less. Another way of putting it is to say that civil liberties in the UK are 'interstitial' in the sense that they exist only in the interstices of the law. The aim of this book is to identify these areas of freedom but before doing so some indications of the theoretical basis of rights and liberties, with possible justifications for their restriction, will be given and this will provide a context within which civil liberties in the UK can be examined. Only a very brief indication of one of the leading theories can be given here as this is a subject on which there is a vast literature and a number of schools of thought.

1.2   The liberal conception of rights

The liberal conception of rights can be seen to owe its antecedents to the school of so-called social contractarians. The school found perhaps its earliest advocate in the writings of John Locke. Locke imagined an actual social contract between individuals and the state at the setting up of civil society in which citizens, in order to secure the protection of their property, handed over certain powers (most importantly a monopoly of coercive force) to the government, in return for the guarantee of certain rights. Locke thus introduced the idea, which is still central to liberalism today, that the overriding purpose of the state is the securing and protection of its citizen's basic liberties.

1.2.1   Rawls' theory of rights

The idea of the social contract is thus clearly an immensely potent one, and it is John Rawls' revival and radical revision of the idea in his *A theory of Justice* (1972) which has almost singlehandedly transformed the face of political theory; as HLA Hart has commented, rights-based theories have replaced utilitarianism as the primary focus of attention.

Rawls imagines not an actual, but a hypothetical social contract taking place in what he terms 'the original position'. The essential feature of this position is that the contractors (Rawls' men) are devising amongst themselves the outlines of 'the foundation charter of their society' whilst behind 'the veil of ignorance'. The men are ignorant not only of what will be their positions in the future social hierarchy, but also of their skills, weaknesses, preferences and conceptions of the good life – whether, for example, they will be a strict Muslim or an humanist academic. Since none of the contractors know what mode of life he will wish to pursue he is bound (if he is rational) to choose a tolerant society, and one which guarantees him the rights necessary to pursue any individual goals he may in future choose. In other words, Rawls' men will wish to put in place the means whereby they will in future be able to pursue their goals rather than adopting structures which might in future prevent them from doing so.

Thus, almost any conception of the good life will require for example freedom from arbitrary arrest, the right to a fair trial and freedom from inhuman treatment. In addition, the man who will become the Muslim might in *future* wish to restrict freedom of speech on religious matters, but at *present*, self-interest dictates that he consider the possibility that his conception of the good life might necessarily include the exercise of freedom of speech. Thus Rawls' men adopt, *inter alia*, 'the first principle,' stating that: 'each person is to have an equal right to the most extensive, total system of equal basic liberties compatible with a similar system of liberty for all'. These basic liberties are identical with any familiar list of civil and political rights.

Although similar to Rawls in political outlook, Ronald Dworkin offers a theoretical construct which derives rights in a different manner, and indeed has criticised Rawls' theory, arguing that a *hypothetical* unlike an *actual* contract provides no grounds for binding actual people to its terms.

1.2.2   Dworkin's thesis: protection for unpopular or minority rights

Dworkin attempts to derive rights from the premise, which he hopes all will agree to, that the state owes a duty to treat all of its citizens with equal concern and respect. Dworkin is not concerned with defending rights from despotic and repressive governments, and indeed he sees no need to protect – by designating them as rights – those individual interests which the *majority* would like to see protected, as these will in any case be ensured by the democratic process which he assumes as a background to his theory. Dworkin's particular concern is to justify the protection of *unpopular* or minority rights – or those whose exercise may on occasion threaten the overall well-being of the community – because such rights would potentially be put at risk if their validity were to be determined through a democratic vote.

For example, if the question whether homosexual acts should be permitted in private between adults were to be decided by a majority vote, homosexuals would express their preference for freedom to perform those acts. Certain heterosexuals, however, would vote against allowing this freedom because their preference is that homosexuals should not be free to commit such acts.

Thus, resolution of the question could be affected by the fact that certain citizens think that the homosexual way of life is not deserving of equal respect; a decision would therefore have been made at least partly on the basis that the way of life of certain citizens was in some way contemptible. If the government enforced this decision through the use of coercive force (the criminal law) it would clearly have failed in its central duty to treat its citizens with equal concern and respect; in other words democracy has an in-built means of undermining its own promise of equality. Since protecting this promise of equality is for Dworkin the central postulate of political morality, he finds that homosexuals should be granted a right to moral autonomy which cannot be overridden even by a majority decision-making process.

1.3   The nature of a right: conflicts with other claims

If a right is conceded to exist, it must next be asked what is and should be the nature and strength of the protection thereby given? If the right is framed or has developed in such a way as to be open-ended in scope with in-built exceptions, how should judges approach conflicts between the right and the claims of society?

1.3.1   The strength of a right

Dworkin has argued persuasively that certain rights which he calls 'strong' or 'trump' rights should almost always prevail against general public interests. The idea of such inviolable rights may seem extreme but is in fact accepted by all civilised countries in the case, for example, of torture. It is not thought to be a sound argument for a government to assert that it is justified in torturing certain of its citizens on the grounds that it can increase the general welfare thereby. The acceptance of this principle is attested to by the lack of exceptions to the right to freedom from torture in all international human rights treaties including the European Convention of Human Rights (see Articles 15(2) and (3)).

Dworkin explains the distinction between 'strong' and 'weak' rights as follows. He gives as an example of the latter a legal right to drive either way on a two-way road; such a right is a 'weak' legal right because it is not an important human interest which is likely to be denied to certain groups through the influence of external preferences. It follows, therefore, that such a right could justifiably be overridden by the government (through making the road one-way) if it thought it in the general interest to do so. By contrast, his conception of the strength of 'trump rights' leads to his insistence that an assertion of (for example) a right to free speech held by citizens 'must imply that it would be wrong for the government to stop them from speaking, even when the government believes that what they say will cause more harm than good'.

It can be seen from the above that Dworkin gives us a very clear prescription for the approach that a judge should take in weighing strong or 'trump' rights against the general welfare of society. He roundly condemns the idea that a judge, in adjudicating upon a right, or a government in framing it, should carefully weigh up the right of the citizen against the possible adverse social consequences, accepting that it may sometimes err on the side of society, sometimes on the side of the individual, but on the whole getting the balance about right. 'It must be wrong', he argues, to consider that 'inflating rights is as serious as invading them'. For to invade a right is to affront human dignity or treat certain citizens as less worthy of respect than others, while to inflate a right is simply to pay 'a little more in social efficiency' than the government *already* has to pay in allowing the right at all. Thus, for Dworkin, if one asserts a 'trump' right, ordinary counter arguments about a decrease in the welfare of society as a whole are simply irrelevant.

In what circumstances, then, might Dworkin consider that a strong individual right may be overridden? His position here is not entirely clear, but it is submitted that three justifications for infringement, which are generally accepted by liberal thought, can be identified.

- Competing rights

  Firstly, there is the situation in which there is a clear competing individual claim, so that the exercise of the original right will directly infringe the competing right. The paradigmatic example of such a collision of individual rights is where one individual uses his right of free speech to defame another. Another is where one incites violence against other, thus infringing his right to security of the person. In such cases, since both rights are as it were from the same class of 'strong' rights, a common sense balancing act is all that may be undertaken.

- The right is not fully at stake

  The second situation in which rights may be overridden is one where the values protected by the right are not at stake in this particular situation. In other words, it may be argued that most rights have a core, the invasion of which will constitute an actual overriding of the right; they also have a penumbra – an area in which the value the right protects is present only in a weaker form. An invasion of the penumbra may be said to constitute only an *infringement* of the right and may therefore be more readily justified. The argument that commercial speech or hard core pornography should not be afforded the same protection as other kinds of speech may rest on the

1.3.2   Rights in conflict with other interests

argument that it is in the penumbra of free speech; by contrast, political speech is clearly in the core of free speech.

- A real risk to society

  The third situation justifying infringement is one in which the exercise of a right may pose a real danger to society. In such cases liberals are unwilling to take danger to mean danger to some abstract attribute to society, such as its moral health, but rather insist that the danger must be ultimately a threat to some concrete aspect of its citizens' well being. Thus, typically, liberals are hostile to characterising the likelihood of shocking or offending citizens as a concrete harm justifying the suppression of the right of free speech. Dworkin's own, very stringent test, is that rights may only be overridden on the basis of a risk to society if the state demonstrates 'a clear and substantial risk' that exercise of the right 'will do great damage to the person or property of others'. This test, due to its stringency, tends not to find expression in Charters of Rights; the criterion laid down, for example, by the European Court of Human Rights for curtailing the right of free expression as set out in Article 10 of the European Convention on Human Rights (ECHR), does not even approach Dworkin's prescription either in stringency or clarity; instead it has adopted the somewhat weak and uncertain phrase, 'a pressing social need'. Dworkin's rights-analysis should not therefore be taken as a description of how rights and liberties are *actually* treated in the UK and under the ECHR, but rather as a particular ideal against which the reality of such 'rights'-protection can be measured.

1.4   Distinguishing rights and liberties

Having given an account of what in general terms an assertion of a right means in the liberal tradition, we may now turn to an analysis of the more specific claims that the assertion of a right may entail, and employ this analysis to make a few general remarks about the nature of 'rights' protection in the UK.

1.4.1   Hohfeld's analysis

One of the more influential attempts to analyse closely the nature of a right was made by the American jurist Wesley Hohfeld. Broadly speaking, Hohfeld attempted to demonstrate how claims of rights in everyday language can in fact be broken down into three more specific claims. Firstly, if it is claimed that X has a right proper, or 'claim right' to A this means that persons generally, or specific persons are under some specific corresponding duty to ensure that X has access to A. Secondly, X may be said to have an immunity as against a particular person or body; this means that they are disabled from interfering with the exercise by X of the interest (A) protected by the immunity. Thirdly, if X has only a liberty (what Hohfeld calls a privilege) to do A, this far weaker claim merely means that X does no wrong in exercising his liberty – the rights of others are not thereby infringed. However, no-one has a duty to allow him to exercise A or assist him to exercise it.

Hohfeld's explanation is a useful analytical tool; it can be seen by utilising it that Dworkin is advocating that rights be set out as a series of immunities – areas of entitlements which even democratically elected governments are disabled from interfering with. The USA constitutions and its amendments represent such a list of immunities. In applying Hohfeld's theory to 'rights' protection in the UK it can be seen that it endows the commentator with the ability to distinguish between the different forms of protection offered towards different freedoms. If Dworkin's analysis is used, all rights in the UK are 'weak', since all are at least theoretically subject to infringement by Parliament, whereas under Hohfeld's view, the picture is more mixed.

1.4.2 Hohfeld applied to the reality of 'rights' protection

- Civil liberties

  Most freedoms in the UK are merely liberties; one does no wrong to exercise them, but there is no positive duty on any organ of the state to allow or facilitate them. For example, the Public Order Act 1986 nowhere places upon Chief Constables a duty to ensure freedom of association and speech (see Chapter 6). These freedoms thus exist, as do most of our liberties, in the interstices of the law – as explained above a liberty is simply an area of human activity which at present is unregulated by the law. As no explicit recognition is in general given to claim rights or immunities judges feel able to allow curtailment of areas of freedom where a competing public interest is in issue even where it does not represent a pressing social need.

- Civil rights

  By contrast, certain UK provisions clearly have the quality of Hohfeldian claim rights, rather than mere liberties, in that they *are* protected by a positive correlative duty. For example, arrestees have the right of access to a solicitor while in police custody as guaranteed by s 58 of the Police and Criminal Evidence Act 1984 (see Chapter 8 at para 8.10).

- No guarantee of permanent freedoms

  Even when a citizen holds a right there are no domestic *legal* guarantees that the legislation providing the positive protection will not be repealed. Similarly, a citizen enjoying a liberty can never be certain that legislation will not be introduced into a previously unregulated area thus destroying or limiting that liberty. Such legal guarantees cannot exist, whilst the doctrine of untrammelled Parliamentary sovereignty remains. Thus in the UK the price we pay for our particular conception of democracy is the quality of potential impermanence which is shared by all our rights and liberties.

Summary of Chapter 1

Civil Rights and Civil Liberties

The term 'civil liberties' is the name used to denote the broad class of rights generally known as civil and political rights as they are recognised in the UK. In many western democracies the rights of citizens are enshrined in a constitutional document sometimes known as a Bill or Charter of Rights. The UK, however, has no Bill of Rights in the modern sense and therefore in order to discover which freedoms are protected and the extent of that protection, it is necessary to examine the common law, statutes and the influence of Treaties to which the UK is a party, especially the European Convention on Human Rights. Once the extent of restraints on liberty created by law are examined the area of freedom which is left can be identified.

The liberal theory of rights

Locke postulated a social contract between individuals and the state at the setting up of civil society in which citizens, in order to secure the protection of their property, handed over certain powers (most importantly a monopoly of coercive force) to the government, in return for the guarantee of certain rights. Rawls took this idea further in putting forward 'the first principle', which states that as part of his imagined social contract: 'each person is to have an equal right to the most extensive, total system of equal basic liberties compatible with a similar system of liberty for all'. These basic liberties are identical with any familiar list of civil and political rights. Dworkin's particular concern, in contrast, was to justify the protection of *unpopular* or minority rights – or those whose exercise may on occasion threaten the overall well-being of the community – because such rights would potentially be put at risk if their validity were to be determined through a democratic vote.

The nature of a right: conflicts with other claims

Dworkin has argued that certain rights which he calls 'strong' or 'trump' rights should almost always prevail against general public interests because to invade a right is an affront to human dignity or a failure to treat humans with equal concern and respect. However, in general, three justifications for curtailment of rights which are generally accepted by liberal thought may be identified. Firstly, there is the situation in which two strong individual rights collide. Speech inciting violence against a certain racial group would provide an example of such a collision. In such circumstances the rights must be balanced against each other. Secondly, there may be circumstances in which the right is not fully at stake. For this reason commercial speech or hard core pornography will not be afforded the same protection as other kinds of speech. The third situation justifying infringement is one in which the exercise of a right may pose a real danger to society. Dworkin's own test requires the state to demonstrate 'a clear and substantial risk' that exercise of the right 'will do great damage to the person or property of others'. This test, due to its stringency, tends not to find expression in Charters of Rights; the criterion laid down, for example, by the European Court of Human Rights for curtailing the right of free expression as set out in Article 10 adopts the weaker and more uncertain phrase, 'a pressing social need'. In considering the protection to be afforded to liberties in the UK, judges will afford precedence to general public interests on an even weaker basis.

Distinguishing rights and liberties

Hohfeld attempted to demonstrate how claims of rights in everyday language can be broken down into three more specific claims. Firstly, if it is claimed that X has a right proper, or 'claim right' to A this means that persons generally, or specific persons are under some specific corresponding duty to ensure that X has access to A. Secondly, X may be said to have an immunity as against a particular person or body; this means that they are disabled from interfering with the exercise by X of the interest (A) protected by the immunity. Thirdly, if X has only a liberty (what Hohfeld calls a privilege) to do A, this far weaker claim merely means that X does no wrong in exercising her liberty – the rights of others are not thereby infringed. However, no-one has a duty to allow her to exercise A or assist her to exercise it. In the UK, broadly speaking, there is no positive legal duty on any organ of the state to allow the exercise of freedoms; moreover, Parliament may at any time abridge them. Thus it may be seen that in the UK what may be termed 'rights proper' or 'immunities' in other democracies, become merely liberties.

Chapter 2

The Protection of Liberties in Britain and the Bill of Rights Issue

The question whether Britain should adopt a Bill of Rights, which has been under discussion in academic and political circles for the last three decades, was initially brought into focus when the UK accepted the right of individual petition under the European Convention on Human Rights: to many it came to appear anomalous that the Strasbourg judges should have the power to require changes in domestic law to ensure respect for Convention rights while domestic judges had no such power. It is probably fair to say that support for a Bill of Rights has grown among lawyers, academics and politicians during the eighties and early nineties; both the present Master of the Rolls and the Lord Chief Justice indicated upon taking office that they shared in this support. However, a number of politicians remain opposed or unconvinced including, it seems, the Conservative Party. However, Labour, which opposed a Bill of Rights during the 1980s and up to and beyond the 1992 election, eventually decided to espouse it as official policy in 1993, while there has been a long history of Liberal and Democrat support for it.

The debate has centred on three questions. Firstly, if the UK has traditionally managed through its unwritten constitution to maintain a reasonable human rights record what factors suggest that there is a need to adopt a Bill of Rights? Is it possible to identify inherent weaknesses in the constitutional protection for civil liberties which have only recently been fully exposed? Secondly, even if it is accepted that some further measures are needed to provide protection for civil liberties, can a compelling case be made out that adoption of a Bill of Rights is an acceptable or effective means of providing it? Thirdly, which Bill of Rights should be adopted, what should its status be and how should it be enforced?

The premise behind the adoption of Bills of Rights all over the world is that citizens can never be fully assured of the safety of their liberties until those liberties are removed out of the reach of government by identifying and enshrining them in a Bill of Rights. It is thought that government cannot be expected to keep a satisfactory check on itself; only some source of power independent of government can do so. In the UK, however, it has been thought until relatively recently that the unwritten constitution as maintained by Parliament and the judiciary is a

2.1   Introduction

2.2   Weaknesses in the protection for civil liberties: introduction

sufficiently effective means of ensuring that power is not abused. The opposing argument, which is now gaining ascendancy, is that the traditional checks on government power have become insufficiently effective, and some consider that an assertion of human rights is needed to prevent further encroachment on them.

2.3 The role of Parliament

It has traditionally been thought that Parliament provides a means of allowing the will of the people to influence government towards the maintenance of liberty through free and secret elections and through the operation of a free press. It can react to the needs of civil liberties by providing specific legislative safeguards and in so doing can take into account the views and expertise of a range of groups. Moreover, it will govern according to the rule of law which will include the notion that it will accept certain limits on its powers based on normative ideals. However, commentators such as Ewing and Gearty, evaluating government in the 1980s, have considered that these traditional checks are beginning to break down: 'Mrs Thatcher has merely utilised to the full the scope for untrammelled power latent in the British constitution but obscured by the hesitancy and scruples of previous consensus-based political leaders'. In particular it is clear that when the government in power has a large majority it may more readily depart from traditional constitutional principles if it is minded to do so because Parliament is likely to be ineffective as a check on its activities.

2.3.1 Government secrecy

Birkinshaw argues that Opposition is hampered by the lack of a Freedom of Information Act in scrutinising the actions of Ministers. This lack means that government can choose what and how much to reveal in response to Opposition questions and therefore – as the *Ponting* case (1985) made clear – is able to present a selective picture of events. Government secrecy is highly significant because, increasingly, decisions affecting civil liberties are taken, not under Parliamentary scrutiny, but by Ministers and officials exercising discretionary powers. For example, the Australian government has accepted that there should be a parliamentary committee charged with scrutiny of the Australian Security Service; in the UK in contrast when the Security Service Bill 1989 was debated the government refused an amendment which would have subjected MI5 to scrutiny by a Select Committee. Britain has of course never had a Freedom of Information Act and unlike other democracies has seen no need to enact one. However, it is arguable that this fact coupled with the lack of a Bill of Rights has become less acceptable due to the increase in executive power in a modern complex democracy.

Aside from these issues which have become particularly pressing over the last decade, it may also be questioned whether Parliament by its nature provides an effective forum for taking the protection of civil liberties into account in passing legislation. It has often been noted that Parliament at times displays a readiness to pass emergency legislation which may go further than necessary in cutting down civil liberties and which is apt to remain on the statute book even after the emergency is over. MPs, whether in government or out of it, tend to respond in an unconsidered fashion to emergencies apparent or real. Government wants to be perceived as acting quickly and decisively while members of the Opposition parties, mindful of their popularity, may not wish to oppose measures adopted in the face of scares whipped up by some sections of the media. Such reactions were seen in the passing of the original Official Secrets Act 1911, passed in one day with all-party support in response to a spy-scare. The far-reaching s 2 which was never debated at all, remained on the statute books for 78 years. Similarly, the Birmingham Pub Bombings on 21 November 1974 led four days later to the announcement of the Prevention of Terrorism Bill which was passed by 29 November virtually without amendment or dissent.

Thus Parliament has demonstrated that it is willing to move quickly to cut down freedoms but it may be argued that it is at the same time slow to bring in measures to protect them because civil liberties issues are perceived as difficult to handle and as doubtful vote-winners. This received Parliamentary wisdom has meant that measures protecting civil liberties are vulnerable to under-funding while Parliament rarely legislates with such protection in mind unless forced to do so by a ruling of the European Court of Human Rights, an EC directive or a ruling of the European Court of Justice.

2.3.2 Parliamentary protection in Emergency Situations

The Diceyan tradition holds that the absence of a written constitution in the UK is not a weakness but a source of strength. This is because the protection of the citizen's liberties are not dependent on vaguely worded constitutional documents but, rather, flow from specific judicial decisions which give the citizen specific remedies for infringement of his or her liberties. He regarded one of the great strengths of the British Constitution as lying in the lack of broad discretionary powers vested in the Executive. Citizens could only be criminalised for clear breaches of clearly established laws. Where there was no relevant law they could know with absolute confidence that they could exercise their liberty as they pleased without fear of incurring any sanction.

2.4 Legal protection of liberty under the unwritten constitution

Dicey's thesis appears to be unconvincing as an analysis of our contemporary legal culture for two main reasons. Firstly, his view of the law as imposing only narrow and tightly defined areas of liability is simply no longer representative given the existence of a number of statutes imposing wide and vaguely drawn offences. Secondly, not only have such statutes rendered his view of the law inaccurate, but the judges in many areas seem to have developed uncertain areas of the law in such a way as to give themselves very wide powers to criminalise conduct; in many cases they have even undermined safeguards for liberties provided by certain statutes. These two themes are developed below.

2.4.1   Coherence and efficacy of legal protection for civil liberties

It is unarguable that in areas such as national security a number of provisions may be found affording very meagre recognition to civil liberties. These include extended detention under the Prevention of Terrorism Act 1989 or powers to use force in order to control demonstrations. Such measures are usually adopted in response to emergency situations but may persist even after the needs of the situation have become less pressing. Alternatively, there may be a continuing pressing need for emergency measures but it may not be clear that the detrimental effect on civil liberties is outweighed by the value of the measures adopted. As there may be no clear mechanism in place allowing such determinations to be made the measures may merely persist. Moreover, powers such as those governing telephone tapping or the keeping of secret records may be contained in quasi-legislation or in unpublished documents so that it is impossible to determine their extent. Discretion might be exercised as to their use but there would be nothing to ensure that it could be relied on.

Robertson has suggested that Parliament and the judges together have created a legal protection for civil liberties which is incoherent in certain areas because they have no idea of the 'ultimate picture'. Aside from areas where judicial scrutiny is *prevented* it may be argued that protection for civil liberties is precarious in some instances due to the number of provisions in UK law which, if fully used, could prevent exercise of a particular liberty. For example, the Public Order Act 1986 contains extensive provisions in ss 11, 12 and 14 placing a potentially grave burden on the organisers of marches and assemblies although these provisions are at present under-enforced. Similarly, s 10(3) of the Broadcasting Act 1990 allows the Home Secretary to prohibit the 'broadcasting of any matter or classes of matter'. Common law doctrines such as private or public nuisance provide further examples of potentially very wide powers.

The existence of such wide provisions means that UK citizens must rely for the existence or extent of certain civil liberties on the forbearance of the authorities, and generally speaking such forbearance is exercised. However, if an emergency or a politically sensitive situation arises, many of the powers government might consider necessary to meet it will already be in place, and troublesome debate and publicity can therefore be avoided. For example, during the miners' strike 1984–5 striking miners shouted abuse at miners going in to work guarded by police; the working miners claimed that such action was unlawful and it was found in *Thomas v NUM* (1985) that although no obvious pigeon hole such as assault could be found for it due to the circumstances, it could be termed 'a species of private nuisance' and injunctions against the striking miners were therefore granted. The use of common law contempt in the *Spycatcher* litigation might provide a further example.

The disorderly nature of the protection for civil liberties may also render it defective. Firstly, in some areas, such as official secrecy or public order, there are a mass of overlapping provisions making it very hard to determine whether an area of freedom still exists. Secondly, where an attempt has been made in a statute to give the law some coherence with a view to ensuring that a particular freedom is protected, as is the case with freedom of speech (in the Obscene Publications Act 1959 and the Contempt of Court Act 1981), it will often be found that the common law begins to take on a role which undermines the statutory provisions. Examples can be found in the common law doctrines of breach of the peace, contempt and conspiracy to corrupt public morals. Ewing and Gearty argue that for this reason a Bill of Rights may be undesirable as the people need Parliament to protect them from the judges, not merely the judges to protect them from Parliament. However, Parliament in the instances mentioned decided to leave the common law intact possibly due to the realisation that it might at times be convenient to invoke.

Further, because a Bill of Rights would affect *all* areas of the common law in contrast to the statutes in question, it might encourage judges to adopt a more rigorous approach to vague common law provisions, testing them against the standards of the Bill of Rights. It is noticeable that when the judges are enjoined in a statute to take account of a value such as freedom of expression – as they are under s 5 of the Contempt of Court Act 1981 – they are much more likely to take such an approach than when dealing with a wide and uncertain power arising at common law.

2.4.2   Contemporary judicial inactivism

It follows from the Diceyan thesis that judges will be concerned to construe legislation strictly against the executive if it conflicts with fundamental liberties arising from the common law, and will interpret the common law so that fundamental freedoms are protected. A rather more modern judicial method of protecting liberties may be seen in the creation of the presumption that law will be interpreted in accordance with International Human Rights Treaties where possible. However, consideration of recent decisions suggests that there does not seem to be a clear conception shared by most members of the judiciary of their role as protecting liberties. A number of decisions documented in Chapter 9 on suspects' rights suggest some concern to protect freedoms, but even within a field such as this in which judges have a fairly good civil liberties record, a lack of consistency is still apparent: compare, for example, the stance taken in *Samuel* (1988) with that of Lord Lane in *Alladice* (1988). Their record in the area of discrimination is also mixed; the judges failed to create a tort of sex discrimination and interpreted statutes in such a way as to exclude women from public office. However, later decisions suggest some determination to uphold the policy of the anti-discrimination legislation, although the decision in *Webb* (1994) may be said to be out of accord with this more recent policy.

Decisions on discrimination or prisoners' rights may be said to lie in a politically uncontentious area of the executive – at least in comparison with decisions taken in the field of national security – but nevertheless do not suggest a clear and general determination to protect liberty. Street in *Freedom the Individual and the Law* argues that 'our judges may be relied on to defend strenuously some kinds of freedom. Their emotions will be aroused where personal freedom is menaced by some politically unimportant area of the executive'.

The Dicyean thesis could however find support in the recent decision of *Derbyshire v Times Newspapers* (1993) which has been acclaimed as 'a legal landmark'. The House of Lords found, without referring to Article 10 of the European Convention, that the importance the common law attached to free speech was such that defamation could not be available as an action to local (or central) government. This decision is certainly to be welcomed, but perhaps it may fairly be said that the threat to free speech was so clear and substantial that any other finding would have been indefensible in a state regarding itself as a free democracy.

In *one* area – judicial review – the judges *have* shown a general determination to develop the common law with the basic aim of preventing the exercise of arbitrary power. However, at present the doctrine is fundamentally limited in that as long as a Minister appears to have followed a correct and fair procedure, to have acted within his or her powers, and to have made a decision which is not clearly unreasonable, the decision must stand regardless of its potentially harmful impact on civil liberties. Thus, the fact that basic liberties were curtailed in the *GCHQ* and *Brind* cases did not in itself provide a ground for review. In other words, the courts are confined to looking back at the method of arriving at the decision rather than forward to its likely effects. In cases which touch particularly directly on national security, so sensitive are the judges to the executives' duty to uphold the safety of the realm, that they may define their powers even to *look back* on the decision as almost non-existent. However, recently the judiciary has shown a determination to use judicial review to protect fundamental rights in a number of instances. In *Secretary of State for the Home Dept ex p Pierson* (1995) The Secretary of State had made a determination that a tariff period of 15 years recommended by the trial judge and the Lord Chief Justice in the case of the applicant's mandatory life sentence, should be increased to 20 years. The applicant sought judicial review of the decision of the Secretary of State on the ground that no adverse factor had been found which would justify the increase in the sentence. The main question at issue was whether the Home Secretary's discretion to increase a life sentence was absolute or whether it had to be exercised fairly. It was found that it was not open to the Home Secretary to fix a longer period for the life sentence if no new adverse factors had emerged. The decision of the Secretary of State therefore had to be quashed.

A similar stance was taken in *Secretary of State for the Home Dept and Another ex p Norney and Others* (1995). The Secretary of State had made a determination that he would not refer the cases of the applicants, IRA life sentence prisoners, to the Parole Board until after the expiry of the tariff period of the sentences. Given the timetable of the parole board this meant that in effect every tariff period was increased by 23 weeks. The applicants sought judicial review of the decision of the Secretary of State not to refer their cases to the Parole Board until after the expiry of the tariff period. This practice flouted the principles of common law and of the European Convention on Human Rights Article 5(4). A declaration was therefore granted that the Home Secretary should have referred the applicants' cases to the Parole Board at such a time

2.4.3   Judicial review

as would have ensured as far as possible that they would be heard immediately after expiry of the tariff period.

These two decisions may be contrasted with that taken in *Secretary of State for Defence ex p Smith and Others* (1995). The applicants had sought judicial review of the policy of the Ministry of Defence in maintaining a ban on homosexuals in the armed forces. The applicants had been dismissed due to the existence of the ban. The Divisional Court dismissed the applications and the applicants appealed from that decision. The court had jurisdiction to grant judicial review of the policy in question since it did not concern national security issues. In conducting such review the court applied the usual *Wednesbury* principles of reasonableness. This meant that the court could not interfere with the exercise of an administrative discretion on substantive grounds save where it was satisfied that the decision was unreasonable in the sense that it was beyond the range of responses open to a reasonable decision maker. However, that in judging whether the decision-maker had exceeded that margin of appreciation the human rights context was seen as important; the more substantial the interference with human rights, the more the court would require by way of justification before it was satisfied that the decision was unreasonable. The court rejected the argument of the Ministry of Defence that a more exacting test than applying *Wednesbury* principles of reasonableness was required. Applying such principles and taking into account the support of the policy in both Houses of Parliament it could not be said that the policy crossed the threshold of irrationality.

The court found that an issue under Article 8 of the European Convention on Human Rights arose but that a decision under the Convention was the responsibility of the European Court on Human Rights. The Master of the Rolls suggested that recourse to Strasbourg might be necessary if all else failed.

Thus the appeal was dismissed. In determining the rationality of the decision, the Master of the Rolls indicated that where human rights were in issue the decision-maker might more readily reach the threshold of irrationality than would be the case in a context unconcerned with such rights. This argument has some affinity with that which has been advanced by Sir John Laws. He has argued that while the courts insist that relevant considerations should be taken into account when making a decision, they tend to hold that the weight to be given to those considerations is entirely for the decision-maker to determine. He has then argued that, on principle, while this may be a reasonable approach when the matter under consideration involves such issues as economic policy, in cases where fundamental rights are at stake, this would mean that the decision maker would be free 'to accord a high or low importance to the right in question, as he chooses' which 'cannot be right'. The courts would therefore insist that the right could only be overridden if an 'objective, sufficient justification' existed so that the infringement was limited to what was strictly required by the situation.

The concept of proportionality as considered by the Master of the Rolls in the instant case was not viewed as a separate head of challenge but merely as an aspect of *Wednesbury* unreasonableness. Further, although it was made clear that fundamental rights should be given a high importance, the really crucial factor in the decision was the determination as to which policy considerations were to be allowed to override rights and which were not. It appears that in making this determination easily satisfied criteria were adopted, suggesting that increased judicial protection offered to basic liberties by means of judicial review is more theoretical than substantive.

These decisions, together with a number of others of a similar nature, reaffirm, it is suggested, the value of judicial review as a means of ensuring that some harmony between UK executive practice and the standards laid down by the European Convention on Human Rights is maintained. However, the decision in *Smith* may also be said to demonstrate the limitations of judicial review in this respect.

2.4.4   Conclusions

Two points seem to emerge from the above discussion. Firstly, the judiciary do not seem to be united around a clear conception of their role. No compelling evidence emerges of a common understanding that they should form a bulwark to protect the citizens' liberties against the burgeoning power of the executive. Secondly, even in the area in which such a clear idea is present – judicial review – the courts seem to lack the determination to continue pushing the limits of the doctrine outwards in order to ensure greater protection for liberties.

In relation to the first point it may be persuasively argued that as judges have no 'textual anchor for their decisions' and have had to 'rely on an appeal to normative ideals that lack any mooring in the common law' it is unsuprising that common practice as regards fundamental freedoms has not emerged. D Oliver points out that what has been termed the 'ethical aimlessness' of the common law – its lack of a sense of clear direction – means that because the judges have no coherent conception as to the direction in which the law should develop, they have not framed any set of 'guiding principles or priorities where civil and political rights clash with public interests'.

The judges in general may therefore be uncertain as to what weight to give to a particular freedom while the more executive-minded amongst them can take advantage of this uncertainty to give little or no weight to a particular civil liberty. This may also mean that debate as to the nature of civil liberties cannot get under way, and that only the most obvious instances of their infringement will receive notice. Of course, even if judges had an 'anchor' to hold on to there might not be common practice among them: judges in the USA Supreme Court and in the European Court of Human Rights may differ very widely as to their conceptions of liberty. However, it seems unarguable that the introduction of a Bill of Rights would achieve an increase in unity amongst English judges; while different judges would give different weights to rights and freedoms at the very least all would be certain about when they had to be taken into account.

In relation to both points it may be argued that the judiciary are not at present able to construct for themselves a clear justification for increasing their powers over government. The introduction of a Bill of Rights which would amount to a public statement from the nation as a whole of the importance which they attach to human rights, would give the judges the mandate for which they may feel the need.

2.5 The influence of Europe

It may be argued that even if further protection for civil liberties is needed, the influence of Europe, through the European Convention on Human Rights and the European Community will provide it, and therefore there is no need to enact a Bill of Rights. It is clear that membership of the EC and the influence of the Convention have had an enormous impact on civil liberties in the UK in the last decade – perhaps more so than the more traditional influences considered above.

2.5.1 Direct influence

The EC, which will have an increasing effect, whether or not the Social Chapter (which lays down minimum rights for workers in the Community countries) eventually becomes part of UK law, has already had an important impact in the areas of sex discrimination and data protection. As this book has demonstrated, the rulings of the European Court of Human Rights have led to better protection of human rights in such areas as prisoners rights, freedom of expression, privacy and discrimination.

2.5.2 Indirect influence

The European Convention on Human Rights has also had, of course, a more covert influence on UK law. As Chapter

3shows, the judges are increasingly prepared to take the European Convention into account in reaching a decision. However, as the House of Lords reaffirmed in *Saunders* (1995) the Convention cannot be utilised where domestic law adversely affecting civil liberties is unambiguous.

Both European influences are necessarily limited in scope. The EC is of its nature concerned more with social and economic than civil rights, while the effect of a ruling of the European Court of Human Rights is dependent on the government in question making a change in the law. The UK government may be able to minimise the impact of an adverse judgment by interpreting defeat narrowly, by avoiding implementation of a ruling or by obeying the letter of the Article in question but ignoring its spirit. The impact of the Convention is also lessened because the process of invoking it is extremely cumbersome, lengthy and expensive. As discussed in Chapter 3, it is unlikely to become less so, despite the imminent merger of the European Court and Commission on Human Rights. While the system of the long trek to Strasbourg (starting with the exhaustion of domestic remedies) remains substantially as it is at present only the most exceptionally determined and resourceful litigants are likely to pursue it.

2.5.3   Limits of European influence

It is fair to say that there is a consensus among commentators that the methods of providing protection for civil liberties which have been considered are insufficiently effective, but not as to the means which should be adopted in order to provide further protection.

2.6   Efficacy and acceptability of a Bill of Rights: introduction

Traditionally, hostility to Bills of Rights sprang from the perception of them as high-sounding documents which are ineffective in practice but dangerous because they create complacency as to liberty. More recently the argument that Bills of Rights *per se* are ineffective or actually inimical to the protection of liberty, has tended to give way to the argument that although some independent restraint on the excess or abuse of power is needed, it would be dangerous or pointless to enact a Bill of Rights because it would not be wise to trust UK judges with such an enormous power. It is thought in some quarters that they would invoke the exceptions in order to interpret it in an executive-minded manner, thus perhaps emasculating the freedoms it was supposed to protect. Commentators such as Lee and Ewing and Gearty have considered that it would be dangerous to trust to a Bill of Rights as interpreted by UK judges, and that there is too great a tendency to regard one as a panacea for all that is wrong with civil liberties in the UK. It could be argued further that whether or not UK judges *in particular* could be trusted with a Bill of Rights, the whole notion of endowing an unelected group with a considerable area of power removed from the reach of the legislature is simply undemocratic.

Thus three aspects of the argument as to trusting the judges may be identified. The first concerns the position of the judges in a democracy, the second the fitness of the British judiciary to adjudicate on civil rights questions and the third the credibility of the doctrine of separation of powers under a Bill of Rights.

2.7	**The argument from democracy and the method of protection**	Whether or not it is acceptable in a democracy that unelected judges should wield the power of a Bill of Rights partly depends on its authority and the availability of review of legislation. The most contentious possibility would arise if judges were empowered to strike down legislation in conflict with an entrenched Bill of Rights because no possibility of correction of judicial decisions by subsequent legislation would arise except in so far as provided for by the method of entrenchment. The argument from democracy has the greatest force only if the Bill of Rights could prevail over subsequent inconsistent legislation. It obviously has much less force if, as is more likely, it was able to prevail only over prior inconsistent legislation.

A further possibility is that a Bill of Rights could be protected by a so-called 'notwithstanding clause' – subsequent legislation would only override it if the intention to do so was clearly stated in the legislation. The perpetrators of the argument against trusting the judges do not always make clear whether their antipathy is to all of these possibilities or only the first. It is obviously a crucial distinction as in the second and third Parliament clearly still retains ultimate power over the content of the law; the third possibility merely requires candour if rights are to be interfered with, which as Dworkin has commented 'is hardly incompatible with democracy.'

2.7.1	Justifying an entrenched Bill of Rights in a democracy	However, the argument that a fully entrenched Bill of Rights *would* be incompatible with democracy should not be too readily conceded. Such an argument seems to proceed from the premise that any restriction upon the freedom of legislative bodies – even those designed to protect fundamental rights – is undemocratic. It should be noted initially that an advocate of absolute democracy ought also to be opposed to UK membership of all international human rights treaties, since the basic premise of all of these is that certain rights of citizens should be placed beyond the power of the majority to infringe them. However, the notion that there should be no limits on the power of the majority arguably amounts to an impoverished

conception of democracy. Such a conception could provide no reason why the majority should not authorise the internment, torture and summary execution of IRA members if it was clear that this would end terrorist attacks and thus immeasurably benefit the mass of the people.

Those who insist that Parliament's power should be untrammelled presumably do *not* think that it should use its powers in this way, and their conviction that it should not do so can only be justified by a belief that there must be limits on what the majority can inflict on even profoundly anti-social individuals and minorities.

The argument against endowing the judges with power under an entrenched Bill of Rights (assuming entrenchment was possible) should also be considered in the light of the experience of America. The most striking feature of the American system is the power of the Supreme Court to render inoperative acts of the elected representatives of the people (first asserted in *Marbury v Madison* (1803)). This power seems alien to UK jurists but the justification offered for it is that the legitimacy of judicial review of legislation derives not from electoral accountability but from the particular positions of the judges within the constitution. Alexander Hamilton has put forward the classic statement of this theory: 'The executive not only dispenses the honours but holds the sword of the community. The legislature not only commands the purse but prescribes the rules by which the duties and rights of every citizen are to be regulated. The judiciary on the contrary has no influence over either the sword or the purse; no direction either of the strength or of the wealth of society.' (Thus it will be) 'the least dangerous to the political rights of the Constitution'.

Entrenchment of a Bill of Rights would be in any event possible in our system only by means of a written constitution (considered below). Such a task would not be undertaken without a referendum; if the people considered such a settlement desirable they would in effect be consenting to be ruled undemocratically within certain defined areas as the price of curbing elected power.

Even if a Bill of Rights were to be unentrenched, it would inevitably contain open-textured provisions which would have to be interpreted, and this raises two further points.

2.8   The judges as policy-makers

2.8.1	Specific statutes should protect liberties?

It has been argued by, *inter alia*, the Labour Party in 1990, that a number of Acts of Parliament, arrived at after full consideration of the issues involved and the likely effects, and covering specific areas, is a better way to protect, for example, the right to privacy than a Bill of Rights containing a provision such as 'Everyone has the right to privacy' followed by certain exceptions. However, it appears that at present this is unlikely to occur. It would be time-consuming to enact such legislation and it might therefore be unlikely to find a place in a legislative programme mainly concerned with social and economic issues. The lack of legislation passed over the last 10 years with the sole or main intention of protecting a particular liberty supports this argument. The legislation that has been passed: the Contempt of Court Act 1981, the Equal Pay Amendment Regulations, 1983, the Data Protection Act 1984 has been Europe-driven. There has clearly been a lack of legislation passed to protect civil liberties which has been enacted without such coercion; the UK, unlike other jurisdictions, has failed to enact a Privacy Act or a Freedom of Information Act.

As mentioned above, government tends not to favour these issues and simply because they are not party political issues they do not find a place in a tight legislative programme. If the party of government tends to abjure its policy-making role in these areas, it may be argued that the only alternative is enactment of a Bill of Rights which would largely hand such a role to the judges. Even if Parliament was prepared to legislate in these areas, it could still be argued that a Bill of Rights would be of value as providing a remedy which would be more flexible than a statute and might adapt to changing social conditions more readily – although whether or not it could do so in actuality would depend on the approach of the judiciary to its interpretation. Moreover, specific pieces of legislation could have the protection they offered to liberties eroded by subsequent legislation through the operation of the doctrine of implied repeal; the protection gained would therefore be far more precarious than that offered by a fully or even partially entrenched Bill of Rights.

2.8.2	Judicial interpretation of the Bill of Rights

The argument about the unsuitability of UK judges to deal with a generally phrased Bill of Rights finds that due to their particular training they would not be at home with a vague concept like the right to privacy. On the other hand, as argued above, the judges in the UK have developed certain presumptions in order to protect liberty and therefore it may be said that they are not incapable of handling indeterminate concepts. An argument has been made by Lester in support of this proposition in the context of the courts' performance in dealing with the task of applying broadly worded EC directives on sex-discrimination. His evaluation is that 'English judges have interpreted and applied these general principles in a manner which recognises their fundamental nature and which gives full effect to their underlying aims,' and from this he concludes that, 'Those sceptics who doubt the ability of British judges to protect the fundamental rights of the (European) Convention should consider their impressive record in translating the fundamental rights of Community law into practical reality.

The judges are largely drawn from a tiny minority group: upper middle class, rich, white, elderly males who were public school and Oxbridge-educated. As positions of power in Britain are often filled by persons drawn from this group it might seem incongruous to suggest that they should be charged with the protection of the rights of the weak or the unpopular. John Griffiths in *The Politics of the Judiciary* argues that the senior judges:

> ... have by their education and training and the pursuit of their professions as barristers, acquired a strikingly homogeneous collection of attitudes, beliefs and principles which to them represent the public interest ... (This is) ... the interest of the state, the preservation of law and order, ... the protection of property rights and ... the promotion of political views normally associated with the Conservative party.

2.9 The conservatism of the judiciary: Griffiths and Old White Males

However, is the causal link between the judges' backgrounds and their decisions as clear as this suggests? Other variables may be present influencing particular decisions and it is clear that judges, despite similar backgrounds, display markedly differing degrees of liberalism: as Lee points out a number of House of Lords decisions on human rights issues have been reached on a three-two majority, while in others a unanimous Court of Appeal has been overturned by a unanimous House of Lords.

2.9.1 Criticism of Griffiths' thesis

This argument does not imply that all judges have a special facility, unknown to normal people, of rooting out of themselves all the unconscious prejudices derived from their backgrounds. Obviously judges will sometimes be influenced, unconsciously or otherwise by the interests of their class. What is apparent, however, is that despite the fact that they largely belong to a particular societal group they do not always display attitudes which tend to be associated with that group. At the least it is fair to say that judges have shown on the whole a greater eagerness to protect the rights of groups such as prisoners or immigrants than have their counterparts in government.

2.9.2   Past record of the Judges

Ewing and Gearty have argued that UK judges have shown how they would acquit themselves under a Bill of Rights and that the results are not promising. They point out that, for example, the Privy Council in considering questions arising from Commonwealth Bills of Rights has given certain guarantees of rights a very restrictive interpretation. In *Attorney General v Antigua Times Ltd* (1976) the Privy Council found that a constitutional guarantee of freedom of speech was not infringed by Antiguan legislation requiring a licence from the Cabinet and a large deposit as a surety against libel in order to publish a newspaper. However, the Privy Council appears recently to have adopted a different approach. In *Guerra v Baptiste* (1995) the Privy Council had to consider delay in carrying out an execution. Guerra was convicted of murder in the Republic of Trinidad and Tobago and sentenced to death. In 1989 Guerra appealed against his sentence but the appeal was not heard until October 1993. The issue before the Privy Council arose from the decision in *Pratt v Attorney General for Jamaica* (1995) in which it was found that where a state wishes to retain capital punishment it must accept the responsibility of ensuring that execution follows as swiftly as possible after sentence, allowing a reasonable time for appeal and consideration of reprieve. If the appeal procedure allows the prisoner to prolong appellate proceedings over a period of years, the fault lies with the appeal procedure, not with the prisoner.

The court suggested that a reasonable target would be to complete the hearings within approximately one year and to carry out the sentence of death within two years. In the present instance there had been substantial delay amounting to nearly five years between sentence and the point at which the sentence was to be carried out. The fact that problems were created by the shortage of court resources did not justify the delay. Such problems had also been a factor in the *Pratt* case. It was therefore found that the sentence must be commuted to one of life imprisonment. This decision and that in *Pratt* suggest that UK judges are quite capable of adopting a broad approach to Bills of Rights. Thus there is some basis for the argument that the judges would take decisions under the European Convention on Human Rights if it was enacted into domestic law which would not emasculate it due to adoption of a narrow and technical approach.

Moreover, where an international treaty has been incorporated into domestic law the English courts have shown a willingness to adopt a broad teleological approach to its provisions. In *The Hollandia* (1983) Lord Diplock said that such provisions:

> ... should be given a purposive rather than a narrow literalistic construction, particularly wherever the adoption of a literalistic construction would enable the stated purpose of the international convention ... to be evaded ...

Further, as mentioned above, UK judges have adapted remarkably quickly to the demands of EC law and have been prepared to take decisions and make pronouncements which were probably unthinkable when the European Communities Act was passed. They have been prepared to be persuaded by the European Court to depart to a very significant extent from the traditional doctrine of parliamentary sovereignty in order to uphold the aims of the Community (see discussion of *Factortame* below).

Thus, there is some basis for the argument that if the judges were enjoined, in an Act of Parliament, to apply the European Convention directly, they would come to feel a loyalty to the jurisprudence of the European Court of Human Rights similar to that which they now appear to feel to the principles of Community law enunciated by the European Court of Justice. Of course, for many of the senior judges the growth of such loyalty to the Convention would only be a development of a process which has already begun. They would also have to acquaint themselves with Convention jurisprudence to a far greater extent than they have already and arguably would therefore be influenced by it towards a more sophisticated conception of human rights than they may already possess.

It should be borne in mind that UK citizens are already trusting to the judges in Strasbourg (and to a certain extent those in Luxembourg) to safeguard their civil liberties. It might seem that once the principle is accepted that individuals should have the right to invoke European Convention rights as interpreted by unelected judges, justice demands that this remedy should be available in UK courts. It may be noted that none of the commentators who distrust UK judges wish to withdraw from the Convention. Such juxtaposition of recognition of the worth of the Convention with fear of its domestic importation has led writers such as Zander to suggest that trust placed in the judges of the European Court of Human Rights (who are after all drawn from a group not dissimilar to that from which British judges are drawn: apart from other factors very few women sit in the court) could and should be extended to UK judges. Dworkin has made the further point that it seems odd to maintain that

2.9.3   Current reliance on Strasbourg judges

it is acceptable for the UK to be bound by interpretations of the Convention made by 'mainly foreign judges' but not by those made by English judges – who are 'trained in the common law and in the legal and political tradition of their own country.'

2.10 Doctrine of the separation of powers

Although there is at present no strict separation of powers, the judges will not, in applying an Act of Parliament, take account (overtly) of the likelihood that the government will not welcome the courts' interpretation. However, there is a theory that the judges under a Bill of Rights would gradually become politicised and that therefore the roles of the judiciary and the legislature would be perceived as being merged with each other. This could happen partly if political influence behind judicial appointments was suspected, and partly because the judges would be more overtly involved in controversy. Both these fears stem from the experience of the Supreme Court of America where appointments are overtly political ones. Whether or not this would occur in the UK it may also be argued that political appointees do not always fulfil the role expected of them. Their views evolve in office as they apply conceptions of civil rights to specific situations. President Eisenhower, when asked about the greatest mistakes of his presidency, reputedly said that they were both sitting in the Supreme Court.

Zander argues that the judges already exhibit bias based on class interest but that the extent of this bias is at present hidden because the judges are thought to be merely applying the existing law. Because a Bill of Rights would be more loosely worded than a Statute any bias might be more easily perceived: 'If the emperor has fewer clothes than had previously been thought, it is not necessarily a bad thing for this to be understood'. Moreover, the overt exhibition of bias, if it occurred, might prompt changes in the system of appointment of judges with a view to creating a more representative body.

Care must of course be used in arguing, as most writers in favour of a Bill of Rights do, at one and the same time for a more representative judiciary and for adopting a Bill of Rights which would have to be applied by the present judges. It might be that a judiciary which included more women and people from ethnic minorities would not hand down decisions which differed enormously from those which the present judiciary would hand down under a Bill of Rights, because the Constitutional tradition under which they were operating would be the same. Moreover, the argument that the judiciary should be representative of the community it serves rests on principles of fairness which bear on issues wider than the question of interpretation of the Bill of Rights. Thus the two arguments in question need not be mutually exclusive.

The overwhelming majority of Human Rights Bills considered by Parliament have advocated incorporation of the European Convention on Human Rights (ECHR) into UK law using the mechanism of an ordinary Act of Parliament. The House of Lords Select Committee on a Bill of Rights was unanimous on this issue: 'To attempt to formulate *de novo* a set of fundamental rights which would command the necessary general assent would be a fruitless exercise.' Starting from scratch and developing a Bill of Rights for the UK might be a burdensome task because the political parties (and the various pressure groups) would have difficulty in reaching agreement on it, while the process of hearing and considering all the representations made by interested parties would be extremely lengthy.

2.11   The European Convention on Human Rights as the UK Bill of Rights

Zander argues that it would be politically and psychologically easier to incorporate the Convention rather than a new tailor-made UK Bill of Rights as it is already binding on the UK internationally, and both major parties have accepted the jurisdiction of the European Court of Human Rights and the right of individual petition. Oliver also notes that incorporation of the ECHR would also make effective protection of the Bill of Rights easier without having to attempt formal entrenchment (see below). Further, if Convention principles continue to encroach on our law at the pace of the last few years incorporation could come to seem almost inevitable.

2.11.1   Advantages of adopting the ECHR

Arguments against incorporating the Convention are based on its defects of both form and content which have often been criticised. It is a cautious document: it is not as open textured as the American Bill of Rights and contains long lists of exceptions to the primary rights – exceptions which suggest a strong respect for the institutions of the state. The most outstanding examples of inadequacy are the limited scope of Article 14, the lack of a due process clause and the dangerous potential of Article 17. These defects and others are dealt with fully in Chapter 1 but the above examples explain why dissatisfaction with the Convention has often been expressed. On the other hand, the decisions of the European Court of Human Rights documented in this book suggest that a great deal has been achieved despite such defects, partly due to the dynamic approach to the Convention. Whether UK judges would be able to emulate such achievements is uncertain, but it may be noted that their counterparts in Canada have adopted a dynamic approach to the Canadian Charter of Rights and Freedoms.

2.11.2   Deficiencies of the ECHR

A Bill of Rights could be drawn up which would be based on the Convention but would improve upon it by using more up to date language and dealing with certain of the inadequacies mentioned. The advantage to be gained by adopting this course would have to be weighed against the possible detriment caused if the jurisprudence of the European Court on Human Rights were seen as less directly applicable. The British judiciary might feel that they had lost the 'anchor' of the authority of the court and the constraints of the need to apply a uniform European standard of human rights.

2.12   The authority of a Bill of Rights: methods of protection/ entrenchment

The adoption of a Bill of Rights intended to be for all time appears to be incompatible with the doctrine of Parliamentary sovereignty because a Bill of Rights with the same status as other enactments is vulnerable to express or implied repeal. Express repeal of all or part of it might be undertaken by a subsequent Parliament out of sympathy with its aims, while implied repeal – which might at times be unintentional – could gradually and insidiously erode it. For example, it would contain a clause protecting the right to privacy – Article 8. If a subsequent enactment dealt with an aspect of privacy (such as the use of newly developed surveillance devices) in terms affording the citizen a very restricted remedy this statute would prevail and the right to privacy could not mean freedom from such devices except to the extent provided for by its provisions. The Bill of Rights might eventually become almost worthless – in fact, worse than worthless because it could be used by government to cloak erosions of freedom while at the same time raising expectations it could not fulfil. However, certain forms of protection for enactments, even, arguably, amounting to a weak form of entrenchment already exist in our constitution. (The word 'protection' is used as being wider than 'entrenchment'.)

2.12.1   A Convention of respect

It is a constitutional truism that Parliament never uses its power to the full; for example, although theoretically able to do so it is inconceivable in 1993 that Parliament would limit the suffrage to those with incomes over a certain level. Similarly, the Bill of Rights, although enacted as an ordinary Act of Parliament, might acquire such prestige that although its express repeal remained theoretically possible it would never be undertaken. Arguably, the Act of Union with Scotland 1706 and perhaps the European Communities Act 1972 provide precedents, but even if government was reluctant to engage in express repeal, implied repeal would still remain a possibility.

The convention of respect for the Bill of Rights would include the presumption that Acts of Parliament should be construed, if possible, in accordance with it on the assumption that Parliament could not have intended to legislate contrary to it. This would be presumed as the courts have already accepted it in relation to the European Convention itself. Thus protection from implied repeal by subsequent ambiguous statutory provisions would be assured.

However, there would remain the possibility of unwitting implied repeal. A provision of a particular statute passed after the Bill of Rights might not appear with any certainty to conflict with it, or the inconsistency might simply go unnoticed. If, under judicial scrutiny, it was determined that the provision did not admit of a construction which would be in accordance with the Bill of Rights the judge would apply the later provision, thereby repealing the Bill of Rights to the extent of its inconsistency.

However, a weak form of entrenchment which could be employed is already known to the British constitution. The form of entrenchment and the possible concomitant weakening of Parliamentary sovereignty is, of course, that contained in s 2(4) of the European Communities Act 1972, which reads as follows:

> any enactment passed or to be passed ... shall be construed and have effect subject to the foregoing provisions of this section ...

'The foregoing' are those provisions referred to in s 2(1) giving the force of law to 'the enforceable Community rights' there defined. The words 'subject to' appear to suggest that the courts must allow Community law to prevail over a subsequent Act of Parliament. This does not, of course, mean that the European Communities Act itself cannot be repealed. The House of Lords in *Pickstone v Freemans* (1988) found that domestic legislation – the Equal Pay Amendment Regulations – made under s 2(2) of the European Communities Act appeared to be inconsistent with Article 119 of European Community law. It held that despite this apparent conflict a purposive interpretation of the domestic legislation would be adopted; in other words the plain meaning of the provision in question would be ignored and an interpretation would be imposed on it which was not in conflict with Article 119. This was done on the basis that Parliament must have intended to fulfil its EC obligations in passing the Amendment regulations once it had been forced to do so by the European Court of Justice. The House of Lords followed a similar approach in *LitsteForth Dry Dock Engineering* (1989).

2.12.2   A favourable rule of construction

2.12.3   Protection by an express favourable rule of construction

2.12.4   **Partial entrenchment of s 2(1) of the 1972 Act?**

It might appear to follow that Parliament has succeeded in partially entrenching s 2(1) of the European Communities Act by means of s 2(4) by – in effect – imposing a requirement of form (express words) on future legislation designed to override Community law. However, the House of Lords in both *Litster* and *Pickstones* cloaked its disregard of statutory words by the finding that they were reasonably capable of bearing a meaning compatible with Community obligations. Dicta of Lord Denning in *Macarthys v Smith* (1981) however, suggest more clearly that partial entrenchment of s 2(1) of the 1972 Act has occurred: ' we are entitled to look to the Treaty ... not only as an aid but as an overriding force. If ... our legislation ... is inconsistent with Community law ... then it is our bounden duty to give priority to Community law'. In other words, the proposition put forward by Lord Denning was to the effect that s 2(4) of the European Communities Act had brought about a variant of the rules of implied repeal but that the rules of express repeal still applied.

In *Secretary of State for Transport ex p Factortame* (1989) in the Court of Appeal Bingham LJ said:

> ... that where the law of the Community is clear 'whether as a result of a ruling given on an Article 177 reference or as a result of previous jurisprudence or on a straightforward interpretation of Community instruments, the duty of the national court is to give effect to it in all circumstances ... To that extent a UK statute is not as inviolable as it once was.

Possibly such a variant of the rules of implied repeal could equally be used to protect the Bill of Rights. The form of words adopted could be similar to those of s 2(4). Clearly, just as it was difficult to predict the effect of s 2(4), so it is to state how the judges would treat such a clause. Possibly the courts would adopt the *Pickstone* approach wherever possible. Where it was not possible the *Macarthy* approach might be used depending on the respect which had been generated for the Bill of Rights. Either approach might protect the Bill of Rights from repeal in most instances, although not of course from express repeal. Parliament might expressly provide that an enactment was to take effect despite the Bill of Rights, it might repeal the whole Bill of Rights or merely the clause giving it some protection against future enactments. However, whether or not such actions became politically impossible Parliamentary sovereignty would have suffered some limitation. The Bill of Rights would have achieved partial entrenchment in that a requirement of form (express words) would be imposed on future Parliaments.

Recently the proposal to protect a Bill of Rights by including in it a clause stating that subsequent legislation would only override it if the intention of doing so were expressly stated in such legislation (together with a provision along the lines of s 2 of the European Communities Act 1972) has gained favour amongst commentators. Oliver notes that such a clause works in Canada to provide effective protection for the Canadian Charter, and offers two reasons why a government would be unwilling to state clearly that it was legislating in breach of the Bill of Rights with the result that a 'notwithstanding clause' would offer it effective protection.

Firstly there would be the general political embarrassment which would be caused to the government if it were seen as directly attacking its citizen's liberties. Secondly, if the ECHR had, as is likely, been adopted as a domestic Bill of Rights, a declaration of intent to infringe constitutional rights would be tantamount to a declaration of the government's intention to breach its obligations under international law; this would undoubtedly provoke widespread international condemnation which would be highly embarrassing.

A Bill which had incorporated the ECHR would, as Oliver notes, be further protected by the legal presumption already discussed that 'Parliament does not intend to act in breach of international law' (*per* Diplock LJ in *Saloman v Commissioners of Custom and Excise* (1967)), so that a reading of the relevant legislation which did not create a breach of rights would be adopted by the courts if such a reading was possible. Oliver concludes that the above methods of protection would provide 'strong protection against legislative encroachment on civil and political rights.' After noting similar arguments, Dworkin comes to a similar conclusion; 'In practice this technically weaker version of incorporation would probably provide almost as much protection as (formal entrenchment)'. This is the method currently favoured by the Labour Party.

Thus it appears that a number of forms of protection might be available to the Bill of Rights even without full formal entrenchment. If the constitutional impact of EC law were used as a model, sovereignty could be regarded as in abeyance during the lifetime of the Bill of Rights as far as questions relevant to its provisions were concerned.

There is, finally, the possibility that the Bill of Rights could be protected from all forms of repeal by full entrenchment. Constitutions throughout the world adopt a number of different forms of entrenchment of codes of rights. The constitution of the USA can be amended only by a proposal

2.12.5   An express 'Notwithstanding Clause'

2.12.6   Partial entrenchment: conclusion

2.12.7   Full entrenchment

which has been agreed by two thirds of each House of Congress or by a convention summoned by Congress at the request of two thirds of the States. The proposed amendment must then be ratified by three-quarters of the States' legislatures. The amendment procedure itself – Article V of the Constitution – can be amended only by the same method.

If a Bill of Rights for the UK were enacted containing a provision that it could not be repealed except in accordance with a procedure such as that discussed above, it is thought that the courts would not give effect to it. However, De Smith suggests that Parliament could redefine itself so as to preclude itself as ordinarily constituted from legislating on a certain matter. The argument is based on the redefinition of Parliament under the Parliament Acts: if Parliament could make it easier for itself to legislate on certain matters equally it could make it harder, thereby entrenching certain legislation.

This analogy however, has come under attack from Munro (*Studies in Constitutional Law* (1987)) on the ground that the Parliament Act procedure introduces no limitation on Parliamentary sovereignty. The only authorities which would support this proposition come from other constitutions; in *Attorney General for New South Wales v Trethowan* (1932) the Privy Council upheld the requirement of a referendum before a Bill to abolish the upper House could be presented for the Royal Assent. Although, as De Smith argues, this decision may be of limited application as involving a non-sovereign legislature it does suggest that a class of legislation exists for which it may be appropriate to delineate the manner and form of any subsequent amendment or repeal. The South African case of *Harris v Minister of the Interior* (1951) is to similar effect. Thus, the point cannot be regarded as settled.

The prospect of such protection for the Bill of Rights is not, at present, in question. However, is it clear that the Bill of Rights could be entrenched within a written constitution? Dicey considered that it would be untenable to espouse 'the strange dogma, sometimes put forward, that a sovereign power such as the Parliament of the UK, can never by its own act divest itself of authority'. On this view the judges would accept the new constitutional settlement; possibly the Judges' Oath might also be amended so that they owed allegiance to the earlier settlement as opposed to a subsequent statute.

2.13 Remedies under a Bill of Rights: judicial review

The scope of judicial review of administrative action would be greatly widened: administrative discretion would have to be exercised within Convention limits, thus reversing the effect of the House of Lord's decision in *Secretary of State for the Home Department ex p Brind* (1991). An official decision could be quashed on the existing grounds but also on the ground that a particular right had been violated. If, for example, a Chief Officer of Police banned marches in a certain area including ones likely to be peaceful under the Public Order Act 1986 s 13, the ban could be challenged in the courts on the basis that Article 11 had been violated. Immigration officials would have to take Article 8, and possibly Articles 6 and 3 into account in discharging their duties, thus reversing the effect of *Salamat Bibi* (1977) and reinstating the principle put forward by Lord Scarman in *Phansopkar* (1977) that immigration officials must have regard to the Convention. The usual remedies of certiorari, mandamus or a declaration would be available.

A claim for, for instance, breach of confidence could be met by the argument that the Article 10 principle should prevail. At present the judges apply a loose defence of public interest in publication in a somewhat idiosyncratic manner. Under Article 10 the public interest in publication would always prevail except where the interest in preserving confidentiality fell within one of the exceptions contained in para 2 of the Article, and met a pressing social need.

2.13.1 A defence in civil proceedings

If a future Sarah Tisdall or Cathy Massiter was prosecuted under the Official Secrets Act 1989, Article 10 could be pleaded as a defence. The European Court and Commission of Human Rights have always been very tender to matters of national security and have therefore developed a policy of allowing a wide margin of appreciation in such matters. However, invocation of Article 10 would at least allow the freedom of expression argument to be heard by the jury. The Act contains no public interest defence; therefore, otherwise, such argument would be irrelevant. If it succeeded the Official Secrets Act would be to that extent modified – to include, in effect, such a defence.

2.13.2 A defence in criminal proceedings

The obvious example is an action for invasion of privacy. If journalists followed, watched, beset a person and bribed neighbours for information, that person could sue them or their employers in tort for invasion of privacy, under Article 8. The journalists' right to gather information as part of the right to freedom of expression would be protected under para 2 of Article 8, but the court would have the opportunity of considering whether there was a genuine public interest in the information thereby gained. Even if a statutory tort of invasion of privacy is eventually enacted in order to cover such a

2.13.3 Creating new rights

situation, the Article 8 guarantee would still be valuable as filling other gaps in the protection for privacy (see Chapter 8).

The Protection of Liberties in Britain and the Bill of Rights Issue

Parliament's support for civil liberties and its ability to check the exercise of government power are perceived as inadequate mainly due to the extent of government secrecy, Parliament's readiness to pass emergency legislation which unnecessarily cuts down civil liberties and the rarity of Parliamentary measures to protect civil liberties in the absence of pressure from Europe.

The need for a Bill of Rights: weak Parliamentary protection for civil liberties

Although the judges have developed the common law so that significantly increased protection for liberties has been created, especially by development of judicial review, there does not seem to be a clear conception shared by most members of the judiciary of their role in protecting liberties. In any event, the protection judges can offer is limited given the existence of a number of statutes imposing wide and vaguely drawn offences or giving Ministers wide discretion to abridge liberties – a discretion the courts are particularly reluctant to challenge if national security considerations are present. Such statutes may not always be used to the full, but if an emergency or a politically sensitive situation arises many of the powers government might consider necessary to meet it will already be in place.

Uncertain judicial protection of civil liberties

Further, in many areas the judges seem to have developed uncertain areas of the common law in such a way as to give themselves very wide powers to criminalise conduct, and in many cases have even undermined safeguards for liberties provided by certain statutes. It can be persuasively argued that the lack of any clear direction in the common law may account for this mixed picture and that the introduction of a Bill of Rights would give the judges the mandate to protect civil liberties for which they may feel the need.

The EC will have an increasing effect on UK law, and has already had an important impact in the areas of discrimination, data protection and laws relating to pornography. The rulings of the European Court of Human Rights have led to better protection for human rights in many areas. However the impact of the European Convention on Human Rights is limited due to the fact that the process of invoking it is extremely cumbersome, lengthy and expensive and is unlikely to become less so.

The influence of Europe: limitations

The European Convention has also had a more covert influence on UK law, because judges are increasingly – though not consistently – prepared to take the European Convention into account in reaching a decision.

Arguments against a Bill of Rights

One of the most important of these arguments questions whether it is acceptable in a democracy that unelected judges should wield the power of a Bill of Rights. This argument depends partly on the authority of the Bill and the availability of review of legislation but in any event arguably represents a limited view of democracy. Another argument questions whether specific Acts of Parliament would not provide better protection than a generally phrased Bill of Rights and is suspicious of entrusting an elitist and unrepresentative judiciary with the protection of our liberties. Finally, some view the adoption of a Bill of Rights as incompatible with the doctrine of the Separation of Powers.

If a Bill of Rights is to be adopted should it be the European Convention?

The overwhelming majority of Human Rights Bills considered by Parliament have advocated incorporation of the European Convention (ECHR) into UK law using the mechanism of an ordinary Act of Parliament; and any other course of action seems fraught with difficulty. Further, although the European Convention has been criticised for both form and content, adopting it would probably be the most politically acceptable course of action and would carry with it a number of other advantages.

The authority of a Bill of Rights

The basic problem here is the apparent incompatibility of an entrenched Bill of Rights with the doctrine of Parliamentary sovereignty. Various other methods of protecting a Bill of Rights have been canvassed, of which the two weakest would be a convention of respect and a favourable rule of construction.

The most favoured method is the use of an express 'Notwithstanding' clause stating that subsequent legislation would only override the Bill of Rights if the intention of doing so were expressly stated in such legislation in tandem with a provision along the lines of s 2(4) above. It is thought that such a clause would offer effective *de facto* protection to a Bill of Rights. A somewhat stronger form of protection which could be employed would rely on a provision similar to that contained in s 2(4) of the European Communities Act 1972 which it is thought could partially entrench a Bill of Rights.

Chapter 3

The European Convention on Human Rights

3.1   Introduction

The European Convention on Human Rights was conceived after the Second World War as a means of preventing the kind of violation of human rights seen in Germany during and before the war. However, it has not generally been invoked in relation to large scale violations of rights, but instead has addressed particular deficiencies in the legal systems of the Member States which on the whole create regimes of human rights which are in conformity with the Convention.

Drafted in 1949, it was based on the United Nations Declaration of Human Rights, and partly for that reason and partly because it was only intended to provide basic protection for human rights, it appears today as quite a cautious document, less far-reaching than the 1966 International Covenant on Civil and Political Rights. Nevertheless, it has had far more effect on UK law than any other Human Rights Treaty due to its machinery for enforcement which includes a court with the power to deliver a ruling adverse to the government of Member States.

Also, the court insists upon the dynamic nature of the Convention and adopts a teleological or purpose-based approach to interpretation which has allowed the substantive rights to develop until they may cover situations unthought of in 1949. The Convention might have been self-defeating had it been a more radical document because it might have failed to secure the necessary acceptance from Member States, both in terms of accepting various parts of it such as the right of individual petition, and in terms of responding to adverse judgments.

The rights and freedoms are largely concerned with civil and political rather than social and economic matters; the latter are governed by the 1961 European Social Charter and the 1966 International Covenant on Economic, Social and Cultural Rights.

3.2   **The status of the Convention in UK law**

Under Article 1 of the Convention the Member States must secure the rights and freedoms to their subjects but they are free to decide how this should be done. Each state decides on the status the Convention enjoys in national law; there is no obligation under Article 1 to allow individuals to rely on it in *national* courts. In some States it has the status of constitutional law; in others ordinary law.

However, in the UK it has no binding force. Successive UK governments have considered that it is not necessary for the Convention to be part of UK law because they have always maintained that the UK's unwritten constitution is in conformity with it. Thus a UK citizen cannot go before a UK court and simply argue that a Convention right has been violated. Nevertheless, the influence of the Convention is rapidly becoming more significant in domestic law through rulings in UK courts, and it may be said that it is encroaching steadily from every direction apart from that of direct incorporation. It can have an impact through domestic courts in the following ways:

3.2.1   Statutory construction

It is a general principle of construction that statutes will be interpreted if possible so as to conform with International Treaties to which the UK is a party on the basis that the government is aware of its international obligations and would not intend to legislate contrary to them. However, as Lord Brandon of Oakbrook made clear in *Re M and H (Minors)* (1988) the English courts are under no duty to apply the Convention's provisions directly. 'While English courts may strive where they can to interpret statutes as conforming with the obligations of the UK under the Convention, they are nevertheless bound to give effect to statutes which are free from ambiguity even if those statutes may be in conflict with the Convention'.

This principle was accepted by the House of Lords in *Secretary of State for the Home Department ex p Brind and Others* (1991) but the possibility of extending the role of the Convention in domestic law by importing it into administrative law was rejected. It was made clear that although the courts would presume that ambiguity in domestic legislation should be resolved by arriving at an interpretation in conformity with the Convention, it did not follow that where Parliament had conferred an administrative discretion on the executive without indicating the precise limits within which it had to be exercised it could be presumed that it had to be exercised within Convention limits. It had been argued that to import such a principle must have been the legislature's intention but the House of Lords considered that this would be an unwarranted step to take, bearing in mind that Parliament had chosen not to adopt the Convention.

However, although importation of the Convention into domestic administrative law or importation by allowing it to override statutory provisions has been prevented, the indirect route to importation – interpretation of ambiguous provisions in conformity with it – still leaves it enormous scope to influence domestic law. The width of this scope was underlined by the ruling of the Court of Appeal in *Derbyshire County Council v Times Newspapers Ltd* (1992) which is considered below. It was delivered in the context of the common law rather than statute but was not expressed to be confined to the common law. It may therefore be relevant to statutory interpretation and if so it could lead to a dramatic increase in Convention-based rulings.

Lord Scarman in *AG v BBC* (1981) considered that the Convention could also influence the common law. He said that where there was some leeway to do so, a court which must adjudicate on the relative weight to be given to different public interests under the common law should try to strike a balance in a manner consistent with the treaty obligations accepted by the government. 'If the issue should ultimately be ... a question of legal policy, we must have regard to the country's international obligation to observe the Convention as interpreted by the Court of Human Rights.'

3.2.2   Influence on the common law

This approach was endorsed by the House of Lords in *AG v Guardian Newspapers (No 2)* (1990), Lord Goff stating that he considered it to be his duty where free to do so to interpret the law in accordance with Convention obligations.

The need to take the Convention into account was emphasised by the Court of Appeal in *Derbyshire County Council v Times Newspapers Ltd* (1992), Ralph Gibson LJ ruling that where a matter 'was not clear [by reference to] established principles of our law ... the court must ... have regard to the principles stated in the Convention'. Butler-Sloss LJ put the matter even more strongly: 'where there is an ambiguity, or the law is otherwise unclear or so far undeclared by an appellate court, the English court is not only entitled but ... obliged to consider the implications of Article 10'. The House of Lords, on the other hand, considered that in the particular instance the *common law* could determine the issues in favour of freedom of speech, but this does not mean that the guidance offered by the Court of Appeal is not of value in an instance in which the common law is uncertain. That guidance suggests that judges have no choice as to whether to consider the Convention where the law is ambiguous or – and this does appear to be a new development – where it is not yet settled in an appellate court.

Thus even where the law is not ambiguous but there is no appellate ruling on a particular point, a judgment should be reached which is in conformity with the Convention. It may therefore be the case that all areas of the common law which are not clearly settled in the House of Lords and which bear on Convention issues, should now incorporate Convention principles.

3.2.3   Influence through EC law

A further means by which the Convention can influence domestic law is clearly becoming increasingly important: according to the European Court of Justice in *Nold v Commission* (1974) the Convention can be a source of general principles of EC Law. This was expressly recognised under the Treaty on European Union signed by the UK in 1993. It is therefore possible that as the influence of EC law becomes more important in the UK, the Convention may also have more influence. EC law can of course have *direct* effect in UK courts; therefore certain Convention principles may come to be of limited binding force in the UK as forming part of EC law. However, the impact of the Convention in the UK by this means is at present of only peripheral importance.

It should be borne in mind that although the Convention may influence European Community law, the two areas of law – European Community law and European Convention law have developed separately and are enforced differently. Thus states which are signatories to the European Convention need not be members of the European Community. In the UK, European Community law can be directly effective and arguably may prevail even over subsequent domestic law; in comparison the European Convention has had less impact and as will be argued below the machinery for enforcement of the Convention in UK law is incomparably weaker.

3.3   The substantive rights and freedoms

In what follows, an outline will be given of the scope of the Articles covering the more significant substantive rights and freedoms. More detailed treatment of cases which are relevant to particular areas of UK law will be undertaken when those areas of municipal law are considered. It will be found that Articles 2–6 cover the most basic human rights and contain, therefore, no exceptions or only narrow exceptions. Also, this group contains the 'non-derogable' articles – those which the state must always adhere to, even in a time of national emergency. Articles 8–11, on the other hand, may be said to cover a more sophisticated or developed conception of human rights and are subject to a range of exceptions. Thus, under the first group of Articles argument will tend to concentrate on the question whether a particular situation will fall within the compass of the right in question, while under the second group it will generally concentrate on determining whether a particular exception will apply.

In general, the Strasbourg authorities will leave Member States a 'margin of discretion' – a certain amount of leeway – in determining what is needed to protect various interests in their own countries. The discretion will not, of course, be unlimited, but it will vary according to the needs of the particular situation and the nature of the interest to be protected.

Article 2 on protection of life states:

1) Everyone's right to life shall be protected by law. No one shall be deprived of his life intentionally save in the execution of a sentence of a court following his conviction of a crime for which this penalty is provided by law.

2) Deprivation of life shall not be regarded as inflicted in contravention of this Article when it results from the use of force which is not more than absolutely necessary:

a) in defence of any person from unlawful violence;

b) in order to effect a lawful arrest or to prevent the escape of a person lawfully detained;

c) in action lawfully taken for the purpose of quelling a riot or insurrection.

3.4   Article 2: protection of life

Article 2 provides non-derogable protection of the right to life. This might seem straightforward – governments are enjoined to refrain from the wanton killing of their subjects – but aside from that instance it is in fact hard to determine what a right to life encompasses. It is difficult to pinpoint the stage at which it may it be said that the responsibility of a state for a person's death is so clear, the causal potency between the state's action or omission and the death so strong, that the right to life has been violated.

3.4.1   Scope of a 'right to life'

Decisions under Article 2 do not yet allow this issue to be clearly determined, but do suggest that Article 2 places two distinct duties on the national authorities although their scope is unclear. Firstly, it implies that the public authorities should refrain from some acts or omissions which in themselves directly endanger life. Thus the state must ensure that any use of force by state agents is subject to careful regulation; aside from capital punishment state agents can only take life where para 2 applies. However, this raises a general question as to how far the individual should have a right to demand the expenditure of resources so that the state can save his or her life. It can be argued that the state bears *some* responsibility in a number of instances: a person might die due to poor housing conditions or due to a failure to impose a particular speed limit in poor driving conditions. The question also arises whether allowing a person – whether a handicapped baby or a patient in a persistent vegetative state – to die would be a breach of Article 2.

Secondly, Article 2 implies a positive obligation on the part of the state authorities to take reasonable steps in order to prevent the deprivation of life by private individuals (*X v UK and Ireland* (1982)). Thus the taking of life by private individuals must generally be illegal and there must be reasonably effective enforcement of the law. However, it was held in *W v UK* (1983) that these enforcement measures will not be scrutinised in detail. Obviously the state may not be able to prevent every attack on an individual without an enormous expenditure of resources. Therefore the Convention will leave a wide margin of discretion to the national authorities in this regard, although the state will be under some duty to maintain reasonable public security.

| 3.4.2 | Exceptions |

The question has arisen in the context of national legislation on abortion whether an unborn baby can fall within the interpretation of 'everyone', but it has been determined that even if the foetus can be protected, its right to life will be weighed against the mother's life and physical and mental health (*X v UK* (1980)). In *Paton v UK* (1980) it was found by the Commission that Article 2 applies only to persons who have been born. Had the Commission found otherwise all national legislation in the Member States permitting abortion would have been in breach of Article 2 as abortion even to save the mother's life would not appear to be covered by any of the express exceptions. *H v Norway* (1992) made it clear that abortion on social grounds was not contrary to Article 2.

The most important exception to Article 2 is that in respect of the death penalty which also includes extradition to a country where the death penalty is in force. Protocol 6 has now removed the death penalty exception but it has not been ratified by the UK. However, it might be possible to challenge use of the death penalty in the UK and other countries which have not ratified Protocol 6 under other Convention provisions such as Article 3.

Generally speaking, para 2, allowing for death resulting from the use of force in certain emergency situations, is reasonably straightforward and is obviously aimed mainly at unintentional deprivation of life. This was explained in *Stewart v UK* (1985) which concerned the use of plastic bullets in a riot. It was found that para 2 is concerned with situations where the use of violence is allowed as necessary force and may as an unintended consequence result in loss of life. On this basis the use of plastic bullets was found to fall within its terms.

However, para 2 would also seem to cover instances where the force used was *bound* to endanger life and/or was bound to do so but was necessary in the circumstances. Thus national laws recognising the right to use self-defence are in harmony with Article 2 under para 2(a). Para 2(a)–(c) provides that in emergency circumstances state agents may take life, but the terms of para 2 must be completely satisfied. In *McCann, Farrell and Savage v UK* (1995) the court found that the state had sanctioned killing by state agents in circumstances in which such killing was not absolutely necessary. SAS soldiers shot three IRA members on the street in Gibraltar; this was justified on the basis that they apparently had with them a remote control device which they might have used to detonate a bomb. The court considered that since they had been shadowed by the SAS soldiers for some time, they could have been arrested at an earlier point.

Article 3 on freedom from inhuman treatment states:

> No one shall be subjected to torture or to inhuman or degrading treatment or punishment.

3.5 Article 3: freedom from inhuman treatment

Article 3 contains no exceptions unlike most of the Articles and it is also non-derogable. Thus, once a state has been found to have fallen within its terms no justification is possible. It has been interpreted widely as to the situations it covers which include some not readily associated with the use of such treatment. In determining the standard of treatment applicable below which a state will be in breach of Article 3 a common European standard is applied, but also all the factors in the situation are taken into account. Thus it does not connote an absolute standard and in its application it allows for a measure of discretion. It is clear that in order to determine this issue *present* views must be considered rather than the views at the time when the Convention was drawn up.

Torture, unlike degrading treatment, was quite narrowly defined in *Ireland v UK* (1978) to include 'deliberate inhuman treatment causing very serious and cruel suffering'. However, treatment which could not come within this restricted definition might well fall within one of the other forms of Article 3 treatment. Degrading treatment will include certain forms of corporal punishment including caning which was found in *Tyrer* (1978) not to amount to torture or inhuman treatment. In contrast, in *Tomasi v France* (1992) physical assault was found to be both degrading and inhuman.

3.5.1 Scope of Article 3 treatment

A number of cases have arisen concerning the position of detainees. In determining whether a particular treatment, such as solitary confinement, amounts to a violation of Article 3 a number of factors must be taken into account. These will include the stringency and duration of the measure, the objective pursued – such as the need to discipline the prisoner (*Hilton v UK* (1972)) in question – and the effect on the person concerned (*Ensslin, Baader and Raspe v FRG* (1979)). If the measure has been adopted as a result of the claimant's own unco-operative behaviour it is probable that no breach will be found.

| 3.5.2 | Risk of Article 3 treatment in another country |

Article 3 can be used in a very broad way to bring rights within the scope of the Convention which are not expressly included, such as admission to a certain country. Violation of Article 3 may occur because of the treatment a person may receive when he or she returns to their own country having been expelled or refused admission. It will have to be clearly established that the danger of such treatment is really present.

The question arose in *Soering* (1989) whether expulsion to a country (the USA) where the applicant risked the death penalty would be compatible with Article 3 because it would subject him to conditions on Death Row which would be likely to cause him acute mental anguish. Of course, as Article 2 specifically excludes the death penalty from its guarantee it cannot in itself create a violation of Article 3 because that would render those words of Article 2 otiose. The Convention must be read as a whole. However, the manner and circumstances of the implementation of the death penalty could give rise to an issue under Article 3. The European Court of Human Rights held that it had to consider the length of detention prior to the execution, the conditions on Death Row, the applicant's age and his mental state. Bearing these factors in mind, especially the very long period of time spent on Death Row and the mounting anguish as execution was awaited, it was found that expulsion would constitute a breach of Article 3. (In response to this ruling the UK and USA agreed to drop the charges to non-capital murder and then extradite the applicant.)

However, for a breach of Article 3 to be established in the context of deportation cases, there must be a clear risk of ill treatment. In *Vilvarajah and four others v UK* (1991) the applicants, Sri Lankan Tamils, arrived in the UK in 1987 and applied for political asylum under the UN Convention of 1951 Relating to the Status of Refugees, contending that they had a well founded fear of persecution if returned to Sri Lanka. The Home Secretary rejected the applications and the applicants sought unsuccessfully to challenge the rejection by means of judicial review. The applicants were then returned to Sri Lanka where, they alleged, four of them were arrested and ill-treated. They alleged that their deportation constituted breaches of Articles 3 and 13.

The European Court of Human Rights considered whether the situation in Sri Lanka at the time the applicants were deported provided substantial support for the view that they would be at risk of Article 3 treatment. The court determined that the general unsettled situation in Sri Lanka at the time did not establish that they were at greater risk than other young male Tamils who were returning there; it established only a possibility rather than a clear risk of ill treatment. No breach of Article 3 could therefore be established. The result of this case means that although an Article 3 issue may arise in asylum cases, the Convention cannot be viewed as a substitute for effective domestic means of determining refugee claims. It should be noted that Article 8 issues may also arise in some immigration claims (see below).

Article 3 could also be invoked in relation to discriminatory treatment on the basis of race and possibly on other bases because such treatment can be termed degrading according to the Commission in *Twenty-five complaints of Afro-Asians v UK* (1970). This possibility could help to compensate for the weakness of the Article 14 guarantee against discrimination which does not create an independent right.

3.5.3   Discrimination as Article 3 treatment

Article 5 states:

1) Everyone has the right to liberty and security of person.

   No one shall be deprived of his liberty save in the following cases and in accordance with a procedure prescribed by law;

   a) the lawful detention of a person after conviction by a competent court;

   b) the lawful arrest or detention of a person for non-compliance with the lawful order of a court or in order to secure the fulfilment of any obligation prescribed by law;

   c) the lawful arrest or detention of a person effected for the purpose of bringing him before the competent legal authority on reasonable suspicion of having committed an offence or when it is reasonably considered necessary to prevent his committing an offence or fleeing after having done so;

   d) the detention of a minor by lawful order for the purpose of educational supervision or his lawful

3.6   **Article 5: right to liberty and security of person**

detention for the purpose of bringing him before the competent legal authority;

e) the lawful detention of persons for the prevention of the spreading of infectious diseases, of persons of unsound mind, alcoholics or drug addicts or vagrants;

f) the lawful arrest or detention of a person to prevent his effecting an unauthorised entry into the country or of a person against whom action is being taken with a view to deportation or extradition.

2) Everyone who is arrested shall be informed promptly, in a language which he understands, of the reasons for his arrest and of any charge against him.

3) Everyone arrested or detained in accordance with the provisions of paragraph 1(c) of this Article shall be brought promptly before a judge or other officer authorised by law to exercise judicial power and shall be entitled to trial within a reasonable time or to release pending trial. Release may be conditioned by guarantees to appear for trial.

4) Everyone who is deprived of his liberty by arrest or detention shall be entitled to take proceedings by which the lawfulness of his detention shall be decided speedily by a court and his release ordered if the detention is not lawful.

5) Everyone who has been the victim of arrest or detention in contravention of the provisions of this Article shall have an enforceable right to compensation.

Although Article 5 speaks of liberty *and* security as though they could be distinguished they are seen as two sides of the same coin; there is no significant distinction between them. Article 5 divides into two parts: firstly exceptions are set out where liberty can be taken away; secondly under paras 2–4 the procedure is set out which must be followed when a person is deprived of liberty. It should be noted that Article 5 is concerned with total deprivation of liberty, not restriction of movement which is covered by Article 2 of Protocol No 4. (The UK is not a party to Protocol 4).

In general it should be noted that the instances when liberty can be taken away under para 5(1)(a)-(f) will be restrictively interpreted although the instances included are potentially wide.

3.6.1   Paragraph 5(1)(a): imprisonment after conviction

This covers lawful detention after conviction by a competent court. Thus the detention must flow from the conviction. This calls into question the revocation of life licences because in such instances a person is being deprived of liberty without a conviction. In *Weeks* case (1987) the European Court of Human Rights considered the causal connection with the original sentence when a life licence was revoked after the applicant was released. The court accepted a very loose link between the original sentence and the revocation of the life licence on the basis that the sentencing judge must be taken to have known and intended that it was inherent in the life sentence that the claimant's liberty would hereafter be at the mercy of the executive. The court would therefore not review the appropriateness of the original sentence.

The second form of permitted deprivation of liberty under para 5(1)(b) denotes deprivation of liberty in order to 'secure fulfilment of an obligation prescribed by law'. This raises difficulties of interpretation and is clearly not so straightforward as the first form of deprivation in para 5(1)(a). It is very wide; it appears to allow deprivation of liberty in many instances without intervention by a court. It might even allow preventive action before violation of a legal obligation. However it has been narrowed down; in *Lawless* (1959) it was found that a specific and concrete obligation must be identified. Once it has been identified, detention can in principle be used to secure its fulfilment.

In *McVeigh v UK* (1981) it was found that specific circumstances, such as the possibility of danger to the public, must be present in order to warrant the use of detention. Identifying an obligation which was un-met was not enough of itself. A requirement to submit to an examination on entering UK was found to be specific enough and in the exigencies of the situation did not breach para 5(1)(b). Moreover, it must be apparent why *detention* rather than some lesser measure is needed to secure compliance with the obligation. Thus the width of para 5(1)(b) has been narrowed down by the use of restrictive interpretation in line with furthering the aims of the Convention.

This provision refers to persons held on remand or detained after arrest. Paragraph 5(3) requires that in such an instance a person should be brought 'promptly' to trial; in other words the trial should occur in *reasonable* time. The part of para 5(1)(c) which causes concern is the ground – 'arrest or detention to prevent him committing an offence'. This is an *alternative* to the holding of the detainee under reasonable suspicion of committing an offence; arguably the two should have been cumulative. This ground would permit internment of persons even if the facts which showed the intention to commit a crime did not in themselves constitute a criminal offence. In *Lawless*

3.6.2   Paragraph 5(1)(b): detention to secure fulfilment of an obligation

3.6.3   Paragraph 5(1)(c): detention before trial

the court narrowed this ground down on the basis that internment in such circumstances might well not fulfil the other requirement in para 5(1)(c) that the arrest or detention should be effected for the purpose of bringing the person before a competent legal authority. It would not be fulfilled if the true purpose was not to do so. This interpretation was warranted because all of Article 5 must be read together.

A level of suspicion below 'reasonable suspicion' will not be sufficient; in *Fox, Campbell and Hartley* (1990) the European Court of Human Rights found that para 5(1)(c) had been violated on the basis that no *reasonable* suspicion of committing an offence had arisen, only an honest belief (which was all that was needed under the Northern Ireland (Emergency Provisions) Act 1987). The court took into account the exigencies of the situation and the need to prevent terrorism; however it found that the country in question must be able to provide *some* information which an objective observer would think justified the arrest. It was found that the information provided was insufficient and therefore a breach of Article 5 had occurred.

3.6.4	Paragraph 5(1)(d): minors

This provision confers far-reaching powers on national authorities with regard to those under the age of 18. This has led the court to interpret 'educational purpose' restrictively. In *Bouamar* (1988) it was found that mere detention without educational facilities will not fulfil Article 5(1)(d)); there had to be educational facilities in the institution and trained staff.

3.6.5	Paragraph 5(1)(e): vagrants and others

This sub-paragraph must of course be read in conjunction with para 5(4) – all the persons mentioned have the right to have the lawfulness of their detention determined by a court. The width of para 5(1)(e) has been narrowed in the *Vagrancy* cases (1971) in which the question arose of the current application of the term 'vagrant'. The court considered whether the applicant was correctly brought within the ambit of the term in the relevant Belgian legislation. The term had been applied to the applicants who had therefore been detained. The court would conduct only a marginal review of municipal law; it separated the question of the interpretation of national law from the application of the Convention. However, the court did then turn to the Convention and conduct a far – reaching review of the meaning of 'vagrant' in accordance with the Convention on the basis of a common European standard; it then asked whether the applicants had been correctly brought within *that* term. It was found that they had not and a breach of Article 5 was therefore found. Thus, ultimately the margin of discretion allowed to the domestic authorities was narrow. This stance prevented too wide an interpretation of the application of the categories of para 5(1)(e).

The importance of this provision is that the Convention does not grant aliens a right of admission or residence in Contracting states, *but* para 5(1)(f) ensures that an alien who is detained pending deportation or admission has certain guarantees; there must be review of the detention by a court and the arrest must be in accordance with national law. Also, because the lawfulness of the detention may depend on the lawfulness of the deportation itself, the lawfulness of the deportation may often be in issue as in *Zamir* (1983).

3.6.6   Paragraph 5(1)(f):
entrants and deportees

Paragraphs 2–4 encapsulate the principle that the liberty of the person is the overriding concern; it can be taken away only in accordance with the exceptions mentioned and only then if paras 2–4 are complied with. If paras 2–4 are not complied with the deprivation of liberty will be unlawful even if it comes within the exceptions. Paragraphs 2–4 provide a minimum standard for arrest and detention.

3.6.7   Safeguards of
paras 2–4

Under para 5(2) the information in question is necessary in order to judge from the moment of arrest whether the arrest is in accordance with the law so that the arrestee could theoretically take action straight away to be released. The Commission's view is that this information need not be as detailed and specific as that guaranteed by para 6(3) in connection with the right to a fair trial.

3.6.8   Paragraph 5(2):
information on arrest

In *Murray v United Kingdom* (1994) soldiers had occupied the applicant's house, thus clearly taking her into detention, but she was not informed of the fact of arrest for half an hour. The question arose whether she was falsely imprisoned during that half hour. The House of Lords found that delay in giving the requisite information was acceptable due to the alarm which the fact of arrest if known, might have aroused in the particular circumstances – the unsettled situation in Northern Ireland. Members of Mrs Murray's family applied to the European Commission on Human Rights, alleging a breach of Article 5 which guarantees liberty and security of the person and of Article 8 which protects the right to privacy.

Article 5(1) requires *inter alia* that deprivation of liberty can occur only if arising from a lawful arrest founded on reasonable suspicion. The European Court of Human Rights found that no breach had occurred even though the relevant legislation (s 14, Northern Ireland (Emergency Provisions) Act 1987) required only suspicion, not reasonable suspicion, since there was some evidence which would provide a basis for the suspicion in question. No breach was found of Article 5(2) which provides that a person must be informed promptly of the reason for arrest. Mrs Murray was eventually informed during interrogation of the reason for the arrest and it was determined that allowing an interval of a few hours between arrest and informing of the reason for it could still be termed prompt. The violation of privacy fell within the exception under Article 8(2) in respect of the prevention of crime.

No violation of the Convention was therefore found. Thus it seems that under Article 5 an arrest which does not comply with all the procedural requirements will still be an arrest as far as all the consequences arising from it are concerned, for a period of time. Therefore the Convention has allowed some departure from the principle that there should be a clear demarcation between the point at which the citizen is at liberty and the point at which her liberty is restrained.

3.6.9   Paragraph 5(3): limits on detention before trial

Paragraph 5(3) confers a right be brought promptly before the judicial authorities; in other words not to be held for long periods without a hearing. It covers both arrest and detention and detainees held on remand. There will be some delay in both situations; the question is therefore what is meant by the term 'promptly'.

Its meaning was considered in relation to arrest and detention in *Brogan* (1990). The European Court of Human Rights had to consider promptness in the case of arrest and detention by virtue of the special powers under s 12 of the Prevention of Terrorism Act 1984. (The UK had entered a derogation as allowed for under Article 15 against the applicability of Article 5 to Northern Ireland but withdrew that derogation in August 1984. Two months later the *Brogan* case was filed.) The applicants complained (*inter alia*) of the length of time they were held in detention without coming before a judge, on the basis that it could not be termed prompt. The court took into account the need for special measures to combat terrorism; such measures had to be balanced against individual rights. However, it found that detention for four days six hours was too long. Following this decision, the UK government ultimately chose to derogate from Article 5 and in *Brannigan and McBride v UK* (1993) it was found that the exigencies of the situation in Northern Ireland warranted the measures taken.

The question whether detainees on remand have been brought to trial or released in a reasonable time has also been considered. The word 'reasonable' is not associated with the processing of the prosecution and trial but with the detention itself. Obviously, if the trial takes a long time to prepare for, there will be a longer delay, but it does not follow that detention for all that time will be reasonable. In the *Neumeister* case (1968) the court rejected an interpretation of 'reasonable' which associated it only with the preparation of the trial. Thus continued detention on remand will be reasonable only so long as the reasonable suspicion of para 5(1)(c) continues to exist. But grounds for continued detention other than those expressly mentioned in para 5(1)(c) could be considered, such as suppression of evidence or the possibility that the detainee will abscond. However, it is clear from *Letellier v France* (1991) that such dangers must persist throughout the period of detention; once they cease, specific reasons for continued detention which have been properly scrutinised must be apparent. Once the accused has been released on bail, Article 5(3) does not apply but Article 6(1) does, as will be seen later. The question of a reasonable time for preparing for the trial can also be considered under Article 6(1).

Paragraph 5(4) provides a right to review of detention. The accused must be able to take proceedings in order to determine whether a detention is unlawful. This is an independent provision: even if it is determined in a particular case by the Commission that the detention *was* lawful there could still be a breach of para 5(4) if no possibility of review of its lawfulness by the domestic courts arose. This was an issue in the cases against the UK regarding discretionary life sentences: obviously there had to be something to review; if the life sentence consisted wholly of a punitive element there could be nothing to review. In *Weeks* case (1984) the sentence consisted of a security element and therefore allowed review of the applicant's progress. In *Thyne, Wilson and Gunnel v UK* (1990), the sentence consisted of both a punitive and a security element. When the punitive element expired a judicial procedure for review of the sentence should have been available because now there was something to review; if it had been purely punitive there would not have been.

3.6.10   Review of detention

Article 5(4) also applies to remand prisoners. It was found in *De Jong, Baljet and Van de Brink* case (1984) that it grants to a person on remand a right of access to a court *after* the decision (in accordance with 5(3)) to detain him or prolong detention has been taken.

Article 5(5) provides for compensation if an arrest or detention contravenes the other provisions of Article 5. This provision differs from the general right to compensation under Article 50 because it exists as an independent right: if a person is found to have been unlawfully arrested under domestic law in the

3.6.11   Article 5(5): compensation

domestic court but no compensation is available, he or she can apply to the European Court on the basis of the lack of compensation. As far as other Convention rights are concerned, if a violation of a right occurs which is found unlawful by the national courts but no compensation is granted, the applicant cannot allege breach of a Convention right.

3.7   Article 6: right to a fair and public hearing

Article 6 states:

1) In the determination of his civil rights and obligations or of any criminal charge against him, everyone is entitled to a fair and public hearing within a reasonable time by an independent and impartial tribunal established by law. Judgment shall be pronounced publicly but the press and public may be excluded from all or part of the trial in the interest of morals, public order or national security in a democratic society, where the interest of juveniles or the protection of the private life of the parties so require, or to the extent strictly necessary in the opinion of the court in special circumstances where publicity would prejudice the interests of justice.

2) Everyone charged with a criminal offence shall be presumed innocent until proved guilty according to law.

3) Everyone charged with a criminal offence has the following minimum rights:

   a) to be informed promptly, in a language which he understands and in detail, of the nature and cause of the accusation against him;

   b) to have adequate time and facilities for the preparation of his defence;

   c) to defend himself in person or through legal assistance of his own choosing, or, if he has not sufficient means to pay for legal assistance, to be given it free when the interests of justice so require;

   d) to examine or have examined witnesses against him and to obtain the attendance and examination of witnesses on his behalf under the same conditions as witness against him;

   e) to have the free assistance of an interpreter if he cannot understand or speak the language used in court.

Most violations arise in respect of this Article. The relationship between paras 1 and 3 is crucial. Paragraph 1 imports a general requirement of a fair hearing applying to criminal and civil hearings which covers all aspects of a fair hearing. Paragraph 3 lists minimum guarantees of a fair hearing in the criminal context only. If para 3 had been omitted, the guarantees contained in it could have arisen from para 1 but it was included on the basis that it is important to declare a minimum standard for a fair hearing. In practice then, para 1 and para 3 may often both be in question in respect of a criminal charge.

As para 3 contains *minimum* guarantees the para 1 protection of a fair hearing goes beyond para 3. In investigating a fair hearing the Commission is not confined to the para 3 guarantees; it can consider further requirements of fairness. Thus if para 1 is *not* violated it will be superfluous to consider para 3 and if one of the para 3 guarantees is violated there will be no need to look at para 1. However if para 3 is not violated it will still be worth considering para 1. It follows that although civil hearings are expressly affected only by para 1, the minimum guarantees will apply to civil hearings too.

Besides the procedural guarantees para 6(1) provides a right of access to a court whether the domestic legal system allows such access in a particular case or not. Obviously that depends on whether an individual instance falls within para 6(1) or not. Whether it will do so depends on the meaning of 'civil rights and obligations' and 'criminal charge'. The meaning of 'civil rights and obligations' does not depend upon the legal classification afforded the right or obligation in question by the national legislator; the question is whether the content and effect of the right or obligation (taking into account the legal systems of all the contracting states) allows the meaning 'civil right' or 'civil obligation' to be assigned to it.

3.7.1   Paragraph 6(1): access to a court

The question of what is meant by a criminal charge has generated quite a lot of case law. 'Charge' has been described in *Eckle* (1982) as 'the official notification given to an individual by the competent authority of an allegation that he has committed a criminal offence'. Further, offences under criminal law must be distinguished from those arising only under *disciplinary* law. In order to do so the court will consider the nature and severity of the penalty the person is threatened with.

In *Campbell and Fell* (1984) the court had to consider whether a prison disciplinary hearing could fall within para 6(1). The applicants, prisoners, were threatened with substantial loss of remission. This was such a serious consequence that the procedure in question could be considered as of a criminal character but the court considered that not *all* disciplinary offences in prison which in fact had an equivalent in the ordinary criminal law would be treated as of a criminal character.

Once it has been determined that a particular instance falls within para 6(1) it must be determined whether the right claimed is covered by the right of access to a court. It seems that, for example, para 6(1) does not confer a right of appeal to a higher court. It may include access to legal advice and by implication legal aid. These issues arise in relation both to *access* to a court hearing and the *fairness* of the hearing. In *Golder* (1975) it was found that a refusal to allow a detainee to correspond with his legal advisor would be contrary to Article 6(1) as in preventing him even initiating proceedings it hindered his right of access to a court.

Access to legal advice may not always imply a right to legal aid. The circumstances in which it will do so were considered in *Granger* (1990). The applicant had been refused legal aid and so did not have counsel at appeal; he only had notes from his solicitor which he read out but clearly did not understand. In particular, there was one especially complex ground of appeal which he was unable to deal with. In view of the complexity of the appeal and his inability to deal with it legal aid should have been granted. It was found that paras 6(1) and 6(3)(c) should be read together and if it would be apparent to an objective observer that a fair hearing could not take place without legal advice then both would be violated.

Granger was concerned with the fairness of the hearing rather than with the ability to obtain access to a court at all. However, in some instances a person unable to obtain legal aid would be unable to obtain legal advice and therefore might be unable to initiate proceedings. In such instances access to a court would be the main issue.

The term a 'fair hearing' encompasses a number of procedural safeguards. For example, it was found in *X v Austria* (1973) that a refusal to summon a witness could constitute unfairness as could a failure to disclose evidence according to the judgment in *Edwards v UK* (1993).

The hearing must take place in 'reasonable time'. These are the same words as are used in Article 5(3), but here the point is to put an end to the insecurity of the applicant who is uncertain of the outcome of the civil action or charge against him or her rather than with the deprivation of liberty. Thus the ending point comes when the uncertainty is resolved either at the court of highest instance or by expiry of the time limit for appeal.

In determining what is meant by 'reasonable' Strasbourg has applied fairly wide time limits so that as much as seven or eight years may be reasonable. The court approved a period of nearly five years in *Buchholz* (1981). It will take into account the conduct of the accused (which may have contributed to the delay) and the need for proper preparation of the case, bearing in mind its complexity (*Ringeisen* (1971)). In order to determine how long the delay has been the point from which time will run must be identified. In criminal cases it will be at the point when the individual is officially notified of the allegation that he or she has committed a criminal offence. In civil cases it will be the moment when proceedings concerned are instituted, not including pre-trial negotiations.

It was said in *Barbéra* (1989) that para 2

3.7.2   Paragraph 6(2): the presumption of innocence

> requires *inter alia* that when carrying out their duties members of a court should not start with the preconceived idea that the accused has committed the offence charged; the burden of proof is on the prosecution, and any doubt should benefit the accused. It also follows that it is for the prosecution to inform the accused of the case that will be made against him so that he may prepare and present his defence accordingly, and to adduce evidence sufficient to convict him.

It follows from the presumption of innocence that the court must base its conviction exclusively on evidence put forward at trial. This provision is very closely related to the impartiality provision of para 6(1).

These sub-paragraphs are very closely related due to the word 'facilities' used in (b). Sub-paragraphs (b) and (c) may often be invoked together: (c) in respect of the assignment of a lawyer, and (b) in respect of the time allowed for such assignment. It is not enough that a lawyer should be assigned; he or she should be appointed in good time in order to give time to prepare the defence and familiarise herself or himself with the case. As has already been noted in relation to *Granger* the legal advice provisions must be read in conjunction with the right to a fair trial. A lawyer must be assigned if otherwise an objective observer would consider that a fair hearing would not occur. However, 6(3)(c) does not merely import a right to have legal assistance; it includes two further rights:

3.7.3   Paragraph 6(3)(b) and (c): preparing the defence

- to choose that assistance;

- if the defendant has insufficient means to pay for that assistance to be given it free if the interests of justice so require.

The Strasbourg case law has left a wide discretion to the national court as to the interpretation of the first limb of para 6(3)(d) – the right to examine witnesses – and so has deprived this right of much of its effect. The 2nd limb – the right to

3.7.4   Paragraph 6(3)(d): cross examination

cross examination – obviously allows for a wide discretion as it only requires that the prosecution and defence should be treated equally as regards summoning witnesses (*X v Austria* (1973)). So conditions and restrictions can be set so long as they apply equally to both sides. This provision relates to the concept of creating equality between parties; it is closely related to the fair hearing principle and therefore will apply in civil cases too.

3.8 Article 8: right to respect for privacy

Article 8 on the right to respect privacy states:

1) Everyone has the right to respect for his private and family life, his home and his correspondence.

2) There shall be no interference by a public authority with the exercise of this right except such as is in accordance with the law and is necessary in a democratic society in the interests of national security, public safety or the economic well-being of the country, for the prevention of disorder or crime, for the protection of health or morals, or for the protection of the rights and freedoms of others.

Article 8 seems to cover four different areas, suggesting that, for example, private life can be distinguished from family life. However, it seems that these rights usually need not be clearly distinguished from each other although sometimes this may be important. There will tend to be a clear overlap between them; for example it is often unnecessary to define 'family' because the factual situation might so obviously fall within the term 'private'. It will be noticed that para 2 contains a large number of exceptions. This is to be expected as the right to privacy conflicts with other convention rights, such as freedom of expression (Article 10), as well as with many other interests.

3.8.1 Informational privacy

An important aspect of private life is that of control over personal information, but the court has approached this issue cautiously, tending to be satisfied if a procedure is in place allowing the interest in such control to be weighed up against a competing interest. Thus in *Gaskin v UK* (1987) the interest of the applicant in obtaining access to the file relating to his childhood in care had to be weighed up against the interest of the contributors to it in maintaining confidentiality because this interference with privacy had a legitimate aim under the 'rights of others' exception. It was held that the responsible authority did not have a procedure available for weighing the two; consequently the procedure automatically preferred the contributors; that was disproportionate to the aim of protecting confidentiality and therefore could not be 'necessary in a democratic society'.

The opposite result was reached but by a similar route in the *Klass* case (1978) brought in respect of telephone tapping. It was found that although telephone tapping constituted an interference with a person's private life, it could be justified as being in the interests of national security, and there were sufficient controls in place (permission had to be given by a Minister applying certain criteria including that of 'reasonable suspicion') to ensure that the power was not abused. In the similar *Malone* case (1982) however, there were no such controls in place and a breach of Article 8 was therefore found which led to the introduction of the Interception of Communications Act 1985.

The same reasoning was applied in *Leander v Sweden* (1987) in respect of a complaint that information about the applicant had been stored on a secret police register for national security purposes and released to the Navy so that it could vet persons who might be subversive. The applicant complained that he had had no opportunity of challenging the information, but the court found that as there were remedies in place – albeit of a limited nature – to address such grievances Article 8 had not been breached because the national security exception could apply. Again, in *Hewitt and Harman v UK* (1989) a breach of Article 8 was found as there was no means of challenging the secret directive which had allowed the storage of information on the applicants.

This aspect of private life may also arise in respect of sexual privacy (see below). It has arisen specifically in two cases brought against the UK by transsexuals. In *Rees* (1987) the applicant, who was born a woman but had had a sex change operation, complained that he could not have his birth certificate altered to record his new sex thereby causing him difficulty in applying for employment. However, the court refused to find a breach of Article 8 because it was reluctant to accept the claim that the UK was under a positive obligation to change its procedures in order to recognise the applicant's identity for social purposes.

3.8.2   Identity

The court followed a similar route in *Cossey* (1990) although it did consider whether it should depart from its judgment in *Rees* in order to ensure that the Convention would reflect societal changes. However, it decided not to do so because developments in this area in the Member States were not consistent and still reflected a diversity of practices. In *B v France* (1992) it was found that although there had been development in the area no broad consensus among Member States had emerged. Nevertheless, the civil position of the applicant in terms of her sexual identity was worse than that of transsexuals in the UK and on that basis a breach of Article 8 could be found.

These rulings suggest that the court is greatly influenced by general practice in the Member States as a body and will interpret the Convention to reflect such practice so that a state which is clearly out of conformity with the others may expect an adverse ruling. However, where practice is still in the process of changing and may be said to be at an inchoate stage as far as the Member States generally are concerned, it may not be prepared to place itself at the forefront of such changes although it will weigh the lack of a consensus against the degree of detriment to the applicant.

3.8.3   Sexual life

The other aspect of privacy which has generated a certain amount of case law has related to sexual privacy and here also the court has adopted a cautious approach. In *Dudgeon* (1982) the Northern Ireland prohibition of homosexual intercourse between consenting males over 21 was found to breach Article 8: clearly there had been an interference with privacy; the question was whether the interference was necessary in order to protect morals. It was found unnecessary as it had not been used recently and no detriment to morals had apparently resulted. Northern Ireland amended the relevant legislation in consequence. It should be noted that this was a gross interference with privacy as it allowed the applicant no means at all of expressing his sexual preference without committing a criminal offence.

3.8.4   Family life

'Family life' is a concept which must be interpreted independently of the laws of the national states. It covers many types of family but if the 'family' in question, such as foster parents, might not fall within the term there might still be an interference with *private* life. Generally a close relationship will be presumed where close ties such as those between parent and child exist; for other relations the presumption will be the other way.

Various aspects of family life have been in issue in cases brought against the UK. *W, B and UK* (1987) concerned a claim that access should be allowed to children in the care of the local authority. The court found that Article 8 does not contain any explicit procedural requirements, but that finding in itself was not conclusive. When the local authority made decisions on children in its care the views and interests of parents should be taken into account and the decision-making process must allow for this. If parents' views were not taken into account then family life was not being respected. Therefore a breach of Article 8 was found on the basis that there was insufficient involvement of the applicants in the process.

In *X v UK* (1980), which was found inadmissible by the Commission, it was determined that 'family life' cannot be interpreted so broadly as to encompass a father's right to be consulted in respect of an abortion. The Commission could have rested the decision on para 2 – the rights of others exception – by taking the rights of the woman in question into account but it preferred to interpret the primary right restrictively.

Family life has also received a narrow interpretation in immigration cases in respect of a right to enter a country. In *Abdulaziz, Cabales and Balkandali v UK* (1985) it was found that 'The duty imposed by Article 8 cannot be considered as extending to a general obligation ... to respect the choice by married couples of the country of their matrimonial residence and to accept the non-national spouses for settlement in that country.' However, where an alien is in contrast faced with expulsion from a country in which he or she has lived for some time and where members of the family are established, the court has recently shown itself willing in *Djeroud v France* (1991) to uphold the right to maintain family ties if satisfied that the ties are clearly in existence.

The cases of *Golder* (1975) and *Silver* (1983) concerned the right of a detainee to correspond with the outside world and led to a steady relaxation of the UK rules relating to stopping and censoring of prisoners' correspondence. In general supervision as such of prisoners' letters is not in breach of Article 8 but particular instances such as stopping a purely personal letter may be.

3.8.5   Correspondence

Article 9 on the freedom of thought, conscience and religion states:

1) Everyone has the right to freedom of thought, conscience and religion; this right includes freedom to change his religion or belief and freedom, either alone or in community with others and in public or private, to manifest his religion or belief, worship, teaching, practice and observance.

2) Freedom to manifest one's religion or beliefs shall be subject only to such limitations as are prescribed by law and are necessary in a democratic society in the interests of public safety, for the protection of public order, health or morals, or for the protection of the rights and freedoms of others.

3.9   Article 9: freedom of thought, conscience and religion

The right under Article 9 of possessing certain convictions is unrestricted. Restrictions are only placed on the *expression* of thought under Article 10(2) and the manifestation of religious belief in para 9(2). Of course, in general, unless thoughts can be expressed they cannot have much impact. However, Article 9 provides a valuable guarantee against using compulsion to change an opinion or prohibiting someone from entering a profession due to their convictions.

Freedom of religion will include the freedom not to take part in religious services, thus particularly affecting persons such as prisoners, but it may also include the opposite obligation – to provide prisoners with a means of practising their religion. However in such instances Strasbourg has been very ready to assume that restrictions are inherent in the detention of prisoners or are justified in para 2. For example, in *Huber v Austria* (1971) broad 'inherent limitations' on a prisoner's right to practice religion were accepted. Similarly in *X v Austria* (1965) the Commission found no violation in respect of a refusal to allow a Buddhist prisoner to grow a beard. It is arguable however that inherent limitations should not be assumed in relation to a right with express exceptions.

3.10	**Article 10: freedom of expression**

Article 10 on freedom of expression states:

1) Everyone has the right to freedom of expression. This right shall include freedom to hold opinions and to receive and impart information and ideas without interference by public authority and regardless of frontiers. This Article shall not prevent States from requiring the licensing of broadcasting, television or cinema enterprises.

2) The exercise of these freedoms, since it carries with it duties and responsibilities, may be subject to such formalities, conditions, restrictions or penalties as are prescribed by law and are necessary in a democratic society in the interests of national security, territorial integrity or public safety, for the prevention of disorder or crime, for the protection of health or morals, for the protection of the reputation or rights of others, for preventing the disclosure of information received in confidence, or for maintaining the authority and impartiality of the judiciary.

Article 10 obviously overlaps with Article 9, but it is broader as it protects the *means* of ensuring freedom of expression; even if the person who provides such means is not the holder of the opinion in question, she or he will be protected. The words used in Article 10 'freedom to hold opinion' cannot be distinguished from Article 9 'freedom of thought'. There is also an obvious overlap with Article 11 which protects freedom of association and assembly.

The stance taken under Article 10 is that all speech is not equally valuable. It was found in *X and Church of Scientology v*

Sweden (1979) that commercial speech is protected by Article 10 but that the level of protection is less than that accorded to the expression of political ideas. This implies that political speech must receive special protection. The motive of the speaker may be significant; if it is to stimulate debate on a particular subject Article 10 will be more readily applicable. The court has stressed that Article 10 applies not only to ideas which are favourably received but also to those which shock and offend. In *Jersild v Denmark* (1992) the Commission accepted that this may include the dissemination of racist ideas although in the instance before it the applicant had not himself expressed such views; his conviction had arisen due to his responsibility as a television interviewer for their dissemination.

Actions in respect of prior and subsequent restraints on freedom of expression may be brought under Article 10, but pre-publication sanctions will be regarded as more pernicious and thus hard to justify as necessary *(Observer and Guardian v UK* (1991)). In relation to post-publication sanctions, criminal actions will be regarded as having a grave impact on freedom of expression, but civil actions which have severe consequences for the individual may also be hard to justify. In *Tolstoy Miloslavsky v United Kingdom* (1995) the European Court of Human Rights considered the level of libel damages which can be awarded in UK courts. Libel damages of £1.5 million had been awarded against Count Tolstoy Miloslavsky in the UK in respect of a pamphlet he had written which alleged that Lord Aldington, a high ranking British army officer, had been responsible for handing over 70,000 people to the Soviet authorities without authorisation, knowing that they would meet a cruel fate. The Count argued that this very large award constituted a breach of Article 10. Was the award necessary in a democratic society as required by Article 10? The court found that it was not having regard to the fact that the scope of judicial control at the trial could not offer an adequate safeguard against a disproportionately large award. Thus a violation of the applicant's rights under Article 10 had been found.

Article 10 includes an additional guarantee of the freedom to receive and impart information. However, the seeking of information does not appear to connote an obligation on the part of the government to make information available; the words 'without restriction by public authority' do not imply a positive obligation on the part of the authorities to ensure that information can be received. So the right is restricted in situations where there is no willing speaker. Article 10 is not therefore a full freedom of information measure. In fact the freedom to *seek* information was deliberately omitted from

Article 10 – although it appears in the Universal Declaration of Human Rights – in order to avoid placing a clear positive obligation on the Member States to communicate information.

Mediums other than written publications can be subjected to a licensing system under Article 10(1), and because these restrictions are mentioned in para 1 it appears that a licensing system can be imposed on grounds other than those outlined in para 2, thereby broadening the possible exceptions. However, any such exceptions must be considered in conjunction with the safeguard against discrimination under Article 14: for example if the state has a monopoly on a media it must not discriminate in granting air time to different groups.

3.10.1   Paragraph 2: exceptions

The restrictions of para 2 are wide, and two of them – maintaining the authority of the judiciary and preventing the disclosure of information received in confidence – are not mentioned in Article 10's companion Articles – Articles 8, 9 and 11. The first of these exceptions was included bearing in mind the contempt law of the UK but it was made clear in the very famous *Sunday Times Case* (1979), that in relation to such law the margin of discretion allowed the Member State should be narrow due to its 'objective' nature. In other words, what was needed to maintain the authority of the judiciary could be more readily evaluated by an objective observer than could measures needed to protect other interests such as morals.

The case in question concerned reporting on a matter of great public interest – the Thalidomide tragedy – and therefore only very compelling reasons for preventing the information being imparted could be justified. It was held that because Article 10 is a particularly important right, and the particular instance touched on the essence of the right, a breach could be found, and in response the Contempt of Court Act 1981 was passed. The rights of others exception has also been given a narrow interpretation in the case of defamation against a public body or person where the applicant was acting in good faith and attempting to stimulate debate on a matter of serious public concern (*Castells v Spain* (1992)).

A very different approach was taken in the *Handyside* case (1976) arising from a conviction under the Obscene Publications Act 1959 and concerning the more subjective nature of the protection of morals exception. The applicant put forward certain special circumstances – that the prohibited material in question was circulating in most other countries and so suppression could not be so evidently necessary in a democratic society – but such circumstances were barely discussed. A wide margin of discretion was left to the national authorities as to what was 'necessary'.

A similar approach was taken in *Muller v Switzerland* (1991), the court stating, 'it is not possible to find in the legal and social orders of the contracting states a uniform European conception of morals. ... By reason of their direct and continuous contact with the vital forces of their countries state authorities are in a better position than the international judge to give an opinion on the exact content of these requirements'. This view echoes the view in *Cossey* (above at para 3.8.2) that where a clear European view does emerge the court may well be influenced by it, but it also suggests a particularly strong reluctance to intervene in this very contentious area.

The lack of a uniform standard was also the key factor in the ruling in *Otto-Preminger Institut v Austria* (1994). The decision concerned the showing of a satirical film depicting God as a senile old man and Jesus as a mental defective erotically attracted to the Virgin Mary. Criminal proceedings for the offence of disparaging religious doctrines were brought against the manager of the Institute which had scheduled the showings of the film. The film was seized by the Austrian authorities while criminal proceedings were pending. The European Court of Human Rights found that the seizure of the film could be seen as furthering the aims of Article 9 of the Convention and therefore it fell within the 'rights of others' exception. In considering whether the seizure and forfeiture of the film was 'necessary in a democratic society' in order to protect the rights of others to respect for their religious views, the court took into account the lack of a uniform conception within the Member States of the significance of religion in society, and therefore considered that the national authorities should have a wide margin of appreciation in assessing what was necessary to protect religious feeling. In ordering the seizure of the film the Austrian authorities had taken its artistic value into account but had not found that it outweighed its offensive features. The court found that the national authorities had not overstepped their margin of appreciation and therefore decided that no breach of Article 10 had occurred. This decision left a very wide discretion to the Member State, a discretion which the dissenting judges considered to be too wide.

The margin of discretion in respect of the protection of morals will not be unlimited, however, even in the absence of a broad consensus. The court so held in *Open Door Counselling and Dublin Well Woman v Ireland* (1992), ruling that an injunction which prevented the dissemination of *any* information at all about abortion amounted to a breach of Article 10.

3.11	**Article 11:** **freedom of** **association and** **assembly**	

Article 11 on freedom of association and assembly states:

1) Everyone has the right to freedom of peaceful assembly and to freedom of association with others, including the right to form and to join trade unions for the protection of his interests.

2) No restrictions shall be placed on the exercise of these rights other than such as are prescribed by law and are necessary in a democratic society in the interests of national security or public safety, for the prevention of disorder or crime, for the protection of health or morals or for the protection of the rights and freedoms of others. This Article shall not prevent the imposition of lawful restrictions on the exercise of these rights by members of the armed forces, of the police or of the administration of the state.

3.11.1   Assembly

The addition of the word 'peaceful' has restricted the scope of para 1; there will be no need to invoke the para 2 exceptions if the authorities concerned could reasonably believe that a planned assembly would not be peaceful. Thus assemblies can be subject to permits so long as the permits relate to the peacefulness of the assembly and not to the right of assembly itself. However, a restriction of a very wide character relating to peacefulness might affect the right to assemble itself and might therefore constitute a violation of Article 11 if it did not fall within one of the exceptions.

It should be noted that freedom of assembly may not merely be secured by a *lack* of interference by the public authorities; they may have to positively intervene in order to prevent an interference with freedom of assembly by private individuals, although as found in *Platform 'Arzte für das Leben' v Austria* (1985) they will have a very wide margin of appreciation in this regard. It has been held in respect of the guarantees of other Articles that states must secure to individuals the rights and freedoms of the Convention by preventing or remedying any breach thereof. If no duty was placed on the authorities to provide such protection then some assemblies could not take place.

3.11.2   Association

'Association' need not be assigned its national meaning. Even if a group such as a trade union is not an 'association' according to the definition of national law it may fall within Article 11. The term connotes a voluntary association, not a professional organisation established by the government. It should be noted that it is only with respect to Trade Unions that the right to form an association is mentioned. However, such a right in respect of other types of association must be implicit – a necessary part of freedom of association.

The question whether freedom of association implies protection against *compulsory* membership of an association was considered in *Young, James and Webster* (1981) and it was found that a measure of freedom of choice is implicit in Article 11. It amounts to a negative aspect of the right to join a Trade Union and is not therefore on the same footing as the positive aspect but it is still a part of freedom of association. The court left open the question whether a closed shop agreement would always amount to a breach of Article 11; in this instance the possibility of dismissal due to refusal to join the union was such a serious form of coercion that it affected the essence of the Article 11 guarantee. It seems that the closed shop practice may be a violation of Article 11 where there is legislation allowing it even if the body enforcing it is not an emanation of the state.

Under para 1 the right to join a Trade Union involves allowing members to have a union that can properly protect the interests of the members. So a union must have sufficient scope for this although this need not mean a right to strike; this right can be subject to the restrictions of the national legislature (*Schmidt* (1976)). Moreover, extra restrictions may be placed on certain groups of employees under para 2 and these do not expressly need to be 'necessary'. However the purposes of Convention imply that they should be.

Article 12 states:

> Men and women of marriageable age have the right to marry and to found a family, according to the national laws governing the exercise of this right.

3.12   Article 12: the right to marry and to found a family

Article 12 contains no second paragraph setting out restrictions but it obviously does not confer an absolute right due to the words 'according to the national laws' which imply the reverse of an absolute right – that Article 12 may be subject to far-reaching limitations in domestic law. The reference to national laws also accepts the possibility that legal systems may vary among contracting states as to, for example, the legally marriageable age. However, this does not mean that the Convention has no role at all; national law can govern the *exercise* of the right, not attack or erode its *essence*. Thus if a person was denied the right to marry due to handicap mental faculties or poverty, the essence of the right would be eroded, assuming that he or she was capable of genuine consent.

The rule that only persons of the opposite sex can marry has caused difficulty. In *Rees* (1987) a woman who had had a sex change complained that she was unable to marry. It was held that there was no violation of Article 12 because the state can impose restrictions on certain men and women due to the social purpose of Article 12 which is concerned with the ability to procreate; marriages which cannot result in procreation may therefore fall outside its ambit. This interpretation was supported on the ground that the wording of the Article suggests that marriage is protected as the basis of the family; thus Article 12 is aimed at protecting the traditional biological marriage. Therefore, preventing the marriage of persons not of the opposite biological sex was not found to impair the essence of the right. This ruling was followed in *Cossey* (1990) on the ground that changes in social values did not indicate a need to depart from the decision in *Rees*.

The right to marry includes placing no sanction on marriage such as sacking a person when he or she marries. But if a priest is sacked when he ceases to be celibate that is not a breach as he has chosen in full freedom not to marry.

The right to divorce or dissolution of marriage is not included under Article 12 so that the state need not provide the means of dissolving a marriage although Article 8 may apply. The right to divorce has been deliberately left out of the Convention, and although the Convention is subject to an evolutive interpretation (in other words changes in social conditions can be taken into account), that will not apply to a right which has been totally omitted.

The right to found a family does not include an economic right to a family allowance or accommodation for the family: it means preventing interference with child-bearing by the non-voluntary use of sterilisation or abortion. Article 3 and possibly Article 2 would probably also apply in such a situation.

3.13	**First protocol (to which the UK is party)**

Article 1

Every natural or legal person is entitled to the peaceful enjoyment of his possessions. No one shall be deprived of his possessions except in the public interest and subject to the conditions provided for by law and by the general principles of international law.

The preceding provisions shall not, however, in any way impair the right of a state to enforce such laws as it deems necessary to control the use of property in accordance with the general interest or to secure the payment of taxes or other contributions or penalties.

It was determined in *James and Others* (1986) that the margin of appreciation open to the legislature in implementing social and economic policies should be a wide one.

Article 2

No person shall be denied the right to education. In the exercise of any functions which it assumes in relation to education and to teaching, the state shall respect the right of parents to ensure such education and teaching in conformity with their own religious and philosophical convictions.

The UK has made the following reservation to Article 2: '... in view of certain provisions of the Education Acts in force in the UK, the principle affirmed in the second sentence of Article 2 is accepted by the UK only so far as it is compatible with the provision of efficient instruction and training, and the avoidance of unreasonable public expenditure.'

In the *Belgium Linguistic* cases 1968 it was held that Article 2 does not require the contracting states to provide a particular *type* of education: it implies the right of persons to 'avail themselves of the means of instruction existing at a given time'.

Article 3

The High Contracting Parties undertake to hold free elections at reasonable intervals by secret ballot, under conditions which will ensure the free expression of the opinion of the people in the choice of the legislature.

Article 3 does not imply an absolute right to vote but that elections should be held at regular intervals, should be secret, free from pressure on the electorate and the choice between candidates should be genuine.

3.14   Later protocols

Certain of the Protocols, including the most recent, Protocol 11, are concerned with the procedural machinery of the Convention. However, certain Protocols, to which the UK is not a party guarantee substantive rights. These are, broadly speaking: freedom of movement (Protocol 4), abolition of the death penalty (Protocol 6), the right of an alien lawfully resident in a state to full review of his or her case before expulsion, rights of appeal, compensation for miscarriages of justice, the right not to be subjected to double jeopardy and sexual equality between spouses as regards private law rights and responsibilities (Protocol 7). A new Protocol on Minority Rights was recommended to the Committee of Ministers in 1993 but at the time of writing it had not been adopted.

3.15   Additional guarantees to the primary rights: Article 13

Article 13 concerns the right to an effective remedy before a national authority:

> Everyone whose rights and freedoms as set forth in this Convention are violated shall have an effective remedy before a national authority notwithstanding that the violation has been committed by persons acting in an official capacity.

In *Leander* (1987) it was found that 'the requirements of Article 13 will be satisfied if there exists domestic machinery whereby, subject to the inherent limitations of the context, the individual can secure compliance with the relevant laws'. This machinery may include a number of possible remedies. It has been held that judicial review proceedings will be sufficient. In *Vilvarajah and four others v the UK* (1991) the applicants maintained that judicial review did not satisfy Article 13 as the English courts could not consider the merits of the Home Secretary's decision in this instance, merely the manner in which it was taken. In holding that the power of judicial review satisfied the Article 13 test the European Court of Human Rights took into account the power of the UK courts to quash an administrative decision for unreasonableness and the fact that these powers were exercisable by the highest tribunal in the UK. Thus no violation of Convention rights was found.

Article 13 does not contain a general guarantee that anyone who considers that his or her rights have been violated by the authorities should have an effective remedy; it can only be considered if one of the substantive rights or freedoms is in question. It does not and cannot connote a requirement that there should be domestic machinery in place to address *any* possible grievance. The words 'are violated' of Article 13 do not mean that the violation has been established before the national courts because obviously it could not be – if it could that would suggest that an effective remedy *did* exist. They mean that a person should have an arguable claim; there will be no breach of Article 13 if the complaint is unmeritorious – in other words, if it is clearly apparent that no violation of the Convention has taken place.

Even if no violation of the other Article is eventually found it can still be argued that the national courts should have provided an effective means of considering the possible violation. Moreover, a claim may eventually be held to be manifestly ill-founded and yet arguable. This is an odd result but, in principle, it is what the case law appears to disclose. In *Klass* it was found that 'Article 13 must be interpreted as guaranteeing an effective remedy before a national authority to everyone who *claims* that his rights and freedoms under the Convention have been violated'. In *Platform Arzte für das Leben*

(1988) it was found that the claim must be arguable. Thus Article 13 can be invoked only if no procedure is available in the domestic courts which can begin to determine whether a violation has occurred. In theory therefore there could be a breach of Article 13 alone and in that sense it protects an independent right. In practice case law tends not to follow this purist approach, and if no violation of the substantive right is found it is likely that no violation of Article 13 will be found either (as it may be argued occurred in the *Arzte für das Leben* case).

In the *Klass* case it was determined that phone tapping did not breach Article 8 as it was found to be in the interests of national security. The applicants claimed that Article 13 could be considered on the basis of their assertion that no effective domestic remedy existed for challenging the decision to tap. The court accepted that the existing remedy was of limited efficacy: it consisted only of the possibility of review of the case by a Parliamentary Committee. Nevertheless, it found that in all the circumstances no more effective remedy was possible. The irony of this case lay in the fact that the tapping was done in order to combat terrorism in its attack on democracy, but the means employed, which included the suspension of judicial remedies, might well be termed undemocratic.

Article 14 on prohibition of discrimination states:

3.16   Additional guarantees: Article 14

> The enjoyment of the rights and freedoms set forth in this Convention shall be secured without discrimination on any ground such as sex, race, colour, language, religion, political or other opinion, national or social origin, association with a national minority, property, birth or other status.

Article 14 does not provide a general right to freedom from discrimination, only that the rights and freedoms of the Convention must be secured without discrimination. An applicant may allege violation of a substantive right taken alone and also that he or she has been discriminated against in respect of that right.

However, even if no violation of the substantive right taken alone is found, and even if that claim is manifestly ill-founded, there could still be a violation of that Article and Article 14 taken together so long as the matter at issue is *covered* by the other Article. This was found in *X v Federal Republic of Germany* (1970)

> 'Article 14 of the Convention has no independent existence ...; nevertheless a measure which in itself is in conformity with the requirement of the Article enshrining the right or freedom in question, may however infringe

this Article when read in conjunction with Article 14 for the reason that it is of a discriminatory nature.

This provision allows more claims to be considered than the 'arguability' provision of Article 13. For example, in *Abdulaziz Cabales and Balkandali* (1985) the female claimants wanted their non-national spouses to enter the UK and alleged a breach of Article 8 which protects family life. That claim was rejected. But a violation of Article 14 was found because the way the rule was applied made it easier for men to bring in their spouses. It was held that: 'Although the application of Article 14 does not necessarily presuppose a breach (of the substantive provisions of the Convention and the Protocols) – and to this extent it is autonomous – there can be no room for its application unless the facts at issue fall within the ambit of one or more of the rights and freedoms'.

Under Article 14 discrimination connotes differential treatment which is unjustifiable. The differential treatment may be unjustifiable either in the sense that it relates to no objective and reasonable aim, or in the sense that there is no reasonable proportionality between the means employed and the aim sought to be realised. In *Abdulaziz* the aim was to protect the domestic labour market. It was held that that was not enough to justify the differential treatment because the difference in treatment was out of proportion to that aim.

3.17   Restriction of the rights and freedoms

All the Articles except Articles 3, 4(1), 6(2) and 7 are subject to certain restrictions, either because certain limitations are inherent in the formulation of the right itself, or because it is expressly stated that particular cases are not covered by the right in question (both these restrictions apply to Articles 2, 4 (except para 1) 5, 6 (except para 2) and 12), or because general restrictions on the primary right contained in the first paragraph are enumerated in a second paragraph (Articles 8–11). Moreover, further general restrictions are allowed under Articles 17, 15 and 64. In considering the restrictions Article 18 must be borne in mind. It provides that the motives of the national authority in creating the restrictions must be the same as the aims appearing behind the restrictions when the Convention was drafted.

3.17.1   Article 15

Article 15 on derogation from the rights and freedoms in case of public emergency:

> In time of war or other public emergency threatening the life of the nation any High Contracting Party may take measures derogating from its obligations under this Convention to the extent strictly required by the exigencies of the situation, provided that such measures

are not inconsistent with its other obligations under international law.

Article 15 allows derogation in respect of most but not all of the Articles. Derogation from Article 2 is not allowed except in respect of death resulting from lawful acts of war, while Articles 3, 4(1) and 7 are entirely non-derogable. The state in question must show that there is a state of war or public emergency, and in order to determine the validity of this claim two questions should be asked. Firstly, is there an actual or imminent exceptional crisis threatening the organised life of the state? Secondly, is it really necessary to adopt measures requiring derogation from the Articles in question? A margin of discretion is allowed in answering these questions because it is thought that the state in question is best placed to determine the facts, but it is not unlimited; Strasbourg will review it if the state has acted unreasonably. However, the court has not been very consistent on the margin allowed to the state. In general if a derogation is entered it must first be investigated and if found invalid the claims in question will *then* be examined.

The UK entered a derogation in the case of *Brogan* (1988) after the European Court had found that a violation of Article 5 which protects liberty had occurred. At the time of the violation there was no derogation in force in respect of Article 5 because the UK had *withdrawn* its derogation. This might suggest that there was no need for it or that the UK had chosen not to derogate despite the gravity of the situation which would have justified derogation.

However, *after* the decision in the European Court the UK entered the derogation stating that there was an emergency at the time. This was challenged in *Brannigan and McBryde v UK* (1993) as an invalid derogation but the claim failed on the basis that the exigencies of the situation did amount to a public emergency, and the derogation could not be called into question merely because the government had decided to keep open the possibility of finding a means in the future of ensuring greater conformity with Convention obligations. The fact that the emergency measures had been in place since 1974 did not mean that the emergency was not still in being. However, it may be argued that a state's failure to enter a derogation need not preclude the claim that a state of emergency did exist. If whenever a state perceived the possibility that an emergency situation might exist it felt it had to enter a derogation as an 'insurance measure' this would encourage a wide use of derogation.

In the *Greek* case (1969) the Commission was prepared to hold an Article 15 derogation invalid. Greece had alleged that the derogation was necessary due to the exigencies of the situation: it was needed to constrain the activities of communist agitators due to the disruption they were likely to cause. There had been past disruption which had verged on anarchy. Greece therefore claimed that it could not abide by the Articles in question: Articles 10 and 11. Apart from violations of those articles violations of Article 3 which is non-derogable were also alleged. The Commission found that the derogation was not needed; the situation at the decisive moment did not contain all the elements necessary under Article 15.

| 3.17.2 | General restrictions on the rights and freedoms contained in Articles 8–11 |

These Articles have a second paragraph enumerating certain restrictions on the primary right. Two general phrases are used in respect of these exceptions: 'prescribed by law' and 'necessary in a democratic society'. This phrase was interpreted in the *Handyside* case (1976) and the *Silver* case (1983) as meaning that to be compatible with the Convention the interference must, *inter alia*, correspond to a pressing social need and 'be proportionate to the legitimate aim pursued'. Taken together these two phrases mean that four steps will be taken if a restriction is to be invoked:

- Is the restriction in accordance with national law?

- Is the law on which the restriction is based aimed at protecting one of the interests listed in para 2; in other words does it fall within one of the exceptions?

- In the particular instance can it be said that the interference is necessary in the sense that although on the face of it the interference may be concerned with a particular restriction such as the protection of morals, is there a real need to protect morals in the particular case – a pressing social need – or is the threat to morals unclear or weak?

- Is the interference in proportion to the aim pursued or does it go further than is needed bearing in mind the objective in question?

The interests covered by the restrictions are largely the same: national security, protection of morals, the rights of others, public safety. The state is allowed a 'margin of appreciation' – a degree of discretion – as to the measures needed to protect the particular interest.

3.18 The doctrine of the 'margin of appreciation'

This doctrine was first adopted in respect of emergency situations but it has gradually permeated all the Articles. It has a particular application with respect to para 2 of Articles 8–11 but it can affect all the guarantees. In different cases a wider or narrower margin of appreciation has been allowed. In other words, the state is allowed more or less leeway in determining how far to protect certain interests which may conflict with convention rights. In considering this area it should be borne in mind that although the doctrine is well established it has not been applied very consistently and therefore only indications as to its application will be given.

A *narrow* margin may be allowed in which case a very full and detailed review of the interference with the guarantee in question will be conducted. This occurred in the *Sunday Times* case (1979); it was held that Strasbourg review was *not* limited to asking whether the state had exercised its discretion reasonably, carefully, and in good faith; it was found that its conduct must also be examined in Strasbourg to see whether it was compatible with the Convention.

If a broader margin is allowed Strasbourg review will be highly circumscribed. For example the *minority* in the *Sunday Times* case (9 judges) wanted to confine the role of Strasbourg to asking only whether the discretion in question was exercised in good faith and carefully and whether the measure was reasonable in the circumstances.

It is quite hard to predict when each approach will be taken but it seems to depend on four factors:

- The nature of the right in question; some are seen as particularly fundamental such as Article 10. Also the particular instance will be considered: does it concern a very important need for free expression; for example is there a great public interest in the subject matter?

- The nature of the restriction. Some are seen as more subjective than others, such as the protection of morals. It is therefore thought more difficult to lay down a common European standard and the European Court and Commission have in such instances shown a certain willingness to allow the exceptions a wide scope in curtailing the primary rights. For example, Article 10 contains an exception in respect of the protection of morals. This was invoked in the *Handyside* case (1976) in respect of a booklet aimed at schoolchildren which was circulating freely in the rest of Europe. It was held that the UK government was best placed to determine what was needed in its own country in order to protect morals and therefore no breach of Article 10 had occurred.

- Some restrictions, particularly national security, appear to fall more within the state's domain than others. It is thought that the state authorities are best placed to evaluate the situation and determine what is needed. In *Council of*

Civil Service Unions v UK (1988) the European Commission, in declaring the Unions' application inadmissible, found that national security interests should prevail over freedom of association even though the national security interest was weak while the infringement of the primary right was very clear: an absolute ban on joining a trade union had been imposed. It is worth noting that the ILO Committee on Freedom of Association had earlier found that the ban breached the 1947 ILO Freedom of Association Convention.

- The positive obligations placed on the state. In order to allow enjoyment of the Convention right in question the state may have to act positively. In such an instance a broad margin will be allowed.

The European Convention on Human Rights

The European Convention on Human Rights can have an impact on domestic law through the interpretation of statutes because it is a general principle of construction that statutes will be interpreted if possible so as to conform with International Treaties to which the UK is a party. The Convention can also influence the common law; if there is some leeway for it to do so, a court which must adjudicate on the relative weight to be given to different public interests under the common law should try to strike a balance in a manner consistent with the Convention. The Convention can also influence domestic law through the medium of EC law. EC law can of course have *direct* effect in UK courts; therefore certain Convention principles may come to be of limited binding force in the UK as forming part of EC law. Finally, a case may be brought against the UK by an individual and the UK government may have to change domestic law in response to an adverse ruling (expected or actual) in the European Court of Human Rights.

Re M and H (Minors) (1988)
R v Secretary of State for the Home Department ex p Brind and Others (1991)
Derbyshire County Council v Times Newspapers Ltd (1992)
AG v BBC (1980)
AG v Guardian Newspapers (No 2) (1990)
Nold v Commission (1974)

Impact on UK law

The most significant rights and freedoms guaranteed are the right to life (Article 2), freedom from torture and other degrading treatment (Article 3), the right to liberty and security of person (Article 5), the right to a fair and public hearing (Article 6), the right to respect for privacy (Article 8), freedom of expression (Article 10) and freedom of association and assembly (Article 11). Further, Article 14 provides that states must not discriminate between citizens in affording them the rights or freedoms, while Article 13 provides that states must provide a remedy for those who think that their Convention rights have been infringed.

X v UK and Ireland (1982)
Stewart v UK (1985)
Soering v UK (1989)
Vilvarajah and four others v UK (1991)

The substantive rights and freedoms

Weeks case (1987)
Fox, Campbell and Hartley (1990)
Neumeister case (1968)
Thyne, Wilson and Gunnel v UK (1990)
Campbell and Fell (1984)
Gaskin v UK (1987)
Klass case (1978)
Malone case (1982)
Rees (1987)
Dudgeon (1982)
W, B and R v UK (1987)
Abdulaziz, Cabales and Balkandali v UK (1985)
Sunday Times case (1979)
Handyside case (1976)
Muller v Switzerland (1991)
Open Door Counselling and Dublin Well Woman v Ireland (1992)
Young, James and Webster v UK (1981)
Leander (1987)
Platform Arzte für das Leben (1988)
X v Federal Republic of Germany (1970)

Restrictions and exceptions

There are a large number of restrictions and exceptions which may mean that the individual is unable to enjoy the right or freedom in question. All the Articles mentioned except Articles 3 and 6(2) are subject to certain restrictions, either because certain limitations are inherent in the formulation of the right itself, or because it is expressly stated that particular cases are not covered by the right in question, or because general restrictions on the primary right contained in the first paragraph are enumerated in a second paragraph (Articles 8-11). Such restrictions mean that the primary right may be infringed but in order to be compatible with the Convention such infringement must correspond to a pressing social need and be proportionate to the legitimate aim pursued. In making a determination as to these matters the court will allow the state a degree of discretion especially in sensitive areas such as national security. Moreover, states can derogate from the rights and freedoms under Article 15 due to a state of emergency. However, derogation from Article 2 is not allowed except in respect of death resulting from lawful acts of war, while Article 3 is entirely non-derogable.

Brogan (1988)
Greek case (1969)
Handyside case (1976)
Silver v UK (1983)
Sunday Times case (1979)
Council of Civil Service Unions v UK (1988)

Chapter 4

Restraining Freedom of Expression on Moral, Political and Religious Grounds

All countries which have a Bill of Rights protect freedom of expression as do international human rights treaties. It is generally accepted that it is one of the most fundamental rights. It is also a freedom which comes into conflict with more other interests than any other liberty and is therefore in more danger of being curtailed. Most Bills of Rights list these interests as exceptions to the primary right of freedom of speech as does the European Convention on Human Rights Article 10. This does not mean that the mere invocation of the other interest will lead to displacement of freedom of speech; it is necessary to show that there is a pressing social need to allow the other interest to prevail.

Although the UK has no Bill of Rights protecting freedom of speech, the European Convention on Human Rights Article 10 will be taken into account by the courts in construing ambiguous legislation on the basis that as Parliament must have intended to comply with its Treaty obligations, an interpretation should be adopted which will allow it to do so. Article 10 provides a surer safeguard for freedom of speech than UK domestic law since its starting point is that the primary right will prevail over competing interests. Article 10 has had some impact on the protection for freedom of speech under UK law through certain significant decisions in the European Court of Human Rights and because it has been taken into account where there is ambiguity in a statute or in common law. However, it has perhaps not had as much impact as might be expected, particularly in relation to the conflict between free speech and the protection of morality. The reasons why this may be so will be considered below.

There are two methods of protecting those interests which tend to come into conflict with freedom of speech: use of prior and subsequent restraints. Prior restraints are seen as more pernicious due to the 'invisibility' of the censorship they effect and therefore countries with a Bill of Rights either outlaw prior restraints or keep them to a minimum. By contrast, subsequent restraints operate *after* publication of the article in question: the persons responsible may face civil or criminal liability. The trial may then generate publicity and the defendants may have an opportunity of demonstrating why they published the article in question. In other words, the case for allowing the speech in question is given a hearing.

4.1 Introduction

However, the distinction between the two kinds of restraint may not be as stark as this implies. Subsequent restraints may have a chilling effect on publications; editors and others may well not wish to risk the possibility of incurring liability and may themselves, therefore, take the decision not to publish without reference to any outside body.

When one turns to consider UK law in this area one confronts a mass of common law and statutory restrictions on freedom of speech. In order to determine how far freedom of speech is protected it is necessary to consider the width of these restrictions in order to determine how much of an area of freedom is left within which freedom of speech can be exercised. It will be found that the law in this area has developed in an incoherent fashion; the lack of a consistent pattern is probably due to the lack of a free speech clause against which the other interests have to be measured. The emphasis will be on the judges' concern to strike a balance between free speech and a variety of other interests and a pervasive critical theme will be the exposure of the judges' readiness to allow freedom of expression to be restricted on uncertain or flimsy grounds.

In considering UK law it will be argued that statutes in this area give in general greater protection to freedom of speech than does the common law. It will be suggested that certain fairly recent common law developments have called into question the Diceyan view that the judges have a significant role as guardians of freedom of speech through their application of the common law, although the recent decision in *Derbyshire CC* (1994) may herald a move towards a more protective approach.

4.2   Free expression and morality

Almost all Bills or Charters of Rights contain an exception to the free speech clause allowing restraint on freedom of speech on the ground of protection of morality. The justification is the harm to be guarded against which seems to include three possibilities: the corruption of persons, particularly the more vulnerable; the shock or outrage caused by public displays of certain material, and the commission of sex crimes. The development of UK law has been based on the avoidance of the first two possibilities mentioned, and on those grounds the public display of certain publications can be regulated, while others can be prohibited entirely, either by punishment of those responsible after publication or by being suppressed or censored before publication.

4.2.1   UK law and theoretical considerations

It should be noted that the legal regulation of free speech on the ground of protection for morality does not reflect an established theoretical position. Laws aimed at protecting individuals from corruption are associated with the conservative view on censorship and morality but the academic expression of this view, Lord Devlin's work, *The Enforcement of Morals* (1965) does not square with existing UK law. In essence, Devlin's view is that since a shared set of basic moral values are essential to society, it is as justified in protecting itself against attacks on these values (mounted, for example, by pornography) as it is in protecting itself against any other phenomena which threaten its basic existence, such as violent public disorder.

This position is clearly *not* compatible with most existing UK law: it could neither support nor even account for the existence of the public good defence in s 4 of the Obscene Publications Act (see below at 4.3.5) or indeed any similar defence: it would seem absurd to argue that material which threatened the very survival of society should be allowed to circulate freely on the ground that it was somehow also in the public good.

If UK law is not compatible with academic conservatism, neither does it reflect a thoroughgoing liberalism. The liberal position on this issue is broadly united around general opposition to censorship in the absence of clear evidence of a concrete harm caused by its free availability.

Mill's argument that free speech is necessary as enabling discovery of the truth was avowedly the basis of the free speech justification adopted by the Williams Committee convened in 1979 to report on obscenity. Interference with the free flow of ideas and artistic endeavour was unacceptable since it amounted to ruling out in advance possible modes of human development, before it was known whether or not they would be desirable or necessary. Since the Committee also reached the conclusion that ' ... no-one has invented, or in our opinion *could* invent, an instrument that would suppress only [worthless pornography] and could not be turned against something ... of [possibly] a more creative kind', they concluded that this risk of suppressing worthwhile creative art ruled out censorship of the written word. (They regarded standard photographic pornography as not expressing anything that could be regarded as an 'idea' and so as unprotected by the argument from truth.) However, although some of the Committee's recommendations in the area of restricting the outlets of pornography have been enacted in legislation, their basic approach has not been enshrined in UK law. Thus, it may be concluded that although some aspects of obscenity and indecency laws reflect certain of these arguments, they have not developed in a manner which reflects a clear and coherent theoretical basis.

4.2.2 Methods of restraint

The type of restraint used to control sexually explicit material tends to depend on the type of publication in question, because it seems to be accepted that the harm which may be caused will vary from medium to medium. Thus printed matter, including magazines, newspapers and books, is not subject to censorship before publication but punishment is available afterwards if indecent or corrupting material is published. Books are less likely to be punished than magazines because it is thought that something which has a *visual* impact is more likely to cause harm. Thus films and broadcasts are censored due to their visual nature and are also subject to punishment. The theatre, however, is in an odd position; it has not been censored since 1968 despite its visual impact. Possibly this may be due to the idea that theatre audiences are more sophisticated and less likely to be affected by what they have seen than cinema audiences.

4.3 Obscenity law

Obscenity law operates as a subsequent restraint and is aimed at books, magazines and other printed material, although theoretically it could be used against broadcasts, films or videos. The harm sought to be prevented is a corrupting effect on an individual. In other words, it is thought that an individual will undergo a change for the worse after encountering the material in question. Of course, if all material which could corrupt were suppressed, a severe infringement of freedom of speech would occur. Thus, the statute which largely governs this area – the Obscene Publications Act 1959 – takes the stance that in preventing material which may deprave and corrupt, a line must be drawn between erotic literature and the truly obscene, on the basis that hard core pornography does not deserve special protection. This echoes the approach in America where hard core pornography is not defined as 'speech' because it is thought that the justification for the constitutional protection for freedom of speech does not apply. In fact, oddly enough, this seems to mean that pornography receives less protection in the USA than in the UK.

4.3.1 The nature of the offence under the Obscene Publications Act 1959 s 1

The 1959 Act was passed in an attempt to clear up uncertainty in this area of the law, although it failed to lay down a clear test for the meaning of the term 'deprave and corrupt'. The *actus reus* of the offence involves the publication of an article which tends, taken as a whole (or where it comprises two or more distinct items the effect of one of the items), to deprave and corrupt a significant proportion of those likely to see or hear it (s 1(1)). This is a crime of strict liability: there is no need to show an intention to deprave and corrupt, merely an intention to publish. Once it is shown that an article is obscene within the meaning of the Act, it will be irrelevant, following the ruling of the Court of Appeal in *Calder & Boyars* (1969), that the defendant's motivation could be characterised as pure or noble. It does not cover live performances on stage which fall within the similarly worded Theatres Act 1968.

The test could be applied to any material which might corrupt; it is clear from the ruling in *John Calder Publications v Powell* (1965) that it is not confined to descriptions or representations of sexual matters, and it could therefore be applied to a disturbing book on the life of a drug addict. This ruling was followed in *Skirving* (1985) which concerned a pamphlet on the means of taking cocaine in order to obtain maximum effect. In all instances the test for obscenity should not be applied to the type of behaviour advocated or described in the article in question but to the article itself. Thus in *Skirving* the question to be asked was not whether taking cocaine would deprave and corrupt but whether the pamphlet itself would.

4.3.2 The 'deprave and corrupt' test: application and attempts at definition

This test is hard to explain to a jury and uncertain of meaning. However, it is clear from the ruling of the Court of Appeal in *Anderson* (1972) that the effect in question must be more than mere shock. The trial judge had directed the jury that the test connoted that which was repulsive, loathsome or filthy. This explanation was clearly defective as it would have merged the concepts of indecency and obscenity, and it was rejected by the Court of Appeal on the basis that it would dilute the test for obscenity which, it was said, must connote the prospect of moral harm, not just shock. The conviction under the Act therefore had to be overturned due to the misdirection.

The House of Lords in *Knuller v DPP* (1972) considered the word 'corrupt' and found that it denoted a publication which produced 'real social evil' – going beyond immoral suggestions or persuasion. This was quite a strict test but it was qualified by the House of Lords in *DPP v Whyte* (1972). The owners of a bookshop which sold pornographic material were prosecuted. Most of the customers were old men who had encountered the material on previous occasions and this gave rise to two difficulties. Firstly, the old men were unlikely to engage in anti-social sexual behaviour and therefore the meaning of 'corrupt' had to be modified if it was to extend to cover the effect on them of the material. It was found that it meant creating a depraved effect on the mind which need not actually issue forth in any particular sexual behaviour. Secondly, it was suggested that the old men were already corrupt and therefore would not be affected by the material. However, it was held that corruption did not connote a once-only process: persons could be 'recorrupted' and on this basis the conviction was sustained.

The test will not be satisfied if the material in question causes feelings of revulsion from the immorality portrayed. This theory is known as the 'aversion theory' from *Calder & Boyars* (1969) which concerned the book *Last Exit from Brooklyn*; it was found that the horrific pictures it painted of homosexuality and drug-taking in New York would be more likely to discourage than encourage such behaviour.

| 4.3.3 | To whom does the test apply? | The 'deprave and corrupt' test must be applied to those likely to see or hear the material in question. In other words, the obscenity or otherwise of material cannot be determined merely by its consideration or analysis but will depend on the character of the consumer. It was found in *DPP v Whyte* (1972) that in order to make a determination as to the type of person in question the court could receive information as to the nature of the relevant area, the type of shop and its location in relation to residential housing or institutions such as schools. The jury must consider the likely reader in order to determine whether the material would deprave and corrupt him or her rather than considering the most vulnerable conceivable reader. In *Penguin Books* (1961), which concerned the prosecution of *Lady Chatterley's Lover*, the selling price of the book was taken into account and the fact that being in paperback it would reach a mass audience. |

The jury has to consider whether the article would be likely to deprave and corrupt a *significant proportion* of those likely to encounter it. It was determined in *Calder and Boyars Ltd* (1969) that the *jury* must determine what is meant by a significant proportion and this was approved in *DPP v Whyte* (1972), Lord Cross explaining that 'a significant proportion of a class means a part which is not numerically negligible but which may be much less than half'. The effect of the article as a whole on persons likely to encounter it should be considered, not merely the effect of specific passages of a particularly explicit nature. However, in *Anderson* (1972) it was made clear that where the article consists of a number of items each item must be considered in isolation from the others. Thus, a magazine which is on the whole innocuous but contains one obscene item can be suppressed although a novel could not be.

| 4.3.4 | Applying the test in practice | It may be reasonably straightforward to identify a group of whom a significant proportion might encounter the material, but it is unclear how it can then be determined that they would be likely to experience depravity and corruption as a result. |

The ruling in *Anderson* (1972) was to the effect that in sexual obscenity cases, and normally in other obscenity cases, the defence cannot call expert evidence as to the effect that an article may have on its likely audience. Thus, the view taken in *DPP v A and BC Chewing Gum Ltd* (1968) that such evidence would be admissible, must be regarded as arising only due to the very specific circumstances of that case. However, following *Skirving* (1985) in cases concerned with alleged depravity and corruption arising due to factors other than the sexual nature of the material, expert evidence as to the likely effect of such material *will*, exceptionally, be admissible.

Thus, generally speaking the jury will receive little help in applying the test. However, it seems clear that a court will take into account changing standards of morality ('the contemporary standards' test from *Calder and Boyars* (1969)) in considering what will deprave and corrupt. Therefore, the concept of obscenity is at least theoretically able to keep up to date. The application of these tests at the present time was seen in the trial for obscenity of the book *Inside Linda Lovelace* in (1976) which suggested that a prosecution brought against a book of any conceivable literary merit would be unlikely to succeed. Thus, in December 1991 the DPP refused to prosecute the Marquis de Sade's *Juliette*, even though it is concerned (fictionally) with the torture, rape and murder of women and children.

The defence of public good, which arises under the 1959 Act s 4 and the Theatres Act 1968 s 3, was intended to afford recognition to artistic merit and thus may be seen as a highly significant step in the direction of freedom of speech. Under the 1959 Act it is a defence to a finding that a publication is obscene if it can be shown that 'the publication of the article in question is justified as for the public good in that it is in the interests of science, literature, art, learning or of other objects of general concern'. Under the 1968 Act the similarly worded defence, which covers 'the interests of drama, opera, ballet or any other art, or of literature or learning' is somewhat narrower as omitting the concluding general words. Expert evidence will be admissible to prove that one of these possibilities can be established, and it may include considering other works.	4.3.5 The defence of public good: application

It was determined in *Penguin Books* (1961) in respect of *Lady Chatterley's Lover* that the jury should adopt a two-stage approach, asking firstly whether the article in question is obscene and if so going on to consider whether the defendant has established the probability that its merits are so high as to outbalance its obscenity so that its publication is for the public good. The failure of the prosecution was seen as a turning point for literary freedom and the jury allowed it to be known that the second stage of the test afforded the basis on which the novel escaped suppression. In *DPP v Jordan* (1977) the House of Lords approved this two-stage approach and the balancing of obscenity against literary or other merit.

In *DPP v Jordan* the attempt was made to widen the test. The main question was whether the articles in question – hard core pornography – could be justified under s 4 as being of psychotherapeutic value for persons of deviant sexuality in that the material might help to relieve their sexual tensions by way of sexual fantasies. It was argued that such material might provide a safety valve for such persons, which would divert them from anti-social activities, and that such benefit could fall within the words 'other objects of general concern' deriving from s 4. The House of Lords, however, held that these words must be construed *ejusdem generis* with the preceding words: 'art, literature learning, science'. As these words were unrelated to sexual benefit the general words which followed them could not be construed in the manner suggested. It was ruled that the jury must be satisfied that the matter in question made a contribution to a recognised field of culture or learning which could be assessed irrespective of the persons to whom it was distributed.

| 4.3.6 | Criticism of the defence |

Although the defence of public good has clearly afforded protection to freedom of expression in relation to publications of artistic merit, it has been criticised: it requires a jury to embark on the very difficult task of weighing a predicted change for the worse in the minds of the group of persons likely to encounter the article, against literary or other merit. Thus an effect or process must be imagined which once established must be measured against an intrinsic quality. Geoffrey Robertson has written: 'the balancing act is a logical nonsense [because it is not] logically possible to weigh such disparate concepts as 'corruption' and 'literary merit'.

The test seems on the face of it to create an almost complete paradox: it assumes that an individual can be corrupted, which suggests a stultifying effect on the mind, and yet can also experience an elevating effect due to the merit of an article. However, such an interpretation of the test is open to two objections. Firstly, a person could experience corruption in the sense that her moral standards might be lowered, but she might retain a sense of literary or artistic appreciation. Secondly – and this might seem the more satisfactory interpretation – the *message* of the article and its general artistic impact (through, for example, its influence on other works which followed it) might be for the public good, although some individuals who encountered it were corrupted. Thus the term 'publication' in s 4 must mean publication to the public at large, not only to those who encounter the article if the test is to be workable – a view apparently taken by the the House of Lords in *Jordan* (1977).

It should be noted that, as discussed below, the defence can be avoided by bringing a charge of indecency at common law; as *Sylveire and Gibson* (1990) demonstrated, the merits of an obscene object may, paradoxically, prevent its suppression while the merits of *less offensive* objects cannot.

Under s 3 of the 1959 Act magazines and other material, such as videos, can be seized in forfeiture proceedings if they are obscene and have been kept for gain. No conviction is obtained; the material is merely destroyed and no other punishment is imposed; therefore s 3 may operate at a low level of visibility. These proceedings may mean that the safeguards provided by the Act can be by-passed: consideration may not be given to the possible literary merits of material seized because the public good defence need not be taken in to account in issuing the seizure warrant. Further, in determining the question of forfeiture there may be a tendancy for magistrates not to take full account of the defence, but may tend to endorse his or her previous decision to issue a seizure warrant. Also, there is not much evidence that magistrates take a very rigorous approach to determining the obscenity of an article. They do not need to read every item but need only look at samples selected by the police (*Crown Court at Snaresbrook ex p Metropolitan Police Comr* (1984)) and seem in any event more ready than a jury to find that an item is obscene. It seems therefore that the protection afforded by the 1959 Act to freedom of speech is flawed in relation to forfeiture and appears to depend too greatly on the exercise of discretion by the police as to the enforcement of s 3, or on the tolerance of magistrates.

However, s 3 can be used only in respect of material which may be obscene rather than in relation to any form of pornography; it was held in *Darbo v DPP* (1992) that a warrant issued under s 3 allowing officers to search for 'sexually explicit material' was bad on its face as such articles would fall within a much wider category of articles than those which could be called obscene.

4.3.7   Forfeiture proceedings

It seems that UK law on obscenity is in harmony with Article 10 of the European Convention on Human Rights. In the *Handyside* case (1976) the European Court of HR had to consider the test of 'deprave and corrupt'. A book called *The Little Red Schoolbook*, which contained chapters on masturbation, sexual intercourse

4.3.8   Compatibility of the 1959 Act with Article 10

and abortion, was prosecuted under the 1959 Act on the basis that it appeared to encourage early sexual intercourse. The publishers applied for a ruling under Article 10 to the European Commission of HR. The Commission considered the protection of morals provision under Article 10(2) – which might allow suppression of the book – in order to determine whether such suppression was necessary.

It was found that the requirements of morals vary from time to time and from place to place, and that the domestic state authorities were therefore best placed to judge what was needed. The fact that the book was circulating freely in the rest of Europe was adjudged irrelevant to this issue. Thus, in finding that para 2 applied, the judgment accepted that domestic legislators would be allowed a wide margin of appreciation in attempting to secure the freedoms guaranteed under the Convention in this area, although this was not to be taken as implying that an unlimited discretion was granted.

4.4   Indecency

The concept of indecency, as opposed to obscenity, arises in certain statutes and exists at common law. The idea of prohibiting indecency is to prevent *public displays* of offensive material. Such prohibition is aimed at protecting persons from the shock or offence occasioned by encountering certain material, rather than at preventing moral deterioration. Therefore, except perhaps in a very broad sense, it may be said not to be aimed at the protection of morals at all. The general lowering of moral standards or attacks on the moral fabric of society must occur – if it is assumed that it is likely to occur at all – through the medium of individual persons who are affected by encountering obscene material; it would seem therefore that the 'moral fabric of society' would be unaffected by material which only serves to shock. If the material is not obscene and is either stored with a view to sale or offered for sale in a way that does not impinge on the general public, it will not attract liability.

Indecency is easier to prove than obscenity because there is no defence of public good, there is no need to consider the whole article, and there is no need to satisfy the difficult test of deprave and corrupt. Prosecuting authorities have taken note of these distinctions and have therefore tended at times to rely on the law against indecency where arguably the article in question could be said to be obscene (a trend reflected in Lord Denning's comments in *GLC ex p Blackburn* (1976)). It will be seen that the existence of these two strands of law has led to some anomalies.

The test for indecency was discussed in *Knuller v DPP* (1973); it was determined by Lord Reid to be satisfied by material which 'an ordinary decent man or woman would find to be shocking, disgusting or revolting'. This statement, coupled with the general tenor of Lord Reid's comments, suggested that the level of shock would have to be fairly high. In *GLC ex p Blackburn* (1976) Lord Denning approved the simple test: 'is this indecent?' as he considered that if jurors were asked the more complex question 'will this deprave and corrupt?' they would allow very offensive articles into circulation. However, Lord Bridge wondered whether asking whether something is shocking or disgusting could be a suitable test of criminality. Sir Robert Megarry has said that 'indecency' is too subjective and emotional a concept to be workable as a legal test.

It seems that the test is not confined to sexual material; Lord Reid in *Knuller* considered that 'indecency is not confined to sexual indecency'. This is supported by the finding in *Sylveire and Gibson* (1990) that the use, or apparent use, of freeze-dried foetuses as earrings on a model of a head was indecent.

4.4.1   General meaning of 'indecency'

Uncertainty arises as to whether the term 'indecency' denotes a relative concept: a concept which like that of relative obscenity, depends on its context or on the nature of the audience or recipient. According to the ruling of the Court of Appeal in *Straker* (1965), which arose under the Post Office Act 1953, such considerations are irrelevant: indecency is an objective quality discoverable by examination in the same way that, for example, a substance might be discovered to be a certain chemical. However, *Wiggins v Field* (1968) suggests otherwise; the ruling specifically demanded that the circumstances in which the alleged indecency occurred should be taken into account. A prosecution was brought in respect of a reading of Allen Ginsberg's poem *America* on the basis of a charge of using indecent language in contravention of a local bye law. The Divisional Court held that if the context was considered – this was the work of a recognised poet, read without any intention of causing offence – the charge of indecency could not be supported. This stance – of viewing the work as a whole and in context – was also taken by the Court of Appeal in *Attorney General v IBA ex p McWhirter* (1973). Thus, it may be that the *Straker* ruling, to the effect that indecency may be treated as an objective concept, is confined to cases arising under the Post Office Act, but the point cannot yet be regarded as settled.

4.4.2   'Indecency' an objective or a relative notion?

4.4.3	Range of offences concerned with indecency	The word 'indecent' is contained in a number of statutes and bye laws. Therefore, only specific areas are covered, but if no statute affects a particular area the gap may be filled by the common law. Taking an indecent photograph of a person under the age of 16 is prohibited under the Protection of Children Act 1978. Offensive displays fall under the Indecent Displays (Control) Act 1981, which covers public displays of anything capable of being displayed, but is limited in its application; it does not apply to the theatre, cinema, broadcasting (which are covered by different provisions), museums, art galleries, local authority or Crown buildings. Shops which display an adequate warning notice are exempted (s 3(b)) as far as adults are concerned; thus, as will be seen below, art galleries are, anomalously, *more* constrained in their displays than sex shops, in that they will fall within the common law on indecency and will not be able to take advantage of this exception. Mailing of sexual literature is covered by the Post Office Act 1953 s 11; sexual literature in luggage is covered by the Customs and Excise Act 1979 s 49.
4.4.4	Importing indecent material	In the seventies Customs officials interpreted the term 'indecency' under the Customs legislation very widely. In 1976, for example, they seized and destroyed 114,000 books and magazines and 4,000 films. It also appeared that the test was being used in an arbitrary and indiscriminate manner. For example, in 1985 books ordered by the bookshop 'Gay's the Word' were impounded, including books by Oscar Wilde and Gore Vidal. The trial was about to commence but the proceedings were withdrawn because of the ruling of the European Court of Justice in *Conegate Ltd v Customs and Excise Commissioners* (1987).

It was held under Articles 30 and 36 of the Treaty of Rome that Britain could not apply a more stringent test – indecency – to imported goods when the equivalent in terms of domestically produced goods could circulate freely because they were not obscene. Thus where obscenity or indecency existed as alternatives the easier test should not be used to favour domestic goods as that would amount to arbitrary discrimination on trade between Member States contrary to Article 36 of the Treaty of Rome. Customs officers now apply this ruling, but not just to EC imports, because it would be too impractical to apply different tests to imports from different countries. This ruling has therefore resulted in a major relaxation on censorship. Hard core pornography is, however, still seized; this is justifiable under Article 36 because it would also be prohibited if disseminated internally, under the Obscene Publications Act.

Anomalies have often arisen from the dichotomy between the tests for indecency on the one hand and obscenity on the other. In *Straker* (1965) obscenity charges which resulted in an acquittal were brought in respect of the sale of artistic nude studies. The defendant then sent the pictures by post to persons interested in photographic art and was prosecuted successfully under the Post Office Act 1953 s 11. In other words, the mere fact that the articles happened to be transferred through the post meant that criminal liability could arise although otherwise it could not have done so. The DPP has recognised the anomalies created by cases of this nature and therefore he indicated – in 1981 – that prosecutions under the Post Office Act would be confined to cases where the indecent material sent through the post was unsolicited.

4.4.5   Anomalies in the law

Apart from statutes prohibiting the promulgation of indecent material in specific situations, the possibility also arises of using the Sexual Offences Act 1956 to prevent displays of indecency in stage plays, and perhaps in the context of other live performances. In 1982 a play, the *Romans in Britain*, which was staged by the National Theatre, included a depiction of the homosexual rape of a young druid priest by three Roman soldiers. Mary Whitehouse was unable to bring a private prosecution under the common law in respect of this scene because under s 2 of the Theatres Act, liability at common law could not arise in respect of a stage performance. Therefore, she invoked s 13 of the Sexual Offences Act 1956 which proscribes the procurement by one male of an act of gross indecency on another, and which was arguably fulfilled by the procurement by the male director of the commission of such an act by one actor on another. It was determined on a preliminary ruling that *prima facie* liability might be established using this method, though the prosecution was then withdrawn: as the point that liability could arise in this way had been made, and there was a risk that it would fail on various grounds.

4.4.6   Indecency on the stage

The artificiality of the proceedings was demonstrated in that had a female director been in charge no prosecution would have been possible. The significance of this possible area of liability should not be over-emphasised; nevertheless it clearly subverts the purpose of the Theatres Act which should therefore be amended to prohibit liability arising under other statutes.

Common law offences arising from the promulgation of sexually explicit material create a wider area of liability than under statute because liability is not confined to specific situations such as using the mail. In *Shaw v DPP* (1962), the

4.4.7   The basis for common law liability

House of Lords determined that the offence of conspiring to corrupt public morals existed, on the basis that the law conferred a general discretion to punish immoral (not merely criminal) conduct which could injure the public. It was found that any subject matter which could lead others astray – although not necessarily mounting to a criminal offence – could be the subject of a prosecution if two or more persons were involved. Lord Reid in his dissenting judgment argued that the decision offended against the principle that the criminal law should be reasonably certain; it would be very difficult to determine beforehand what a jury would consider to fall within the area of liability created.

The DPP has used this form of liability in instances where the material in question appeared to fall outside the Obscene Publications Act, or has added a charge of conspiracy to corrupt public morals to a charge of obscenity as an alternative in case the obscenity charge failed.

4.4.8	The requirements of the offences

In *Knuller v DPP* the House of Lords confirmed the existence of the offence of conspiring to corrupt public morals, although it was found that the definition from *Shaw* was too broad and that the offence would only be committed if the conduct in question threatened the very fabric of society.

The existence of the substantive offence of outraging public decency and conspiring to commit it was also confirmed. It was found that the indecency need not be immediately visible but must in some way be projected; there must be an express or implied invitation to open the material and partake of the lewd contents; therefore there must be a reference on the cover to the contents.

Furthermore, the contents must be so offensive that the sense of decency of the public would be outraged by seeing them. Whether or not a member of the public would be so outraged, would be determined by reference to that section of the public likely to frequent the place where the publication in question was sold. The motive in offering the article would be irrelevant although it would be necessary to show that the defendant was aware both of the lewd nature of the material in question and that it was being placed on public sale. However, in *Gibson* (1990), it was held that no intent to outrage public decency or recklessness as to the risk of such outrage need be established; it was only necessary to prove that a defendant had intentionally done an act which *in fact* outraged public decency; he could not escape liability merely because his own standards were so base that he could not appreciate that outrage might be caused.

In two significant respects, after Knuller, conspiracy to outrage public decency may differ from conspiracy to corrupt public morals: the latter requires that the defendants should intend that the morals of readers should be corrupted and may be open to a defence of public good. The need to show *mens rea* means that in one respect this offence is harder to establish than a charge of obscenity.

In the *Gibson* case, the Court of Appeal reaffirmed the ruling of the House of Lords in *Knuller* as to the ingredients of the offence of outraging public decency in considering an allegedly indecent sculpture. The defendants were convicted of the offence after displaying in an art gallery a model of a human head with earrings made out of freeze-dried human foetuses of three to four months gestation. Argument on appeal centred on s 2(4) of the 1959 Act which provides that where a prosecution is brought in respect of an obscene article it must be considered within the Act, not at common law 'where it is of the essence of the offence that the matter is obscene'. 'Obscene' could denote something which disgusted the public or something which had a tendency to corrupt; if it carried the first meaning the prosecution failed as there was no suggestion that the exhibition of the earrings had a tendency to corrupt. If the second, more restricted meaning were accepted, it was argued that that would undermine the defence contained in s 4 of the Act which could be invoked if the material in question was, *inter alia*, of artistic worth.

4.4.9   Indecency and artistic expression

However, Lord Lane held that the words of s 1(1) were plain and clearly indicated that the *restricted* meaning of 'obscene' applied throughout the Act. If the defence argument on the meaning of obscene had been accepted, the sculpture would have fallen within the Obscene Publications Act and could have benefited from the s 4 defence. As it is, the anomaly has been continued that the artistic merit of objects which more seriously breach normal moral standards – objects which may corrupt – can prevent their suppression while the merits of less offensive objects cannot. A further anomaly arises due to the exclusion from the Indecent Displays Act of art galleries which, as noted above, are actually more restricted under common law.

Although there are obvious similarities between these two forms of common law conspiracy, and they are usually considered together in textbooks (such as Smith and Hogan's *Criminal Law* (1992)), they are each aimed at a distinct mischief. Conspiracy to corrupt public morals clearly stems from the same roots as the offence under the Obscene Publications Act, rather than forming a part of the laws against indecency. Its

4.4.10   Conclusions

existence is therefore perhaps even less defensible than that of conspiracy to outrage public decency as it covers an area of liability which is very hard to distinguish from that covered by the 1959 Act, and it is therefore most likely to allow escape from the statutory safeguards.

On the other hand, it may be argued that the protection of morals answers to a more weighty public interest than the prevention of shock or outrage; Article 10 contains an exception expressed in terms of the former interest but not the latter. However, when the defendants in *Gibson* applied to the European Commission alleging a breach of Article 10, the application was found inadmissible, suggesting either that in the particular circumstances the conviction might have appeared to have the effect of protecting morals as opposed to merely preventing outrage, or that the 'protection of morals' exception *does* cover material which merely shocks. It must be said that at present the European Court of Human Rights has not drawn a clear distinction between the two mischiefs: in *Muller v Switzerland* (1991) paintings found to offend against morals under Swiss law fell within Article 10(2) as likely to 'grossly offend the sense of sexual propriety of persons of ordinary sensitivity'. This sounds like indecency rather than corruption but the court did not make anything of this distinction.

It may be noted that the development of the wide ranging and flexible doctrines of common law indecency and conspiracy to corrupt public morals bears some resemblance to that of common law contempt: both doctrines work in tandem with statutes which create a narrower and more precise area of liability and which provide a defence which may ensure compatibility with Article 10 of the European Convention on Human Rights. In both instances therefore the common law tends to undermine the safeguards for free speech provided by the statute.

4.5   Censorship of broadcasting

In part the Broadcasting Acts and the Cinemas Act 1985 were passed because it was thought that due to their particular impact on audiences, a special regime was needed for the moving image, and so it required a system of prior restraints whereas books and other printed material did not. This was also the view of the Williams committee although it can be argued that the evidence that films have a very different impact from books or magazines is not strong, and that the difference in treatment may be due to the relative youth of the medium; it has not yet gained the acceptance accorded to traditional mediums and is still viewed with some suspicion. The Williams Committee considered that in the light of some psychiatric evidence to the effect that violent films might induce violent behaviour a policy based on caution was justified. Due to the availability of censorship, it is very unlikely that a broadcast could attract liability under the Obscene Publications Act; nevertheless it provides a further possibility of restraint and can also be used as a guide as to the minimum standards censorship will observe.

Government influence over broadcasting is of enormous significance due to the importance of broadcasting as the main means of informing the public as to matters of public interest. The openly partisan nature of the popular press means that broadcasting provides the only impartial source of information for many people. Government may exert control over broadcasting by overt means, which can include the operation of parts of the Broadcasting Act 1990, in particular s 10(3), or through more subtle means such as the criteria used to determine appointments to the BBC governors. The recent 'de-regulation' of television under the 1990 Broadcasting Act might appear to suggest a movement away from governmental influence, but it raises other questions about the influence of the new owners of broadcasting stations who might wish to use broadcasting as a means of exerting political influence. However, the 1990 Act contains provisions designed to preserve political neutrality in broadcasting.

4.5.1   Broadcasting: general considerations

As part of the 'de-regulation' of television the 1990 Act sets up the Independent Television Commission (ITC) to replace the Independent Broadcasting Authority (IBA) as a public body charged with licensing and regulating non-BBC television services. The ITC is required, under a new impartiality clause introduced by s 6 of the 1990 Act, to set up a Code to require that politically sensitive programmes must be balanced in order to ensure impartiality. Such programmes can be balanced by means of a series of programmes; it is not necessary that any one programme should be followed by another specific balancing programme. However, the requirement may mean that some politically controversial programmes are not made: the expense and difficulty of setting up balancing programmes may prove to have a deterrent effect. In interpreting this Code, the companies may act cautiously and may interpret what is meant by 'bias' broadly. Thus, although this new provision may seek to balance a need for impartiality against the need to protect freedom of expression it may not achieve that balance in practice.

4.5.2   Control over broadcasting on political grounds

Obviously s 6 can only affect a *positive* decision to broadcast a programme dealing with a sensitive issue; there is nothing in the arrangements for the franchising of independent television and radio to affect a decision to ignore some such issues on political grounds. The franchises went to the highest bidder once a 'quality control threshold' was satisfied. Nothing was done to attempt to ensure that a political balance between franchise holders was achieved at that stage.

The impartiality clause only affects non-BBC broadcasting, although the BBC has undertaken to comply generally with the statutory duties placed on the IBA (replaced by the ITC). However, this undertaking is unenforceable and instead BBC censorship operates by a process of 'reference up' the Corporation management hierarchy: producers refer to middle management who may seek direction from departmental heads who may then consult the Managing Director or even the Director General.

Thus censorship is largely self-imposed; the government cannot bring *direct* influence to bear. However, the Board of Governors of the BBC are appointed by the government, and although they usually leave editorial matters to the Director General, they may occasionally intervene. They did so in 1985 in relation to a programme about an IRA sympathiser in Belfast, 'Real Lives', after condemnation of it by the Prime Minister – an incident perceived as damaging to the BBC's reputation for independence from the government. On the other hand, certain incidents such as coverage of the USA bombing of Libya, have led to expressions of concern from the Conservative party about BBC 'bias' against the government, although this may have been partly mollified by the banning of a documentary on the Zircon spy satellite project in 1987 and a documentary on the workings of Cabinet government. Both films were eventually shown with modification, the latter by Channel 4 in 1991.

4.5.3   Direct governmental censorship

Apart from the restraints already mentioned, government has a direct power of censorship (under s 10(3) Broadcasting Act 1990) which is of the widest possible nature. Its predecessor was invoked by the Secretary of State in 1988 in order to issue directives requiring the IBA to refrain from broadcasting words spoken by persons representing certain extremist groups or words spoken supporting or inviting support for those groups. The very similar power under clause 13(4) of the 1981 licence and agreement between the Home Secretary and the BBC was invoked in order to apply the same ban to the BBC. The ban remained in place until September 1994 when it was lifted after the IRA declared the cessation of violence. The ban was challenged by the National Union of Journalists and others but not by the broadcasting organisations themselves in *Regina v Secretary of State for the Home Department ex p Brind and*

Others (1991). The ban covered organisations proscribed under the Northern Ireland (Emergency Provisions) legislation and also Sinn Fein, Republican Sinn Fein and the Ulster Defence Association. The applicants submitted that the Home Secretary in exercising discretionary powers was under a duty not to act in a way incompatible with Article 10 of the European Convention as it was presumed that this would be contrary to the intention of the enabling legislation. Given this duty, it followed that in curtailing freedom of expression where there was no pressing social need to do so the directives contravened Article 10 so that the Minister had acted *ultra vires*.

The House of Lords held that the issuing of the directives could not be seen as *ultra vires*. It could not be presumed that discretionary powers were limited by the terms of the Convention since this would amount to assuming that Parliament had intended to import the text of the Convention into domestic administrative law. Since in fact Parliament had never incorporated the Convention into domestic law an intention to do so could not be presumed.

A further submission that the Minister's directives were disproportionate to the mischief at which they were aimed, and subject to review on that basis also failed. It was held that lack of proportionality was merely to be regarded as one aspect of *Wednesbury* unreasonableness, not as a separate head of challenge. The question to be asked was therefore whether the Minister's decision was one which no reasonable Minister could have made. Taking into account the fact that the directives did not restrict the reporting of information but merely the manner of its presentation, it was found that this ground of challenge had not been made out.

Although the challenge failed, it would be over-stating the matter to say that broadcasters' freedom of expression will now depend more on the forbearance of the Home Secretary than on the law. The House of Lords indicated that the challenge might have succeeded had the interference been more wide ranging. Nevertheless the ban meant that a Sinn Fein or IRA member could not be forced to justify their policies and therefore it offended against the notion that flawed or evil speech is best combated by further speech.

Under s 6(1)(a) of the 1990 Act the ITC must attempt to ensure that every licensed television service includes nothing in its programmes 'which offends against good taste and decency'. The ITC published a Programme Code dealing with these matters in 1991 which attempts to strike a balance between preserving good taste and decency on the one hand and avoiding too great a restraint on freedom of speech on the

4.5.4   Censorship on grounds of taste and decency

other. It therefore allows sexual scenes so long as they are presented with tact and discretion. As far as films are concerned it follows the guidelines laid down by the BBFC (see below); '18' rated films may be shown but only after 10.00 pm. Further, the BBFC standards are to be regarded as minimum ones; the mere fact that a film has an '18' certificate is not to be taken as implying that it would be proper to broadcast it. The role of the ITC in this respect is to an extent duplicated by the Broadcasting Standards Council (BSC), set up in 1988 to monitor the standards being maintained in programmes. Section 152 of the 1990 Act required the BSC to draw up a Code relating to broadcasting standards which covered the BBC and independent broadcasting. Thus, it seems that as far as independent television is concerned, a dual and overlapping system is in place imposing an onerous burden on the companies.

In some respects the new arrangements could be said to represent a slackening of restraint on what may be broadcast in the sense that the television companies will no longer have to submit their controversial programmes to an outside body for preview and censorship. As the Annan Committee pointed out in 1977, the old system meant that programmes might be subject to dual censorship in being considered first by the IBA and then by the company concerned. However, although such censorship is now solely in the hands of the companies themselves, the ITC has a number of sanctions to use against a company which fails to abide by the Programming Code, ranging from a requirement to broadcast an apology to the power to revoke its licence. The financial penalties available are very severe and may deter the companies from taking risks in their interpretation of what is allowed by the Code.

4.6   Censorship of the cinema

Censorship of films operates on two levels: firstly the British Board of Film Classification, a self-censoring body set up by the film industry in 1912, may insist on cuts before issuing a certificate allowing the film to be screened, or it may refuse to issue a certificate at all. It was set up in response to the Cinematograph Act 1909 which allowed local authorities to grant licences in respect of the films to be shown in their particular area; the idea was that the film industry would achieve a uniformity of decision-making by local councils. Thus it would have a guide as to whether a film would be shown and as to where to make cuts in order to achieve a wider audience.

In order to protect children, films are classified by age: U films are open to anybody as in effect are PG (parental guidance) classified films but thereafter restrictions are effected by the 12, 15 or 18 rating for films. R18 films (restricted viewing) may be viewed only on segregated premises. An R18 certificate means that the BBFC considers that the film would survive an Obscene Publications Act prosecution; it will refuse a certificate if it is thought that a film might not so survive, even in a 'cut' form. In coming to its decision the BBFC may take the restricted 'public good' defence under s 4(1A) of the Obscene Publications Act 1959 into account and may grant a certificate on the grounds of artistic merit to a film which contains some obscene matter. Under the Criminal Justice and Public Order Act 1994 s 90 the BBFC must have 'special regard' to harm which may be caused to film viewers or through their behaviour to society by the manner in which the film deals with criminal activity, violent or horrific incidents or behaviour and sexual behaviour. Videos are censored in the same way, and under the Video Recordings Act 1984 it is an offence to supply an uncensored video.

The second level of censorship is operated by local authorities under the Cinemas Act 1985 which continues their old power arising under the Cinematograph Act 1909. The local authority will usually follow the BBFC's advice but may choose not to grant a licence to a film regardless of its decision. Films which have been licensed but which nevertheless have been banned in some areas include: *A Clockwork Orange*, *The Life of Brian*, and *The Last Temptation of Christ*. There is no requirement of consistency between authorities and thus discrepancies have arisen between different local authority areas.

If there is to be reform of the law relating to the protection of morals the government will have to take the initiative. After the decisions in the *Handyside* case (1976) and in *Muller v Switzerland* (1991), it seems unlikely that any UK move towards greater protection of freedom of speech in this area will be brought about by recourse to the European Convention on Human Rights because the UK position in respect of restraints on freedom of speech in the name of protection of morality does not appear to breach Article 10 of the Convention. It seems that the exception contained in Article 10(2) in respect of the interpretation of morals will continue to be widely interpreted because the court will wish to allow a wide margin of appreciation to Member States in this very sensitive area.	**4.7** **Reform of the law relating to protection of morals**
The Williams Committee recommended in 1979 that the printed word should not be subject to any restraint and that other material should be restrained on the basis of two specific tests: first, material which might shock should be available only through restricted outlets; second, material should not be prohibited unless it could be shown to cause specific harm.	4.7.1 The Williams Committee recommendations

Clearly, these proposals would give greater weight to freedom of speech than the protection of morals in that they would allow greater differentiation between the kind of harm which might be caused by the various media. They emphasise a fundamental difference between prohibition and restriction of the sale of obscene articles.

The Committee's proposals have found partial expression in The Indecent Displays Act 1981, the provisions under the Local Government (Miscellaneous Provisions) Act 1982 for regulating 'sex establishments' and the Cinematograph (Amendment) Act 1982 which changed the classification of films and introduced the R18 rating. However, the proposal as to removing the prohibition, as opposed to restriction, from the *written* word and from much other pornographic material has not been implemented, and therefore the uncertain deprave and corrupt test remains as an arguably unacceptable restraint on artistic freedom.

4.8 Blasphemy and religious hatred

The basis of the offence of blasphemous libel which derived from *Taylor's* case (1676), was that the defendant had aspersed the Christian religion and, more particularly, Anglicanism. By the middle of the 19th century and in particular after the case of *Ramsay and Foote* (1883) it became clear that the basis of blasphemy had changed: it required a scurrilous attack on Christianity rather than merely reasoned and sober arguments against it.

4.8.1 The present offence of blasphemy

It was thought by 1950 that the offence was a dead letter but it re-emerged in *Lemon* (1979). *Gay News* published a poem – *The love that dares to speak its name* – by a Professor of English literature, James Kirkup. It expressed religious sentiment in describing a homosexual's conversion to Christianity, and it metaphorically attributed homosexual acts to Jesus and made an explicit reference to sodomy. A private prosecution was brought against *Gay News* and the editor and publishing company were convicted of the offence of blasphemous libel.

The Court of Appeal held that the intention or motive of the defendants was irrelevant as blasphemy was a crime of strict liability, and the Lords confirmed that mere intention to publish the material constituted the *mens rea* of the offence. Moreover, it could be committed by a Christian as there was no need to show that the material had mounted a fundamental attack on Christianity (as had been thought). There was no defence of publication in the public interest; serious literature could therefore be caught. The work in question need not be considered as a whole. All that needed to be shown was that the material in question, which was published with the defendant's knowledge, had crossed the borderline between moderate criticism on the one hand and immoderate treatment of objects sacred to Christians on the other. There was no need to show indecent or offensive treatment of such objects, nor was it necessary to show that resentment would be likely to be aroused. The past requirement to show that a breach of the peace might be occasioned by publication of the material was also no longer necessary.

This decision has been much criticised as it inhibits juxtaposition of sexuality with aspects of the Anglican religion by writers and broadcasters. In common with other parts of the common law it allows the Obscene Publications Act to be circumvented because it admits of no public good defence. Moreover, there are already various areas of liability arising at common law and under statute which could be used to prevent offence being caused to Christians.

Gay News applied to the European Commission on Human Rights on a number of grounds including that of a breach of Article 10. This application was ruled inadmissible in a cautious judgment. It was found that the Article 10 guarantee of freedom of expression had been interfered with but that the interference fell within the 'rights of others' exception of Article 10(2). Was the interference necessary in a democratic society? It was found that once it was accepted that the religious feelings of citizens may deserve protection if attacks reach a certain level of savagery, it seemed to follow that the domestic authorities were best placed to determine when that level was reached. In other words, the argument used in the *Handyside* case (1976) that a very wide margin of appreciation was required was invoked.

It seems fairly clear that this offence will not be extended beyond Anglicanism. The Law Commission in their 1985 Report concluded that an offence of wounding the feelings of	4.8.2 The future of blasphemy: extension of the law?

adherents of any religious group would be impossible to construct because the term 'religion' could not be defined with sufficient precision. The argument in favour of extension of the offence was put and rejected in *Chief Metropolitan Magistrates' Court ex p Choudhury* (1991) a case which arose out of the publication of Salman Rushdie's *The Satanic Verses*. The applicants applied for judicial review of the refusal of a magistrate's court to grant summonses against Salman Rushdie and his publishers for *inter alia* the common law offence of blasphemous libel. The Court of Appeal determined after reviewing the relevant decisions that the offence of blasphemy was clearly confined only to publications offensive to Christians. Extending the offence would, it was determined, create great difficulties as it would be virtually impossible to define the term 'religion' sufficiently clearly. Freedom of expression would be curtailed as authors would have to try to avoid offending members of many different sects.

The applicants did not, however, rely only on domestic law; during argument that the offence should be extended it was said that UK law must contain a provision to give effect to the Convention guarantee of freedom of religion under Article 9. In response it was argued and accepted by the Court of Appeal that the Convention need not be considered because the common law on the point is not uncertain. However, the respondents nevertheless accepted that in this particular instance the Convention should be considered. It was found that the UK was not in breach of the Convention because extending the offence of blasphemy would breach Articles 10 and 7; the exceptions of Article 10(2) could not be invoked as nothing in the book would support a pressing social need for its suppression. Furthermore, it was uncertain that Article 9 was applicable; it would be infringed if Muslims were prevented from exercising their religion, but such restrictions were not in question. Moreover, Article 9(2) contains a number of exceptions including that of protection for the rights of others which would be relevant.

The applicants put forward the further argument that UK blasphemy law discriminated against Muslims and therefore a violation of Article 14 read in conjunction with Article 9 had occurred. This interpretation of Article 9, read alongside Article 14, had been rejected by the European Commission in the *Gay News* case (1982). In this case it also failed on the ground that the envisaged extension of UK law to protect Islam would involve a violation of Article 10 which guarantees freedom of expression. Such an extension was not therefore warranted. It seems clear from this ruling and from statements made by Lord Scarman in the House of Lords in *Lemon* which were relied upon in the *Choudhury* case, that the judiciary are not minded to extend this offence.

It also seems that extension of blasphemy law is unlikely to come about due to decisions of the European Court or Commission of Human Rights. In *Choudhury* (1991) the applicants in the *Choudhury* case argued before the Commission that Article 9 required states to take steps to protect the religious feelings of Muslims. This argument failed, but the ruling in *Otto-Preminger Institut v Austria* (1994) that Article 9 requires that religious feelings should be protected by banning material which might cause offence to religious adherents may be inconsistent with the finding of the Commission in relation to the Satanic Verses. It might be argued in future on the basis of *Otto-Preminger Institut v*

Austria that states are *required* to put in place measures to protect religious feelings. Nevertheless, at present it appears that failure to extend blasphemy law beyond Christianity does not constitute a breach of Article 9.

It is clear that some change is needed in the current law for at least two reasons. Firstly, from a pragmatic point of view, the present situation, since it is perceived by Muslims as unfair, is a considerable source of racial tension; it both engenders feelings of anger and alienation in the Muslim community and, when these feelings are expressed through such activities as book-burning and attacks on booksellers stocking the *Satanic Verses*, increased feelings of hostility towards Muslims in certain sections of the non-Muslim population. Secondly, it is indefensible that the state should single out one group of citizens and protect their religious feelings while others are without such protection. Since extension of the law does not seem a realistic alternative, it would appear that abolition of blasphemy as an offence would be the simplest way of remedying the current unfairness of the law in this area. However, it is arguable that abolition should be coupled with creation of a new offence of religious hatred as suggested below.

4.8.3   Abolition of the offence

The International Covenant on Civil and Political Rights, of which the UK is a signatory, requires contracting states to prohibit the advocacy of 'national, racial or *religious* hatred that constitutes incitement to discrimination, hostility or violence.' (Article 20). In practical terms, it would be fairly straightforward to amend ss 17, 18, 19 and 23 of Part III of the Public Order Act 1986 which prohibit incitement to racial hatred, to include religious groups. This would remedy the present situation, which permits the advocacy of hatred against Muslims, while Sikhs and Jews (as racial groups) are protected from such speech. The problem of defining religion of course still remains; however, since such incitement represents a far narrower area of liability than blasphemy, the danger that a wide interpretation of 'religion' would lead to the courts being overrun by claims from obscure groups is accordingly less great. Furthermore, prosecutions in this area can only be brought with the consent of the DPP, so the possibility of frivolous prosecutions being brought would be slight. There appears therefore to be an arguable case for extending the offence of incitement to racial hatred to cover religious groups.

4.8.4   The case for creating an offence of incitement to religious hatred

The acceptability of the proposal to create such a new offence is dependant on the assumption that the prohibition of incitement to racial hatred under the Public Order Act does not already create an unacceptable infringement of freedom of speech. It may be argued however, that the offences as currently conceived go beyond the mischief they are intended to prevent. There is an argument that some provision should be available to prevent racist speech due to its special propensity to lead to disorder, and that such protection should be extended to religious groups, but it is suggested that one could comfortably support the addition of incitement to religious hatred to the Public Order Act offences only once they had been reformed to encompass a much narrower area of liability.

Restraining Freedom of Expression on Moral, Political and Religious Grounds

Obscenity

Obscenity law operates as a subsequent restraint and is mainly aimed at books, magazines and other printed material. The offence requires the publication of an article (which need not be of a sexual nature) which tends to deprave and corrupt a significant proportion of those likely to see or hear it. There is no need to show an intention to deprave and corrupt, merely an intention to publish. The effect on the reader must be more than mere shock, but there is no need to show a likelihood that the material will cause anti-social conduct. The test will not be satisfied if the material in question causes feelings of revulsion from the immorality portrayed. It is a defence to show that the publication of the article in question is justified as for the public good, a test which has been criticised as requiring impossible judgments to be made. The Act also creates a limited power of forfeiture.

John Calder Publications v Powell (1965)

R v Anderson (1972)

Knuller v DPP (1972)

DPP v Jordan (1977)

Indecency under statute

Statutory offences of indecency are concerned with the dissemination and public display of material including non-sexual material. The test for indecency is vague but probably satisfied by material which 'an ordinary decent man or woman would find to be shocking, disgusting or revolting'; jurors will have considerable discretion and there is no defence of public good although context and the total impact of the article may be taken into account. Offences of public display are not specifically covered by statute in a number of situations (although the common law will apply) and shops may be required only to display warnings. The Sexual Offences Act 1956 may create liability in the context of drama and live performance. The dissemination of indecent material is controlled by provisions relating to the mailing of sexual literature and to such literature when carried in luggage.

R v Straker (1965)

Knuller v DPP (1972)

Under common law

The common law offences of conspiring to corrupt public morals and of outraging public decency and conspiring to do so create a far wider area of liability than under statute. The offences, particularly the latter, are in general easier to establish than obscenity charges and they have been used as an alternative to such charges.

Conspiracy to corrupt public morals

Conspiracy to corrupt public morals will occur if two or more defendants agree to publish material in order to procure the advancement of conduct which will corrupt public morals in the sense of threatening the very fabric of society. A defence of public good may be available.

Outraging public decency

An item must be so offensive that the sense of decency of that section of the public likely to frequent the relevant place would be outraged by seeing it. It has been held that the indecency need not be immediately visible but must in some way be projected. No intent to outrage public decency or recklessness as to the risk of such outrage need be established; it is necessary only to prove that a defendant intentionally did an act which *in fact* outraged public decency. Prosecutions have been brought in respect of artistic material which – anomalously – is unprotected by its possible merit. These offences have been criticised as being both unacceptably vague and as undermining statutory protection for freedom of expression.

Shaw v DPP (1962)

Knuller v DPP (1972)

R v Gibson (1990)

Censorship of broadcasting and film broadcasting

Non-governmental control over broadcasting on political grounds is effected through the Independent Television Commission (ITC) which is required to ensure impartiality in the area of politically sensitive programs. The ITC must also ensure that television services do not offend against good taste and decency, a role which is to an extent duplicated by the Broadcasting Standards Council. The government has a direct statutory power of censorship over broadcasting which is of the widest possible nature. It appears that judicial review will be of limited efficacy in protecting free speech in the face of this power.

R v Secretary of State etc ex p Brind (1990)

Censorship of films operates initially through the British Board of Film Classification which may refuse a certificate or insist on cuts before issuing a certificate allowing the film to be screened; the BBFC will take the 'public good' defence under the 1968 Act into account. In addition, censorship is operated by local authorities and although they will usually follow the Board's advice they may choose not to; discrepancies have thus arisen between different local authority areas.

The offence of blasphemous libel is committed by one who publishes an immoderate treatment of aspects of the Anglican religion. Intention or motive of the defendant is irrelevant: it is merely necessary to show an intention to publish the material. There is no defence of publication in the public interest and the work in question need not be considered as a whole. It seems fairly clear that this offence will not be extended beyond Anglicanism and that the European Convention does not require such extension. Abolition of the offence seems the most acceptable way of remedying the present unfairness of the law. Extension of the law of incitement to racial hatred to include religious hatred would seem to be another reasonable course of action, although the scope of the present racial hatred offences under the Public Order Act 1986 is arguably too wide.

Blasphemy and religious hatred

R v Lemon (1979)

R v Chief Metropolitan Magistrates Court ex p Choudhury (1991)

Chapter 5

Freedom of Expression and Contempt of Court

5.1 **Introduction**

In this chapter we will be concerned with two conflicting interests: the interest in protecting the administration of justice and in the free speech principle. The main effect of criminal contempt is to limit the freedom of the media to report on or comment on issues arising from the administration of justice. Such restriction answers to a genuine public interest in ensuring that justice is properly administered and is unaffected by bodies who are unlikely to judge the merits of a case fairly. If, for example, a large section of the media, in pursuance of a good story, takes the view that a defendant is guilty it may slant stories and pictures so that they seem to give that impression and clearly there is a risk that such coverage may affect jury members. If at trial the risk materialises, the conviction will have been influenced by the partial views of a certain group of people who do not have all the evidence available to them and are influenced by concerns other than the concern to ensure fairness in decision-making. If a trial seems to be have been prejudiced by unfair reporting a successful appeal may be brought on that basis but this method only creates a remedy for the defendant; it does not punish the media or deter them from such behaviour in future. No-one would argue that this is a desirable method of preventing prejudice to the administration of justice. Contempt law may properly have the effect of deterring newspapers from such behaviour, but on the other hand it should not prevent accurate reporting of trials and debate in the media as to issues relevant in trials.

5.2 **Prejudicing proceedings: the development of the common law prior to 1981**

This particular area of criminal contempt arose at common law and curtailed the freedom of the media to discuss and report on issues arising from criminal or civil proceedings on the basis that those proceedings might suffer prejudice. However, it went further than was necessary to deal with very clear risks of interference with the administration of justice. The media was restricted in their reporting of issues relevant to civil or criminal proceedings which were or were soon to be in being. It is apparent that more weight was given to protecting the administration of justice rather than free speech from the ease with which it was possible to satisfy the common law tests.

5.2.1	Tests at common law	The elements of common law contempt consisted of the creation of a real risk of prejudice (the *actus reus*) and an intention to publish; in other words, it was a crime of strict liability. The *actus reus* could be fulfilled if it were shown that the publication had created a *risk* that the proceedings in question might be prejudiced; it was irrelevant whether they actually had been. This distinction was clearly illustrated by *Thomson Newspapers Ltd ex p Attorney General* (1968). While the defendant was awaiting trial the *Sunday Times* published his photograph and commented on his unsavoury background as a brothel keeper. This was held to amount to contempt. He was convicted and then appealed on the ground that the trial had been prejudiced by the article. His appeal failed on the basis that jurors had not in actuality been so prejudiced. This case further illustrates the nature of the *actus reus*: it was not necessary to publish *very* damaging comments in order to create the risk in question.
5.2.2	The *sub judice* period	At common law there was a certain time before and a certain time after the trial, known as the *sub judice* period, when there was a risk that any article published relevant to the trial might be in contempt. The starting point of this period occurred when the proceedings were 'imminent' (*Savundranayagan and Walker* (1968)). This test attracted much criticism due to its vagueness and width; it was obviously capable of applying a long time before the trial and it therefore had an inhibiting effect on the media out of proportion to its value. In particular it gave rise to the restriction caused by so-called 'gagging writs'. A newspaper might be discussing corruption in a company. If a writ for libel was then issued – although there was no intention of proceeding with the case – the newspaper might then find itself in contempt if it continued to discuss the issues. Thus this method could be used to prevent further comment.
5.2.3	The *Sunday Times* case: House of Lords ruling	The need for reform, which would in particular address the width of the imminence test, was apparent and led to the setting up of the Phillimore Committee in 1974, but it might not have come about without the influence of the European Court of Human Rights. The ruling that UK contempt law breached Article 10 arose due to the decision of the House of Lords in *AG v Times Newspapers Ltd* (1974). The case concerned litigation arising out of the Thalidomide tragedy. The parents of the Thalidomide children wished to sue Distillers, the company which had manufactured the drug, because they believed that it was responsible for the terrible damage done to their unborn children. Distillers resisted the claims and entered into negotiation with the parents' solicitors. Thus the litigation was dormant while the negotiations were taking place.

Meanwhile the *Sunday Times* wished to publish an article accusing Distillers of acting ungenerously towards the Thalidomide children. The article came close to saying that Distillers had been negligent, although it was balanced in that it did consider both sides.

The Attorney General obtained an injunction in the Divisional Court preventing publication of the article on the ground that it amounted to a contempt of court. The Court of Appeal then discharged the injunction in a ruling which weighed up the public interest in freedom of speech against the need to protect the administration of justice, and found that the former value outweighed the latter: the article concerned a matter of great public interest and as the litigation in question was dormant it would probably be unaffected by the article.

The House of Lords then restored the injunction on the ground that the article dealt with the question of negligence and therefore prejudged the case pending before the court. It held that such prejudgment was particularly objectionable as coming close to 'trial by media' and thereby leading to an undermining of the administration of justice: a person might be adjudged negligent by parts of the media with none of the safeguards available in court. The confidence of the public in the courts might be undermined, thus creating a long term detriment to the course of justice generally.

This ruling seemed to create two possible new tests for the *actus reus* of contempt:

- The prejudgment test, which seemed to be wider than the test of real risk of prejudice, in that little risk to proceedings might be shown, but it might still be possible to assert that they had been prejudged. This test was heavily criticised by the Phillimore Committee; it had a potentially grave effect on freedom of speech because it was very difficult to draw the line between legitimate discussion in the media and prejudgment.

- The risk of creation of a long term effect on the course of justice. It seemed that this test could be satisfied even where it could not be shown that any particular proceedings might be affected (perhaps because they were clearly even *more* unlikely to be affected than in the *Sunday Times* case); it therefore appeared to operate as an alternative to the first test, not as a definitional element of it.

Because it might be easier to satisfy these tests than it was as far as the old test for the *actus reus* of common law contempt was concerned, the Phillimore Committee considered that the *Sunday Times* ruling strengthened the case for reform.

Meanwhile the case was on its way to the European Court of Human Rights. The editor of the *Sunday Times* applied to the European Commission on Human Rights seeking a ruling that the imposition of the injunction breached Article 10 of the European Convention, and five years after the judgment of the House of Lords the case came before the European Court (*Sunday Times* case (1979)).

5.2.4   The *Sunday Times* case: the Strasbourg ruling

Article 10 creates a principle of freedom of expression which is subject to exceptions to be narrowly construed. The court found that the injunction clearly infringed Article 10 para 1 and that this was not a trivial infringement; the free speech interest involved was very strong because the matter was one of great public concern. However, the injunction fell within Article 10(2) because it had an aim permitted by one of exceptions – maintenance of the authority of the judiciary.

The next question was whether the injunction was *necessary* in a democratic society in order to achieve the aim in question: it was not enough merely to show that the injunction was covered by an exception. In order to make a determination on this point the court considered the meaning of the term 'necessary'. It ruled that this did not mean indispensable but connoted something stronger than 'useful', 'reasonable' or 'desirable'. It implied the existence a of 'pressing social need'. Was there such a need? The court employed the doctrine of proportionality in determining the meaning of 'need': it weighed up the strength of the free speech interest against the strength of the threat to the authority of the judiciary.

It found that although courts are clearly the forums for settling disputes, this does not mean that there can be no newspaper discussion before a case. The article was couched in moderate terms; it explored the issues in a balanced way, and moreover the litigation in question was dormant and therefore unlikely to be affected by the article. Thus on the one hand there was a strong free speech interest; on the other there was a weak threat to the authority of the judiciary. If the free speech interest had been weaker it might have been more easily overcome. The court therefore concluded that the interference with justice did not correspond to a social need sufficiently pressing to outweigh the public interest in freedom of expression. A breach of Article 10 had therefore taken place. It may be noted that the court was divided 11 to 9 in reaching this determination.

The UK government had to respond to this decision and it did so in the enactment of the Contempt of Court Act 1981 which was supposed to take account of the ruling of the

European Court of Human Rights and was also influenced to an extent by the proposals of the Phillimore Committee.

The 1981 Act was designed to modify the common law without bringing about radical change. It introduced various liberalising factors but it was intended to maintain the stance of the ultimate supremacy of the administration of justice over freedom of speech, while moving the balance further towards freedom of speech. In particular it introduced stricter time limits, a more precise test for the *actus reus* and allowed some articles on matters of public interest to escape liability even though prejudice to proceedings was created. In order to determine whether liability is created the following steps must be taken.

5.3   The tests under the Contempt of Court Act 1981

Conduct will be contempt if it interferes with the administration of justice in particular proceedings regardless of intent to do so. Thus, not all publications which deal with issues touching on litigation will fall within the 1981 Act. The starting point under s 1 is to ask whether the publication touches upon *particular* legal proceedings.

It is important to note that it is not necessary to show that the defendant *intended* to prejudice proceedings: the 'strict liability rule' under s 1 continues the position as it was at common law. After establishing that the publication might affect particular proceedings, a number of other tests must be satisfied if the strict liability rule is to be established. If the publication *does* affect particular proceedings, but one of these tests is unsatisfied, it might still be possible to consider it at common law.

5.3.1   The publication falls within s 1 of the Act

This test, which arises under s 2(3), determines the period during which there is a risk that liability under the 1981 Act will arise. It is more clearly defined than the test at common law and therefore proceedings are 'active' (or *sub judice*) for shorter periods. Thus the test is intended to have a liberalising effect. The starting and ending points for civil and criminal proceedings are defined in Schedule 1. For criminal proceedings the starting point (Schedule 1 s 4(a–e)) is: the issue of a warrant for arrest, an arrest without warrant, the service of an indictment (or summons or an oral charge), while the ending point is acquittal, sentence, any other verdict or discontinuance of the trial.

5.3.2   The proceedings are 'active'

The starting point for civil proceedings occurs when the case is set down for a hearing in the High Court or a date for the hearing fixed (Schedule 1 ss 12 and 13). This provision was clarified in *Attorney General v Hislop* (1991): it was found that s 2(3) was fulfilled because the proceedings in question (an action for defamation) had come into the 'warned' list at the time the articles in question were published. This starting point addresses the problem of gagging writs: the mere issuance of a writ would not mean that any further comment could give rise to an action for contempt because the issue of a writ is *not* the starting point. The end point of the active period for civil proceedings comes when the proceedings are disposed of, discontinued or withdrawn.

Perhaps surprisingly, appellate proceedings are also covered by Schedule 1. The starting point occurs when leave to appeal is applied for, by notice of appeal or application for review or other originating process; the end point occurs when the proceedings are disposed of or abandoned.

5.3.3	**The publication creates 'a substantial risk of serious prejudice' (s 2(2))**

According to the Court of Appeal in *AG v News Group Newspapers* (1987) both limbs of this test must be satisfied: showing a slight risk of serious prejudice or a substantial risk of slight prejudice would not be sufficient. The question to be asked under the first limb could be broken down as follows: can it be argued that there is a substantial risk that a person involved in the case in question such as a juror would (a) encounter the article, (b) remember it and (c) be affected by it so that he or she could not put it out of his or her mind during the trial? Clearly a person cannot be affected at all by something he or she has never encountered or has forgotten about.

Thus a number of factors may be identified which will be relevant to one or more of these questions. Four such factors are identified below which will also be relevant at the stage of considering whether serious prejudice has occurred. In considering them it should be noted that Lord Diplock in *AG v English* (1983) interpreted 'substantial risk' as excluding a 'risk which is only remote'. If this should be taken to mean that fairly slight risks are sufficient it is open to question as seeming not to further the policy of the Act which is to narrow down the area of liability covered by criminal contempt. However, it seems to have been interpreted in later cases such as *AG v Times Newspapers Ltd* (1983) as excluding such risks, creating in effect a test, it is submitted, of fairly or reasonably substantial risk.

• If an article is published in a national newspaper it is possible that jurors and others may encounter the article; however if it has a very small circulation this risk might be seen as too remote. This point was considered in *AG v Hislop and Pressdram* (1991) which concerned the effect of an article in *Private Eye* written about Sonia Sutcliffe, wife of the Yorkshire Ripper. *Private Eye* had published two articles making serious allegations against Sonia Sutcliffe and in response she began an action for defamation.

Shortly before the hearing of the action *Private Eye* published two further articles defamatory of Mrs Sutcliffe. The Attorney General brought proceedings for contempt of court in respect of the second articles and on appeal it was determined that as *Private Eye* had a large readership, many of whom might live in London where the libel action was held, it could not be said that the risk of prejudice was insubstantial. In *AG v Independent TV News and Others* (1995) TV News and certain newspapers published the fact that a defendant in a forthcoming murder trial was a convicted IRA terrorist who had escaped from jail where he was serving a life sentence for murder. It was found that s 2(2) was not satisfied since the trial was not expected to take place for nine months, there had only been one offending news item and there had been limited circulation of only one edition of the offending newspaper items. The risk of prejudice was found to be too small to be termed substantial.

- The ruling in *AG v Newsgroup Newspapers* (1986) made it clear that the proximity of the article to the trial will also be relevant to the question of risk. The Court of Appeal held that a gap of 10 months between the two could not create the substantial risk in question because the jury would be likely to have forgotten the article by the time the trial came on. Even if the article were faintly recollected at the time of the trial it might be likely to have little impact. Similarly in *AG v Independent TV News and Others* (1995) one of the factors founding the ruling that s 2(2) was not satisfied was that the trial was not expected to take place for nine months, and therefore the risk that any juror who had seen the offending item would remember it was not seen as substantial. In contrast, in *AG v Hislop and Pressdram* (1991) a gap of three months between publication of the article and the trial of the libel action did create such a risk. Of course, this factor cannot be considered in isolation from the others: the subject matter of the publication or language used may be more likely to ensure that it is remembered even over a substantial period of time.

- If the case will be very much in the public eye due to the persons or issues involved (as was the case in respect of the article in *Hislop and Pressdram* concerning Sonia Sutcliffe, wife of the Yorkshire Ripper) the article is more likely to make an impact, although the mere fact that the issue attracts a great deal of media coverage will not mean that jurors will be unable to put it from their minds. In *AG v Times Newspapers* (1983) it was found that jurors were able to ignore possibly prejudicial comment in newspapers; however, that case concerned a relatively trivial incident which happened to attract publicity due to the fame of one of the persons involved.

• The language used in the publication will clearly be relevant. An article of a relatively mild nature not couched in particularly vitriolic language might have little influence and might in any event be blotted out by the immediacy of the trial. However, it is also possible that very specific pieces of information soberly conveyed such as previous convictions of the defendant might make even more impact than a forceful opinion couched in more emotive language. Photographs accompanying an article will also be relevant especially where they are used to create a misleading impression. In *Taylor* (1993) certain tabloids published a photograph which was taken of one of the defendants in a murder trial giving the husband of the victim a polite kiss on the cheek; it was distorted in such a way as to give the impression that it was a passionate mouth to mouth kiss and was captioned 'cheats kiss'. It was found that this was part of 'unremitting, extensive, sensational, inaccurate and misleading press coverage' and had led to a real risk of prejudice to the trial. This determination was not however made in contempt proceedings, although it would obviously be relevant to them, but in overturning the convictions of the two defendants.

Having established a substantial risk that jurors and others will be influenced by the article it will be necessary to ask whether there is a substantial risk that the effect of such influence will be of a prejudicial nature. A publication which was in some way relevant to a trial might be likely to create a substantial risk that it would influence persons involved in the trial, bearing the factors identified in mind, but without leading to prejudice to it. An article published in every national newspaper in the land on the day of the trial and discussing certain issues relevant to it in a striking and interesting but fair and impartial manner would have an influence but, it is submitted, not a prejudicial one. In considering whether it would be prejudicial the two limbs of the test must be considered together: it must be shown that the language used, the facts disclosed or sentiments expressed would lead an observer to conclude that a substantial risk had been established that persons involved in the proceedings might be prejudiced, before going on to consider whether that effect could properly be described as serious.

Prejudice and its seriousness can be established in a number of ways: the article might have the effect of influencing persons against or in favour of the defendant; it might affect either the outcome of the proceedings in question or their very existence – as where pressure is placed on one party to discontinue the proceedings as in *Hislop and Pressdram*. The proximity in time between the article and the trial can affect this limb of s 2(2) also, as can the extent to which it may be said that the trial concerns a person in the public eye.

If the article is published some time before the trial as in *AG v News Group Newspapers* (1986) its likely effect on the minds of jurors will be lessened because it may only exist there as a faint memory: any effect it has is unlikely to be of a *seriously* prejudicial nature. This might be the case even though the article would have been likely to have such an effect had it been fresh in their minds. In the *Hislop* case however, the vitriolic nature of the article did suggest that it would be likely to have a seriously prejudicial effect. The serious allegations in question were held to blacken the plaintiff's character and might well have influenced the jurors against her. The fact that Peter Sutcliffe was well known also made it more likely that the article would have an impact.

Courts will not be quick to assume that jurors are incapable of ignoring prejudicial publications. In *AG v Guardian Newspapers* (1992) the publication of the fact that one unidentified defendant out of six in a Manchester trial was also awaiting trial elsewhere was not found to satisfy s 2(2) since it was thought that it would not cause a juror of ordinary good sense to be biassed against the defendant.

5.3.4 The article amounts to 'a discussion in good faith of public affairs or other matters of general public interest' and 'the risk of impediment or prejudice to particular legal proceedings is merely incidental to the discussion' (s 5)

If it appears possible to put forward a reasonable argument to the effect that s 2(2) is fulfilled it must next be established that s 5 does *not* apply. *AG v English* (1983) is the leading case on s 5 and is generally considered to provide a good example of the kind of case for which s 5 was framed. After the trial had begun of a consultant who was charged with the murder of a Downs Syndrome baby, an article was published in the *Daily Mail* which made no direct reference to him but was written in support of a pro-life candidate, Mrs Carr, who was standing in a by-election. Mrs Carr had no arms; the article referred to this fact and continued: 'today the chances of such a baby surviving are very small – someone would surely recommend letting her die of starvation. Are babies who are not up to scratch to be destroyed before or after birth?' The trial judge referred the article to the Attorney General who brought contempt proceedings against the *Daily Mail*. Firstly, it was determined that the article did fulfil the test under s 2(2) on the basis that jurors would be likely to take the comments to refer to the trial; therefore the assertion that babies were often allowed to die if handicapped might influence them against the consultant, Dr Arthur.

The burden then fell on the prosecution to show that s 5 did *not* apply. Lord Diplock adopted a two stage approach in determining this issue. Firstly, could the article be called a 'discussion'? The Divisional Court had held that a discussion must mean the general airing of views and debating of principles. However, Lord Diplock considered that the term 'discussion' could not be confined merely to abstract discussions but could include consideration of examples drawn from real life. Applying this test, he found that a discussion could include accusations without which the article would have been emasculated and would have lost its main point. Without the implied accusations it would have become a contribution to a purely hypothetical issue. It was about Mrs Carr's election and also the general topic of mercy killing. The main point of her candidature was that killing of sub-standard babies did happen and should be stopped; if it had not asserted that babies were allowed to die she would have been depicted as tilting at imaginary windmills. Thus the term 'discussion' could include implied accusations.

Secondly, was the risk of prejudice to Dr Arthur's trial merely an incidental consequence of expounding the main theme of the article? Lord Diplock held that in answering this the Divisional Court had applied the wrong test in considering whether the article could have been written without including the offending words. Instead the court should have looked at the actual words written. The main theme of the article was Mrs Carr's election policy; Dr Arthur was not mentioned. Therefore this article was the antithesis of the one considered in the *Sunday Times* case which was concerned entirely with the actions of Distillers. Clearly, Dr Arthur's trial could be prejudiced by the article, but that prejudice could properly be described as incidental to its main theme.

Thus s 5 applied; the article did not therefore fall within the strict liability rule. This ruling was generally seen as giving a liberal interpretation to s 5. Had the narrow interpretation of the Divisional Court prevailed it would have meant that all debate in the media on the topic of mercy killing would have been prevented for almost a year – the time during which the proceedings in Dr Arthur's case were active from charge to acquittal. (It may be noted that Dr Arthur was acquitted; therefore the article presumably did not influence the jurors against him. That fact, however, as already pointed out, did not preclude a finding that there was a substantial risk of serious prejudice to his trial.)

Lord Diplock's test under s 5 may be summed up as follows: looking at the actual words written (as opposed to considering what could have been omitted) is the article written in good faith and concerned with a question of general legitimate public interest which creates an incidental risk of prejudice to a particular case? It seems that the discussion may have been triggered off by the case itself; it need not have arisen prior to the case.

This ruling gave an emphasis to freedom of speech which tended to bring the strict liability rule into harmony with Article 10 as interpreted by the European Court of Human Rights ruling in the *Sunday Times* case. However, despite this broad interpretation of s 5 the media obviously does not have *carte blanche* to discuss issues arising from or relating to any particular case during the 'active' period.

The *AG v English* ruling did not concern a direct reference to a particular case and therefore it was uncertain until the ruling in *AG v Times Newspaper* (1983) whether s 5 would cover such direct references. The *Sunday Times* and four other newspapers commented on the background of the intruder into the Queen's bedroom, Michael Fagin, at a time when he was about to stand trial. The comments of the *Mail on Sunday* about Fagin which included the allegation that he had had a homosexual liaison with the royal bodyguard and that he was a 'rootless penniless neurotic' satisfied the s 2(2) test as it was thought that they would affect the jury's assessment of his honesty. However, they fell within s 5 as they were part of a discussion of the Queen's safety which was a matter of general public concern. In contrast, the *Sunday Times'* allegation that Fagin had stabbed his stepson could not fall within s 5 as it was irrelevant to the question of the Queen's safety but had nevertheless been considered in detail.

Finally it must be shown that the article was written in good faith. In *AG v Hislop and Pressdram* (1991) the articles in question did not fall within s 5 because it could not be said that they were published in good faith: the finding – relevant to the question of contempt at common law – that the editor had intended to prejudice the relevant proceedings was held to be incompatible with a finding of good faith under s 5.

Section 5 clearly requires some fine lines to be drawn. Where a piece merely discusses a particular case and makes no attempt to address wider issues s 5 will not apply (*AG v Liverpool Daily Post* (1984)), but where there *is* some discussion of wider issues this will not mean that s 5 will always apply.

This issue can only be resolved by looking at the subject matter of the discussion and asking how closely it relates to the trial in question. In *AG v TVS Television; AG v HW Southey & Sons* (1989) it was determined that a TVS programme concerned with the possibility that Rachmanism had arisen in the South of England but focused on landlords in Reading, which coincided with the charging of a Reading landlord with conspiring to defraud the DHSS, could not create a merely incidental risk.

Similarly, in *Pickering v Liverpool Daily Post and Echo Newspapers plc* (1991) where the discussion centred on the case itself s 5 did not apply. This issue was further considered in *AG v Guardian Newspaper* (1992) and it was determined that the term 'merely incidental' should receive a wide interpretation. However, it is suggested that it would be to misunderstand s 5 to say that a discussion which arose from and concerned the case itself would never be able to take advantage of s 5 protection: s 5 impliedly accepts that the *discussion*, but not the risk of prejudice it creates, need not be merely incidental to the trial. Obviously, given that it will already have been shown that the article in question creates a risk of serious prejudice, it might be hard to show that this is merely incidental if the article relates largely to the case. However, it might not be impossible if the thrust of the discussion could not be said to cause prejudice while the part which did could be said to be incidental to the rest.

5.3.5   Section 5:
          further reform?

Due largely to the operation of s 5 the strict liability rule seems to have created a fairer balance than was the case at common law between freedom of speech and protection for the administration of justice. However, the uncertainty as to the application of s 5 where the article focuses on the case itself, means that s 5 will allow some legitimate debate in the press to be stifled and therefore it might be argued that further relaxation is needed such as a general public interest defence.

However, the experience of America, where the existence of the First Amendment has meant that there is far less restraint, has demonstrated that a very liberal approach can give rise to problems. Witnesses' statements may be obtained pre-trial, while assertions of guilt or confessions may all be made public. In *Nebraska Press Association v Stuart* (1976) the Supreme Court held that adverse publicity before a trial would not necessarily have a prejudicial effect on it and therefore a prior restraint would not be granted. Barendt argues further that a conviction would not be obtained in respect of an already published article which created a risk of prejudicial effect. In response to this stance procedural devices such as delaying the trial or changing its venue have been adopted, but they are not always very effective, leaving open the possibility that defendants may appeal against conviction and obtain an acquittal due to the publicity. Nevertheless, some broadening of s 5 or possibly development of a public interest defence at common law might be desirable if it clearly allowed discussion focusing mainly on the particular case. Miller favours the Australian approach which allows a balancing exercise between the public interest in publication and the interest in a fair trial to be carried out, and which does allow suppression of material where the risk it creates to a fair trial is very clear.

The principle at stake here is that justice should be openly administered. Thus courts are open to the public and therefore a fair and accurate factual report of the proceedings will not amount to a contempt under s 4(1) of the 1981 Act. The reverse is true of private sittings, a report of which will *prima facie* amount to a contempt. However, at common law a judge could order postponement of a publication in order to prevent, for example, the disclosure of the identity of a witness.

The leading authority is *AG v Leveller Magazine Ltd* (1979) in which it was accepted that if in the course of regulating its own proceedings a court made an order designed to protect the administration of justice then it would be incumbent on those who knew of it not to do anything which might frustrate its object. The position is now regulated by s 4(2) of the 1981 which provides that during any legal proceeding held in public a judge may make an order postponing reporting of the proceedings if such action 'appears necessary for avoiding a substantial risk of prejudice to the administration of justice in those proceedings', thus creating an exception to s 4(1). This might typically involve the reporting of matters which the defence wished to argue should be ruled inadmissible. A right of appeal against such orders in relation to trials on indictment has been created by s 159 of the Criminal Justice Act 1988.

The position of the media when a s 4(2) order is made in respect of reporting a *summary* trial is less clear; however, it was established in *Clerkenwell Metropolitan Stipendiary magistrates' court ex p the Telegraph and Others* (1992) that in such circumstances the media have a right to be heard and must be allowed to put forward the case for discharging the order. When the applicants, publishers of national newspapers, became aware of the existence of the order they were granted a hearing before the magistrate at which they submitted that the court had power to hear representations from them as to why the order should be discharged. The magistrate held that the court had no power to hear from

5.4   Restrictions on reporting of court proceedings

5.4.1   Summary trials

anyone but the parties to the proceedings. The applicants sought a declaration that the court did have the power to hear their representations and it was determined, relying on *Horsham Justices ex p Farquharson* (1982), that they had sufficient standing to apply for judicial review. It was found to be implicit in s 4(2) that a court contemplating use of the section should be able to hear representations from those who would be affected if an order was made. In determining whether the order should be maintained it would be necessary to balance the interest in the need for a fair trial before an unprejudiced jury on the one hand and the requirements of open justice on the other. In performing this balancing exercise the magistrate would need to hear representations from the press as being best qualified to represent the public interest in publicity.

5.4.2	Restrictions on use of postponing orders

The ruling of the Court of Appeal in *Horsham Magistrates ex p Farquharson and Another* (1982) was to the effect that such orders should be made sparingly; judges should be careful not to impose a ban on flimsy grounds where the connection between the matters in question and prejudice to the administration of justice was purely speculative. If other means of protecting the jury from possibly prejudicial reports of the trial were available they should be used. Moreover, it must be ensured that the ban covers only the matters in question. This ruling was reinforced by the decision in *Re Central Independent Television plc and Others* (1990). During a criminal trial the jury had to stay overnight in a hotel and in order that they could watch television or listen to the radio, the judge made an order under s 4(2) postponing reporting of the proceedings for that night.

The applicants, broadcasters, appealed against the order under s 159 of the Criminal Justice Act 1988 on the basis that there was no ground on which the judge could have concluded that there was a substantial risk of prejudice to the administration of justice. Further, the judge had incorrectly exercised his discretion under the subsection and failed to take proper account of the public interest in freedom of expression and in the open administration of justice. The Court of Appeal found that it had not been necessary to make the order as there was little, if any, evidence of a risk to the administration of justice: the previous reporting of the case had not suggested that reporting on the day in question would be anything other than fair and accurate. Even had there been a substantial risk it might have been possible to adopt alternative methods of insulating the jury from the media. Where such alternative methods were available they should be used. Accordingly, the appeal was allowed.

The emphasis in this case on the need to restrict reporting only where clearly necessary is to be welcomed; certainly the convenience of the jury is not a sufficient reason for invoking the subsection. Similarly, in *Ex p the Telegraph plc* (1993), the Court of Appeal found that even where a substantial risk to proceedings might arise this need not mean that an order must be made. The court based this finding on the need to consider the two limbs of s 4(2) separately; firstly a substantial risk of serious prejudice to the administration should be identified flowing from publication of matters relating to the trial, and, secondly, whether it was necessary to make an order in order to avoid the risk. In making a determination as to the second limb a judge should consider whether in the light of the interest in open justice the order should be made at all and if so with all or any of the restrictions sought.

This case suggests a concern on the part of the judiciary to prevent an unrestricted use of s 4(2) orders which would be prejudicial to the principle of open justice. Incidentally, it is of some interest to note that this decision followed closely on that in *AG v Guardian Newspaper* (1992) which concerned an article written after a ban on reporting of a major fraud trial had been imposed criticising the alleged propensity of judges in such trials to impose bans. It was held that the article did not constitute a contempt under the strict liability rule and Justice Brooke took the opportunity of re-emphasising the importance of the news media as the eyes and ears of the general public.

Section 11 of the 1981 Act allows a court, which has power to do so, to make an order prohibiting publication of names or other matters if this appears necessary. Thus s 11 does not itself confer such a power and therefore refers to existing powers. At present there are signs that a robust interpretation will be given to s 11 similar to that being taken to s 4(2): the fundamental importance of open justice will be outweighed only by very clear detriment which may answer to a general public interest flowing from publication of the matters in question. It was found in *Dover Justices ex p Dover District Council and Wells* (1992) that economic damage to the interests of the defendant would not suffice.	5.4.3 Prohibiting publication of names etc
Section 6(c) of the 1981 Act preserves liability for contempt at common law if intention to prejudice the administration of justice can be shown. 'Prejudice (to) the administration of justice' clearly includes (and may solely denote: see below) prejudice to particular proceedings. Once the requirement of intent is satisfied it is easier to establish contempt at common law rather than under the Act as it is only necessary to show 'a	**5.5 Common law contempt**

real risk of prejudice' and proceedings need only be imminent, not 'active'. Clearly, liability can be established at common law in instances when it might also be established under the 1981 Act as occurred in the *Hislop* case, and also in instances when the Act will not apply because proceedings are inactive. Possibly it might also be established where one of the statutory tests *other than* the 'active' requirement was not satisfied.

A publication will fall within the area of liability preserved by s 6(c) if the following three elements are present.

5.5.1   Intention to prejudice
          the administration
          of justice

The test for intention to prejudice the administration of justice was established in *AG v Newspaper Publishing plc* (1990) and *AG v News Group Newspapers* (1988). It was made clear that 'intention' connotes specific intent and therefore cannot include recklessness. The test may be summed up as follows: did the defendant either wish to prejudice proceedings or foresee that such prejudice was a virtually inevitable consequence of publishing the material in question? Thus it is not necessary to show a *desire* to prejudice proceedings or that where there was such a desire it was the *sole* desire. This test is based on the meaning of intent arising from two rulings on the *mens rea* for murder from *Hancock and Shankland* (1986) and *Nedrick* (1986).

This is a subjective test but the Court of Appeal in *AG v Newspaper Publishing plc* (1987) (*Spycatcher* case) appeared to be asking whether or not the consequences in question were 'foreseeable', suggesting not that the defendant should actually have foreseen them, but that an objective observer would have done so. This would of course be an easier test to satisfy although as in practice it will be necessary to *infer* that the defendant foresaw the consequences, the difference between the two tests may be of only theoretical importance. This may be argued on the basis that in general if an objective observer would have foreseen a risk of prejudice it will be hard for an editor to show that he or she did not, because unlike some defendants to whom this test is applied (in other areas of criminal law) an editor must make a decision as to publication unaffected by mental incompetence (it is assumed!), emotion or by the need to act in the heat of the moment. Nevertheless, a concept of 'objective intent' is not distinguishable from recklessness; and as it is clear that recklessness will not suffice for common law contempt it is clear that intention should be interpreted to mean subjective intent.

A number of circumstances may allow the inference of intention to prejudice the proceedings to be made. In *AG v News Groups Newspapers plc* (1989) the newspaper's support for the prosecution in its columns and in funding a private prosecution allowed the inference to be made. A Dr B was questioned about an allegation of rape made against him by an eight year old girl but eventually the county prosecuting solicitor decided that there was insufficient evidence to prosecute him. *The Sun* got hold of the story and decided that it should offer the mother financial help in order to fund a private prosecution.

It published various articles attacking Dr B: 'Rape Case Doc: Sun acts'; 'Beast must be named says MP' etc. The Attorney General brought a prosecution against *The Sun* for contempt. The articles could not come within the strict liability rule under the 1981 Act because the proceedings in question – the private prosecution – were not active. The contempt alleged therefore arose at common law. It was found that intention could be established, either on the basis of a desire to prejudice the proceedings (presumably in order to vindicate *The Sun*'s stance) or because *The Sun* must have foreseen that Dr B would almost certainly not receive a fair trial.

The judgment would support either view but probably favours the former: in his ruling Watkins LJ said, 'they could only have printed articles of such a kind if they were campaigning for a conviction as they clearly were'. However, although it may well seem that *The Sun* had acted reprehensibly in using its power to attempt to influence a trial it had become itself involved in, it is arguable that intent should not have been so readily established. The proceedings were clearly not going to occur for some time; therefore, although the defendants probably foresaw some risk of prejudice to them it was not clear that such prejudice could be said to be a virtually inevitable consequence of publication. In fact Dr B was acquitted; the jury were clearly able to put out of their minds any influence *The Sun* articles may have had.

The Sun case may be contrasted with *AG v Sport Newspapers Ltd and Others* (1991) in which the test for intention was more strictly interpreted. One David Evans who had previous convictions for rape was suspected of abducting Anna Humphries. He was on the run when the *Sport* published his convictions; the proceedings were not therefore active and so the case arose at common law. Could it be said to be foreseeable as a virtual certainty that prejudice to Evans' trial would occur as a result of the publication? It was held that there was a risk of such prejudice of which the editor of the *Sport* was aware, but that such awareness of risk was not sufficient. Clearly, had the *mens rea* of common law contempt included recklessness it would have been established.

5.5.2	Imminence	At common law the *sub judice* period began when proceedings could be said to be imminent (*Savundranayagan* (1968)). This test would of course be readily satisfied where proceedings were active. However, it may not always be necessary even to establish imminence. In *AG v Newsgroup Newspapers plc* (1989) it was held *obiter* that where it is established that the defendant intended to prejudice proceedings it is not necessary to show that proceedings are imminent. It was found that even if the trial of Dr B was too far off to be said to be pending or imminent, the conduct of *The Sun* in publishing stories at the same time as assisting the mother in the private prosecutions could still amount to contempt.

Bingham LJ concurred with this dilution of the imminence test in *AG v Sport* (1991) although in the same case Mr Justice Hodgson considered that proceedings must be 'pending'. He interpreted 'pending' as synonymous with 'active', an interpretation which would have greatly curtailed the scope of common law contempt. (As noted above the *Sport* was found not to be in contempt on other grounds.) This point therefore remains unresolved, leaving the media without a clear guide as to the period during which publication of matter relevant to proceedings will be risky. If proceedings need not even be imminent it appears that reporting of matters which may give rise to proceedings at some point in the future will be severely circumscribed.

The test of imminence is itself too wide and uncertain but would be preferable to the uncertainty on this point which was exacerbated by *AG v Sport*. It is uncertain what the alternative test contemplated by Lord Bingham could be. There cannot be an intention to prejudice something which cannot even be identified as a possibility. Thus the test at its least stringent must be that proceedings can be identified as a possibility before this head of common law contempt can be in question. This development in common law contempt may significantly curtail press freedom as it clearly does nothing to help editors who wish to determine whether or not a publication might attract a criminal prosecution.

5.5.3	A real risk of prejudice	It must be shown that the publication amounts to conduct which creates a real risk of prejudice to the administration of justice (*Thomson Newspapers* (1968)). There may be a number of different methods of fulfilling this test. In *AG v Hislop and Pressdram* (1991) it was found that the defendants who were one party in an action for defamation had interfered with the administration of justice because they had brought improper pressure to bear on the other party, Sonia Sutcliffe by published material in *Private Eye* intended to deter her from

pursuing the action. There was a substantial risk that the articles might have succeeded in their aim; had they done so the course of justice in Mrs Sutcliffe's action would have been seriously prejudiced as she would have been deterred from having her claim decided in a court.

Counsel for *Private Eye* had argued that defamatory material which the defendant seeks to justify should not be restrained, because until it is clear that the alleged libel is untrue it is not clear that any right has been infringed (*Bonnard v Perryman* (1891)). This argument was rejected because the question of deterrence did not depend on the truth or falsity of the allegations. The possibility of justification was thus irrelevant. In this instance it might also be noted that the relevant tests under the 1981 Act had been satisfied; therefore it would seem that *a fortiori* common law contempt could be established, it having already been accepted that the articles had been published with the intention of putting pressure on Mrs Sutcliffe to discontinue the defamation action thereby satisfying the *mens rea* requirement at common law.

The 'real risk of prejudice' test may also be fulfilled in certain circumstances if part of the media frustrates a court order against another part. This highly significant extension of common law contempt arose from part of the *Spycatcher* litigation. In 1985 the Attorney General commenced proceedings in Australia in an attempt to restrain publication of *Spycatcher* by Peter Wright. The book included allegations of illegal activity engaged in by MI5. In 1986 after the *Guardian* and the *Observer* published reports of the forthcoming hearing which included some *Spycatcher* material, the Attorney General obtained temporary *ex parte* injunctions preventing them from further disclosure of such material.

While the temporary injunctions were in force the *Independent* and two other papers published material covered by them. It was determined in the Court of Appeal (*AG v Newspaper Publishing plc* (1990)) and confirmed in the House of Lords (*Times Newspapers and Another v AG* (1991)) that such publication constituted the *actus reus* of common law contempt on the basis that publication of confidential material, the subject matter of a pending action, damaging its confidentiality and thereby probably rendering the action pointless, created an interference with the administration of justice.

The case therefore affirmed the principle that once an interlocutory injunction has been obtained restraining one organ of the media from publication of allegedly confidential material the rest of the media may be in contempt if they publish that material, even if their intention in doing so is to bring alleged iniquity to public attention. This case thus created an inroad into the general principle that a court order should only affect the party to which it is directed as only that party will have a chance to argue that the making of the order would be wrong. In creating such an inroad this case allowed the laws of confidence and contempt to operate together as a significant prior restraint on media freedom.

5.6 Relationship between the 1981 Act and the common law

Common law contempt presents not only an alternative but also, where proceedings are active, an *additional* possibility of establishing liability. It presents such an alternative in all instances in which proceedings are not active, assuming, of course, that the *mens rea* requirement can be satisfied, and it has proved to be of great significance in this context due to the readiness with which it is sometimes accepted that the common law tests have been fulfilled. The doctrine has therefore attracted criticism as circumventing the 1981 Act but it may also, even more controversially, present an alternative in instances where proceedings *are* active but liability under the Act could not be established, thus opening up the possibility that the Act, and in particular the provisions of s 5, could be undermined. This is of particular significance given that s 5 was adopted to take account of the ruling in the European Court of Human Rights that UK contempt law breached the Article 10 guarantee of freedom of speech.

Common law contempt was established in the *Hislop* case in an instance where proceedings were active and therefore the relationship between the concept of good faith under s 5 and the question of intention under s 6(c) came under consideration. It appeared that a finding of intention to prejudice the administration of justice necessary to found liability for contempt at common law would probably preclude a finding of good faith under s 5. This finding seemed to obviate the possibility of proceeding at common law in appropriate instances in order to avoid the operation of s 5 which would have undermined the policy of the Act as providing some safeguards for media freedom.

However, the point is open to argument. It could be said that in the majority of cases a finding of good faith under s 5 would indeed preclude a finding of intention to prejudice proceedings but in one instance it might not. It might be shown that where a newspaper recognised a strong risk that proceedings would be prejudiced but did not desire such prejudice (as may have been the case in *AG v Newspaper Publishing plc* (1990)) a finding of good faith might not be precluded. An editor might argue that his or her recognition of the risk to proceedings was outweighed (in his or her own mind) by the need to bring iniquity to public attention. Section 5 might cover such a situation, thereby preventing liability under statute although it might still arise at common law. In other words, the principle arising from *AG v Newspaper Publishing plc* might apply even where proceedings were active and where publication of material covered by an injunction fell within s 5. Thus in this sense common law contempt clearly has the ability to undermine the statutory protection for freedom of speech.

This possibility may be unlikely to arise. However, this does not mean that a prosecution at common law could never succeed in an instance in which proceedings were active but prosecution under the 1981 Act failed. For example, s 5 might be irrelevant because it might be clear that the article did not concern a discussion in good faith of public affairs. However, s 2(2) might not be satisfied on the basis that although some risk of prejudice arose it could not be termed serious enough. In such an instance there appears to be no reason why the common law could not be used instead on the basis that the test of showing 'a real risk of prejudice' is less difficult to satisfy. If so it would be possible to circumvent the more stringent s 2(2) requirement. Of course it would be necessary to prove an intention to prejudice the administration of justice.

The concern here is with publications interfering with the course of justice as a continuing process as opposed to publications affecting particular proceedings. The forms which a risk to justice as a continuing process could take are considered below; the first issue to be considered concerns the mental element under this form of contempt. Such publications must fall outside the Contempt of Court Act, which according to s 1 is concerned only with publications which may affect particular proceedings. They must therefore arise at common law; the question is whether *mens rea* must be shown. It could be argued that the words 'administration of justice' used in s 6(c) could be interpreted to mean 'in particular proceedings only' in which case forms of strict liability contempt may still exist at common law.

Support could be found for such an interpretation on the basis that s 6(c) is concerned to demonstrate that where intention can be shown nothing prevents liability arising at common law. Given the context in which this statement is made (appearing to present a contrast to the strict liability rule) it might seem that the area of liability preserved by s 6(c) would cover the same ground as s 1 but only in instances in which *mens rea* could be shown.

If, on the other hand, s 6(c) covers all interferences with the administration of justice at common law, whether of a long term nature or not, it would appear to cover the form of

5.7   Protecting justice as a continuing process

contempt known as 'scandalising the court' (considered below) which would run counter to the ruling of the Divisional Court in *Editor of New Statesman* (1928) and to persuasive authority from other jurisdictions. Nevertheless, this might be the more satisfactory approach as it would be more likely to allow the UK to fulfil its obligations under Article 10. Otherwise common law contempt might have too wide a potential and the intention of the European Court of Human Rights in the *Sunday Times* case (1979) would not be given full effect. This would mean that liability for 'scandalising the court' would arise only where *intention* to interfere with the course of justice generally was shown. This point is not settled: there is no post-Act authority on it.

5.7.1   Scandalising the court

This type of contempt arose to protect the judicial system from media attacks. The idea behind it is that it would be against the public interest if the media could attack judges and cast doubt on their decisions – suggest for example that a judge has shown bias – because the public confidence in the administration of justice would be undermined. It has not been affected by the 1981 Act because there are normally no proceedings which could be affected; any relevant proceedings will usually be concluded.

If an attack on a judge occurred during the 'active' period it would probably fall outside the Act as any risk it created would be to the course of justice as a continuing process rather than to the particular proceeding.

Prosecutions are rare (and in recent times unheard of in the UK) but Lord Hailsham said in *Baldry v DPP of Mauritius* (1982), a Privy Council decision, that though it was likely that only the most serious or intolerable instances would be taken notice of by courts or Attorney Generals, nothing had happened in the intervening 80 years to invalidate the analysis of this branch of contempt put forward in the leading case in the area, *Gray* (1900). Thus this branch of contempt law is still alive and cannot merely be disregarded by the media.

As noted above, the weight of authority is probably to the effect that this is a form of strict liability contempt arising at common law but this point cannot be regarded as settled. If the view taken in *Editor of New Statesman* (1928) is correct there would be no need to show an intention to lower the repute of the judge or court in question, merely an intention to publish. The *actus reus* of this form of contempt consists of the publication of material calculated to lower the reputation of a court or judge, thereby creating a real risk of undermining public confidence in the due administration of justice.

There are two main means of fulfilling this *actus reus*. Firstly, a publication which is held to be scurrilously abusive of a court or judge may provide the classic example of scandalising the court. The leading case is *Gray* (1900) which arose from the trial of one Wells on a charge of obscene libel in which Justice Darling warned the press not to publish a full account of court proceedings (because details of obscene matter would have been included). After they were over the *Birmingham Daily Argus* published an article attacking him and referring to him as an 'impudent little man in horsehair' and 'a microcosm of conceit and empty-headedness' (who) 'would do well to master the duties of his own profession before undertaking the regulation of another'. This article was held by the Divisional Court to be a grave contempt as it was 'not moderate criticism; it amounted to personal, scurrilous abuse of the judge in his capacity of judge'.

On the other hand in *Ambard v AG for Trinidad and Tobago* (1936) reasoned criticism of certain sentences was found by the Privy Council not to constitute contempt on the basis that 'Justice is not a cloistered virtue: she must be allowed to suffer the scrutiny and respectful, even though outspoken, comments of ordinary men'. In a more recent case, *Metropolitan Police Commissioner ex p Blackburn* (1968), the Court of Appeal reaffirmed this position.

Secondly, a publication may scandalise a court if it imputes bias to a judge – even if it does so in a moderate way – on the basis that allegations of partiality will undermine confidence in the basic function of a judge. The leading case in this area is *Editor of New Statesman* (1928). The pioneer of birth control, Dr Marie Stopes, lost a libel action, and an article commenting on the case stated: 'the verdict represents a substantial miscarriage of justice ... we are not in sympathy with Dr Stopes but prejudice against her aims should not be allowed to influence a Court of Justice as it appeared to influence Mr Justice Avory in his summing up. Such views as those of Dr Stopes cannot get a fair hearing in a court presided over by Mr Justice Avory'. The editor was found to be in contempt because, although the article was serious and seemingly respectful, it imputed unfairness and lack of impartiality to the judge in the discharge of his judicial duties.

The most extreme example of this variety of scandalising the court occurred in *Colsey* (1931). A moderate article had imputed unconscious bias to a judge because in making a determination as to the meaning of a statute he might have been influenced by the fact that he had himself earlier, as Solicitor General, steered it through Parliament. This was the last successful prosecution for this form of contempt in the UK. Prosecutions may have been discouraged due to the attacks on the *Colsey* ruling which had clearly laid itself open to the charge of amounting to an unjustified encroachment on the free speech principle.

5.7.2   Scandalising the court: conclusions

It will not be surprising to learn that this is an area of contempt law which has attracted particular criticism from writers such as Borrie and Lowe. It has been argued that the offence of scandalising the court should be abolished altogether on the grounds that the rationale of the offence – undermining public confidence in administration of justice – is too vague to justify imposing restrictions on freedom of speech. It is argued that a system of justice should not be so lacking in self-confidence that it must suppress attacks on itself. Harold Laski has written:

> To argue that the expression of doubts ... as to judicial impartiality is an interference in the course of justice because the result is to undermine public confidence in the judiciary is to forget that public confidence is undermined not so much by the comment as by the habit which leads to the comment.

It may be argued that the public will have *more* confidence in the judiciary if it can be freely discussed. Moreover, because no jury sits in such cases the judicial system is in a sense prosecution and judge in the same case, thereby giving rise to a suggestion of bias. It may be asked why only *judges* and not, for example politicians or members of the clergy, should receive this special protection from criticism? Why single out judges for such insulation? The position may be compared to that in America where this form of contempt is a dead letter due to the ruling in *Bridges v California* (1941); it was held that the evil of displaying disrespect for the judiciary should not be averted by restricting freedom of expression since enforced silence on a subject is more likely to engender resent, suspicion and contempt.

On the other hand it might be said that allowing certain sections of the press complete *carte blanche* to attack judicial decisions and perhaps impute bias *does* create a risk of undermining public confidence, and that an action for defamation is not a sufficient remedy because it would place a judge in an invidious position while the action was being held. Also it might be argued that the singling out of judges can be justified on the basis that unlike other public figures judges have no forum from which to reply to criticism. A compromise between these two positions could be effected by adopting the course advocated by the Law Commission – replacement of this form of liability with a narrowly drawn offence covering the distribution of false matter with intent that it should be taken as true and knowing or being reckless as to its falsity when it imputes corrupt conduct to any judge.

Section 8 of the 1981 Act provides that disclosure of jury deliberations will amount to a contempt of court and it is clear from the ruling in *AG v Associated Newspapers Ltd and others* (1992) that this provision must be interpreted literally. In that instance jury deliberations were not disclosed directly to the defendant newspaper but to researchers who made a transcript of them. The paper then used the transcript in order to gather information for the article in question. It was argued on behalf of the defendants that the word 'disclose' used in s 8 is capable of bearing two meanings; it could mean disclosure by anyone or it could mean disclosure by a member of the jury to the defendant.

5.8   Jury deliberations

Where a statute contains an ambiguous provision and affects freedoms protected by the European Convention on Human Rights it should be construed so as to conform with the Convention. Thus the narrower meaning should be adopted allowing the defendants to escape liability. However, it was found that the word 'disclose' was not ambiguous: in its natural and ordinary meaning, which Parliament clearly intended it to bear, it denoted disclosure to anyone; the defendants therefore clearly fell within its provisions. The closing up of a potential loophole in s 8 achieved by this ruling means that the important institution of the jury is largely immune from scrutiny at least as regards the manner in which it discharges its role.

The section does not prevent interviewing of jurors which does not touch upon their deliberations in the jury room; however, such deliberations are clearly a matter of public interest and it may be argued that s 8 should have been framed less widely. Exceptions could have been included (as they were under the clause as originally drafted) which would clearly have allowed approaches to jurors as part of academic research so long as the proceedings and jurors were not identified. The Divisional Court in *AG v New Statesman* (1981) indicated that disclosure of jury-room secrets which did not identify the persons concerned could have no adverse effects on the administration of justice. The only constraint is the requirement of the Attorney General's consent to a prosecution, but even this is not necessary where proceedings are instituted on the motion of a court.

In general very little recognition is given in UK law to the constitutional role of the press. However, an exception to this rule is afforded by s 10 of the 1981 Act which provides that 'no court may require a person to disclose ... the source of

5.9   Refusing to disclose sources

information contained in a publication for which he is responsible, unless it be established to the satisfaction of the court that disclosure is necessary in the interests of justice or national security or for the prevention of disorder or crime'. Thus s 10 creates a presumption in favour of journalists who wish to protect their sources, which is however subject to four wide exceptions, of which the widest arises where the interests of justice require that disclosure should be made.

| 5.9.1 | Circumstances in which disclosure will be ordered |

It was found in *Secretary of State for Defence v Guardian Newspaper* (1985) that disclosure of the identity of the source would only be ordered where this was necessary in order to identify him or her; if other means of identification were reasonably readily available they should be used. On the other hand this did not mean that all other means of inquiry which might reveal the identity of the source must be exhausted before disclosure would be ordered.

The term 'necessary' was found in *Re an Inquiry under the Companies Security (Insider Dealing) Act 1985* (1988) to mean something less than indispensable but something more than useful. The House of Lords clarified the nature of the balancing exercise to be carried out under s 10 in *X v Morgan Grampian Publishers and Others* (1990) in its finding that when a journalist relies on s 10 in order to protect a source it must be determined whether the applicant's right to take legal action against the source is outweighed by the journalist's interest in maintaining the promise of confidentiality made to him or her. These decisions suggest that s 10 may provide a further protection for journalists than was previously available but cannot be said to be a dramatic development in the direction of furthering press freedom.

| 5.9.2 | Relevance of the Prevention of Terrorism Act |

It is possible to circumvent s 10 under Schedule 7 para 3(5) of the Prevention of Terrorism (Temporary Provisions) Act 1989 (PTA) which provides for the production of material if such production would be in the public interest; the making of such an order would seem to preclude a s 10 defence. The potential danger of Schedule 7 was shown by *Director of Public Prosecutions v Channel Four Television Co Ltd and Another* (1992). Channel 4 screened a programme in its 'Dispatches' series called 'The Committee' which was based on the allegations of an anonymous source (Source A) that the RUC and Loyalist paramilitaries had colluded in the assassination of Republicans. The police successfully applied under Schedule 7 para 3(5) for orders disclosing information which would probably uncover the identity of Source A. Channel 4 was committed for contempt of court when it refused to comply with the orders on the ground that to do so would expose Source A to almost certain death.

Channel 4 attempted to rely on the public interest provision of Schedule 7 in arguing that it was in the public interest for the identity of Source A to be protected, but this was rejected on the following grounds. It should not have given an unqualified assurance of protection to the source even though had it not done so the programme could probably not have been made, because so doing was likely to lead to flouting of the provisions of the PTA. Thus giving such assurances could inevitably undermine the rule of law and therefore, it was held, help to achieve the very result that terrorists in Northern Ireland were seeking to bring about. A fine was therefore imposed for non-compliance with the orders. In determining the amount of the fine it was borne in mind that Channel 4 might not have appreciated the dangers of giving an unqualified assurance, but a warning was given that this consideration would be unlikely to influence courts in future cases of this nature.

It may be argued that this ruling fails to accord sufficient weight to the public interest in the protection of journalistic sources in order to allow the media to fulfil its role of informing the public. The comment that the assurances given to Source A as a necessary precondition to publication of this material would undermine the rule of law, ignores the possibility that such undermining might be most likely to flow from the behaviour alleged in the programme: it might appear that nothing would be more likely to undermine the rule of law than collusion between state security forces and terrorists. The decision not to impose a rolling fine on Channel 4 or make a sequestration order may be welcomed in the interests of press freedom, but it is clear that such indulgence may be refused in future, thereby creating a significant curb on investigative journalism.

Freedom of Expression and Contempt of Court

A publication will be in contempt under the Act due to its effect on particular proceedings if the proceedings are 'active', the publication creates a substantial risk of serious prejudice to them and the article does not amount to 'a discussion in good faith of public affairs or other matters of general public interest' which creates a merely incidental risk of prejudice to the proceedings. A fair and accurate factual report of the proceedings will not amount to a contempt under s 4(1) but a judge may make an order postponing reporting of the proceedings if such action 'appears necessary for avoiding a substantial risk of prejudice to the administration of justice in those proceedings'.

Prejudicing proceedings under the Contempt of Court Act 1981

AG v Hislop (1991)
AG v News Group Newspapers (1986)
AG v Times Newspapers Ltd (1983)
AG v English (1983)
Pickering v Liverpool Daily Post and Echo Newspapers plc (1991)
AG v Leveller Magazine Ltd (1979)
Ex p the Telegraph plc (1993)
AG v Independent TV News and Others (1995)

Section 6(c) of the 1981 Act preserves liability for contempt at common law if *intention* to prejudice the administration of justice can be shown. Once such intention is established it is only necessary to show that the publication created 'a real risk of prejudice' to the proceedings which were imminent at the time. It may even be unnecessary to show that the proceedings were imminent but this point cannot yet be regarded as settled.

Prejudice to proceedings under common law

AG v Newspaper Publishing plc (1990)
AG v News Group Newspapers (1988)
Hancock and Shankland (1986)
AG v Sport Newspapers Ltd and Others (1991)
R v Savundranayagan (1968)
Hislop and Pressdram (1990)
Times Newspapers and Another v Attorney General (1991)

This seems to be a form of strict liability contempt arising at common law, the *actus reus* of which consists of the publication of material calculated to lower the reputation of a court or

Protecting justice as a continuing process: scandalising the court

judge, thereby creating a real risk of undermining public confidence in the due administration of justice. Such a risk may be created by publications which are held to be scurrilously abusive of a court or judge or which impute bias to a judge.

Baldry v DPP of Mauritius (1982)
R v Gray (1900)
R v Editor of New Statesman (1928)
Ambard v AG for Trinidad and Tobago (1936)
R v Metropolitan Police Commissioner ex p Blackburn (1968)
R v Colsey (1931)

Disclosure of jury deliberations

Section 8 of the 1981 Act provides that disclosure of jury deliberations will amount to a contempt of court although this does not prevent interviewing of jurors which does not touch upon their deliberations in the jury room.

AG v Associated Newspapers Ltd and others (1992)
AG v New Statesman (1981)

Refusing to disclose sources

Section 10 of the 1981 Act provides that 'no court may require a person to disclose ... the source of information contained in a publication for which he is responsible, unless it be established to the satisfaction of the court that disclosure is necessary in the interests of justice or national security or for the prevention of disorder or crime'. It will be a contempt to refuse to disclose a source if one of the exceptions applies. Thus s 10 creates a presumption in favour of journalists who wish to protect their sources which is however subject to four wide exceptions. Moreover, Schedule 7 para 3(5) of the Prevention of Terrorism Act 1989 provides for the production of material which might have the effect of disclosing the identity of a source if such production would be in the public interest.

Secretary of State for Defence v Guardian Newspaper (1985)
Re an Inquiry under the Companies Security (Insider Dealing) Act 1985 (1988)
X v Morgan Grampian Publishers and Others (1990)
DPP v Channel Four Television Co Ltd and Another (1992)

Chapter 6

Freedom of Information and 'Open' Government

6.1   Introduction

A 'freedom of information' scheme might cover many situations in which the citizen might wish to receive information, including that of the individual who wishes to obtain and publicise government information. The Campaign for Freedom of Information wants access rights to information in all relevant fields including education, welfare benefits, consumer protection, social work. However, freedom of information is most readily associated with the demand for the receipt of information with a view to placing it in the public domain; thus the rights of the individual who wishes to receive information for his or her *private* purposes will be considered in Chapter 8 on Privacy.

Probably the most important value associated with freedom of information is the need for the citizen to understand as fully as possible the working of government, partly in order to render it accountable and partly in order to participate fully in the democratic process. The main concern of this chapter is therefore with the methods employed by government to ensure that official information cannot fall into the hands of those who might place it in the public domain, and with methods of preventing or deterring persons from publication when such information has been obtained. Its emphasis is on the degree to which a proper balance is struck between the interest of the individual in acquiring government information and the interest of the state in withholding it, often on grounds of national security.

6.1.1   Provisions enforcing secrecy: general

Clearly, there is a genuine public interest in keeping *some* information out of the public domain; the question is whether other interests which do not correspond with and may even be opposed to the interests of the public are also at work. As will be seen, the central instrument influencing the balance struck is the Official Secrets Act 1989 but this is reinforced by the civil service conduct code, by around 80 statutory provisions engendering secrecy in various areas, and by the civil action for breach of confidence. Initially, it may be said that the area of control over government information is one in which in the UK, the state's supposed interest in keeping information secret often seems to prevail very readily over the individual interest in question; often the reasons put forward for denying the individual 'right' could not conceivably be brought within one of the justifications broadly accepted by liberal political theory as allowing the infringement of individual freedoms.

| 6.1.2 | The UK tradition of secrecy |

It has often been said that the UK is more obsessed with keeping government information secret than any other Western democracy. It is clearly advantageous for the party in power to control the flow of information in order to prevent public scrutiny of certain official decisions and in order to be able to release information selectively at convenient moments. However, the citizen's right to know is recognised in the USA, Canada, Australia, New Zealand, Denmark, Sweden, Holland, Norway, Greece and France. In such countries the general principle of freedom of information is subject to exceptions where information falls into specific categories.

Perhaps responding to the general acceptance of freedom of information, there has been a shift in the government attitude to freedom of information in the UK recently: that is, the principle appears to have been accepted but the traditional stance as to the role of the law has not changed radically. The UK has always resisted freedom of information legislation and until 1989 criminalised the unauthorised disclosure of any official information at all, however trivial, under s 2 of the Official Secrets Act 1911, thereby creating a climate of secrecy in the civil service which greatly hampered the efforts of those who wished to obtain and publish information about the workings of government.

6.2 The Official Secrets Act 1989: introduction

When the decision to reform the area of official secrecy was taken an opportunity was created for radical change which could have included freedom of information legislation along the lines of the instruments in America and Canada. However, it was made clear from the outset that the legislation was unconcerned with freedom of information. It de-criminalises disclosure of some official information (although an official who makes such disclosure may of course face an action for breach of confidence as well as disciplinary proceedings) but it will not allow the release of any official documents into the public domain. Thus claims made, for example, by Douglas Hurd (the then Home Secretary) that it is 'a great liberalising measure' clearly rest on the other aspects of the Act which will be considered.

The categories of information covered and the harm tests (excepting the provisions of s 1(1)) all concern unauthorised disclosures by any present or former crown servant or government contractor of information which has been acquired in the course of his or her employment. If a civil servant happened to acquire by *other* means information falling within one of the categories which he or she disclosed, the provisions of s 5 would apply. Section 7 (below) governs the meaning of 'authorisation'.

This category arises under s 1 and covers 'the work of, or in support of, the security and intelligence services' and includes 'references to information held or transmitted by those services or by persons in support of ... those services'. It is therefore a wide category and is not confined only to work done by members of the Security Services. Section 1(1) is intended to prevent members or former members of the Security Services (and any person notified that he is subject to the provisions of the subsection) disclosing anything at all relating or appearing to relate to the operation of those services. All such members thus come under a lifelong duty to keep silent even though their information might reveal serious abuse of power in the Security Service or some operational weakness. There is no need to show that any harm will or may flow from the disclosure and so all information, however trivial, is covered.

6.2.1   Security and intelligence

Section 1(3), which criminalises disclosure of information relating to the security services by a former or present crown servant as opposed to a member of the Security Services, does include a harm test under s 1(4) which provides that

a disclosure is damaging if –

(a) it causes damage to the work of, or any part of, the security and intelligence services; or

(b) it is of information or a document or other article which is such that its unauthorised disclosure would be likely to cause such damage or which falls within a class or description of information, documents or articles the unauthorised disclosure of which would be likely to have that effect.

Taken at its lowest level it is clear that this test may be very readily satisfied: it is not necessary to show that disclosure of the actual document in question has caused harm or would be likely to cause harm, merely that it belongs to a class of documents disclosure of which would be likely to have that effect. Disclosure of a document containing insignificant information and incapable itself of causing the harm described under s 1(4)(a) can therefore be criminalised, suggesting that the importation of a harm test for crown servants as opposed to members of the security services may not in practice create a very significant distinction between them.

However, harm must be likely to flow from disclosure of a specific document where due to its unique nature it cannot be said to be one of a class of documents, and in such an instance the ruling of the House of Lords in *Lord Advocate v Scotsman Publications Ltd* (1989) suggests that the test for harm will be quite restrictively interpreted: it will be necessary to show quite a strong likelihood that harm will arise, and the nature of the harm must be specified. The ruling was given in the context of civil proceedings for breach of confidence but the House of Lords decided the case on the basis of the principles under the 1989 Act even though it was not then in force.

The ruling concerned publication by a journalist of material relating to the work of the intelligence services. Thus the test for harm had to be interpreted, according to s 5, in accordance with the test under s 1(3) as though the disclosure had been by a Crown servant. The Crown conceded that the information in question was innocuous but argued that harm would be done because the publication would undermine confidence in the Security Services. The House of Lords, noting that there had already been a degree of prior publication, rejected this argument as unable alone to satisfy the test for harm. The case therefore gives some indication as to the interpretation the harm tests may receive.

Even taken at its highest level the harm test is potentially extremely wide due to its open-textured wording. It states, in effect, that a disclosure of information in this category is damaging if it causes damage to the area of government operation covered by the category. No clue is given as to what is meant by 'damage'; in many cases it would therefore be impossible for a Crown servant to determine beforehand whether or not a particular disclosure would be criminal. The only safe approach would be non-disclosure of almost all relevant information; the position of Crown servants under the 1989 Act in relation to information in this category is therefore only with difficulty to be distinguished from that under the 1911 Act.

6.2.2   Defence

What is meant by defence is set out in s 2(4):

(a) the size, shape, organisation, logistics, order of battle, deployment, operations, state of readiness and training of the armed forces of the Crown;

(b) the weapons, stores or other equipment of those forces and the invention, development, production and operation of such equipment and research relating to it;

(c) defence policy and strategy and military planning and intelligence;

(d) plans and measures for the maintenance of essential supplies and services that are or would be needed in time of war.

It must be shown that the disclosure in question is or would be likely to be damaging as defined under s 2(2):

(a)   it damages the capability of, or of any part of, the armed forces of the Crown to carry out their tasks or leads to loss of life or injury to members of those forces or serious damage to the equipment or installations of those forces; or

(b)   otherwise than as mentioned in paragraph (a) above, it endangers the interests of the UK abroad, seriously obstructs the promotion or protection by the UK of those interests or endangers the safety of British citizens abroad; or

(c)   it is of information or of a document or article which is such that its unauthorised disclosure would be likely to have any of those effects.

The first part of this test under (a), which is fairly specific and deals with quite serious harm, may be contrasted with (b) which is much wider and clearly covers part but – due to the addition of the word 'abroad' – not all of the harm envisaged in (a). Thus as far as disclosures concerning UK armed forces operating *abroad* are concerned, it would seem that (b) may render (a) partly redundant, so that (a) will tend to play a role only where the disclosure concerns operations within the UK. It may be noted that parts of this test are mere verbiage; it would be hard to draw a significant distinction between 'endangering' and 'seriously obstructing' the interests of the UK abroad. In fact, the overlapping of the harm tests within the categories and across the categories is a feature of this statute; the reasons why this may be so are considered below.

This category, which arises under s 3(1)(a), covers disclosure of 'any information, document or other article relating to international relations'. Clarification of this provision is undertaken by s 3(5) which creates a test to be used in order to determine whether information falls within it. Firstly, it must concern the relations between states, between international organisations or between an international organisation and a state; secondly it is said that it may affect the relation between the UK and another state or between the UK and an international organisation. Presumably information concerning international relations which failed to satisfy this test could be disclosed without fear of a criminal sanction unless it was caught by one of the other categories. The harm test arises under s 3(2) and is identical to that arising under s 2(2)(b) and (c).	6.2.3 International relations
This category also arises under s 3 but under s 3(1)(b). It covers: 'any confidential information, document or other article which was obtained from a state other than the UK or an international organisation'. Clearly, the substance of this	6.2.4 Confidential information emanating from other states or international organisations

information might be completely different from that covered under s 3(1)(a) although some documents might fall within both categories. Under s 3(6) the information will be confidential if it is expressed to be so treated due to the terms under which it was obtained or if the circumstances in which it was obtained impute an obligation of confidence.

The harm test under this category contained in s 3 is somewhat curious: the mere fact that the information is confidential or its nature or contents 'may' be sufficient to establish the likelihood that its disclosure would cause harm within the terms of s 3(2)(b). In other words, once the information is identified as falling within this category a fiction is created that harm may automatically flow from its disclosure. Presumably the only ingredient which the prosecution *must* prove is that the information falls within the category.

| 6.2.5 | Crime and the detection of crime |

Section 4 is headed 'crime and special investigation powers' but in fact the information covered under the rubric 'special investigation powers' is completely different in substance from that relating to crime. Thus such information should be treated as falling within a separate category. Section 4(2) covers any information the disclosure of which:

> results in the commission of an offence; or facilitates an escape from legal custody or the doing of any other act prejudicial to the safekeeping of persons in legal custody; or impedes the prevention or detection of offences or the apprehension or prosecution of suspected offenders; or which is such that its unauthorised disclosure would be likely to have any of those effects.

'Legal custody' includes detention in pursuance of any enactment or any instrument made under an enactment (s 4(6)). In contrast to s 3(3) in which the test for harm may be satisfied once the information is identified as falling within the category, in s 4(2) once the test for harm has been satisfied the information will necessarily be so identified. As with s 2 parts of this test could have been omitted, such as 'facilitates an escape' which would have been covered by the succeeding general words.

| 6.2.6 | Information obtained by use of Intercept and Security Service warrants |

This category of information arises under s 4(3). It applies to:

(a) any information obtained by reason of the interception of any communication in obedience to a warrant issued under s 2 of the Interception of Communications Act 1985, any information relating to the obtaining of information by reason of any such interception and any document or other article which is or has been used or held for use in, or has been obtained by reason of any such interception; and

(b) any information obtained by reason of action authorised by a warrant issued under s 3 of the Security Service Act 1989, any information relating to the obtaining of information by reason of any such action and any document or other article which is or has been used or held for use in or has been obtained by reason of any such action.'

There is no harm test under this category. It therefore creates a wide exception to the general need to show harm under s 1(3) when a Crown servant who is not a member of the Security service makes a disclosure about the work of those services.

Section 5 is headed, 'Information resulting from unauthorised disclosures or entrusted in confidence'. This is not a new category. Information will fall within s 5 if it falls within one or more of the previous categories and it has been disclosed to the defendant by a Crown Servant or falls within s 1 of the Official Secrets Act 1911.

6.3   The position of non-Crown Servants

Section 5 is primarily aimed at *journalists* who receive information leaked to them by Crown Servants although it could of course cover anybody in that position. It is also aimed at the person to whom a document is entrusted by a Crown servant 'on terms requiring it to be held in confidence or in circumstances in which the Crown servant or government contractor could reasonably expect that it would be so held' (s 5(1)(ii)). The difference between entrusting and disclosing is significant in that in the one instance the document – but not the information it contains – will have been entrusted to the care of the person in question.

If the Crown servant has disclosed or entrusted it to another who discloses it to the defendant this will suffice (s 5(1)(a)(i) and (iii)). This provision is presumably intended to catch the journalist who receives the information from another journalist who received it from the civil servant in question. However this does not apply where the information must be *entrusted* to the defendant; in that case it must come directly from the civil servant, not from another person who had it entrusted to him or her. The disclosure of the information or document by the person into whose possession it has come must not already be an offence under any of the six categories.

In contrast to disclosure of information by a Crown servant under one of the six categories, s 5 *does* import a requirement of mens rea under s 5(2) which, as far as information falling within ss 1, 2 and 3 is concerned, consists of three elements.

6.3.1   The *mens rea* requirement

The defendant must disclose the information knowing or having reasonable cause to believe that it falls within one or more of the categories, that it has come into his possession as mentioned in subsection (1) above and that it will be damaging (s 5(3)(b)).

As far as information falling within s 4 and probably s 3(1)(b) is concerned, only the first two of these elements will be relevant. Under s 5(6) only the first of these elements need be proved if the information came into the defendant's possession as a result of a contravention of s 1 of the Official Secrets Act 1911. Thus, as far as disclosure of such information is concerned, the *mens rea* requirement will be fulfilled even though the defendant believed that the disclosure would not be damaging and intended that it should not be.

The requirement of *mens rea*, although not as strict as may at first appear, represents the only means of differentiating between journalists and Crown servants.

| 6.3.2 | The harm test |

The test for damage will be determined as it would be if the information was disclosed by a Crown servant in contravention of ss 1(3), 2(1) or 3(1) above. Section 4 is not mentioned because the information will not fall within s 4(1) unless the harm test is satisfied. As already mentioned there is no harm test under s 4(3).

| 6.3.3 | The receiver of information |

Another apparent improvement which might tend to affect journalists more than others is the decriminalisation of the receiver of information. If he or she refrains from publishing it, no liability will be incurred. Of course, this improvement might be said to be more theoretical than real in that it was perhaps unlikely that the mere receiver would be prosecuted under the 1911 Act even though that possibility did exist.

| 6.3.4 | Conclusions |

The fact that journalists were included at all in the net of criminal liability under s 5 has been greatly criticised on the basis that some recognition should be given to the important role of the press in informing the public about government actions. A comparison could be drawn with the constitutional role of the press recognised in America by the *Pentagon Papers* case (1971): the Supreme Court determined that no restraining order on the press could be made so that the press would remain free to censure the government.

Section 6 deals with prior publication abroad of information which falls into one of the other substantive categories apart from crime and special investigation powers. It covers the leak to a UK citizen of information which has been received in confidence from the UK by another state or international organisation. Typically, the section might cover a leak of such information to a foreign journalist who then passed it on to a UK journalist. However, liability will not be incurred if the state or organisation (or a member of the organisation) authorises the disclosure of the information to the public (s 6(3)).

Again, as this section is aimed at journalists a requirement of *mens rea* is imported: it must be shown under s 6(2) that the defendant made 'a damaging disclosure of [the information] knowing, or having reasonable cause to believe that it is such as is mentioned in subsection (1) above and that its disclosure would be damaging.' However, it is important to note that under s 6(4) the test for harm under this section is to be determined 'as it would be in relation to a disclosure of the information, document or article in question by a Crown servant in contravention of ss 1(3), 2(1) and 3(1) above'.

Thus, although it appears that *two* tests must be satisfied in order to fulfil the *mens rea* requirement, the tests may in fact be conflated as far as s 3(1)(b) is concerned because proof that the defendant knew that the information fell within the category may satisfy the requirement that he or she knew that the disclosure would be damaging. The requirement that *mens rea* be established is not therefore as favourable to the defendant as it appears to be because – as noted in respect of s 5 – it may be satisfied even where the defendant believes that no damage will result.

The requirement that the information, document or article is communicated in confidence will be satisfied as under s 3 if it is communicated in 'circumstances in which the person communicating it could reasonably expect that it would be so held' (s 6(5)).

The meaning of 'authorised disclosures' is determined by s 7. A disclosure will be authorised if it is made in accordance with the official duty of the Crown servant or a person in whose case a notification for the purposes of s 1(1) is in force. As far as a government contractor is concerned, a disclosure will be authorised if made 'in accordance with an official authorisation' or 'for the purposes of the functions by virtue of which he is a government contractor and without contravening an official restriction'. Further, it must be made to a Crown servant for the purposes of his functions as such; or in accordance with an official authorisation.

6.4 Information entrusted in confidence to other states or international organisations

6.5 Authorised disclosures

6.6 Harm tests and categorisation: general

The claim that the 1989 Act is an improvement on its predecessor rests partly on the substance or significance of the information it covers. Such substance is made relevant firstly by the use of categorisation; impliedly, trivial information relating to cups of tea or colours of carpets in government buildings is not covered (except in Security Service buildings), and secondly because even where information *does* fall within the category in question its disclosure will not incur liability unless harm will or may flow from it. Thus, on the face of it, liability will not be incurred merely because the information disclosed covers a topic of significance such as defence. In other words, it seems to be assumed that although there is a public interest in keeping information of the particular type secret, it will not always operate to prevent disclosure of a particular piece of information.

However, in relation to many disclosures it is in fact misleading to speak of using a *second* method to narrow down further the amount of information covered because, as noted above, establishing that the information falls within the category in question is in fact (or may be; no guidance is given as to when this will be the case) synonymous with establishing that harm will occur in a number of instances.

6.6.1 Levels on which the harm test operates

Clearly, if only to avoid bringing the criminal law into disrepute, 'harm tests' which allow the substance of the information to be taken into account are to be preferred to the width of s 2 of the 1911 Act. However, although the 1989 Act embodies and emphasises the notion of a test for harm in its reiteration of the term 'damaging', there is no requirement at any point to show that harm has *actually occurred*. Bearing this important point in mind it can be seen that the test for damage actually operates on four different levels:

(1) The lowest level arises in two categories, s 1(1) and s 4(3) where there is no explicit test for harm at all – a disclosure is deemed to be automatically damaging.

(2) In one category, s 3(1)(b), the test for harm is more apparent than real in that it may be identical to the test determining whether the information falls within the category at all.

(3) In s 1(3) there *is* a harm test but the harm need not flow from or be likely to flow from disclosure of the specific document in question.

(4) In three categories, ss 2, 3(1)(a) and 4(2), there is a harm test but it is only necessary to prove that harm would be *likely* to occur due to the disclosure in question, whether it has occurred or not.

Even in categories where it is necessary to show that the actual document in question would be likely to cause harm, the task of doing so is made easy due to the width of the tests themselves. Under s 2(2) for example, a disclosure of information relating to defence will be damaging if it is likely to seriously obstruct the interests of the UK abroad. Thus, the harm tests may be said to be concerned less with preventing damaging disclosures than with creating the *impression* that liability is confined to such disclosures.

One of the objections to the old s 2 of the 1911 Act was the failure to include a requirement to prove *mens rea*. The 1989 Act includes such a requirement only as regards the leaking of information by non-crown servants; in all other instances it creates a 'reversed *mens rea*' which is considered below: the defence can attempt to prove that the defendant did not know (or have reasonable cause to know) of the nature of the information or that its disclosure would be damaging.

6.7   *Mens rea*

However, under ss 5 and 6 the prosecution must prove *mens rea* in the sense that it must be shown that the disclosure was made in the knowledge that it would be damaging. This is a step in the right direction and a clear improvement on the 1911 Act; nevertheless, the burden of proof on the prosecution would be very easy to discharge if the information fell within ss 1(3) or 3(1)(b) due to the nature of the tests for damage included in those sections; it would be necessary to do little more than show that the journalist knew that the information fell within the category in question. In the other categories it would be necessary to show that the journalist appreciated a risk or deliberately shut his or her eyes to the fact that the information might cause some harm.

The Act appears to provide three defences for Crown servants: firstly, that the defendant did not know and had no reasonable cause to believe that the information fell into the category in question, secondly, that he or she did not realise that the information would cause harm and thirdly, that s/he believed that s/he had lawful authorisation to make the disclosure *and* had no reasonable cause to believe otherwise (s 7). However, it is unclear whether or not there are *three* defences or only two; the Act may be read as requiring the defendant to prove that he or she did not know that the information fell into a particular category *and* that it was not realised that it would cause harm. In other words, lack of knowledge in respect of both factors might be necessary: it might be irrelevant that the defendant was unaware of one only. Even assuming that there *are* three defences, the first two may in any event be conflated

6.8   Defences under the 1989 Act: actual and potential

in certain categories, largely because the second defence is intimately tied up with the harm tests and therefore, like them, operates on a number of levels.

6.8.1   Operation of the defences: relationship with harm tests

Where the harm test operates at its lowest level only the first defence is available. Thus a person falling under ss 1(1) or 4(3) would have no opportunity at all of arguing that, for example, the triviality of the information had given rise to an expectation that its disclosure would cause no harm at all. At the next level under s 3(1)(b), because the test for harm *may* be satisfied merely by showing that the information falls within the subsection, the second defence may be more apparent than real and should perhaps therefore be categorised along with the defence under s 1 as non-existent. Under s 1(3) the second defence is extremely circumscribed. It would not necessarily avail the defendant to prove that for various reasons it was known before the disclosure took place that it would not cause harm. So long as the prosecution could prove a likelihood that harm would be caused from disclosure of documents falling into the same class, the harm test under the section would be satisfied and would preclude significant use of the second defence.

Generally speaking, under all the other categories the harm test allows for argument under both the first and second defences assuming that they are expressed disjunctively. However, under s 4(4) both defences apply to information falling within category (a) but oddly enough not to information likely to have those effects. In such an instance, the only defence would be to prove that it was not known that the information fell within the category. This is anomalous as it means that the disclosure of information which had had the effect of preventing an arrest could be met by the defence that it was not expected to have that effect while information which had not yet had such an effect but might have in future would be susceptible to no such defence. Thus the second defence would be available in respect of the more significant disclosure but not in respect of the less significant. Further, it should be noted that under s 4(1) the first defence is contained in the second due to the use of the harm test as the means of identifying the information falling within the section.

6.8.2   Lack of a public interest defence

The Act contains no explicit public interest defence and it follows from the nature of the harm tests that one cannot be implied into it; any good flowing from disclosure of the information in question cannot be considered, merely any harm that might be caused. Thus, while it may be accepted that the Act at least allows argument as to a defendant's state of knowledge (albeit of very limited scope in certain instances) in making a disclosure to be led before a jury, it does not allow for argument as to the good intentions of the persons concerned, who may believe with reason that no other effective means of exposing iniquity exists. In particular, the information may concern corruption at such a high level that internal methods of addressing the problem would be ineffective. Of course, good intentions are normally irrelevant in criminal trials: not many would argue that a robber should be able to adduce evidence that he intended to use the proceeds of his robbery to help the poor. However, it is arguable that an exception to this rule should be made in respect of the Official Secrets Act: a statute aimed specifically at those best placed to know of corruption or malpractice in government, should, in a democracy, allow such a defence. The fact that it does not argues strongly against the likelihood that it will have a liberalising impact.

The situation of the civil servant in the UK who believes that disclosure as to a certain state of affairs is necessary in order to serve the public interest may therefore be contrasted with the situation of his of her counterpart in the USA where he or she would receive protection from detrimental action flowing from whistle-blowing under the Civil Service Reform Act 1978.

Similarly, no general express defence of prior publication is provided by the 1989 Act; the only means of putting forward such argument would arise in one of the categories in which it was necessary to prove the likelihood that harm would flow from the disclosure; the prosecution might find it hard to establish such a likelihood where there had been a great deal of prior publication because no further harm could be caused.

6.8.3   No defence of prior publication?

Obviously, once again, this will depend on the level at which the harm test operates. Where it operates at its lowest level, prior publication would be irrelevant. Thus, if a member of the security services repeated information falling within s 1 which had been published all over the world and in the UK, a conviction could still be obtained. If such publication had occurred but the information fell within s 1(3), the test for harm might be satisfied on the basis that, although no further harm could be caused by disclosure of the *particular document*, it nevertheless belonged to a class of documents disclosure of which was likely to cause harm. However, where harm flowing from publication of a specific document which is unique is relied on *Lord Advocate v Scotsman Publications Ltd* (1989) suggests that a *degree* of prior publication may tend to defeat the argument that further publication can still cause harm. However, this suggestion must be treated with care as the ruling was not given under the 1989 Act and the link between the Act and the civil law of confidence may not form part of its *ratio*. It should also be noted that s 6 expressly provides that information which has already been leaked abroad can still cause harm if disclosed in the UK.

6.9	The 1989 Act: conclusions

Although the attempt to decriminalise disclosure of some official information is to be welcomed, it must be remembered that prosecution under the 1911 Act, theoretically possible in respect of extremely trivial disclosures, was not in practice undertaken. Therefore, given the nature of the harm tests, it could be said that very little has changed. It may be said – bearing in mind the scarcity of prosecutions under the 1911 Act – that these statutes were put in place largely, although, of course, not wholly, in order to create a deterrent effect and as a centrepiece in the general legal scheme engendering government secrecy. It is hard to resist the suggestion that the Act sets out *not* to establish clear and well defined categories of information which should not be disclosed, but to appear convincing and authoritative to persons who come into contact with it. It is therefore suggested that its liberalising effect is likely to be insignificant.

6.9.1   Efficacy in maintaining secrecy

The Act may, however, be more effective as a means of creating government credibility in relation to official secrecy than its predecessor. In this respect it appears to fulfil three roles. Firstly, it allows the claim of liberalisation to be made and gives the impression that the anomalies in existence under the 1911 Act have been dealt with. Secondly, it appears complex and wide-ranging, partly due to overlapping between and within the categories, and therefore will be likely to have a chilling effect since civil servants and others will be uncertain as to the information covered except in very clear-cut cases. It may prove more effective than the 1911 Act in deterring the press from publishing the revelations of a future Peter Wright in respect of the workings of the Security Service. Thus, it may rarely need to be invoked and in fact may have much greater symbolic than practical value. Thirdly, because it is less easy to decode than the 1911 Act, it may not so readily begin to engender contempt in those it is meant to affect. This could also mean that its credibility may be more easily maintained before a jury than was possible in respect of its predecessor.

6.9.2   Context in which the 1989 Act operates

In considering the impact of the Act, it must be borne in mind that many other criminal sanctions for the unauthorised disclosure of information exist, and some of these clearly overlap with provisions of the 1989 Act. Sections 1 and 4(3) work in conjunction with the provisions of the Security Services Act 1989 to prevent almost all scrutiny of the operation of the Security Service. Even where a member of the public has a grievance concerning the operation of the Service it will not be possible to use a court action as a means of bringing such operations to the notice of the public: under s 5 of the Security Services Act complaint can only be made to a tribunal and under s 5(4) the decisions of the tribunal are not questionable in any court of law.

Furthermore, the Act provides for no real form of Parliamentary oversight of the Security Service. In a similar manner s 4(3) of the Official Secrets Act 1989, which prevents disclosure of information about telephone tapping, works in tandem with the Interception of Communications Act 1985. Under the 1985 Act complaints can be made only to a tribunal (set up under the Act) with no possibility of scrutiny by a court. Furthermore, tribunal decisions are not published and although an annual report must be made available giving some information on the number of intercept warrants issued, it is first subject to censorship by the Prime Minister (see further Chapter 7 at 7.13).

Moreover, around 80 other statutory provisions already invoke such sanctions to enforce secrecy on civil servants in the particular areas they cover. For example, s 11 of the Atomic Energy Act 1946 makes it an offence to communicate to an unauthorised person information relating to atomic energy plant. Further, s 1 of the Official Secrets Act 1911 is still available to punish spies. Thus, it is arguable that s 2 of the 1911 Act could merely have been repealed without being replaced.

6.10   Breach of confidence: introduction

Breach of confidence is a civil remedy affording protection against the disclosure or use of information which is not generally known, and which has been entrusted in circumstances imposing an obligation not to disclose it without authorisation from the person who originally imparted it. This area of law developed as a means of protecting secret information belonging to individuals and organisations. However, it can also be used by government to prevent disclosure of sensitive information and is in that sense a back up to the other measures available to government including the Official Secrets Act 1989. The government has made it clear that actions for breach of confidence will be used against civil servants in instances falling outside the protected categories.

In some respects breach of confidence actions may be more valuable than the criminal sanction provided by the 1989 Act. Their use may attract less publicity than a criminal trial, no jury will be involved and they offer the possibility of quickly obtaining an interim injunction. The latter possibility is very valuable because in many instances the other party (usually a newspaper) will not pursue the case to a trial of the permanent injunction as the secret will probably be stale news by that time.

| 6.10.1 | The public interest defence |

However, where government as opposed to a private individual is concerned, the courts will not merely accept that it is in the public interest that the information should be kept confidential. Government will have to show that the public interest in keeping it confidential due to the harm its disclosure would cause is not outweighed by the public interest in disclosure. Thus, in *AG v Jonathan Cape* (1976), when the Attorney General invoked the law of confidence to try to stop publication of Richard Crossman's memoirs on the ground that they concerned Cabinet discussions, the Lord Chief Justice accepted that such public secrets could be restrained but only on the basis that the balance of the public interest came down in favour of suppression. As the discussions had taken place ten years previously it was not possible to show that harm would flow from their disclosure; the public interest in publication therefore prevailed.

The nature of the public interest defence – the interest in disclosure – was clarified in *Lion Laboratories v Evans and Express Newspapers* (1985). The Court of Appeal held that the defence extended beyond situations in which there had been serious wrongdoing by the plaintiff. Even where the plaintiff was blameless, publication would be excusable where it was possible to show a serious and legitimate interest in the revelation. Thus, the *Daily Express* was allowed to publish information extracted from the manufacturer of the intoximeter (a means of conducting breathalyser tests) even though it did not reveal iniquity on the part of the manufacturer. It did, however, reveal a matter of genuine public interest: that wrongful convictions might have been obtained in drink driving cases due to possible deficiencies of the intoximeter.

| 6.10.2 | The *Spycatcher* litigation: the temporary injunctions |

The leading case in this area is now the House of Lords decision in *AG v Guardian Newspapers Ltd (No 2)* (1990) which confirmed that the *Lion Laboratories Ltd v Evans* approach to the public interest defence is the correct one, and also clarified certain other aspects of this area of the law. In 1985 the Attorney General commenced proceedings in New South Wales in an attempt (which was ultimately unsuccessful) to restrain publication of *Spycatcher* by Peter Wright. The book included allegations of illegal activity engaged in by MI5. In the UK on 22 and 23 June 1986 the *Guardian* and the *Observer* published reports of the forthcoming hearing which included some Spycatcher material, and on 27 June the Attorney General obtained temporary *ex parte* injunctions preventing them from further disclosure of such material. *Inter partes* injunctions were granted against the newspapers on 11 July 1986. On 12 July 1987 the *Sunday Times* began publishing extracts from *Spycatcher* and the Attorney General obtained an injunction restraining publication on 16 July.

On 14 July 1987 the book was published in the United States and many copies were brought into the UK On 30 July 1987 the House of Lords decided (relying on *American Cyanamid Co v Ethicon Ltd* (1975)) to continue the injunctions against the newspapers on the basis that the Attorney General still had an arguable case for permanent injunctions. In making this decision the House of Lords were obviously influenced by the fact that publication of the information was an irreversible step. This is the usual approach at the interim stage: the court considers the balance of convenience between the two parties and will tend to come down on the side of the plaintiff because of the irrevocable nature of publication. However, as an interim injunction represents a prior restraint and as it is often the most crucial, and indeed sometimes the *only*, stage in the whole action, it may be argued that a presumption in favour of freedom of expression should be more readily allowed to tip the balance in favour of the defendant. This may especially be argued where publication from other sources has already occurred which will be likely to increase, and where the public interest in the information is very strong.

This judgment will do nothing to curb the use of 'gagging injunctions' in actions for breach of confidence where there has not been prior publication of the material. In any such action, even if the claim is of little merit, it is at present possible to argue that its subject matter should be preserved intact until the merits of the claim can be considered. Even if the claimant then decides to drop the action before that point, publication of the material in question will have been prevented for some substantial period of time. The House of Lords' decision has now been found to be in breach of Article 10 of the European Convention on Human Rights; the effect of that decision will be considered below.

In the trial of the permanent injunctions (*AG v Guardian (No 2)* (1990)) the Crown argued that confidential information disclosed to third parties does not thereby lose its confidential character if the third parties know that the disclosure has been

6.10.3   *Spycatcher*: the permanent injunctions

made in breach of a duty of confidence. A further reason for maintaining confidentiality in the particular instance was that the unauthorised disclosure of the information was thought likely to damage the trust which members of the Security Service have in each other and might encourage others to follow suit. These factors, it was argued, established the public interest in keeping the information confidential.

On the other hand, it was argued on behalf of the newspapers that some of the information in *Spycatcher*, if true, disclosed that members of MI5 in their operations in England had committed serious breaches of domestic law in, for example, bugging foreign embassies or effecting unlawful entry into private premises. Most seriously, the book included the allegations that members of MI5 attempted to de-stabilise the administration of Mr Harold Wilson, and that the Director General or Deputy Director General of MI5 was a spy. The newspapers contended that the duty of non-disclosure to which newspapers coming into the unauthorised possession of confidential state secrets may be subject, does not extend to allegations of serious iniquity of this character.

It was determined at first instance and in the Court of Appeal that whether or not the newspapers would have had a duty to refrain from publishing *Spycatcher* material in June 1986 before its publication elsewhere, any such duty had now lapsed. Thus the mere making of allegations of iniquity was insufficient, of itself, to justify overriding the duty of confidentiality, but the articles in question published in June 1986 had not contained information going beyond what the public was reasonably entitled to know, and in so far as they went beyond what had been previously published, no detriment to national security had been shown which could outweigh the public interest in free speech, given the publication of *Spycatcher* that had already taken place.

Thus, balancing the public interest in freedom of speech and the right to receive information against the countervailing interest of the Crown in national security, continuation of the injunctions was not necessary. The injunctions, however, continued until the House of Lords rejected the Attorney General's claim on the basis that the interest in maintaining confidentiality was outweighed by the public interest in knowing of the allegations in *Spycatcher*. It was further determined that an injunction to restrain future publication of matters connected with the operations of the Security Service would amount to a comprehensive ban on publication and would undermine the operation of determining the balance of public interest in deciding whether such publication was to be prevented; accordingly an injunction to prevent future publication which had not yet been threatened was not granted.

It appears likely that the permanent injunctions would have been granted but for the massive publication of *Spycatcher* abroad. That factor seems to have tipped the balance in favour of the newspapers. It is clear that the operation of the public interest defence involves a value judgment by the judge rather than application of a clear legal rule and the danger is that without a Bill of Rights to protect freedom of speech judges may be too prone to be swayed by establishment arguments.

The judgment also made it clear that once the information has become available from other sources, even though the plaintiff played no part in its dissemination and indeed tried to prevent it, an injunction would be unlikely to be granted. This principle was affirmed in *Lord Advocate v Scotsman publications Ltd* (1989) which concerned the publication of extracts from *Inside Intelligence* by Antony Cavendish. The interlocutory injunction sought by the Crown was refused by the House of Lords on the ground that there had been a small amount of prior publication and the possible damage to national security was very nebulous. The case suggests that the degree of prior publication may be weighed against the significance of the disclosures in question: if less innocuous material had been in issue an injunction might have been granted.

6.10.4   Prior publication

This issue has now come before the European Court of Human Rights in relation to the temporary injunctions granted in the *Spycatcher* case (*The Observer, Guardian and Sunday Times v UK* (1991)) but, although the newspapers 'won', the judgment is unlikely to have a significant liberalising influence on the principles governing the grant of temporary injunctions on the grounds of breach of confidence. All three newspapers applied to the European Commission of Human Rights alleging *inter alia* a breach of Article 10 of the Convention, which guarantees freedom of expression. Having given its opinion that the temporary injunctions constituted a breach of Article 10 the Commission referred the case to the court.

6.10.5   *Spycatcher* in the European Court of Human Rights

It was found that the injunctions clearly constituted an interference with the newspapers' freedom of expression; the question was whether the interference fell within one of the exceptions provided for by para 2 of Article 10. The injunctions fell within two of the para 2 exceptions: maintaining the authority of the judiciary and protecting national security. However those exceptions could be invoked only if the injunctions were necessary in a democratic society in the sense that they corresponded to a pressing social need and were proportionate to the aims pursued.

The court considered these questions with regard firstly to the period from 11 July 1986 to 30 July 1987. The injunctions had the aim of preventing publication of material which, according to evidence presented by the Attorney General, might have created a risk of detriment to MI5. The nature of the risk was uncertain since the exact contents of the book were not known at that time because it was still only available in manuscript form. Further, they ensured the preservation of the Attorney General's right to be granted a permanent injunction; if *Spycatcher* material had been published before that claim could be heard, the subject matter of the action would have been damaged or destroyed. In the court's view these factors established the existence of a pressing social need.

Were the actual restraints imposed proportionate to these aims? The injunctions did not prevent the papers pursuing a campaign for an enquiry into the operation of the Security Services and, though preventing publication for a long time – over a year – the material in question could not be classified as urgent news. Thus it was found that the interference complained of was proportionate to the ends in view.

The court then considered the period from 30 July 1987 to October 30 1988, after publication of *Spycatcher* had taken place in the USA. That event changed the situation: in the court's view the aim of the injunctions was no longer to keep secret information secret; it was to attempt to preserve the reputation of MI5 and to deter others who might be tempted to follow Peter Wright's example. It was uncertain whether the injunctions could achieve those aims and it was not clear that newspapers who had been unconcerned with the publication of *Spycatcher* should be enjoined as an example to others.

Further, after 30 July it was not possible to maintain the Attorney General's rights as a litigant because the substance of his claim had already been destroyed; had permanent injunctions been obtained against the newspapers that would not have preserved the confidentiality of the material in question. Thus the injunctions could no longer be said to be necessary either to protect national security or to maintain the authority of the judiciary. Maintenance of the injunctions after publication of the book in the USA therefore constituted a violation of Article 10.

6.10.6   The Strasbourg ruling: conclusions

This was a cautious judgment. It suggests that had the book been published in the USA after the House of Lords' decision to uphold the temporary injunctions, no breach of Article 10 would have occurred, despite the fact that publication of extracts from the book had already occurred in the USA and the UK. The court seems to have been readily persuaded by the Attorney General's argument that a widely framed injunction was needed in July 1986, but it is arguable that it was wider than it needed to be to prevent a risk to national security. It could have required the newspapers to refrain from publishing Wright material which had not been previously published by others until (if) the action to prevent publication of the book was lost. Such wording would have taken care of any national security interest; therefore wording going beyond that was disproportionate to that aim.

The minority judges in the court also set themselves against the narrow view that the authority of the judiciary is best preserved by allowing a claim of confidentiality set up in the face of a strong competing public interest to found an infringement of freedom of speech for over a year. Judge Morenilla argued that prior restraint should be imposed in such circumstances only where disclosure would result in immediate, serious and irreparable damage to the public interest.

It might be said that such a test would impair the authority of the judiciary in the sense that the rights of litigants would not be sufficiently protected. However, at present the test at the interlocutory stage allows a case based on a weak argument to prevail on the basis that the court cannot weigh the evidence at that stage and must grant an injunction in order to preserve confidentiality until the case can be fully looked into. As noted above, this may mean that the other party does not pursue the case to the permanent stage and therefore freedom of speech is suppressed on very flimsy grounds. Thus a greater burden to show the well-founded nature of the claim of danger to the public interest even if not as heavy as that under the test proposed by Judge Morenilla should be placed on the plaintiff.

The result of the ruling in the European Court appears to be that where there has been an enormous amount of prior publication an interim injunction should not be granted, but can be when there is at least *some* evidence of a threat to national security posed by publication coupled with a lesser degree of prior publication. Thus the action for breach of confidence is still of great value as part of the legal scheme bolstering government secrecy.

Moreover, recent developments in common law contempt discussed in Chapter 5 (at 5.5) will allow breach of confidence a greater potential than it previously possessed to prevent	6.10.7 Confidence and contempt

dissemination of government information. While the temporary injunctions were in force the *Independent* and two other papers published material covered by them. It was determined in the Court of Appeal (*AG v Newspaper Publishing Plc* (1990)) that such publication constituted the *actus reus* of contempt. The case therefore affirmed the principle that once an interlocutory injunction has been obtained restraining one organ of the media from publication of allegedly confidential material, the rest of the media may be in contempt if they publish that material.

Thus the laws of confidence and contempt were allowed to operate together as a significant prior restraint on media freedom, and this principle was upheld by the House of Lords (*Times Newspapers and Another v Attorney General* (1991)). Arguably this ruling afforded insufficient recognition to the public interest in knowing of the allegations made in *Spycatcher* which should have outweighed the possibility that publication of the allegations would constitute an interference with the administration of justice.

It may be that the House of Lords did not appreciate the extent to which this decision, in combination with the possibility of obtaining a temporary injunction where an arguable case for breach of confidence had been made out, would hand government an effective and wide-ranging means of silencing the media when publication of sensitive information was threatened.

However, the potential of this method should already have been apparent. In 1987 the BBC wished to broadcast a programme to be entitled *My Country Right or Wrong* which was to examine issues raised by the *Spycatcher* litigation. The Attorney General obtained an injunction preventing transmission on the ground of breach of confidence (*AG v BBC* (1987)). According to the Attorney General the injunction then affected every organ of the media because of the July ruling of the Court of Appeal in *AG v Newspaper Publishing plc* (1987) (this was a preliminary ruling on the *actus reus* of common law contempt which was affirmed as noted above).

6.10.8   Breach of confidence: conclusions

It seems fairly clear that although the government eventually lost in the *Spycatcher* litigation the decision will not have any liberalising impact as far as enhancing the ability of newspapers to publish information about government is concerned. The most pernicious aspect of breach of confidence – the ease with which interim injunctions may be obtained – remains largely unaffected by the outcome of the litigation, and where such an injunction is obtained it will affect all of the media in the sense that they probably will not wish to risk criminal liability for contempt of court.

Thus, these developments in the use of the common law as a means of preventing disclosure of information provide a further means of ensuring secrecy where information falls outside the categories covered by the Official Secrets Act, or where it is thought appropriate not to invoke criminal sanctions. *AG v Guardian Newspapers* (1987) has demonstrated that temporary injunctions may be obtained to prevent disclosure of official information even where prior publication has ensured that there is little confidentiality left to be protected.

Government and the media may normally avoid the head-on confrontation which occurred in the *Spycatcher* litigation by means of a curious institution known as the 'D' Notice system. This system, which effectively means that the media censor themselves in respect of publication of official information, may obviate the need to seek injunctions to prevent publication. The 'D' Notice Committee was set up with the object of letting the Press know which information could be printed and at what point: it was intended that if sensitive political information was covered by a 'D' notice an editor would decide against printing it.

6.11   Other measures affecting government secrecy

The system is entirely voluntary and in theory the fact that a 'D' notice has not been issued does not mean that a prosecution under the Official Secrets Act 1989 is precluded, although in practice it is very unlikely. Press representatives sit on the Committee as well as civil servants and officers of the armed forces.

The value and purpose of the system was called into question due to the injunction obtained against the BBC in respect of '*My Country Right or Wrong*' mentioned above. The programme concerned issues raised by the *Spycatcher* litigation; the BBC consulted the 'D' notice Committee before broadcasting and were told that the programme did not affect national security. However, the Attorney General then obtained an injunction preventing transmission on the ground of breach of confidence, thereby disregarding the 'D' Notice Committee.

It may appear that although the 'D' notice system is itself objectionable in some respects it is to be preferred to this heavyhanded use of injunctions which leaves the media with very little guidance as to what to publish or broadcast. Of course, it may be argued that the broad sanctions available to deter the media from publication, either on the ground of breach of confidence or under the Official Secrets Act, are at the root of media fears as to what may be published and that it is therefore these measures and particularly the Act itself which demands reform. Such arguments, as suggested above, have validity. However, given the width of the Act, it is probably better that the media should have guidance as to what may safely be published; if such guidance is not available the Act may have an even more 'chilling' effect than its provisions warrant due to uncertainty as to which information it covers. Thus it may be argued that decisions of the 'D' notice Committee should be accepted and should preclude prosecutions or the use of injunctions. However, as the Committee has no official role or legal recognition there is at present no means of ensuring this.

Some criticism has been levelled at the system: in the Third Report from the Defence Committee 1980 the 'D' Notice System was examined and it was concluded that it was failing to fulfil its role. It was found that major newspapers did not consult their 'D' notices to see what was covered by them and that the wording of 'D' notices was so wide as to render them meaningless. The system conveyed an appearance of censorship which had provoked strong criticism. It was determined that the machinery for the administration of 'D' notices and the 'D' notices themselves needed revision. The review which followed this reduced the number of notices and confined them to specific areas.

6.11.1   The Public Records Acts

The UK Public Records Act 1958, as amended by the Public Records Act 1967, provides that public records will not be transferred to the Public Records Office in order to be made available for inspection until the expiration of 30 years, and longer periods can be prescribed for 'sensitive information'. Such information will include personal details about persons who are still living, and papers affecting the security of the state. Some such information can be withheld for a hundred years or for ever and there is no means of challenging such decisions. For example, at the end of 1987 a great deal of information about the Windscale fire in 1957 was disclosed although some items are still held back. Robertson argues that information is withheld to prevent embarrassment to bodies such as the police or civil servants rather than to descendants of persons mentioned in it; and in support of this he cites examples such as police reports on NCCL (1935–41), flogging of vagrants (1919), decisions against prosecuting James Joyce's *Ulysses* (1924) as instances of material which in January 1989 was listed as closed for a century.

6.11.2   Public interest immunity

One area in which there is a general right to acquire information will be where discovery is needed by one party to an action of document held by the other in order to allow the action to proceed. However, the government may claim that it is immune from the duty to make such disclosure, asserting public interest immunity, a privilege based on the royal prerogative. The immunity is expressly preserved in the Crown Proceedings Act 1947 but this means that the courts have had to determine its scope. Section 28(1) of the 1947 Act, which provides that the court can make an order for discovery of documents against the Crown and require the Crown to answer interrogatories, is qualified by s 28(2) which preserves Crown privilege to withhold documents on the grounds of public interest in a variety of cases.

It was therefore thought in 1947 and for some time afterwards, that s 28(2) created important qualifications arising from the prerogative: it did not prevent the withholding of documents or refusal to answer questions on the ground that disclosures would be injurious to the public interest. Certain cases demonstrate the development there has been in determining the scope of this privilege. The House of Lords in *Duncan v Camell Laird & Co* (1942) held that documents otherwise relevant to judicial proceedings are not to be produced if the public interest requires that they be withheld. Crown Privilege as formulated here was an exclusionary rule of evidence based on public interest and the Minister was deemed the sole judge of what that constituted. In *Ellis v HO* (1953), a prisoner on remand, who was severely injured by a mentally disturbed prisoner in the prison hospital, sued the Crown for negligence. Privilege was claimed to prevent the disclosure of medical reports on his assailant and so the action had to fail.

However, in *Conway v Rimmer* (1968) a police constable was prosecuted for theft. The charge was dismissed but he was dismissed from the police force. He brought an action for malicious prosecution against his former superintendent but the Home Office objected to the disclosure of reports relevant to the case. The House of Lords in a landmark decision overruled the Minister's claim of Crown privilege and ordered disclosure. This substituted judicial discretion for executive discretion regarding disclosure of documents. However, the judges have tended to exercise this discretion cautiously and it seems that disclosure is unlikely to be ordered unless the party seeking it can show firstly that the material is clearly relevant to a specific issue in the case and secondly that it will be of significant value in assisting him or her. These tests were satisfied in the *Matrix Churchill* case (1992) in which there had been an attempt to exclude relevant evidence in the prosecution of Matrix Churchill executives in relation to the sale of defence equipment to Iraq.

The need to show that the material in question will be of *substantial* assistance was emphasised in *Bookbinder v Tebbit* (1992). Even where these tests may be satisfied discovery may be refused due to the nature of the material in question, even where it clearly falls outside the protected categories covered by the 1989 Official Secrets Act. In *Halford v Sharples* (1992) the applicant claimed sex discrimination in that she had not been recommended for promotion, and sought discovery of documents from *inter alia* the relevant police authority. The Court of Appeal found that all documents of any type relating to police discipline were protected by public interest immunity and therefore production of the files would not be ordered.

6.12   Freedom of information in other countries

All these measures may be contrasted with the situation in other democracies which have introduced freedom of information legislation within the last 10 or 20 years. Canada introduced its Access to Information Act in 1982 while America has had such legislation since 1966. Its Freedom of Information Act (FOIA) applies to all parts of the Federal Government unless an exemption applies. Exempted categories include information concerning defence, law enforcement and foreign policy. The exemptions can be challenged in court and the onus of proof will be on the agency withholding the information to prove that disclosure could bring about the harm the exemption was intended to prevent.

However, although the principle of freedom of information in America has attracted praise, its application in practice has often been criticised. In particular the American business community considers that the system is being abused by persons who have a particular financial interest in uncovering commercial information. A number of reforms have been suggested since 1980 and in 1986 a major FOIA reform was passed which extended the exemption available to law enforcement practices.

In general, the attitude to secrecy exemplified by the many democracies which have freedom of information legislation, such as that in Canada or the USA with its presumption that information must be disclosed unless specifically exempted, can be contrasted with that in the UK which takes the opposite stance: no general provision is made for such disclosure; the starting point is to criminalise disclosure in certain categories. American freedom of information provision can in particular be contrasted with provision under the UK Public Records Act 1958. Considering all the various and overlapping methods of preventing disclosure of official information in the UK and bearing in mind the contrasting attitude to this issue evinced in other democracies, it may seem that the UK is being increasingly isolated in its stance as a resister of freedom of information legislation. The freedom of information debate in the UK has not yet been able to grips with issues which are preoccupying other democracies because it is still at the stage of attempting to make an impact on the secrecy surrounding central government.

Nevertheless, certain recent developments suggest that some movement towards more open government has occurred in the UK over the last few years and that such movement is gradually gaining momentum in the early nineties. The Campaign for Freedom of Information has from 1985 onwards brought about acceptance of the principle of access rights in some areas including local government (see Chapter 8 at 8.8). Limited scrutiny of interception of communications was made possible under the Interception of Communications Act 1985. Disclosure of a range of information was decriminalised under the 1989 Official Secrets Act; MI5 was acknowledged to exist and placed for the first time on a statutory basis in 1989 as was MI6 in 1994. The Interception of Communications Act, the Security Service Act 1989, the Intelligence Services Act 1994 and the Official Secrets Act cannot be termed freedom of information measures. However, it might be argued that although in themselves they will not allow the citizen access to government information, they appear to be in accord with a trend towards more open government.

6.13   'Open' government in the UK

The Environmental Protection Regulations 1992 mean that the UK now has in effect an environmental freedom of information Act, although subject to wide ranging exceptions. After the 1992 election the Prime Minister promised a review of secrecy in Whitehall to be conducted by William Waldegrave, the Minister with responsibility for the Citizen's Charter which would concentrate on the large number of statutory instruments which prevent public disclosure of government information in various areas, with a view to removing those which did not appear to fulfil a pressing need. It was also promised that a list of secret Cabinet Committees with their terms of reference and their ministerial membership would be published. The government published a White Paper in July 1993 which set out its intentions in relation to freedom of information. These included means of allowing citizens access to some government information and reform of the Official Secrets Act 1989 so that disclosure of a specific document would be criminalised as opposed to disclosure of a document belonging to a class of documents which might cause harm.

Most significantly, the *Code of Practice on Access to Government Information* came into effect from 4 April 1994 as

6.13.1   Voluntary access to information

promised in the White Paper. The Code provides that certain government departments will provide information on request. The Parliamentary Commissioner for Administration has agreed to consider complaints that information has been improperly withheld by government departments. However, no legal remedies are provided for citizens if the Code is breached. Further, a number of matters were excluded from it, including defence, security and international relations, internal discussion and advice, law enforcement and legal proceedings, management of the economy and of the public service, information given in confidence, information covered by statutory and other restrictions.

This Code has been criticised on a number of grounds. It is apparently based on the presumption that all useful government information will be released unless there are pressing reasons why it is in the public interest that it should remain secret. This is the general principle on which freedom of information is based. However, the Code promises only to afford release of information as opposed to documents and in relation to major policy decisions (Part I s 3(i)) it only covers information considered relevant by the government. In countries which have freedom of information the usefulness or relevance of documents containing information is determined by the person who seeks it rather than by government ministers or civil servants. Usefulness is not an objective quality but depends on the purposes of the seeker which only he or she can appreciate and therefore it may be argued that both these limitations undermine the principle of 'openness'.

Challenge via an MP to the Ombudsman is clearly unlikely to be as effective as challenge in a court and no avenue of challenge to the exclusions from the Code is available. Thus, the Code is perhaps most open to criticism due to its lack of 'teeth'. The case for a voluntary Code as opposed to a general statutory right of access is not a strong one, mainly because voluntary open government asks the citizen to trust government to act against its own interests. Clearly government departments may be readily prepared to release voluntarily some information which is out of date or innocuous for some other reason, but this may be less likely where the information will cause political embarrassment and may enable the Opposition to make a more informed and therefore more damaging attack on the governing party.

6.13.2   Directions for the future

Once the value of the open government principle is accepted the argument against enshrining it in legislation begins to look unconvincing. Legislation would only clarify and make more certain a process which under voluntary open government would already be in being; it would not mean that matters which might be seriously damaging to the public interest would be disclosed since they would fall within exception clauses. At present the UK is almost isolated among democracies as regards freedom of information but at present there are no plans to enact legislation allowing full freedom of information except in specific and narrow protected categories with a right of challenge to denial of access in a court.

Although a general access right may not become available yet, freedom of information, like a Bill of Rights, may be said to be gradually arriving in the UK by default in the shape of a number of limited rights. Each one creates a breach in resistance to freedom of information and so anomalies become more readily apparent: for example if access to environmental information is available why not consumer protection information? Gradually the areas in which access is not allowed will come to seem more embattled and the case for general freedom of information with specific exceptions, as opposed to a myriad of provisions each governing a small area, may come to seem overwhelming. Thus it may be that now that the principle of freedom of information has been conceded it is likely that acceptance of the need for legislation cannot be long following.

Freedom of Information and 'Open' Government

The 1989 Act creates six categories of information the unauthorised disclosure of which will attract liability if the relevant test for harm is satisfied, *mens rea* is shown in the case of a non-Crown servant – it must be shown that the disclosure was made in the knowledge that it would be damaging – and none of the defences apply. However, in two categories, ss 1(1) and 4(3) a disclosure is deemed to be automatically damaging and in one category, s 3(1)(b), the test for harm is more apparent than real in that it may be identical to the test determining whether the information falls within the category at all. The Act appears to provide three defences: firstly that the defendant did not know and had no reasonable cause to believe that the information fell into the category in question, secondly that he or she did not realise that the information would cause harm and thirdly that he or she believed that he had lawful authorisation to make the disclosure *and* had no reasonable cause to believe otherwise (s 7). However the first two may be conflated in certain categories, largely because the second defence is intimately tied up with the harm tests and therefore, like them, operates on a number of levels. The Act contains no defence of disclosure in the public interest.

The operation of the Official Secrets Act 1989

Lord Advocate v Scotsman Publications Ltd (1989)

Breach of confidence is a civil remedy affording protection against the disclosure or use of information which is not generally known, and which has been entrusted in circumstances imposing an obligation not to disclose it without authorisation from the person who originally imparted it. Where government wishes to keep official information secret it will have to show that the public interest in keeping it confidential due to the harm its disclosure would cause is not outweighed by the public interest in disclosure.

Breach of confidence

AG v Jonathan Cape (1976)
Lion Laboratories v Evans and Express Newspapers (1985)
AG v Guardian Newspapers Ltd (No 2) (1990)
American Cyanamid Co v Ethicon Ltd (1975)
AG v Guardian (No 2) (1990)
Lord Advocate v Scotsman publications Ltd (1989)
The Observer, Guardian and Sunday Times v UK (1991)

Other measures affecting government secrecy

The 'D' Notice system, which is entirely voluntary, was set up in order to let the Press know which information could be printed and at what point. If information is covered by a 'D' Notice an editor will probably decide not to print it.

The Public Records Acts

The UK Public Records Act 1958, as amended by the Public Records Act 1967, provides that public records will not be transferred to the Public Records Office in order to be made available for inspection until the expiration of 30 years, and longer periods can be prescribed for 'sensitive information'.

Public Interest Immunity

Discovery may be needed by one party to an action of documents held by the other in order to allow the action to proceed. However the government may claim that it is immune from the duty to make such disclosure, asserting public interest immunity, a privilege based on the royal prerogative which was expressly preserved in the Crown Proceedings Act 1947. This means that documents otherwise relevant to judicial proceedings will not be produced if the public interest as assessed by the judge requires that they be withheld.

Conway v Rimmer (1968)
Bookbinder v Tebbit (1992)

Freedom of information in the UK

Most other democracies have introduced freedom of information legislation within the last 10 or 20 years. Such legislation presumes that information must be disclosed unless specifically exempted. Recently a movement towards freedom of information has occurred in the UK. The principle of access rights in some areas, including information held on computer files and information held by local government, has been accepted. The Queen's Speech following the 1992 General Election indicated a desire to move towards more open government and this was followed by publication of a White Paper on freedom of information in 1993 setting out the means to be adopted in order to allow citizens access to some government information. The *Code of Practice on Access to Government Information* came into effect from 4 April 1994 as promised in the White Paper, but it did not amount to a full freedom of information measure which would include a statutory right of access to official information, except in specific protected categories, with a right of challenge to such categorisation in a court.

Chapter 7

Freedom of Assembly

All free societies recognise the need to allow citizens to assemble in order to express their views publicly. In order to allow citizens to do so, it is necessary for the state to maintain a reasonable degree of public order, but at the same time public protest itself may come into conflict with the legitimate interest of the state in maintaining order. In order to determine how far freedom of assembly, including the freedom to engage in public protest, exists, it is necessary to consider both the law relating to public order and the use made of the law in practice. Therefore this chapter focuses on those provisions of the criminal law most applicable in the context of demonstrations, marches or meetings. These restraints are not aimed specifically at assemblies but generally at keeping the peace. However, freedom of assembly is affected by them and, as it has no special constitutional protection, is in a very vulnerable position due to their number and width.

The Public Order Act 1986, together with the public order provisions of the Criminal Justice and Public Order Act 1994, has a strong influence on the legal framework within which freedom of assembly operates, but it is not the only influence, and possibly in practice it is not the most significant due to the impact of vague, ill defined, and sometimes archaic powers which spring partly from a mix of statutory provisions, partly from the common law and partly from the royal prerogative. It will be found that while the 1986 and 1994 Acts confer on the police greater powers to keep the peace it gives virtually no recognition to freedom of assembly, and therefore in so far as such a freedom exists it relies for its protection largely on police discretion in using these new powers. The Act makes no attempt to differentiate between groups of hooligans and legitimate demonstrations; such failure argues strongly for constitutional protection for freedom of assembly.

The law takes the view that greater constraints are needed in respect of certain types of assemblies than others in proportion to the risk they seem to pose to public order. Thus indoor meetings require less control than public outdoor meetings, while marches require most control. The Public Order Act 1986 extended the existing controls over marches contained in its predecessor the 1936 Act and created entirely new controls over open air meetings. In passing the 1986 Act the government apparently intended to uphold the freedom to protest peacefully without infringing the rights of others.

7.1 Freedom of assembly: introduction

7.2	**Legal recognition of freedom of assembly?**	UK law affords virtually no recognition to any right to meet or march apart from a very limited right to hold meetings applying only to Parliamentary candidates before a general election, which arises under the Representation of the People Act 1983 ss 95 and 96. This right will be upheld even when it appears that it is being abused by a minority group: in *Webster v Southwark London BC* (1983) the Labour Council had wished to deny it to a National Front candidate, but the court upheld the statutory right of the group to meet.

There is a convention that there is a right to meet in certain places such as Trafalgar Square or Hyde Park but it is a fallacy that there is any legal right to do so. Once a meeting is in being the law will afford a limited protection: it is an offence under the Representation of the People Act 1983 s 97 to use disorderly conduct in order to break up a lawful public election meeting, and this will include meetings held on the highway. Thus a very limited positive obligation is placed on the state to allow meetings to take place, but apart from this provision, a group which is prevented from holding an effective meeting due to the activities of other groups has no special protection. This limited provision may be compared with more general provisions from other jurisdictions making it an offence to disrupt any meeting which has not been prohibited.

On the other hand the law affords great prominence to the freedom to pass and repass along the highway. From this, it may be argued that the freedom to meet publicly is virtually non-existent and depends largely on the discretion of the police in withholding prosecutions. If this argument is accepted, assemblies are placed in an even more precarious position than marches because it may appear that any fairly large stationary meeting is *prima facie* unlawful.

However, it could be argued that the Public Order Act 1986 s 14 impliedly recognises the freedom to meet so long as the statutory requirements are complied with, and this argument may be supported by the existence of certain specific statutory prohibitions on meetings in certain places or at certain times such as the Seditious Meetings Act 1817 s 3 which prohibits meetings of 50 or more in the vicinity of the Westminster during a Parliamentary session. Such restrictions impliedly support the existence of a general freedom to meet or march which will exist if not specifically prohibited. The decision in *Burden v Rigler* (1911) that for the purposes of s 97 of the Representation of the People Act the fact that the meeting is held on the highway will not of itself render it unlawful, also supports this view.

7.3	**Prior restraints: under the 1986 Act**	The imposition of prior restraints may mean that an assembly cannot take place at all or that it can take place only under

various limitations. A variety of prior restraints are available of which the most significant arise from the provisions of ss 12, 13 and 14 of the Public Order Act 1986 as amended by ss 70 and 71 of the 1994 Act. Prior restraints obviously have great potential effect. If a march takes place and subsequently some of its members are prosecuted for public order offences the march will have achieved its end in gaining publicity and will in fact have gained greater publicity due to the prosecutions. If the march never takes place its object will probably be completely defeated.

Section 12 of the 1986 Act which allows the police to impose controls on marches, is underpinned by s 11 which provides that the organisers of a march (not a meeting) must give advance notice of it to the police in the relevant police area six clear days before the date when it is intended to be held. This national requirement is an entirely new measure although in some districts a notice requirement was already imposed under local Acts. It represents the first step to involving the police so that they will have an opportunity to impose conditions. It should be remembered of course that organisers of a sizeable march would probably have to involve the police in any event as they might need traffic to be held up while crossing busy roads. As the main purpose of s 11 is to allow conditions to be imposed on marches which might disrupt the community, but as those are the very marches which the police would know of in any event, the need for a new provision of this nature is questionable.

Advance notice must be given if the procession is held 'to demonstrate support or opposition to the views or actions of any person or body of persons, to publicise a cause or campaign, or to mark or commemorate an event'. This provision was included in order to exempt innocuous crocodiles of children from the requirement. Processions customarily held are expressly exempted. The notice must specify the date, time and proposed route of the procession and give the name and address of the person proposing to organise it. Under s 11(7) the organisers may be guilty of an offence if the notice requirement has not been satisfied or if the march deviates from the date, time or route specified.

Clearly, s 11 may prove of some deterrence value to organisers due to the heavy burden of responsibility such persons now bear in ensuring that any deviation does not occur. If it does an organiser may have a defence under s 11(8) or (9) that he or she either had no reason to suspect that it had occurred or that it arose due to circumstances outside his or her control. Obviously it may be difficult for an organiser to

7.3.1   Advance notice of public processions

discharge this burden. Section 11 therefore criminalises what may be trivial administrative errors. Clearly, police officers will use a discretion in bringing prosecutions under the section, but it can be argued that this leaves the power open to abuse and means that potentially at least it could be more rigidly enforced against marchers espousing unpopular causes.

However, it may be noted that prosecutions under s 11 are not being brought at present; therefore its deterrence value to organisers may become minimal. For example, the organisers of a large Peace March held on the date the UN Security Council ultimatum against Iraq expired, failed to comply with the notice requirements under s 11, but no prosecution was brought.

The notice requirement does not apply under s 11(1) if it was not reasonably practicable to give any advance notice. This provision was intended to exempt spontaneous demonstrations from the notice requirement but is defective due to the use of the word 'any'.

Strictly interpreted, this word would suggest that a phone call made five minutes before the march sets off would fulfil the requirements, thereby exempting very few marches. In most circumstances, even though a march sets off suddenly, it might well be reasonably practicable to make such a phone call. However, it can be argued that the word 'any' should not be interpreted so strictly as to exclude spontaneous processions where a few minutes was available to give notice, because to do so would defeat the intention behind including the provision. If read in combination with the requirements as to giving notice by hand or in writing it should be interpreted to mean any written notice.

If it were not so interpreted it might be argued that s 11 breaches the guarantee of freedom of assembly under Article 11 of the European Convention on Human Rights. Section 11 may be said to fall within the ruling from In *Re M and H (minors)* (1988) that where statutes are ambiguous they should be interpreted so as to conform with the UK's Convention obligations.

| 7.3.2 | Imposing conditions on processions |

Sections 12 and 13 grew out of the power under the Public Order Act 1936 s 3 allowing the Chief Officer of Police to impose conditions on a procession or apply for a banning order if he apprehended serious public disorder. However, the power to impose conditions under s 12 may be exercised in a much wider range of situations than the old power.

The power arises in one of four situations which may be known as 'triggers'. In making a determination as to the existence of one of these 'triggers' the senior police officer in question will take into account the time or place at which and the circumstances in which, any public procession is being held or is intended to be held, and its route or proposed route. Bearing these factors in mind he or she must reasonably believe that serious public disorder, serious damage to property or serious disruption to the life of the community may be caused by the procession (s 12(1)(a)).

'Serious disruption to the life of the community' is a very wide phrase which clearly offers police officers wide scope for interpretation and may be said to render the other two 'triggers' redundant. Serious obstruction of traffic might arguably amount to some disruption of the 'life of the community'. The phrase might be interpreted widely if police officers wished to cut down the cost of the policing requirement for an assembly because the conditions then imposed, such as requiring a limit on the numbers participating, might lead to a reduction in the number of officers who had to be present. In answer to some of these fears it can be noted that in *Reid* (1987) it was determined that the 'triggers' should be strictly interpreted: the words used should not be diluted.

The fourth 'trigger', arising under s 12(1)(b), consists of an evaluation of the purpose of the assembly rather than an apprehension that a particular state of affairs may arise. The senior police officer must reasonably believe that the purpose of the assembly is 'the intimidation of others with a view to compelling them not to do an act they have a right to do or to do an act they have a right not to do'.

This requires a police officer to make a political judgment as to the purpose of the group in question because it must be determined whether the purpose is coercive or merely persuasive. Asking police officers to make such a judgment clearly lays them open to claims of partiality in instances where they are perceived as out of sympathy with the aims of the group in question. It should be noted that the fourth 'trigger' requires a reasonable belief in the presence of *two* elements – intimidation and coercion. Therefore, a racist march through an Asian area would probably fall outside its terms as the element of coercion would probably be absent. It might however fall within the terms of the third 'trigger'.

On the other hand, a march might be coercive without being intimidatory. In *Reid* (1987) the defendants shouted, raised their arms and waved their fingers; it was determined that such behaviour might cause discomfort but not intimidation and that the two concepts could not be equated. In *News Group Newspapers Ltd v SOGAT* (1982) it was held that mere abuse and shouting did not amount to a threat of violence for the purposes of intimidation under the Conspiracy and Protection of Property Act 1875 s 7. Thus behaviour of a fairly threatening nature would have to be present in order to cross the boundary between discomfort and intimidation.

The conditions that can be imposed if one of the above 'triggers' is thought to be present are very wide in the case of processions: *any* condition may be imposed which appears necessary to the senior police officer in order to prevent the envisaged mischief occurring. It should be noted from the ruling in *Secretary of State for Education v Tameside* (1977) that the use of such subjective wording does not oust the jurisdiction of the courts to assess the legality of the decision made. Thus, at least in theory, it is not the case that *any* decision which appears necessary to that officer will in fact be lawful. However it must be noted that in dealing with police action to maintain public order, the courts will tend to be unwilling to find that police decisions were unlawful.

The conditions imposed may include changes to the route of the procession or a prohibition on it entering a particular public place. If the march is already assembling the conditions may be imposed by the senior police officer present at the scene who may be a constable; if the conditions are being considered some time before this point they must be determined by the Chief Officer of Police. In contrast, the conditions which may be imposed on assemblies under s 14 are much more limited in scope, presumably because it was thought that marches presented more of a threat to public order than meetings.

The scope for challenging the conditions is very limited: there is no method of appealing from them and it is only possible to have them reviewed for procedural errors or unreasonableness in the High Court. Applying the rule from *Kent v Metropolitan Police Commissioner* (1981) one can infer that such a challenge would succeed only where an officer had evinced a belief in the existence of a 'trigger' which no reasonable officer could entertain: no presumption in favour of freedom of assembly would be imported.

7.3.3	Prohibiting public processions and assemblies

Under s 13 of the 1986 Act a ban must be imposed on a march if it is thought that it may result in serious public disorder. This power arises under s 13(1) and is exercised as follows:

> If at any time the chief officer of police reasonably believes that, because of particular circumstances existing in any district or part of a district, the powers under s 12 will not be sufficient to prevent the holding of public processions in that district or part from resulting in serious public disorder, he shall apply to the council of the district for an

order prohibiting for such period not exceeding three months as may be specified in the application the holding of all public processions (or of any class of public procession so specified) in the district or part concerned.

In response, the council may make the order as requested or modify it with the approval of the Secretary of State.

It should be noted that once the Chief Officer of Police has come to the conclusion in question he *must*, not may, apply for a banning order. This power is exercised in respect of London by the Commissioner of Police for the City of London or the Commissioner of Police of the Metropolis. A member of the march or a person who organises it knowing of the ban will commit an offence under s 13(7) and (8) and can be arrested under s 13(10).

Section 13 reproduces the old power under s 3 of the Public Order Act 1936. Assuming that a power was needed to ban marches expected to be violent, this power was nevertheless open to criticism in that once a banning order had been imposed it prevented all marches in the area it covered for its duration.

Thus a projected march likely to be of an entirely peaceful character would be caught by a ban aimed at a violent march. The Campaign for Nuclear Disarmament attempted to challenge such a ban after it had had to cancel a number of its marches (*Kent v Metropolitan Police Commissioner* (1981)) but failed due to the finding that an order quashing the ban could be made only if there were no reasons for imposing it at all. The court found that the Commissioner had considered the relevant matters, and further that CND had a remedy under s 9(3) (now s 13(5) of the 1986 Act) as they could apply to have the order relaxed.

It is arguable that the 1986 Act should have limited the banning power to the particular marches giving rise to fear of serious public disorder, but this possibility was rejected by the government on the ground that it could be subverted by organisers of marches who might attempt to march under another name. It would therefore, it was thought, have placed too great a burden on the police who would have had to determine whether or not this had occurred.

However, in making this decision it is arguable that too great a weight was given to the possible administrative burden placed on the police and too little to the need to uphold freedom of assembly. This power was being used with increased frequency up to the mid-eighties: there were 11 banning orders in the period 1970 to 1980 and 75 in the period 1981 to 1984 (39 in 1981, 13 in 1982, 9 in 1983 and 11 in

1984). Interestingly, however, use of the banning power seems to have declined since the passing of the 1986 Act and few bans have been imposed in the rest of the country.

It might seem that the banning power would be in breach of Article 11 in that the banning of a march expected to be peaceful would not appear to be justified under para 2 in respect of the need to prevent disorder. However, in *Christians Against Racism and Fascism v UK* (1984) the applicants' argument that a ban imposed under s 3(3) of the Public Order Act 1936 infringed *inter alia* Article 11 was rejected by the Commission as manifestly ill-founded on the ground that the ban was justified under the exceptions to Article 11 contained in para 2, as there was a real danger of disorder which it was thought could not be 'prevented by other less stringent measures'. Thus it may be irrelevant that a particular march affected by the ban was unlikely in itself to give rise to disorder.

Originally, the 1986 Act contained no power to ban assemblies, possibly because it was thought that such a power would be too draconian, but provision to allow for such bans has been inserted into it by s 70 of the Criminal Justice and Public Order Act 1994. The new banning power, arising under s 14A, provides that a Chief Officer of Police may apply for a banning order if he reasonably believes that an assembly is likely to be trespassory and may result in serious disruption to the life of the community or damage to certain types of buildings and structures. If an order is made, it will subsist for four days and operate within a radius of five miles around the area in question.

Apart from these two restrictions in terms of length of order and area affected, this is a much wider power than that arising under s 13 since it is based on the very broad and uncertain concept of 'serious disruption to the life of the community'. Since it uses the same 'trigger' as that operating under s 14 (see below, at 7.3.4), it appears to leave a complete discretion to the police as to whether to ban or to impose conditions. Section 14A is backed up by s 14C (inserted into the 1986 Act by s 71 of the 1994 Act). Section 14C provides a very broad power to stop persons within a radius of five miles from the assembly if a police officer reasonably believes that they were on their way to it and that it is subject to a s 14A order. Thus this power operates before any offence has been committed and hands the police a very wide discretion.

It should be pointed out that a banned march or assembly might occur in an aggravated form due to discontent generated by the ban. This may partly account for the cautious use of the banning power; police officers may well prefer to police a meeting or march known about for some time as opposed to one formed hastily in response to a ban which is hostile, unpredictable and disorganised.

Such considerations may account for the police refusal to ban the Third Anti Poll Tax march to Trafalgar Square, although such a march had previously led to a riot, and despite fierce pressure to ban from Westminster City Council, local MPs and the Home Secretary. However, the power to ban and to impose conditions gives the police bargaining power to use in negotiating with marchers and enables them to adopt a policy of strategic under enforcement as part of the price of avoiding trouble when a march occurs.

Power to impose conditions on public assemblies arises under s 14. Conditions may be imposed only if one of four 'triggers' under s 14(1) – identical to those arising under s 12 – is present. However, once it is clear that one of the 'triggers' is present, the conditions which may be imposed are much more limited than those which may be imposed on marches. They are confined to 'directions ... as to the place at which the assembly may be (or continue to be) held, its maximum duration, or the maximum number of persons who may constitute it' as appear to the senior police officer necessary to prevent the disorder, damage, disruption or intimidation. The defences available if there is a failure to comply with the conditions are identical to those under s 12, as is the power of arrest arising under s 14(7).

7.3.4 Controlling public assemblies

There are some similarities in the provisions applying to processions and assemblies but there are also certain important distinctions. An assembly is not subject to the no notice requirement, and the conditions which may be imposed are much more limited. It is therefore important to be able to distinguish between a march and an assembly. Under s 16 an assembly consists of 20 or more people in a public place; a public place is defined as one which is wholly or partly open to the air. Section 16 defines a public procession as one in a place to which the public have access. No further guidance is given. Presumably the procession must be moving and will become an assembly if it stops and if it consists of 20 or more people, in which case different rules will apply.

The Act does not define the term 'organiser' and there is no post-Act case law on the issue; therefore questions as to the meaning of the term cannot be settled with certainty. However, it is submitted that on the dictionary definition of the term, stewards and others who have some role as marshals will be organisers. This contention is supported by the ruling from *Flockhart v Robinson* (1950) that a person who indicated the route to be followed should be designated an organiser as

7.3.5 Liability of organisers

well as the person who planned the route. Thus it appears likely that the term includes stewards.

An organiser will incur liability if he or she knowingly fails to comply with the conditions imposed, although he or she will have a defence if it can be shown that the failure arose from circumstances beyond his or her control. An organiser may also incur liability if he or she incites another knowingly to participate in a march in breach of a condition (s 12(6)). According to the Court of Appeal in *Hendrickson and Tichner* (1977) incitement requires an element of persuasion or encouragement; moreover, following *Krause* (1902), the solicitation must actually come to the notice of the person intended to act on it. Therefore, merely assuming the position of leader of a march which is knowingly in breach of a condition is not sufficient of itself to amount to incitement. However, once implied encouragement including leading the group is undertaken this might amount to incitement if the leader was aware of the breach of the condition.

7.4   Prior restraints: breach of the peace and binding over

Binding over is an old but still very significant power which arises under the Justices of the Peace Act 1361. Under its provisions if a police officer suspects that a breach of the peace is likely to be committed – a march is expected to be disorderly – a person or persons can be arrested without a warrant and can be bound over to keep the peace, in other words not to continue the behaviour thought likely to lead to the breach of the peace. Thus the march could be prevented from occurring.

If the person refuses the binding over order he or she can be imprisoned. This power was used extensively during the miners' strike and this is discussed below in relation to use of breach of the peace as a subsequent restraint. In fact it is not possible to make a neat division between breach of the peace used as a subsequent and as a prior restraint: it may be used as indicated below where persons are many miles from their objective. However, for the purposes of discussion in this chapter it will be given full consideration in its role as a subsequent restraint in the sense that some relevant behaviour has occurred before it is invoked.

7.5   Prior restraints: bail conditions

Persons charged with any offence may be bailed so long as they promise to fulfil certain conditions. This aspect of criminal procedure can readily be used by the police against protesters or demonstrators; they can be charged with a low level public order offence or bound over to keep the peace, thus allowing the imposition of conditions which may prevent participation in future protest. If the conditions are broken the bailee can be imprisoned.

The Bail Act 1976 requires that applications for bail should be individually assessed in order to determine whether conditions should be imposed, thereby reflecting concern that the bailing procedure should not result in any further deprivation of liberty than is necessary. Despite this, during the miners' strike there was evidence that conditions were being routinely imposed without regard to the threat posed by the individual applicant. The Divisional Court however found that such practices were lawful (*Mansfield Justices ex p Sharkey* (1985)).

So far only *prior* restraints have been considered; these are particularly pernicious as they attract less publicity than restraints imposed once an assembly is in being and may, in the case of a ban, mean that the whole purpose of the march – to gain support for a cause – is lost. The use of subsequent restraints occurs publicly and may at least receive publicity.

7.6   Subsequent restraints on public processions or assemblies under the 1986 Act

It may be argued that the role of the 1986 Act in allowing prior restraints to be imposed on assemblies is more crucial than its role in providing *subsequent* restraints as so many other subsequent restraints arise from a very wide range of common law and statutory powers, while in contrast the notice requirement and the power to ban marches arising under the Act is unique. Subsequent restraints arising from other powers can be used as an alternative or in addition to the powers arising under the 1986 Act and as will be seen many of the powers overlap. In fact, it will be found that other powers and, in particular the common law doctrine of breach of the peace, have been used extensively while the subsequent restraints arising under ss 12 and 14 of the Act are, as noted above, strikingly under-used.

Everything that has been said as to ss 12 and 14 applies *during* the assembly: the senior police officer present, who may of course be a constable, can impose the conditions mentioned if after the assembly has begun it is apparent that one of the 'triggers' is in being or is about to come into being.

7.6.1   Imposing conditions

Threatening behaviour is specifically catered for under the low level public order offences arising under the 1986 Act ss 4 and 5, but sometimes it might equally well be dealt with under common law powers to deal with breaches of the peace or, in the case of a march, by imposing stringent conditions.

7.6.2   Threatening behaviour: s 5

Section 5 is the lowest level public order offence contained in the Act and the most contentious, since it brings behaviour within the scope of the criminal law which was previously seen as too trivial to justify the imposition of criminal liability. It criminalises 'threatening, abusive or insulting words or behaviour or disorderly behaviour' which takes place in the hearing or sight of a person likely to be caused harassment, alarm or distress thereby'. It was included as a measure aimed at anti-social behaviour generally, but its breadth and vagueness have given rise to the criticism that the police have been handed too broad a power.

The word 'likely' imports an objective test into the section: it is necessary to show that a person was present at the scene but not that he or she actually experienced the feelings in question, although it must be shown that in all the circumstances he or she would be likely to experience such feelings. Similarly, whether the words used were insulting etc is a question of fact for the magistrates. There is no need to aim the words or behaviour at a specific individual. The terms used must be given their ordinary meaning (*Brutus v Cozens* (1973)). It was determined in *DPP v Orum* (1988) that a police officer may be the person mentioned who is caused harassment, alarm or distress, but in such instances Lord Justice Glidewell thought it might be held that a police officer is less likely to experience such feelings than an ordinary person. It was found in *DPP v Fidler* (1992) that a person whose own behaviour would not satisfy the requirements of s 5 may be guilty as aiding and abetting this offence if he or she is part of a crowd who are committing it.

Thus, taken at its lowest level, s 5 criminalises a person in the company of others who display disorderly behaviour which may cause a person to experience harassment. However, the *mens rea* requirements of the offence may offer some protection to free expression. Because under s 6(4) it is required that the defendant intended his words or behaviour to be threatening, abusive or insulting – or was aware that they might be, s 5 may not catch persons participating in forceful demonstrations; they may be able to show that behaviour which could be termed disorderly and which might be capable of causing harassment to others was intended only to make a point, and that it had not been realised that it might be threatening etc.

In *DPP v Clarke* (1992) it was found that to establish liability, it is not sufficient to show only that the defendant intended or was aware that he might cause the forbidden harm; it must also be clearly shown that he intended his conduct to be threatening abusive or insulting, or was aware that it might be. Thus, for example, showing that the defendant was aware that he might cause distress is not equivalent to showing that he was aware that his speech or behaviour might be insulting; the latter mental state must be established independently. The burden imposed by this decision on prosecutors is to be welcomed if it means that an offence which strikes directly at freedom of expression and can only doubtfully be justified will be harder to make out.

A further defence available to demonstrators shouting at passers-by to support their cause, whose behaviour could readily be termed disorderly and likely to cause one of the passers-by harassment, is available under s 5(3)(c). This defence is made out if the demonstrators can show that their behaviour was 'reasonable', although the Act gives no guidance as to the meaning of the term.

However it was determined in *DPP v Clarke* that the defence is to be judged objectively and it will therefore depend on what a bench of magistrates considers reasonable. Possibly this defence could be invoked on the basis that in the context of a particular demonstration which had a legitimate political aim such behaviour is reasonable. An argument for giving such a wide interpretation to the term 'reasonable' can be supported on the basis that, as argued above, to criminalise such behaviour would arguably amount to a very far-reaching curb on the freedom to protest; such a curb might be in breach of Article 11 of the European Convention bearing in mind the need to interpret ambiguous statutory provisions in conformity with the Convention. Whether a forceful demonstration which included some disorderly behaviour could fall within Article 11 which extends only to peaceful protest is debatable, but there is at least room to argue that liability would not be incurred under s 5 in the circumstances described.

Section 154 of the 1994 Act inserts s 4A into the 1986 Act and thereby provides a new and wide area of liability which to some extent overlaps with s 5. The *actus reus* under s 4A is the same as that under s 5 with the proviso that the harm in question must actually be caused as opposed to being likely to be caused. The *mens rea* differs somewhat from that under s 5 since the defendant must intend the person in question to suffer harassment, alarm or distress. Section 4A provides another possible level of liability with the result that using offensive words is now imprisonable without any requirement (as under s 4, below) to show that violence was intended or likely to be caused. It may therefore offend against the protection for freedom of speech under Article 10 of the European Convention on Human Rights which clearly includes protection for forms of forceful or offensive speech.

7.6.3   Intentional harassment

Section 4 of the Act covers somewhat more serious behaviour than s 5. It is couched in the same terms except for the omission of 'disorderly behaviour' and with the added need to

7.6.4   Threatening behaviour: s 4

show 'intent to cause that person to believe that immediate unlawful violence will be used against him or another by any person, or to provoke the immediate use of unlawful violence by that person or another, or whereby that person is likely to believe that such violence will be provoked'.

One or more of these possibilities must be present. The behaviour in question must be specifically directed towards another person. Following *Ambrose* (1973) rude or offensive words or behaviour may not necessarily be insulting while mere swearing may not fall within the meaning of 'abusive'. However, threatening gestures such as waving a fist might suffice. If the defendant does not directly approach the person being threatened he or she might be unlikely to apprehend immediate violence. However, there might remain the possibility that the defendant intended his or her words to provoke others to violence against the victim.

Following the ruling in *Horseferry Road Metropolitan Stipendiary Magistrate ex p Siadatan* (1991) 'violence' in this context must mean immediate and unlawful violence. This strict interpretation was confirmed in *Winn v DPP* (1992) and it was made plain that the prosecution must ensure that all the ingredients of the particular form of the offence charged under s 4 are present. It is clear from the provision of s 7(2) of the Act that s 4 creates only one offence; however, due to the provisions of ss 4 and 6(3) it is clear that the offence can be committed in one of four ways. Common to all four are the requirements firstly, that the accused must intend or be aware that his words or behaviour are, or may be threatening, abusive or insulting, and secondly, that they must be directed to another person. The offence charged was based on the fourth way it could be committed: that the defendant used threatening and abusive words and behaviour whereby it was likely that violence would be provoked. The charge therefore required proof of a likelihood that the recipient of the threats would be provoked to immediate unlawful violence and as there was no evidence to that effect the charge under s 4 should have been dismissed.

It is also necessary to satisfy the *mens rea* requirement under s 6(3): the defendant must be aware or intend that his words or behaviour are threatening, abusive or insulting. Whether or not the words are insulting is not a purely subjective test and therefore the mere fact that the recipient finds them so will not be sufficient. The House of Lords so held in *Brutus v Cozens* (1973) in respect of disruption of a tennis match involving a South African player by an anti-apartheid demonstrator. Some of the crowd were provoked to violence but the conduct of the demonstrator could not be described as insulting. The conviction of the defendant under the predecessor of s 4 was therefore over-turned. The test appears to be whether a reasonable person sharing the characteristics of the persons at whom the words in question are directed would find them insulting. However, whether or not the speaker *knows* that such persons will hear the words is immaterial as far as this ingredient of s 4 is concerned (*Jordan v Burgoyne* (1963)).

The Criminal Justice and Public Order Act 1994 creates in addition to all these existing powers the new offence of aggravated trespass under s 68 which is aimed at certain groups such as hunt sabateurs or motorway protestors. Section 68 creates a two-stage test. Firstly it must be shown that the defendant trespassed on land in the open air, and secondly that he or she did there anything intended to have the effect of either intimidating, obstructing or disrupting persons about to engage in a lawful activity so as to deter them from the activity or disrupt or obstruct it. No defence is provided and it is not necessary to show that the activity was affected.

7.6.5   Aggravated trespass

This is a very broad power since a great many peaceful demonstration are intended to have some impact of an obstructive nature on lawful activities (such as, for example, export of veal calves or closure of schools or hospitals). It is, however, limited in that it does not apply to demonstrations on a metalled highway, although it does include public paths such as briodleways and excludes most but not all buildings. Section 69 provides an extremely wide power as a back up to s 68; it provides at its lowest level that if the senior officer present at the scene reasonably believes that a person intends to commit the offence under s 68, he can direct them to leave the land and refrain from re-entering it within three months. If the person in question does so re-enter it, he or she commits an imprisonable offence. Thus, where a person is in receipt of the direction under s 69, even though it was erroneously given (since in fact the person did not have the purpose of committing the s 68 offence), he or she will still commit an offence if thereafter he or she re-enters the land in question during the specified time. In other words, under s 69 persons may commit an offence merely by walking peacefully onto land in order to engage in non-obstructive and entirely innocuous public protest.

The 1936 Act was amended in order to include this offence but the 1986 Act extends the powers arising under it. However, it does not provide a power to ban processions organised by

7.6.6   Incitement to racial hatred under the Public Order Act 1986

racialist organisations unless s 13 applies. The s 18 provision, which is most likely to be used in respect of processions and assemblies, provides that liability will arise if threatening, abusive or insulting words or behaviour are used, or written material of that nature displayed, intended by the defendant to stir up racial hatred or which make it likely that racial hatred will be stirred up against a racial group (not a religious group) in Great Britain.

There is no need to show disorder, or an intent to cause disorder, or to stir up racial hatred, and there is no need to show that racial hatred is actually stirred up. It would be sufficient to show that hatred *might* actually be stirred up whether or not the accused realised that it would be. However, the term 'hatred' is a strong one: merely causing offence or bringing into ridicule would not be enough.

If the words in question are only used to the group they are aimed at, this will not constitute the offence because they are unlikely to be stirred to racial hatred against themselves. If a bystander of another racial group is likely to be stirred up to racial hatred against the group being attacked that would, however, fulfil the terms of the offence. The Commission for Racial Equality has criticised these provisions as ineffective as a means of curbing the activities of racist groups, but the government has taken the view that uttering words attacking other racial groups – even in scurrilous terms – should not be criminalised as this would represent too severe a curtailment of freedom of expression. However, in certain circumstances, where members of a particular racial group felt threatened by a demonstration ss 4 or 5 might be applicable. The government has declined so far to create a new crime of racial attack or harassment which might sometimes be applicable to racist marches.

| 7.7 | **Obstructing the highway** | The Highways Act 1980 s 137 provides that a person will be guilty of an offence if he 'without lawful authority or excuse in any way wilfully obstructs the free passage of the highway'. The only right in using the highway is to pass and re-pass along it – to make an ordinary reasonable use of it as a highway. As obstruction of the highway is a criminal offence it might therefore be said that all assemblies are *prima facie* unlawful and can only take place if the police refrain from prosecuting. The courts, however, seem to take the stance that not every procession will be unlawful; the main issue will be what was reasonable in the circumstances. |

In *Arrowsmith v Jenkins* (1963) it was determined that minor obstruction of traffic can lead to liability under the

1980 Act. A pacifist meeting was held in a certain street which linked up two main roads. The meeting blocked the street and the organiser cooperated with the police in unblocking it. It was completely blocked for five minutes and partly blocked for 15. The police had advance notice of the meeting and the organiser was under the impression that the proceedings were lawful. Other meetings had been held there on a number of occasions without attracting prosecutions. Nevertheless, the organiser was convicted.

This use of the Highways Act places such meetings in a very precarious position as it seems to hand a power to the police to licence them, thereby seriously undermining freedom of assembly. However, in *Nagy v Weston* (1966) it was held that a reasonable user of the highway will constitute a lawful excuse, and that in order to determine its reasonableness or otherwise, the length of the obstruction must be considered, its purpose, the place where it occurs and whether an actual or potential obstruction took place. The *purpose* of the obstruction, mentioned in *Nagy*, was given greater prominence in *Hirst and Agu v Chief Constable of West Yorkshire* (1986): it was said that courts should have regard to the freedom to demonstrate. On that basis the purpose of an assembly as a means of legitimate protest may suggest that it can amount to a reasonable user of the highway.

7.8 Public nuisance

The common law offence of public nuisance is arguably too wide and vague to form part of the criminal law. It will arise if something occurs which inflicts damage, injury or inconvenience on all members of a class who come within the sphere or neighbourhood of its operation. Liability for committing a public nuisance may arise by blocking the highway; however, according to *Clarke* (1964) the disruption caused must amount to an unreasonable user of the highway in order to found such liability.

Thus, once obstruction has been shown the question of reasonableness arises. It would appear from *News Group Newspapers Ltd v SOGAT* (1986) that to cause a minor disruption for a legitimate purpose such as a march does not constitute an unreasonable user of the highway and will not therefore amount to a nuisance. It might seem that an assembly could not constitute a reasonable user of the highway under the Highways Act and yet nevertheless amount to a public nuisance. However, in *Gillingham Borough Council v Medway Dock Co* (1992) it was suggested that this might, exceptionally, be possible.

7.9   Breach of the peace

The flexible common law power to prevent a breach of the peace overlaps with a number of the powers arising under the 1986 Act and is in one sense more useful to the police than they are as its definition is so vague. This vagueness means that it can be used in such a way as to undermine attempts in statutory provisions to carve out more clearly defined areas of liability.

The leading case is *Howell* (1981) in which it was determined that breach of the peace will arise if an act is done or threatened to be done which either: harms a person or *in his presence* his property, or is likely to cause such harm, or which puts a person in fear of such harm. Threatening words are not in themselves a breach of the peace but they may lead a police officer to apprehend a breach of the peace.

In a later case, *Chief Constable for Devon and Cornwall ex p CEGB* (1982), Lord Denning offered a rather different definition of the offence. His view was that violence is unnecessary; he considered that 'if anyone unlawfully and physically obstructs a worker – by lying down or chaining himself to a rig or the like – he is guilty of a breach of the peace'. On this view peaceful protest could be severely curtailed. It is generally considered that the view taken in *Howell* is the correct one but the fact that as eminent an authority as Lord Denning could offer such a radically different definition of the offence from that put forward in *Howell* only a year earlier, epitomises the disturbingly vague parameters of breach of the peace.

Such flexibility means that the offence can be used to curtail freedom of assembly in situations in which statutory powers might be inapplicable. *Piddington v Bates* (1961) illustrated how unwilling the courts sometimes are to disagree with the finding of the police officer on the ground. In that case the defendant wished to join other pickets at a printer's works but was told by police officers that only two men were to be allowed to picket each of the main entrances. The defendant then tried to push 'gently' past the police officer and was arrested for obstructing a police officer in the course of his duty.

On appeal it was held that the officer had reasonably apprehended that a breach of the peace might occur and the limiting of the number of the pickets was designed to prevent it; however, the main reason for fearing trouble was apparently merely that there were 18 pickets at the works. In effect, therefore, a condition was imposed on a static assembly, reducing its numbers to four. It is interesting to note that if that situation were to occur today, with the 1986

Act in force, the powers under s 14 to control assemblies could not be used since less than 20 people were present, and even had more than 20 pickets been there, it seems probable that none of the trigger conditions would have been satisfied. The case illustrates the readiness of the common law to sanction police interference with free assembly on production of what can only be described as minimal evidence of a risk of disorder.

This power, in conjunction with the offence of obstruction of an officer in the execution of his duty was used extensively during the miners strike. The most notorious instance of its use occurred in *Moss v McLachlan* (1985). A group of striking miners were stopped by the police a few miles away from a number of collieries; the police told them that they feared a breach of the peace if the miners reached the pits, and that they would arrest the miners for obstruction if they tried to continue. After some time, a group of miners tried to push past the police and were arrested and convicted of obstructing a police officer in the course of his duty.

Their appeal on the ground that the police had not been acting in the course of their duty was dismissed. It was said that there was no need to show that individual miners would cause a breach of the peace, nor even to specify at which pit disorder was expected. A reasonable belief in a real risk that a breach would occur in close proximity to the point of arrest (the pits were two to four miles away) was all that was necessary. In assessing whether a real risk existed, news about disorder at previous pickets could be taken into account; in other words there did not appear to be a requirement that there was anything about these *particular* miners to suggest they might cause a breach of the peace. Thus a number of individuals were lawfully denied their freedom of movement and assembly apparently on no more substantial grounds than that *other* striking miners had caused trouble in the past, without having *themselves* provided grounds on which violence could be foreseen.

7.10 Obstruction of the police

This offence is not of course confined to public order situations but it is frequently used in them and provides police with a useful general power to bring to bear on persons assembling in a group who refuse to move on or disobey other police instructions. It arises under s 51(3) of the Police Act 1964 and under *Rice v Connolly* (1966) three tests must be satisfied if it is to be made out. Firstly, it must be shown that the constable was in the execution of his or her duty. Secondly, it must be shown that the defendant did an act which made it more difficult for the officer to carry out her or his duty. This means that a police officer must actually be impeded in some way. Thirdly it must be shown that the defendant behaved wilfully in the sense that he or she acted deliberately with the knowledge and intention that the effect would be to obstruct the police officer. (See further Chapter 8.)

7.11   Serious public order offences

The Public Order Act 1986 s 9 abolished the common law offences of riot, unlawful assembly and affray, and replaced them with similar statutory offences of riot (s 1), violent disorder (s 2) and affray (s 3). Each of these offences may be committed in a public or a private place and it is not necessary that any person should actually have feared unlawful violence.

7.11.1   Affray

In order to establish an affray it must firstly be shown that the defendant used or threatened unlawful violence towards another and secondly that his conduct was such as would cause a person of reasonable firmness present at the scene to fear for his personal safety. Under s 3(3) a threat cannot be made by the use of words alone. A demonstration in which threatening gestures were used might fulfil the first limb of s 3(1) but a strong argument can be advanced that it does not fulfil the second. If the gestures are part of a demonstration, it is probable that a person of reasonable firmness would not fear unlawful violence even though such a person might feel somewhat distressed. In *Taylor v DPP* (1973) Lord Hailsham, speaking of the common law offence, said 'the degree of violence ... must be such as to be calculated to terrify a person of reasonably firm character'. The Act of course refers to 'fear' as opposed to terror but this ruling suggests that 'fear' should be interpreted restrictively.

7.11.2   Violent disorder

This was a completely new offence which was aimed at preventing violent pickets. It is couched in the same terms as affray but requires that three or more persons are involved. In order to establish violent disorder it must firstly be shown that the defendant was one of three or more persons who used or threatened unlawful violence, secondly that his conduct was such as would cause a person of reasonable firmness present at the scene to fear for his personal safety, and thirdly that he actually used or threatened violence. It may be argued that in the context of a demonstration, threatening gestures would not be termed a threat of violence. 'Violence' is a strong term which should not be watered down. If no threats are used a defendant could incur liability under s 2 only if it was found that he encouraged violence by others.

7.11.3   Riot

Riot is the highest level public order offence created by the 1986 Act and is similar to the offence of violent disorder.

However, it requires that 12 or more persons who are present together use or threaten unlawful violence for a common purpose and the conduct of them (taken together) is such as would cause a person reasonable firmness present at the scene to fear for his personal safety.

Apart from powers of arrest what powers are conferred on the police to quell a protest which is becoming disorderly? In 1981 the Home Secretary announced that stocks of CS gas, water cannon and plastic bullets would be held in a central store available to Chief Officers of Police for use in situations of serious disorder. The conditions under which these weapons may be used are not defined in any statute and it may be that their use is unreviewable by the courts.

7.12   **Prerogative powers to keep the peace**

In *Secretary of State to the Home Dept ex p Northumbria Police Authority* (1989) a local police authority tried to prevent the Chief Constable applying for plastic bullets from the central store. The Court of Appeal declared that the Crown had a prerogative power to keep the peace which allowed the Home Secretary to 'do all that was reasonably necessary to preserve the peace of the realm'. As the power is undefined it appears to render lawful any measures taken by the Home Secretary which can be termed 'reasonably necessary' in order to keep the peace. Thus it appears that while protesters can at least know when and on what grounds conditions can be imposed limiting or preventing protest, they are denied such knowledge as to the power to use weapons against them.

So far the emphasis has been on meetings in public places. The provisions of ss 11, 12, 13 and 14 of the Public Order Act 1986 do not cover private meetings, although the general public order offences do. Any meeting held in wholly enclosed premises will be a private meeting (s 16) including a meeting held in a town hall although the town hall is owned by a public body. The control of indoor public meetings is generally speaking the responsibility of the persons holding the meeting and to that end a reasonable number of stewards should be appointed (Public Order Act 1936 s 2(6)) who may use reasonable force to control disorder and to eject members of the public whose behaviour does not constitute reasonable participation in the meeting.

7.13   **Meetings on private premises**

The power of the police to enter indoor meetings is uncertain. It was generally thought that the police had no power to enter unless they were invited in. However, such a power may derive from the decision in *Thomas v Sawkins* (1935). A meeting was held in a hall to protest regarding the provisions of the Incitement to Disaffection Bill which was then before Parliament. The police entered the meeting and its leader, who considered that they were trespassing, removed one of the officers who resisted the ejectment.

In response the leader brought a private prosecution against the officers for assault and battery. He sought to show that the officers were trespassers and that therefore he had a right to eject them in which case their resistance would amount to assault and battery. The court found that the officers had not been trespassing. Although the meeting had not constituted or given rise to a breach of the peace the officers had reasonably apprehended a breach because seditious speeches and incitement to violence might have occurred. The police had therefore been entitled to enter the premises. This decision has been much criticised. Nevertheless, it does not hand the police *carte blanche* to enter private meetings; it should mean that the police can enter the meeting only if there is a clear possibility that a breach of the peace may occur.

A more narrow right to enter premises which might be applicable in respect of some meetings arises under s 17(1)(c) of the Police and Criminal Evidence Act 1984. A police officer has the right to enter and search premises with a view to arresting a person for the offence arising under s 1 of the Public Order Act 1936 of wearing a uniform in connection with a political object. Furthermore, the police can enter premises in order to arrest a person for an offence under s 4 of the Public Order Act 1986. It should be noted that the offence under s 4 (discussed above at 7.6.4) can be committed in a private or public place although not in a dwelling. Presumably it could therefore be committed in a town hall. Thus a meeting during which violence might be threatened to persons present would give police officers the right to enter if they had reasonable suspicion that such could be the case.

| 7.14 | **Private remedies: the civil law** |

Apart from control by the police, meetings and demonstrations can be prevented by private persons who seek injunctions in order to prevent them. An interim injunction may be obtained very quickly in a hearing in which the other party is not represented. Even if a permanent injunction is not eventually granted the aim of the demonstration may well have been destroyed by that time. In *Hubbard v Pitt* (1976) the defendants mounted a demonstration outside an estate agents in order to protest at what was seen as the ousting of working class tenants in order to make way for higher income buyers, thereby effecting a change in the character of the area. They therefore picketed the estate agents. The plaintiffs sought an injunction to prevent this on various grounds including that of nuisance. At first instance it was held that a stationary meeting would not constitute a reasonable user of the Highway; the grant of the interim injunction was then upheld by the Court of Appeal, Lord Denning dissenting on the ground that the right to demonstrate is so closely analogous to freedom of speech that it should be protected.

Freedom of Assembly

There are very few restrictions under UK law on the freedom to join or form groups which do not constitute conspiracies. Restraint does however arise in two areas: firstly in relation to groups associated with the use of violence and secondly in relation to trade union membership. Any 'quasi military' group as defined under the Act will be prohibited under s 2 of the Public Order Act 1936. Certain named groups are prohibited under the Prevention of Terrorism (Temporary Provisions) Act 1989 (PTA) which makes it an offence under s 1 to belong to a proscribed organisation. Also certain means of signalling support for such groups will attract liability; under s 2 of the PTA it is an offence to wear any item which arouses a reasonable apprehension that a person is a member or supporter of a proscribed organisation.

Three issues have arisen in relation to restrictions on trade union membership: the freedom not to join a Trade Union, freedom to choose between Unions, and the limits of the basic freedom to belong to a Union. UK legislation has been amended in order to comply with the Article 11 of the European Convention guarantee of freedom of association, so that where a closed shop is operating an employee need not join the trade union on grounds of political conviction. However, Article 11 dos not appear in general to demand complete freedom of choice as between trade Unions, while the need to allow union membership will give way before the demands of national security.

Jordan and Tyndall (1963)
McEldowney v Forde (1971)
DPP v Whelan (1975)
Young, James and Webster v UK (1981)
Sibson v United Kingdom (1993)
Council of Civil Service Unions v Minister for the Civil Service (1984) (the GCHQ case)
Civil Service Unions v UK (1988)

Marches and public meetings are affected by a number of legal constraints, of which some are aimed directly at them and some generally at keeping the peace. Some of these restraints can operate before the assembly (the term 'assembly' will be used here to mean a march or meeting) has begun, perhaps

Freedom of assembly

Freedom of assembly: prior restraints

some days before it is due to begin; these are known as prior restraints. They include those arising from the provisions of ss 11, 12, 13 and 14 of the Public Order Act 1986, as amended by the Criminal Justice and Public Order Act 1994, ss 70 and 71. As will be found most restraints operate in relation to marches, not stationary meetings. Section 11 ensures that the police will have notice of a march; then, if it seems that it might be disorderly or intimidatory conditions may be imposed on it under s 12, or it could be banned under s 13 if the disorder apprehended was seen as serious. The banning order affects all marches in the area over the period covered. Of course, the police are not dependent on the notice given in order to make a determination as to the peacefulness of the march, but if the notice requirement is not complied with the organisers will incur liability. Section 14 can be used to impose conditions on meetings if it is thought that they are likely to be disorderly or intimidatory. Under s 14A a meeting can now be banned for up to four days if it is likely to be both trespassing and seriously disruptive to the life of the community, or likely to result in damage to certain types of building or structure. Common law powers arising under the breach of the peace doctrine might be used instead of the powers under the 1986 Act or perhaps even in addition to them to prevent certain persons taking part in the march or meeting.

Subsequent restraints under the 1986 and 1994 Acts

There are a very large number of restraints which can be used when the march or meeting is in being or as persons are assembling to take part. Conditions can be imposed under ss 12 and 14 during the assembly if it seems to be becoming disorderly or intimidatory. There are also a mass of other powers which might be used against members or organisers of a disorderly assembly. These arise under a variety of statutory provisions and at common law. The 1986 Act contains a number of provisions other than those already considered which may be used in respect of disorderly or violent behaviour during a march of assembly. These offences ascend in order of seriousness, beginning with s 5 in relation to threatening or insulting behaviour, followed by s 4A, then by s 4, affray under s 3, violent disorder s 2 and riot under s 1. Section 68 of the 1994 Act also creates a new offence of aggravated trespass. The 1986 Act contains a special area of liability aimed at racist meetings and marches of an inflammatory nature: incitement to racial hatred under s 18.

In Re M and H (minors) (1988)
Reid (1987)
News Group Newspapers Ltd v SOGAT (1982)
Kent v Metropolitan Police Commissioner (1981)

Christians Against Racism and Fascism v UK (1984)
Flockhart v Robinson (1950)

Other statutory provisions which overlap with these include obstruction of the highway under the Highways Act 1980 s 137, and of the police under the Police Act 1964 s 51(3) and intimidation under the Conspiracy and Protection of Property Act 1875 s 7. There are also certain common law powers available to use against members of assemblies which show signs of disorder: breach of the peace and public nuisance. Apart from these areas of criminal law civil remedies such as trespass and nuisance will be available to landowners who wish to prevent meetings or demonstrations on their land.

Subsequent restraints under other provisions

Brutus v Cozens (1973)
DPP v Orum (1988)
DPP v Fidler (1992)
DPP v Clarke (1992)
R v Ambrose (1973)
R v Horseferry Road Metropolitan Stipendiary Magistrate ex p Siadatan (1991)
Winn v DPP (1992)
Jordan v Burgoyne (1963)
Arrowsmith v Jenkins (1963)
Nagy v Weston (1966)
Hirst and Agu v Chief Constable of West Yorkshire (1986)
R v Clarke (1964)
Gillingham Borough Council v Medway Dock Co (1992)
Howell (1981)
Chief Constable for Devon and Cornwall ex p CEGB (1982)
Piddington v Bates (1961)
Moss v McLachlan (1985)
Rice v Connolly (1966)
Taylor v DPP (1973)
R v Secretary of State to the Home Dept ex p Northumbria Police Authority (1987)
Hubbard v Pitt (1976)

Meetings on private premises are not affected by the special provisions of ss 11,12,13 and 14 of the Public Order Act 1986. However, the police have the power to enter such a meeting if a breach of the peace is apprehended.

Meetings on private premises

Thomas v Sawkins (1935)

Chapter 8

Privacy

The right to privacy is a well accepted part of the domestic law of a number of countries such as France, Canada and Germany, and of international human rights instruments including the European Convention on Human Rights. However, it has been found to cover such a wide range of concepts that any proffered definition of privacy is likely to be very broad. In particular, numerous issues have been accommodated within the concept of privacy arising under Article 8 of the European Convention on Human Rights: they range from the right to engage in homosexual practices to the right to receive information about oneself.

This chapter will take Article 8 jurisprudence as a guide and will assume that privacy as recognised under Article 8 may be said to encompass two broad interests which will be termed: control over intrusions and control over personal information. The term 'control' is used here to mean conferring a power of choice rather than merely allowing determination as to the degree of interference once it is taking place. It may be apparent that these two broad interests need not be treated as entirely distinct from each other; as will be seen both will be in question in relation to resistance to the gathering by others of personal information. These two interests may be protected if the state and others come under negative obligations to leave the individual alone, or even positive obligations to act in order to enable the individual to retain the power of choice in relation to aspects of his or her personal life.

Boundaries round these areas of choice may be breached if another sufficiently pressing claim is put forward: privacy, like freedom of expression, is not treated as an absolute right under Article 8 and competes not only with a number of public interests, such as the prevention of crime but also with other individual freedoms such as freedom of expression.

At present UK law recognises no general right to privacy, although there is some evidence, as will be seen, that judges consider this to be an evil which should be remedied. It can be argued that various areas of tort or equity such as trespass, breach of confidence, copyright and defamation are instances of a general right to privacy, but it is reasonably clear from judicial pronouncements in cases such as *Kaye v Robertson* (1991) that these areas and others must be treated as covering specific and distinct interests which may only incidentally

8.1   Introduction

offer protection to privacy – despite the fact that the term 'privacy' is used in a number of rulings. In such instances it will be found that a recognised interest such as property actually formed the basis of the ruling. Thus it will be found that UK law offers only piecemeal protection to privacy and therefore a number of privacy interests are largely unprotected. In so far as protection for privacy has been broadened recently, the initiative has largely come not from the courts or the government but from Europe – either from European Community directives or from claims under the European Convention on Human Rights.

8.2   **The control of personal information: freedom from interference by the media**

No tort of invasion of privacy exists in the UK as in the USA to control the activity of the media in obtaining information regarding an individual's private life and then publishing the details possibly in exaggerated, lurid terms. However, certain legal controls do exist although they are not aimed directly at the invasion of privacy, and they can be used against the media when private information is published. These controls affect both the publication of the information and the methods used to obtain it.

When personal information such as a photograph is obtained, there may be some kind of intrusion on property, albeit of a nebulous kind, such as long range surveillance, but the real grievance may well be in the obtaining of the information even if it is not published, rather than the intrusion itself. However, for the sake of simplicity the legal control of intrusions which is relevant in this area will be considered separately below and only the legal controls relevant to the publication of information will be considered here. These are found in the laws of confidence, copyright, defamation and malicious falsehood. However, it will be argued that these controls are limited in scope and are aimed at the protection of other interests making them ill-suited to the protection of privacy.

8.3   **Breach of confidence and public disclosure of personal information**

The common law doctrine of breach of confidence will protect some confidential communications, and its breadth has supported the view that it could provide a general means of protecting personal information. The Younger Committee, which reported on the legal protection of privacy in 1972, considered that confidence was the area of the law which offered most effective protection of privacy. It has a wider ambit than defamation in that it prevents *truthful* communications, and appears to protect confidential communications whether or not their unauthorised disclosure causes detriment to the reputation of any person. It may be that detriment is in fact caused to the reputation of the person who is its subject when personal information is disclosed as in *Woodward v Hutchings* (1977) or *Lennon v News Group Newspapers Ltd* (1978), but the rulings do not rest on the need to demonstrate such detriment. However, it must be remembered that confidence, while quite closely associated with it, has traditionally protected a somewhat different interest from that of privacy; it is concerned with the *preservation of confidentiality* and therefore has not appeared apt to cover all possible circumstances in which private life is laid bare.

This area of law developed largely as a means of protecting commercial secrets. Its ingredients, according to Lord Greene MR in *Saltman Engineering Co Ltd v Campbell Engineering Co Ltd* (1963), are: information which has a quality of confidence as it is not in the public domain, transmission of the information in circumstances importing an obligation of confidence, and unauthorised use of that information.

As *Duke of Argyll v Duchess of Argyll* (1965) demonstrated, these ingredients may arise when confidential information is imparted in a relationship of trust not of a contractual nature and therefore personal information is clearly covered. However, that ruling was delivered in the context of a formal relationship – marriage – and combined with other rulings such as that in *Thompson v Stanhope* (1774) suggests that beach of confidence is relevant only where a formal relationship could be identified. In *Stephens v Avery* (1988), however, which concerned information communicated within a close friendship, it was not found necessary to identify a formal relationship between the parties at the time when the information was communicated, thus suggesting that the confidential nature of the information was the important factor: 'The basis of equitable intervention to protect confidentiality is that it is unconscionable for a person who has received information on the basis that it is confidential, subsequently to reveal that information ... The relationship between the parties is not the determining factor.' Thus it appears that no particular pre-existing relationship is needed.

These comments might appear to cover a communication of confidential information by one complete stranger to another so long as the communicator informed the recipient that the information was confidential. However, it may be going too far to suggest that the *Stephens v Avery* ruling would support the use of confidence in relation to secrets passed between strangers. The *ratio* of the case would seem to be merely that no pre-existing *formal* relationship is needed; as the information was passed within a close friendship it was not

8.3.1   A duty of confidence in personal relationships

necessary for the decision to state that there was no need to identify any relationship at all. The comment to that effect was therefore only *obiter* and so it is doubtful whether courts in future would be prepared to accept that confidences passed between slight acquaintances or strangers should be protected. Possibly they would be reluctant to do so since the betrayal of trust for which the law of confidence has traditionally sought to provide a remedy would be less apparent in such instances. Nevertheless, support for imposition of a broad duty of confidence not dependent on the relationship between the parties also comes from *Francome v Mirror Group Newspapers* (1984), in which the information was obtained by means of a telephone tap, and from *AG v Guardian Newspapers (No 2)* (1990). Lord Goff considered *obiter* that confidentiality would be imposed in instances where, for example, '... an obviously confidential document is wafted by an electric fan out of the window into a crowded street, or when an obviously confidential document ... is dropped in a public place and is then picked up by a passer-by ...'.

Following *Hellewell v Chief Constable of Derbyshire* (1995) a duty of confidence will also be imposed where the defendant acquired the information with the awareness but without the consent of the plaintiff. The case concerned police officers who acting under a legal power in acquiring the information for investigative purposes but disclosed it to persons operating a Shopwatch scheme. It was found that a duty of confidence could arise on the facts. It is concluded that a duty of confidence will be imposed more readily and in a wider range of circumstances than was previously the case, but that the parameters of confidence are at present unclear. Thompson observes, '... the early emphasis in breach of confidence actions was to protect the secrecy of information confided by one person to another ... the law seems to be moving beyond this, to afford protection to secret information *which may not have been confided to anyone*' (*Confidentiality and the Law* London (1990), p 73). Thus, it is suggested that this doctrine may be moving towards a position where the cause of action may be termed confidence but the interest protected is that of privacy.

Stephens v Avery also demonstrated that a newspaper which was not a party to the original relationship but was directly involved in that it had been approached by one of the parties, could have obligations associated with a relationship of trust imposed upon it. *AG v Guardian Newspaper Ltd* (1987) (the *Spycatcher* case: see Chapter 5) took this a stage further in making it clear that if an editor of a newspaper is not directly approached but has merely acquired the information he or she can be held to be under the same duty of confidence if aware that the information is confidential. However, it must be possible to identify a duty of confidence (in the *Stephens and Avery sense*) involving the source at some point in the transaction. In the *Spycatcher* litigation the duty of confidence arose from the relationship of trust originally subsisting between Peter Wright and M15.

The need to identify a duty of confidence places a limitation on the use of this remedy: it must exist at some point, but there will be circumstances in which the media will investigate and acquire facts outside any such duty. Even where it can be identified and one party then discloses a story to the media, the courts have placed limitations on this remedy which arise from the 'public interest' defence. In *Woodward v Hutchings* (1977) intimate facts about Tom Jones and another pop star were revealed to the *Daily Mirror* by a former agent who had been their confidante. The plaintiffs sought an injunction on the ground of breach of confidence. There had been a relationship of trust and they claimed that the agent should not be able to take unfair advantage of that confidence.

8.3.2   The 'public interest' defence

The Court of Appeal failed to uphold the claim on the basis that the plaintiffs had sought to publicise themselves in order to present a certain 'image' and therefore could not complain if the truth were later revealed. This decision has been criticised on the basis that a need to reveal the truth about the plaintiffs was irrelevant to the breach of confidence on the part of the agent, but it has not been overruled. The public interest in knowing the truth about the plaintiffs seemed to rest on a refusal to use the law to protect their attempt to mislead the public, and therefore would not usually be in question in relation to the disclosure of personal information.

It is said that there is no confidence in *iniquity*; in other words the plaintiff cannot use this remedy to cover up his or her own wrong doing and therefore the public interest in disclosure will prevail. However it is uncertain whether this 'public interest defence' is limited to cases of iniquity. The House of Lords considered *obiter* in *British Steel Corpn v Granada Television* (1981) that publication of confidential information could legitimately be undertaken only where there was misconduct, but on the other hand in *Lion Laboratories v Evans* (1985) Lord Justice Stephenson said that he would reject the 'no iniquity, no public interest rule' on the basis that 'some things are required to be disclosed in the public interest in which case no confidence can be prayed in aid to keep them secret and [iniquity] is merely an instance of just cause and excuse for breaking confidence'.

These rulings concerned confidential information held by private companies and seem to leave open the possibility of a broad public interest defence which, it seems from *Woodward*, may also sometimes apply in the case of public figures. Where personal information relating to an ordinary individual is in issue, it would seem from the ruling in *X v Y* (1988) that the public interest defence is confined to cases of iniquity, although a proviso to this principle may arise where the plaintiff due to no fault of his own creates a danger to the public. This proviso may be said to arise either as a variant of the public interest defence – although the plaintiff due to a particular mental state is not responsible for it, wrong doing is likely to arise through his agency if the information is suppressed – or as a specific exception to it. The general principle can be supported on the basis that private persons have a greater interest in maintaining confidentiality of information than have private companies or public figures.

| 8.3.3 | A public interest in maintaining confidence? |

The above discussion should not be taken as assuming that the public interest will always require disclosure of information and will therefore invariably be in competition with the interest of the plaintiff in suppressing it. In certain circumstances, such as those which arose in *X v Y*, there may be a *public* interest in maintaining confidentiality. A newspaper wished to publish information deriving from confidential hospital records which showed that certain practising doctors were suffering from the AIDS virus. In granting an injunction preventing publication, Rose J took into account the public interest in *disclosure* but weighed it against the private interest in confidentiality *and* the public interest in encouraging AIDS patients to seek help from hospitals, which would not be served if it was thought that confidentiality might not be maintained.

| 8.3.4 | Disclosure to whom? |

In *Francome v Mirror Group Newspapers* (1984) it was unclear that publication to the public at large, as opposed to the racing authorities, was warranted and this appears to have persuaded the Court of Appeal to allow a remedy. Otherwise, reporting of breaches of the race rules might not have attracted a remedy due to the iniquity defence.

| 8.4 | **Defamation and malicious falsehood** |

Defamation tends to provide limited protection for privacy since the defence of justification is available, and therefore it will not usually affect the situation in which true facts are disclosed. Moreover, the interest protected by defamation – the interest in preserving one's reputation – is not synonymous with the interest in preserving privacy. A reputation may not suffer but private facts may nevertheless be spread abroad which is in itself hurtful for the individual affected.

In *Corelli v Wall* (1906) the defendants had published without the plaintiff's permission postcards depicting imaginary events in her life. This was held not to be libellous and no remedy lay in copyright as the copyright was in the creator of the cards. Thus no remedy was available. *Kaye v Robertson and Another* (1990), which was of a similar nature, may be said to have made clear the inadequacy of defamation as a remedy for invasions of privacy. Mr Kaye, a well-known actor, was involved in a car accident and suffered severe injuries to his head and brain. While he was lying in hospital two journalists from the *Sunday Sport*, acting on Mr Robertson's orders, got into his room, photographed him and interviewed him. Due to his injuries, he did not object to their presence and shortly after the incident had no recollection of it.

The resultant article gave the impression that Mr Kaye had consented to the interview. His advisers sought and obtained an injunction restraining the defendants from publishing the photographs and the interview. On appeal by the defendants the Court of Appeal ruled that the plaintiff's claim could not be based on a right to privacy as such a right is unknown to English law. His true grievance lay in the 'monstrous invasion of privacy' which he had suffered but he would have to look to other rights of action in order to obtain a remedy, namely libel and malicious falsehood.

The basis of the defamation claim was that the article's implication that Mr Kaye had consented to a first 'exclusive' interview for a 'lurid and sensational' newspaper such as the *Sunday Sport* would lower him in the esteem of right thinking people. The Court of Appeal held that this claim might well succeed but that as such a conclusion was not inevitable it could not warrant grant of an interim injunction, basing this ruling on *Herbage v Times Newspapers and Others* (1981).

The court then considered malicious falsehood. Firstly it had to be shown that the defendant had published about the plaintiff words which were false. It was found that any reasonable jury would find that the implication contained in the words of the article was false. As the case was, on that basis, clear cut, an interim injunction could in principle be granted. Secondly, it had to be shown that the words were published maliciously. Malice would be inferred if it was proved that the words were calculated to produce damage and that the defendant knew them to be false. The reporters clearly realised that Mr Kaye was unable to give them any informed consent. Any subsequent publication of the falsehood would therefore be malicious. Thirdly, damage must have followed as a direct result of the publication of the falsehood. The words had produced damage in that they had diminished the value of Mr Kaye's right to sell the story of his accident at some later date. That ground of action was therefore made out.

Therefore, an injunction restraining the defendants until trial from publishing anything which suggested that the plaintiff had given an informed consent to the interview or the taking of the photographs was substituted for the original order. However, this was a limited injunction which allowed publication of the story with certain of the photographs. Thus it seemed that no effective remedy was available for the plaintiff. Legatt LJ concluded his ruling by saying: 'We do not need a First Amendment to preserve the freedom of the Press, but the abuse of that freedom can be ensured only by the enforcement of a right to privacy'.

8.5 Power of the court to protect minors

The privacy of children receives some protection from the courts' inherent jurisdiction to protect the privacy of minors. This was confirmed in *Central Independent Television* (1995). A programme was made depicting the work of the police which included an investigation into a man subsequently convicted of offences of indecency. The plaintiff recognised him as her husband in a trailer shown of the programme. She did not wish her daughter, aged five, who knew nothing of his convictions to know what had occurred and therefore sought to have the programme altered so that it would not be possible to recognise her husband.

The House of Lords refused the injunction despite accepting that it had an inherent jurisdiction to protect the privacy of minors. It found that the protection for the privacy of children would not extend to covering publication of facts relating to those who were not carers of the child in question and which occurred before the child was born.

8.6 Further press regulation

Proposals for further press regulation can be divided into three main areas which will be considered in turn: firstly, the various experiments with methods of self regulation and proposals for their improvement, or for a statutory tribunal to regulate the press; secondly, proposals for a statutory tort of invasion of privacy; thirdly, proposals to remedy various kinds of intrusion made with the intent to obtain personal material for publication, together with suggestions as to how the existing law could provide a remedy in this area.

8.6.1 Self-regulation/regulation by tribunal

Until recently it was thought that the press should regulate itself as regards protection of privacy rather than using civil or criminal sanctions. Self-discipline was preferred to court regulation in order to preserve press freedom, and to this end the Press Council was created in 1953. It was supposed to regulate the Press and therefore issued guidelines on privacy and adjudicated on complaints. It could censure a newspaper and require its adjudication to be published. In practice, however, a number of deficiencies became apparent in this system; the council did not issue clear enough guidelines, its decisions were seen as inconsistent and in any event ineffective: it had no power to fine or award an injunction. Moreover, it was seen as too lenient; it would not interfere if the disclosure in question could be said to be in the public interest, and what was meant by the public interest was uncertain.

Its inefficacy led the Younger Committee, convened in 1972, to recommend a number of proposals offering greater protection from intrusion by the press. These proposals were not implemented, but recently a perception again began to arise, partly influenced by *Kaye*, that further measures might be needed to control the tabloid newspapers, although at the same time there was concern that they should not prevent legitimate investigative journalism. This perceived need led eventually to the formation of the Committee on Privacy and Related Matters (hereafter 'Calcutt I') in 1990 which considered a number of measures, some relevant to actual publication and some to the means of gathering information. The Committee decided that improved self-regulation should be given one final chance and recommended the creation of the Press Complaints Commission which was set up in 1991.

The Commission agreed a Code of Practice which the newspapers accepted. It can receive and pronounce on complaints of violation of the Code and can demand an apology for inaccuracy, or that there should be an opportunity for reply. Intrusion into private life is allowed under the Code only if it is in the public interest; this is defined as including 'detecting or exposing seriously anti-social conduct' or 'preventing the public being misled by some statement or action of that individual'. Harassment is not allowed. The Code makes special mention of hospitals and requires that the press must obtain permission in order to interview patients. The Commission does not require the complainant to waive any legal right of action as the Press Council was criticised for doing. However, it has the same limited sanctions as the Press Council.

The Broadcasting Complaints Commission (BCC) has a similar role in adjudicating on complaints of infringement of privacy 'in or in connection with the obtaining of materials included in BBC or independent licensed television or sound broadcasts'. The term 'privacy' will receive quite a wide interpretation according to the ruling in *Broadcasting Complaints Commission ex p Granada Television Ltd* (1993). Granada television challenged a finding of the BCC that matters already in the public domain could, if republished, constitute an invasion of privacy. In judicial review proceedings it was found that privacy differed from confidentiality and went well beyond it because it was not confined to secrets; the significant issue was not whether material was or was not in the public domain, but whether, by being published, it caused hurt and anguish. There were grounds on which it could be considered that publication of the matters in question had caused distress and therefore the BCC had not acted unreasonably in the *Wednesbury* sense in taking the view that an infringement of privacy had occurred.

After self-regulation under the new Code had been in place for a year, Sir David Calcutt (hereafter 'Calcutt II') reviewed its success and determined that the Press Complaints Commission 'does not hold the balance fairly between the press and the individual ... it is in essence a body set up by the industry ... dominated by the industry'. He therefore proposed the introduction of a statutory tribunal which would draw up a code of practice for the press and would rule on alleged breaches of the code; its sanctions would include those already possessed by the Press Complaints Commission and in addition the imposition of fines and the award of compensation. When the matter was considered by the National Heritage Select Committee in 1993 it rejected the proposal of a statutory tribunal in favour of the creation of another self-regulatory body to be known as the Press Commission, which would monitor a Press Code and which would have powers to fine and to award compensation. At the time of writing this proposal has not been adopted; at present the government favours strengthening the sanctions available to the Press Complaints Commission. In 1994 it was given the power to institute disciplinary action against editors who breach the Press Code.

8.6.2   Tort of invasion
          of privacy

Proposals for such a tort which have been put forward centre around the protection of personal information. As was noted above, *Stephens v Avery* may herald the development of the existing tort of breach of confidence with the result that greatly increased protection for control of personal information would be effected. However, such development is not certain and in any event, as argued above, it may be preferable that protection should be achieved by a statutory tort balanced by wide ranging and carefully drawn specific public interest defences, rather than through the development of the common law of confidence with its far vaguer public interest defence.

However, support for a statutory tort has been far from unanimous in the relevant committees. Thus while the

Younger Committee recommended the introduction of a tort of disclosure of information unlawfully acquired, Calcutt I decided against recommending a new statutory tort of invasion of privacy relating to publication or personal information, although the committee considered that it would be possible to define such a tort with sufficient precision. Calcutt II recommended only that the government should give further consideration to the introduction of such a tort, but the Heritage Select Committee made a more positive recommendation and this view was adopted by Lord Mackay in his Green Paper published in July 1993. However, the White Paper published in June 1995 found against creation of a statutory tort.

Turning now to the substantive merits of such a tort, it may be noted that the possible definition put forward by Calcutt I was designed to relate only to personal information which was published without authorisation. Such information was defined as those aspects of an individual's personal life which a reasonable person would assume should remain private. The main concern of the Committee was that true information which would not cause lasting harm, was already known to some, and was obtained reputably might be caught by its provisions.

The Committee did not consider that liability should be subject to a general defence of public interest although it did favour a tightly drawn defence of justified disclosure. The difficulty here is that it might not always be possible for a journalist trying to investigate corruption in public life to show that there was a clear justification for gathering the relevant information if the investigation was still at an inchoate stage; as discussed above, to be effective in protecting worthwhile journalism, any defences would have to require only an honest belief by the journalist that his or her investigations had one of the justificatory purposes. The Green Paper suggested a defence of public interest which would cover the same areas as discussed below in relation to criminal liability. However, even with such a defence, various causes for concern remain.

Perhaps the most important of these is that since this tort would cover *all* personal information instead of being confined to material gained through intrusion, it would represent a far greater restriction on the kind of information that could be published than would the Calcutt offence of intrusion considered above. Countries which have specific legal protection for privacy often also have freedom of information measures. If the UK were to enact a right to privacy without such a measure and without any other protection for the freedom of the press, the detriment caused might outweigh the value of such a right. It might also be pointed out that the Green Paper did not suggest that legal aid should be available to those seeking redress under the new civil privacy liability. If a tort of invasion of privacy is enacted in the future without the provision of legal aid the new provisions might merely be used – as arguably defamation has been – by powerful figures to protect their activities from scrutiny, while the ordinary citizen might be unable in practice to obtain redress for invasions of privacy.

Legatt LJ asserted confidently in *Kaye* that a right to privacy exists in the USA which will be enforced and suggested that such a right should be imported into UK law, but this proposition has come under attack from Bedingfield, on the basis that the scope of USA privacy rights is limited by a general defence of 'newsworthiness' which allows many stories disclosing embarrassing and painful personal facts to be published. This perhaps suggests that there is little value in looking to the USA for a model if a UK right to privacy is to have any efficacy. At present two divergent models of privacy law seem to confront law reformers in the UK: on the one hand a claim of invasion of privacy might be met by such a general defence of public interest or newsworthiness that it had in most instances very little chance of success, while on the other a narrow defence of public interest or 'justified publication' might allow invasion of privacy too much scope.

Arguably an acceptable middle way forward until and if freedom of information and speech receive further protection, may be to enact very specific and narrowly defined areas of liability relating to particularly intrusive invasions of privacy, which differentiate between the lives of ordinary citizens who happen to come into the public eye, and the lives of public figures. It is to consideration of proposals for such measures that we now turn.

8.6.3	Remedies for intrusion

The kinds of particularly clear invasions of privacy which arguably require some kind of statutory response are as follows: physical intrusion by reporters both onto the individual's own property or onto other private property where he or she happens to be as in *Kaye*; the taking of photographs for publication without the subject's consent, and the use of bugging devices. The Younger Committee proposed the introduction of a tort and crime of unlawful surveillance by means of a technical device, and both Calcutt committees recommended the creation of a specific criminal offence providing more extensive protection – a recommendation which was backed by the National Heritage Select Committee when it considered the matter. At the time of writing it is thought that the offence as framed in Calcutt II will probably form part of a forthcoming Criminal Justice Bill.

The clause creating the offence also offers the individual whose privacy has been invaded, the possibility of obtaining injunctions in the High Court to prevent publication of material gained in contravention of the clause provisions; damages will also be available to hold newspapers to account for any profits gained through publication of such material.

Criminal liability under the clause is made out if the defendant does any of the following with intent to obtain personal information or photographs, in either case with a view to their publication: entering or remaining on private property without the consent of the lawful occupant; placing a surveillance device on private property without such consent; using a surveillance device *whether on private property or elsewhere* in relation to an individual who is on private property without his or her consent; taking a photograph or recording the voice of an individual who is on private property without his or her consent and with intent that the individual should be identifiable. This offence seems to specify the forbidden acts fairly clearly and to be aimed at preventing what would generally be accepted to be undesirable invasions of privacy; it is worth noting that France, Germany, Denmark and the Netherlands all have similar offences on the statute books. (It should be noted that the offence would *not* cover persistent telephoning although the decision in *Khorasandjian v Bush* (1993) might offer some protection in this area as it might to photographing, interviewing or recording the voice of a vulnerable individual such as a disaster victim or a bereaved relative in a *public* place.)

Under Calcutt II it would be a defence to any of the above to show that the act was done: (a) for the purpose of preventing, detecting or exposing the commission of a crime or other seriously anti-social conduct; or (b) for the purpose of preventing the public from being misled by some public statement or action of the individual concerned; or (c) for the purpose of informing the public about matters directly affecting the discharge of any public function of the individual concerned; or (d) for the protection of public health or safety; or (e) under any lawful authority.

Under the Green Paper the words 'seriously anti-social conduct' would have been removed from defence (a) and defences (b) and (c) would have been curtailed, possibly with a view to protecting politicians who may have improperly accepted favours or in some way misled the public. The interpretation given to the defences would of course be crucial in safeguarding media freedom, but it is suggested that the proposed offence may have merit as an addition to self-regulation of the media; it provides a remedy against some unjustifiable invasions of privacy, but coupled with the defences as suggested under Calcutt II would not risk the deterrence of serious journalism and the concomitant loss of public accountability vital to a healthy democracy. Retention of *all* the defences is, however, crucial in creating this balance.

8.7 **Conclusions**	In conclusion, although it seems that there are gaps in the protection offered to privacy by the common law it does not follow that broad statutory measures to protect it should be adopted. The main difficulty is to ensure that such measures do not cover the public lives of public figures in a way which might keep matters of public interest from the press. If the UK were to enact a right to privacy without enacting freedom of information legislation, and without any other protection for the freedom of the press, the detriment caused might outweigh the value of such a right. Thus while freedom of information and speech are without constitutional protection, the best way forward seems to be, it is submitted, enactment of narrowly defined areas of liability relating to intrusion which, coupled with broad defences may be able to differentiate reasonably well between the lives of ordinary citizens who happen to come into the public eye and the lives of public figures.

8.8 **The control of personal information: freedom from interference by the state**

In contrast to the attention which is paid to preventing access to government information under the Official Secrets Act 1989 (see Chapter 6) legal regulation of state surveillance and information gathering is ineffective in protecting the privacy of personal information. Until recently such activities operated outside any legal framework, and many aspects of state surveillance remain entirely unregulated such as bugging and infiltration of pressure groups. However, the interception of communications – as opposed to electronic surveillance or bugging generally – is subject to certain controls arising under the Interception of Communications Act 1985, which was introduced as a direct result of a ruling in the European Court of Human Rights that the existing British warrant procedure violated the Article 8 guarantee of privacy in the European Convention (*Malone v UK* (1985)).

8.8.1 **The interception of communications: legal regulation**

In 1979 Mr James Malone was on trial for receiving stolen goods. During his trial, evidence that his phone had been tapped was revealed in court when a police witness read extracts from his notebook of an intercept which had been authorised by the Home Secretary on Malone's phone. Malone sought a declaration in the High Court that it was unlawful for anyone to intercept another's telephone conversations without consent (*Malone v MPC No 2* (1979)). This line of argument failed as did the argument, based on Article 8 of the European Convention, that there was a right to privacy which had been violated by the tapping. The judge, Sir Robert Megarry, concluded that the Convention did not give rise to any enforceable rights under English law and that therefore there was no direct right of privacy. However, he commented 'This is not a subject on which it is possible to feel any pride in English law ... telephone tapping is a subject which cries out for legislation.'

Malone took his case to the European Court of Human Rights which, in 1985, finally held that the existing warrant procedure violated the Article 8 guarantee of privacy. Article 8(2) reads: 'There shall be no interference by a public authority with the exercise of this right *except such as is in accordance with the law*' etc. The European Court of Human Rights held that UK domestic law did not regulate the circumstances in which telephone tapping could be carried out sufficiently clearly or provide any remedy against abuse of the power. This meant that it did not meet the requirement of being 'in accordance with the law'. However, the decision only required the UK government to introduce legislation to regulate the circumstances in which the power to tap could be used rather than giving guidance as to what would be acceptable limits on the right to privacy.

Before the Interception of Communications Act came into force, CND brought a High Court action challenging the decision to tap the phones of its members (*Secretary of State for Home Affairs ex p Ruddock* (1987)) on the ground that the government had aroused a legitimate expectation through published statements that it would not use tapping for party political purposes. The action failed but did establish the principle that the courts were entitled to review unfair actions by government arising from the failure to live up to legitimate expectations created in this way. The judge, Mr Justice Taylor, also stated that the jurisdiction of the court to look into such a complaint against a Minister should not be totally ousted. It had been argued on behalf of the Crown that the court should not entertain the action because to do so would be detrimental to national security. Mr Justice Taylor, however, ruled that such ousting of the courts' jurisdiction in a field where the citizen could have no right to be consulted would be a 'dangerous and draconian step indeed'. That case was the last time such statements would be heard publicly in respect of telephone tapping: s 9 of the 1985 Act then precluded the possibility of their repetition and of course brought about the very danger Mr Justice Taylor wanted to avert.

The response of the UK government to *Malone* in the Interception of Communications Act 1985 was to provide very wide grounds under s 2 on which warrants for the purposes of interception could be authorised by the Home Secretary: they include warrants necessary 'in the interests of national security' for the purpose of preventing *or* detecting serious crime; or 'for the purpose of safeguarding the economic well being of the UK'. These seem to be significantly wider than the old Home Office guidelines previously relied on in respect of the authorising of warrants. The warrants must be personally signed by the Home Secretary or in urgent cases by a Home Office official with express authorisation from the Home Secretary.

The warrants are issued for an initial period of two months and may be renewed for longer periods. There is no overall limit on renewals and some warrants are undoubtedly very longstanding. The warrants are supposed to be *precise*; they must specify a person and an address. However, there have been allegations – which are denied – that blanket warrants have been issued, and it does appear that 'a person' can equal an organisation. Once a warrant is obtained telephone tapping and mail interceptions are conducted by Post Office employees at the request of the police and security service members. At the end of 1989, 315 warrants were in force and 522 were issued during the year.

The Act establishes a tribunal to consider complaints from people who believe that their telephone may have been tapped or their mail interfered with. The tribunal has a duty to investigate whether a warrant has been issued and if so, whether it was properly issued – whether there were adequate grounds for issuing the warrant and whether statutory procedures were complied with. The tribunal can order quashing of the warrant and payment of compensation to the victim, but in fact, none of the first 68 complaints to the tribunal were upheld. Indeed, no contraventions of the Act were found during its first 18 months. In addition to the tribunal (which consists of five senior lawyers) there is a Commissioner – a senior judge appointed by the PM on a part-time basis to assist the tribunal and generally monitor the warrant procedure. He has two specific duties: to notify the PM of any breach of the rules and to publish an annual report. The tribunal has no power to deal with the problem of tapping without a warrant, ie unauthorised tapping.

Telephone tapping will be used for the purposes of gathering information which may be relevant in criminal prosecutions. However, it has generally been assumed that intercept information would not be proffered directly as evidence, although it might lead to the uncovering of other evidence.

If an unauthorised telephone tap does occur will the information gained be admissible in evidence? In *Effick* (1992) the defendants were prosecuted for conspiracy to supply controlled drugs. Police officers obtained part of the evidence against them by means of intercepting and taping their telephone calls. The appellants were convicted and appealed on the ground that the intercepted telephone calls should have been ruled inadmissible under s 9 of the Interception of Communications Act 1985 or under s 78 of the Police and Criminal Evidence Act 1984 (PACE) as they were made without a warrant for interception.

It was determined that argument under s 9 failed because its provisions are aimed at preventing disclosure of information which tends to suggest that the offence of unauthorised interception (under s 1(1) of the 1985 Act) has been committed by specified persons or that a warrant has been or is to be issued to such persons: they were not intended to render inadmissible all evidence obtained as a result of an interception. Clear statutory language would have been needed to oust the principle that all logically probative evidence should be admitted. As this was not the case, and as the instance in question did not appear to fall within s 9, the evidence was admissible.

The submission in respect of s 78 PACE failed because it was not suggested that the police officers had deliberately contravened the 1985 Act. It was found that no unfairness to the defendants had occurred due to the admission of the evidence. This begs the question whether the very fact that the evidence was obtained unlawfully could lead to unfairness at the trial. However, it is now fairly clear that, except in the case of confession or identification evidence, evidence obtained illegally will not be excluded unless the illegality was deliberately perpetrated (see Chapter 9). However, in *Preston* (1993) the House of Lords found that material gained directly by an intercept would be inadmissible; s 9 would relate only to background material.

Section 1 of the 1985 Act deals with *unauthorised* interceptions and makes it a criminal offence to intentionally intercept a postal communication or telecommunication without authorisation. This applies to persons in the public or private sectors and would therefore catch, for example, newspaper

8.8.2 Admissibility of evidence deriving from an intercept

8.8.3 Unauthorised tapping and surveillance devices

reporters although such persons could use electronic bugging devices with impunity. It should be remembered that the Act does not deal with electronic surveillance generally; its scope is limited to interceptions of telephone calls: mail electronic bugs and surveillance devices require no authorisation at all.

8.8.4   The interception of communication: conclusions

The main criticism of the statutory scheme is that there is no judicial scrutiny of the warrant procedure at any stage and only limited Parliamentary scrutiny. Further, the Tribunal does not have to give any reasons for its decisions and they cannot be questioned. Tribunal decisions on individual cases are not published and although the Commissioner's annual report giving some information on the number of intercept warrants issued must be made available, it may be censored by the PM before publication if it is thought to be 'prejudicial'. Thus the whole scheme operates at a low level of visibility. The absence or inadequacy of control in this area has often been criticised. Clearly, telephone tapping and electronic surveillance techniques offer an important weapon to the police and security services in the maintenance of law and order and protection of national security. However, it may be suggested that the balance created at present between this interest and that of protecting privacy is unsatisfactory in a democratic society. It is possible that progress may be made in this area as a result of European pressure but the European Court of Human Rights has a fairly weak record in national security cases.

8.9   Access to personal information

In the UK there is no statute equivalent to the Privacy Act in the USA which enables persons to obtain access to information held on them in government files. The starting point in the UK is that certain categories of information covered by the Official Secrets Act 1989 cannot be disclosed. Moreover, if information falls outside the categories created by the 1989 Act there is no general right of access to it. The government holds a vast amount of personal information in files controlled by bodies including the DSS and NHS. The Police use a national computer which stores an immense amount of personal information, as does the Inland Revenue. Until recently the citizen had no means of knowing what information was held on him or her, and no control over the nature or use of such information.

However, an inroad into the principle of secrecy was made in 1984 by the Data Protection Act which was adopted in response to a European Community Directive. Once access to computerised files became possible, access rights to manual files were bound to follow although a large amount of personal information still remains inaccessible.

The Data Protection Act 1984 was seen as a measure to protect privacy and a first step to freedom of information. However, it must be questioned whether it was clear that there was a pressing need to allow access to electronically held information as opposed to a need for access to *all* personal information.

It may be argued that the electronic storage of information presents a particular threat to privacy because computers *exacerbate* problems which also exist with respect to manual files. For example, an error may creep into information held on manual files, but where information is collated from a large number of sources as may be more likely in respect of computerised files, an error may be more likely to occur.

Moreover, once it does occur the speed with which information can be retrieved and disseminated means that an error can reach far more persons and may do more damage than a record on a manual file. The ease of linkage and transference of information may in itself create problems aside from the rapid dissemination of errors. It is possible to transmit data from one data bank to another much more easily than can be done using manual files. For example, particulars of licensed vehicles and drivers are automatically transferred from the Driver and Vehicle Licensing Centre to police National Computers and can be to the Inland Revenue. Information can be linked and thus present a distorted picture, particularly if speculative data and opinion are linked in with factual data. Information gathered for one purpose can be used for another without the subject of the information or its contributor consenting to it or even realising what has occurred.

There is a danger that the confidentiality of information may be placed at risk. Information may be given to an employer by an employee on the understanding that because there is a confidential relationship between the parties it will go no further. If it is then stored in a data bank there is a danger that the confidentiality will be lost. An action for breach of confidence could lie but the individual affected would have to be aware of the breach. The retention of data may also create disadvantages. Although a person's circumstances or behaviour may change, old data may not be up-dated but may follow him or her around with the result that (for example) he or she is refused credit. Manually held information is less likely to follow an individual so effectively.

Perhaps it may be concluded that no difference in principle between problems associated with the storage of manually held and computerised information can be discerned, but that there is a difference of degree. The Data Protection Act 1984

8.9.1   Access to information held on computer: threat to privacy

8.9.2   Preservation of privacy under the 1984 Act

attempts to address these problems by placing certain obligations on the data user. Under ss 4 and 5 of the Act any person using a computerised system in order to store data relating to people is designated the 'data user', while the person who is the subject of the data is the 'data subject'. Any data relating to a living person is termed 'personal data'. The data user must register with the Data Protection Registrar. Under s 5 the data user must not use the data for any purpose other than the one it was collected for, and under Schedule 1 it must be kept up to date. Also, it must be adequately protected; appropriate security measures must be taken. Under ss 10 and 11 if the Data Registrar is satisfied that the data user is not complying with the Act he can serve an enforcement notice, and if this measure is not adequate he can serve a de-registration notice. It is a criminal offence for an unregistered person or body to store personal data.

Section 21 provides that if the Data User is asked by the data subject whether personal data is held on her or him, that information must be given and the data subject must be allowed access to such data. Schedule 1 also provides that if the data is found to be inaccurate, the data subject can have it corrected or erased. If the data user does not comply the subject can apply to court under s 24 for an order erasing or rectifying the data. Under s 22 compensation can be awarded if loss or damage has resulted from inaccurate data. However, compensation is available only if the data user compiled the inaccurate information, not if the data user compiled inaccurate material supplied by a malicious or careless third party. No compensation is available for circulating the inaccurate data; nor may the data subject know the third party's name.

The Act has not been without difficulties of interpretation. For example, the opinion of an employer about an employee falls within the Act but not an expression of intention. The two may be hard to distinguish; it is unclear whether the statement 'she is unpromotable' would be termed an expression of intention or an opinion. The Data Protection Registrar has accepted that this uncertainty creates a large grey area.

Certain aspects of the Act have attracted particular criticism, especially the wide subject access exemptions which include information relating to crime, national security, and a person's physical or mental health. A broad interpretation is given to these exemptions; thus the difficulties mentioned earlier may still operate in those categories. Moreover, there is still the possibility of transferring data to manual files and as provisions relating to manual files are narrow in scope, there is the possibility that the manual file will not be covered by them. The transfer of data from a registered data user such as the Department of Employment to an unregistered user such as the Security Service will remain secret, and national security is exempt from the principle that data users cannot allow data to be used for a purpose other than the original one.

Further, the budgetary restraint on the Data Protection Registry makes it impossible to keep a check on all Data Users. In any event it is considered relatively straightforward to devise an information retrieval system which only provides an incomplete copy of an individual's record; it is probable that no action for breach of the Act would follow due to the inability of the Data Registrar Officer to check up. It would take a specialist a long time to work out what had happened, and given the constraints on the Data Registrar that time is unlikely to be available. Thus it may be said that the Act is certainly a step in the direction of control over personal information but it does contain many loop-holes.

Unauthorised access to information electronically held falls within the Computer Misuse Act 1990 which criminalises such conduct whether or not the 'hacker' has a sinister purpose. It may be wondered why it should be an offence to access files held on an office computer but not files held in the filing cabinet. One answer is that hacking seems to present a more widespread and pernicious danger: it is possible to access the files from a different part of the country – there is no need for the would-be hacker to break into the office as in the case of the unauthorised seeker of information in manual files. The possibility that persons may gain unauthorised access to computer-held personal information should now be diminished.

8.9.3   The Computer Misuse Act 1990

In the wake of the 1984 Act access rights to manual files were gradually extended under the influence of the Campaign for Freedom of Information, although without government support. The Access to Personal Files Bill was put forward as a Private Members Bill and would have allowed access to a wide range of personal information. However, the government forced its proponents to accept an eviscerated Bill covering only Housing and Social Security files. Thus, the Bill was restricted to local government because central government was resistant to any measure allowing individuals access to personal files. The Bill became the Access to Personal Files Act 1987. It allowed access to 'accessible information' and therefore provided for the rectification of errors. However, it was acknowledged in the passage of the Bill that there was

8.9.4   Access to manually held files: government information

nothing to prevent the keeping of a secret file behind the accessible file. Moreover, the Act does not have retrospective effect; thus it does not apply to information collected before it came into effect.

The *Gaskin case* (1989) which went to the European Court of Human Rights illustrated the inadequacy of the available measures. Graham Gaskin wanted to gain access to the personal files on his childhood in care kept by Liverpool City Council because he wanted to sue the council in negligence. However, the files did not fall under the Data Protection Act as they were manually held; nor did they fall within the Access to Personal Files Act 1987 because they were collected before it came into force. Thus Gaskin wished to invoke Article 8 which protects the right to privacy.

The first question to be determined under Article 8 was whether it could apply to such a situation. The essential object of Article 8 is to protect the individual from arbitrary interference by the authorities. However, the court considered that there could also be a positive obligation on the authorities to act in certain situations. Here the information consisted of the only coherent record of the whole of Gaskin's early childhood. It was therefore found that *prima facie* an obligation to protect privacy arose because individuals should not be obstructed by the authorities from obtaining information so closely bound up with their identity as human beings. Thus a positive obligation could arise although Article 8 would not normally import such an obligation.

The court then considered whether the exception under Article 8(2) in respect of the rights of others could apply. On the one hand there was the need to demonstrate respect for Gaskin's privacy; on the other the contributors of the information wanted it kept confidential. It was found that the two interests should be weighed against each other by invoking the principle of proportionality. However, the local authority had not put in place any means of independently weighing the two values; thus the preference would automatically be given to the interest in maintaining confidence. Therefore the principle of proportionality was offended and a breach of Article 8 was found. Gaskin was awarded damages on the basis of the distress he had suffered.

The government complied with this ruling by introducing the Access to Personal Files Regulations 1989, which provide that social services departments must give personal information to individuals unless the contributor of the information can be identified and he or she does not consent to the access. Certain personal health information is also exempted. Thus local authorities should now be able to weigh the two values considered by the Court of Human Rights. One further possible result of this case may be that test cases will be encouraged in relation to *central* government files.

A further method of obtaining access to information relating to oneself arises under the Access to Medical Reports Act 1988 which also started life as a Private Members Bill. It provides for limited circumstances in which a person can obtain access to personal medical information: if an insurance company or prospective insurer asks for a medical report for employment purposes the individual in question can see it beforehand to read it and check it for errors. For example, a mis-diagnosis might remain on a medical record and never be corrected. This possibility is of particular significance because a medical record contains information on a person's sexual habits and family circumstances; it does not merely contain purely medical information.

The Act however creates only a limited right of access; it does not mean that a person has a general right of access to all his or her medical files. Doctors argue, paternalistically, that patients who do not have medical knowledge will not be able to place medical notes in their context, and moreover that knowing of certain conditions may exacerbate their illness as they may worry or come under greater stress. Doctors also consider that a general right of access might increase the likelihood of a negligence action; clearly such an action might fail but they do not welcome the waste of time and energy which fighting an action even successfully would entail. The darker side to this argument is of course that lack of access might preclude a legitimate negligence action: in some instances a patient might never realise that a mistake had been made.

The Access to Health Records Act 1990, which came into force on 1 November 1991, took the principle of access in this area much further. Since the introduction of the Data Protection Act 1984, patients had been entitled to have access to their *computerised* health records but the 1990 Act aims to provide an equivalent right of access to information recorded in manually held health records. Access to health records will allow people to examine exactly what has been recorded about them – thus satisfying personal curiosity – but, more importantly, it will allow for mistakes to be noted and rectified. The emphasis of the Act is on an individual's *control* of personal and private information.

However, several exceptions curb the actual scope of the access. Firstly, as in the Access to Personal Files Act, no pre-

8.9.5   Access to manually held files: medical records

commencement material must be shown, unless it is necessary for a full understanding of something which has been shown. It was found in *Mid-Glamorgan Family Health Services and Another ex p Martin* (1993) that no right of access to pre-commencement material arises at common law. Secondly, if the holder of the information – the doctor – considers that disclosure of information would result in serious physical or mental harm to the patient, access can be denied. Thirdly, patients need not be told when information is being withheld. Although the Act is a move in the direction of enabling individuals to enjoy a degree of control over personal medical information and should ensure higher standards of accuracy and objectivity on the part of doctors and other record holders, it remains the case that patients whose documents are held on computerised records enjoy greater legal protection.

8.9.6	Conclusions

In general it may be concluded that although the statutes mentioned here have opened up access to personal information in both computerised and manually held files, such access is still limited and, in the case of manual records, has still to find general application.

8.10 Freedom from intrusion: bodily and sexual privacy

Bodily and sexual privacy may be seen as encompassing two main interests. Firstly, individuals have an interest in preventing actual physical intrusions on the body. This interest consists of a negative right to be 'left alone' in a physical sense, but may also encompass a positive claim on the state to ensure that bodily integrity is not infringed. Secondly, individuals have an interest in retaining autonomy as regards freedom of choice in decisions as to the disposal or control of his or her own body. Usually the individual is, in effect, asking the state to leave him or her alone to make such decisions in order to preserve autonomy. In some instances however, the individual will be requiring the assistance of the authorities in ensuring that he or she is able to exercise autonomy. Thus, personal privacy at its simplest level may be defined as the freedom from physical intrusion but arguably the concept may be expanded to encompass individual autonomy.

8.11 Control over physical intrusions

The law determines that in certain circumstances bodily privacy may give way to other interests. Thus the Police and Criminal Evidence Act 1984 s 55 allows intimate strip searches but recognises that the violation they represent may occur only in well defined circumstances. Examination may occur only if there is reasonable suspicion that drugs or implements which might be used to harm others may be found. The examination may only be carried out by a nurse (or a medical practitioner in respect of drugs or a weapon) or if that is not practicable it can be carried out by a police officer who must be of the same sex as the person to be searched.

The question as to how far clothing could be removed for other purposes in police custody was considered in *Lindley v Rutter* (1980) and a general order to remove the bras of all female detainees in the police station was challenged. Justification was put forward for the order on the grounds that the detainees might otherwise injure themselves. However, it was found that such treatment constituted an affront to human dignity and therefore needed a clearer justification which could be derived only from the specific circumstances of the arrestee: something particular about the individual in question must support a suspicion that she might do herself an injury. It was found that in removing a detainee's bra where such specific justification did not exist, the police officer in question had acted outside her duty. Thus the court evinced a reluctance to accept a general invasion of privacy.

Certain forms of punishment may be seen as an unjustified intrusion onto bodily integrity. Corporal punishment was outlawed in state schools after the decision of the European Court of Human Rights in *Campbell and Cosans v UK* (1982) which was determined not on the basis of Articles 3 or 8 but under Article 2 of the First Protocol, which protects the right of parents to have their children educated according to their own philosophical convictions.

However, corporal punishment in private schools was not outlawed, and in *Costello-Roberts v UK* (1993) the European Court of Human Rights found that the UK had a responsibility to ensure that school discipline was compatible with the Convention even though the treatment in question was administered in an institution independent of the state. However, although the court considered that there might be circumstances in which Article 8 could be regarded as affording protection to physical integrity which would be broader than that afforded by Article 3, in the particular circumstances the adverse effect on the complainant was insufficient to amount to an invasion of privacy.

8.12 Personal autonomy and bodily privacy

Personal autonomy has been clearly recognised for some time in the USA as a legitimate privacy interest; in *Doe v Bolton* (1973) Douglas J, said: 'The right to privacy means freedom of choice in the basic decisions of one's life respecting marriage, divorce, procreation, contraception, education and upbringing of children.' Personal autonomy connotes an interest not in preventing physical intrusion by others, but with the extent to which the law allows an individual a degree of control over his or her own body.

Recognition of the need to allow self-determination has arguably become more prominent this century. Abortion and suicide are no longer crimes under the Abortion Act 1967 and the Suicide Act 1961. However, limits as to self-determination are represented by the Prohibition of Female Circumcision Act 1985 and the Surrogacy Act 1985 (although it should be noted that surrogacy is only curbed by the Act, not outlawed: it only prevents commercial surrogacy arrangements). Such measures may reflect the notion that the individual should apply his or her own moral standards in relation to decisions affecting his or her own body except when this allows something particularly abhorrent in British society to occur, such as female circumcision. Then the law will impose the wider social standard on the particular individual.

8.12.1   Medical treatment

The question of self-determination has arisen most frequently in the context of medical treatment, but the law has not so far made much progress in the direction of granting it recognition. It has particularly arisen in the context of medical negligence; it was argued in *Sidaway v Board of Governors of the Bethlem Royal Hospital* (1985) that a patient who was not fully informed as to the risks associated with the operation she was to undergo should be able to succeed against the doctor when one of those risks did materialise. However, it was found that so long as the doctor had acted in accordance with practice accepted as proper by a body of medical practitioners (the test deriving from *Bolam v Friern HMC* (1957)) with regard to disclosure of risks the action must fail.

It may be argued that this stance fails to accord sufficient weight to the personal autonomy of the patient. For example, if a patient had a serious cancerous condition there might be two main options: radical treatment which would be disfiguring but might prolong life, or conservative treatment which would not prolong life but would not disfigure. Length of life would have to be weighed against quality of life. It might appear that only the patient who knows intimately which of the options fits with his or her own aspirations and lifestyle and who must live for the rest of his or her life with the decision taken, can make it. Thus, all the information needed to make that choice should be disclosed to the patient.

The law has not however recognised any general right to self autonomy even where elective operations are concerned. The *Sidaway* case concerned an operation which might be not be termed elective in that it was aimed at pain relief, but where a purely elective operation was in question in *Gold v Haringey*

Health Authority (1987) the same principles applied. Clearly, in order that a patient can exercise self-determination he or she must know of the options for treatment and of the likely outcome in each instance. The patient can then give or withhold consent to the proposed course of treatment and, further, can question it. This should be particularly the case where one of the options is to have no treatment at all as in pain-relieving or cosmetic operations. However, the test to be applied as to whether a doctor has been negligent in failing to inform the patient of certain possibilities – the *Bolam* test – does not lay a heavy burden upon doctors in terms of the amount of information which must be given. This test may be acceptable in respect of decisions as to diagnosis and treatment (although it may be argued that it puts the plaintiff in medical negligence cases in an extremely difficult position) but arguably it is unacceptable in respect of the duty to disclose information so that the patient can give an informed consent to the treatment proposed. It appears that judges have put their fear of defensive medicine and a flood of medical litigation before the need to uphold the right of the patient to retain control over his or her own body.

Self-determination as regards the body in areas relating to sexuality may be regarded as a separate interest because it goes beyond freedom to use one's body as one chooses and raises questions as to choice of sexual identity. The first matter to be addressed concerns the extent to which individuals have the power of choice in relation to the expression of sexuality. At present sexual freedom is restricted by the criminal law which prohibits certain acts between consenting participants. The rationale for such prohibition seems to depend partly on use of the criminal law as the means of affirming and upholding a certain moral standard, and partly on the need to prevent certain specific harms. The debate as to whether or not the proper function of the criminal law is to interfere in the private lives of citizens in order to enforce a particular pattern of behaviour where no clear harm will arise from the prohibited behaviour remains unresolved. The main objection to allowing it to do so is, it is suggested, that the interests of the minority whose sexual self-expression differs from that of the majority may receive no protection. The law may be said to be in danger of enshrining and perpetuating prejudice.

8.13 Personal autonomy and sexual privacy

The offence of buggery consists at common law of intercourse *per annum* by a man with a man or woman and intercourse *per anum* or *vaginum* with an animal, and until 1994 it could be committed by a husband with his wife. An exception was provided by the Sexual Offences Act 1967 s 1 which permitted

8.13.1 Homosexuality

consensual buggery between males, both of whom were 21 or over, done in private. The position is now governed by s 145 of the Criminal Justice and Public Order Act 1994 which lowers the age of consent for male homosexual intercourse to 18. Heterosexual buggery is decriminalised by s 143 so long as both parties are over 18. Thus, the current law governing the sexual freedom of homosexuals is at present in accord with Article 8 of the European Convention on Human Rights, at least in this respect.

The European Court of Human Rights has accepted that restriction of sexual freedom may create a violation of Article 8. The issue arose in *Dudgeon v UK* (1981) in respect of the law in Northern Ireland (the Offences against the Person Act 1861) which made buggery between consenting males of any age a crime. Dudgeon, who was suspected of homosexual activities, was arrested on that basis and questioned but the police decided not to prosecute. He applied to the European Commission of Human Rights on the grounds of a breach of the right to privacy under Article 8. The European Court held that the legislation in question constituted a continuing interference with his private life which included his sexual life. He was forced either to abstain from sexual relations completely or to commit a crime.

However, the court considered that some regulation of homosexual activity was acceptable; the question was what was necessary in a democratic society. The court took into account the doctrine of the margin of appreciation (the discretion of member state governments as to what measures are necessary) as considered in the *Handyside* case (1976) where it was held that state authorities were in the best position to judge the requirements of morals in their own particular situations. However, the court found that the instant case concerned a very intimate aspect of private life. A restriction on a Convention right cannot be regarded as necessary unless it is proportionate to the aim pursued. In the instant case there was a grave detrimental interference with the applicant's private life and on the other hand there was little evidence of much damage to morals. The law had not been enforced and no evidence had been adduced to show that this had been harmful to moral standards. So the aim of the restriction was *not proportional* to the damage done to the applicants' privacy and therefore the invasion of privacy went beyond what was needed.

In response to this ruling Northern Irish law was changed under the Homosexual Offences (NI) Order 1982. *Dudgeon* demonstrates that the European Court is prepared to uphold the right of the individual to choose to indulge in homosexual practices and suggests that the term 'private life' in Article 8 may be used to cover a wide range of situations where bodily or sexual privacy is in question. The next challenge may be to the point at which the age of consent for homosexual sex is fixed which is, at 18, one of the highest levels in the European Community.

Some types of sado-masochistic behaviour are held to be unlawful whether or not the participants consent to it. The level of behaviour which will be unlawful despite consent is of a surprisingly minor nature; in *Donovan* (1934) it was defined as 'any hurt of injury calculated to interfere with health or comfort ... it need not be permanent but must be more than merely transient or trifling'. However, such interference may be justified as in the public interest, thus exempting blows given in the course of friendly athletic contests which, following the ruling in *Coney* (1882), are seen as being for 'good reason'.

8.13.2   Sado-masochism

In *Brown* (1993) a group of sado-masochistic homosexuals had regularly, over 10 years, willingly participated in acts of violence against each other for the sexual pleasure engendered in the giving and receiving of pain. It was found that the inflicting of injuries amounting to actual bodily harm could not fall within the category of 'good reason' and therefore, despite the consent of all the participants, the defendants were convicted of actual bodily harm under the Offences Against the Person Act 1861.

This decision may be criticised for its subjectivity; it is unclear why it is acceptable that boxing contests may be carried out which can result in serious permanent injury or even death, while activities such as those in *Brown* are criminalised although they may result in a lesser degree of harm. The activities in question were carried on privately and there was no suggestion that any of the 'victims' were coerced into consenting to them: all had chosen freely to participate and none seemed to be in a more powerful position than the others. It may perhaps be inferred that while boxing is regarded as a 'manly' sport homosexual activity, although legal, is barely tolerated. The House of Lords may have considered that it was reflecting a general moral standard but whether there is general support for interfering in such activities when carried out in private is unclear. Even if such general support exists, it is clear that this decision shows a lack of concern and respect for sexual minorities.

8.14	**Freedom from intrusion: property**	As with intrusion on the body, privacy of property may be infringed, it will be suggested, both by actual physical intrusions and by violations of the integrity of property, which might include surveillance by methods involving no physical intrusion on property and occurring some distance from it.

8.14.1   Civil law remedies

Traditionally, the law has viewed intrusions on property as being less serious than physical intrusion on the body and therefore remedies are found in the civil as opposed to the criminal law. A number of private persons such as reporters, as well as agents of the state, might wish to undertake such intrusion and therefore the right to be left alone to enjoy one's property may impose positive or negative obligations on the state.

The term 'intrusion' as used here is being given a wide meaning; it is intended to connote not just physical intrusion but any activity emanating from an external source which results in diminishing the privacy of the home or other private property. In this sense many methods of invasion of the home may be seen as intrusion: trespassing, harassing, photographing, watching, lurking, or snooping using long range electronic surveillance devices. Many sophisticated devices are now available to someone who wants to place a person's home under surveillance and therefore at the present time there is no need for the snooper or watcher actually to invade the territory as in the past. However, it is apparent that a law which grew up before use of such technology became possible has not caught up with it. As noted below, the use of surveillance devices is not covered by the Interception of Communications Act 1985.

8.14.2   Trespass

The main protection for such intrusion is afforded by actions for the torts of trespass or nuisance but it may be argued that the protection offered is limited. Trespass is defined as entering on to land in the possession of another without lawful justification. It is confined to instances in which there is some physical entry; prying with binoculars is not covered and obviously nor is electronic eavesdropping. The limitations of the law have been determined by a certain group of cases. In *Hickman v Maisey* (1900) the defendant, who was on the highway, was watching the plaintiff's land. It was found that the plaintiff owned the land under the highway and that the defendant was entitled to make ordinary and reasonable use of it. Such watching was held not to be reasonable; the defendant had gone outside the accepted use and therefore had trespassed. Thus it was made clear that intention in such instances is all important, but that unless behaviour could be linked to some kind of physical presence on land, trespass would not provide a remedy.

This case can be contrasted with that of *Bernstein v Skyviews & General Ltd* (1978) in order to determine the limits of trespass. The defendants flew over the plaintiff's land in order to take photographs of it, and the question arose whether the plaintiff had a right in trespass to prevent such intrusion. It was held that either he had no rights of ownership over the air space to that height, or, alternatively, if he did have such rights, the Civil Aviation Act 1942 s 40 exempted reasonable flights from liability. The court was not prepared to find that the taking of one photograph was unreasonable and a remedy could not be based solely on invasion of privacy as, of course, there is no such tort. The distinction between this decision and *Hickman* arises partly because the plaintiff could not show that he had an interest in what was violated – the air space – and so he fell outside the ambit of trespass.

How far can nuisance provide a means of protecting privacy? Nuisance involves disturbing a person in the enjoyment of his or her land to an extent that the law regards as unreasonable. There is a dearth of authority on the issue of surveillance but in an Australian case, *Victoria Park Racing Company v Taylor* (1937), where a platform was erected in order to gain a view of a racecourse which diminished the value of the plaintiff's business, no remedy in nuisance was available. The activity was held not to affect the use and enjoyment of the land but *dicta* in the case suggested that there would in general be no remedy in nuisance for looking over another's premises.

8.14.3   Nuisance

However, *dicta* in *Bernstein* favoured the possibility that grossly invasive embarrassing surveillance would amount to a nuisance and that possibility was followed up, though not explicitly, in somewhat different circumstances in *Khorasandijan v Bush* (1993). An injunction was granted against the defendant restraining him from using violence to, harassing, pestering or communicating with the plaintiff, the child of the owner of the property in question. The defendant argued before the Court of Appeal that apart from the restraint as to violence the judge had had no jurisdiction to grant the injunction as the other words used did not reflect any tort known to the law.

The Court of Appeal noted the decision of the Alberta Supreme Court in *Motherwell v Motherwell* (1976) that the legal owner of property could obtain an injunction to restrain persistent harassment by unwanted telephone calls to his home, and that the partner of the owner also had such a right. It considered that it would be ridiculous if such harassment was only actionable in the civil courts if the recipient of the calls happened to be the owner of the property, and that there was no reason why a child of the house should not have the same right as the owner's partner. Thus the injunction granted was in principle justified. The court did not make it clear whether harassment as an area of tortious liability should be seen as a head of private nuisance or as a distinct tort, but in any event it seems clear that some forms of grossly invasive activity will be actionable. Nevertheless, it is still fair to conclude that trespass and nuisance offer only protection in this area only from the crudest or clearest forms of invasions of privacy.

8.14.4 Statutory protection	It should further be noted that various statutes afford piecemeal protection from certain specified types of intrusion. Intrusion by creditors is regulated under the Administration of Justice Act 1970 s 40 and by landlords under the Rent Act 1965 s 30. Obscene phone calls are prohibited under the Post Office Act 1953 s 66 as are unsolicited obscene publications under the Unsolicited Goods and Services Act 1971 s 4.

8.15 Private property and official intrusions

If state officials physically enter property where there is no power allowing them to do so, they will commit a trespass. However, if they engage in certain types of surveillance they may commit no tort and therefore may not need to operate under a specific power although they may infringe privacy. Police officers may enter property to search and to seize goods; the powers under which they operate are fully discussed in Chapter 9. Members of the Security Services may also intrude physically upon property or may place the property under surveillance. It is suggested that two questions should be asked in relation to such intrusions. Firstly, do the powers provided create a reasonable balance between respecting individual privacy and the needs of internal security? The answer to this question depends on the breadth of the powers themselves and the extent to which they are subject to independent scrutiny. Secondly, what is the extent of the unregulated area of operation? This section will concentrate on these two questions.

8.15.1 The Security Services

Chapter 9 deals with the powers of the police to enter private property to search and seize items under PACE and at common law. However, a power also arises under the Security Services Act 1989 and the Intelligence Services Act 1994. These statutes were introduced partly in order to place the powers of the Security Services to interfere with individual privacy on a statutory basis. The perception that some control on the Security Services was needed arose partly due to the fear aroused by the *Spycatcher* case that the Services were insufficiently accountable and should be subject to controls in respect of their intrusions on private individuals, but also partly due to the challenge to the legality of the tapping of the phones of CND members already mentioned in *Secretary of State for the Home Dept ex p Ruddock* (1987) which proved embarrassing to the government although it failed.

However, introduction of the 1989 Act was finally forced upon the government as a response to the finding of the European Commission on Human Rights that a complaint against MI5 was admissible (*H and H v UK* (1986)). The case was brought by two former NCCL officers, Patricia Hewitt and Harriet Harman, who were complaining of their classification as 'subversive' by MI5 which had placed them under surveillance. Part of their complaint concerned a breach of Article 13 of the European Convention on the basis that no effective remedy for complainants existed. In response the Security Services Act placed MI5 on a statutory basis but prevented almost all effective scrutiny of its operation.

If a member of the public has a grievance concerning the operation of the Act complaint to a court is not possible: under s 5 it can only be made to a tribunal and under s 5(4) the decisions of the tribunal are not questionable in any court of law. The volume of complaint will be inherently limited: citizens may often be unaware that surveillance is taking place, while service personnel who feel that they have been required to act improperly in bugging or searching a person's property are not permitted to complain to the Tribunal. The provision of s 5(4) was criticised in 1992 by Mr Justice Kennedy in refusing an application for review of the Security Service Tribunal's decision not to investigate allegations that MI5 is still holding files on Harriet Harman, the shadow Health Minister; he considered that in some circumstances the courts certainly would have jurisdiction to intervene.

Given the width of the powers conferred on members of the Security Service under this legislation this lack of accountability is disturbing. Any private individual can have surveillance devices placed on his or her premises or can be subject to a search of the premises even though engaged in lawful political activity which is not intended to serve any foreign interest. An amendment to the Security Services Bill was put forward which would have exempted such a person from the operation of the legislation but it was rejected by the government. If Security Service members wish to enter property the Home Secretary can issue a warrant authorising the 'taking of any such action as is specified in the warrant in respect of any property so specified'. In other words, members of MI5 can interfere in any way with property so long as it appears that they are doing so in order to discharge any of their functions. These functions are set out in s 1 of the Act and include 'the protection of national security and in particular, its protection from ... actions intended to overthrow or undermine parliamentary democracy by political, industrial or violent means'. This Act provided a model for the Intelligence Services Act 1994 which placed MI6 and GCHQ on a statutory basis. Section 5 of the 1994 Act provides that a warrant will be issued by a Minister if the action it covers 'would be of substantial value in assisting the Services to carry out their functions'. It is apparent that the powers provided under both Acts are very broad and might arise in a wide range of circumstances.

Furthermore, the 1989 Act provides for no real form of Parliamentary oversight of the Security Service. However, the 1994 Act set up, under s 10, a Parliamentary Committee to oversee the administration and policy of MI5, MI6 and GCHQ. Since the Committee is not a Select Committee, its powers will be limited; therefore, although this was a welcome move, the oversight provided may have, in practice, little impact on the work of the Services.

The ease with which warrants may be obtained under the 1989 and 1994 Acts, and the concomitant disregard for individual privacy may be contrasted with the position in Canada regarding the powers of the Canadian Security Intelligence Service (the CSIS). The CSIS can only be granted warrants on the authorisation of a judge, thus ensuring a measure of independent oversight. Moreover, the warrant will not be issued unless the facts relied on to justify the belief that a warrant is necessary to investigate a threat to national security are set out in a sworn statement. Clearly, the Canadian system places greater emphasis on the privacy of the citizen and therefore appears to strike a fairer balance between privacy on the one hand and the security of the state on the other.

| 8.15.2 | The Official Secrets Act 1989 |

The 1989 Act and the 1985 Act will work in tandem with the Official Secrets Act 1989, s 1 of which prevents members or former members of the Security Services disclosing anything at all about the operation of those services. All such members come under a lifelong duty to keep silent even though their information might reveal serious abuse of power by the security services. These provisions also apply to anyone who is notified that he or she is subject to the provisions of the subsection. Similarly, s 4(3) of the Act prohibits disclosure of information obtained by or relating to the issue of a warrant under the Interception of Communications Act 1985 or the Security Services Act 1989.

The wide grounds on which intrusion may be authorised, the secrecy surrounding the issuing of intercept and burgling warrants, and the lack of an effective complaints procedure suggest that the balance has tipped too far away from concern for the privacy of the individual. It does not appear that the Security Services Act, like the Interception of Communications Act, will open up the workings of internal security to greater scrutiny. The nature of both statutes reflects a perception that no breach of the European Convention will occur so long as a mechanism is in place able to consider the claims of aggrieved citizens, however ineffective that mechanism might be. If, for example, the Security Services had to obtain authorisation of a burgling warrant from a judge and had to specify where practicable the items to be seized; if, most importantly, the use of intercept and burgling warrants was more open to public scrutiny it might be possible to feel that the safeguards in place allowed sufficient weight to be given to the need to maintain privacy.

8.15.3   Conclusions

The most effective general remedy for invasions of privacy might be a privacy clause under a UK Bill of Rights, but because privacy covers so many varied issues such a clause would have to be accompanied by the enactment of specific pieces of legislation over and above those, such as the Data Protection Act, already in existence. A privacy clause alone would probably be too nebulous to be effective unaccompanied by such legislation, but it may be argued that it would be necessary given the disparate issues covered which could otherwise fall between different statutory provisions. Also such provisions would, of course, be open to express or implied repeal while, as discussed in Chapter 2, a Bill of Rights might have some protection from repeal. Most importantly, a privacy clause might allow the judiciary to consider the provisions relating to telephone tapping and other activities of the Security Services. The decision of Mr Justice Taylor in *Ruddock* and of Mr Justice Kennedy in relation to s 5(4) of the Security Services Act underline the inefficacy of judicial review as a means of safeguarding individual privacy in this context, even assuming that review is not entirely ousted. Of course, importing the European Convention on Human Rights into domestic law would not provide a simple panacea. It is unlikely that review conducted by the judiciary of the activities of the Security Services under Article 8 would be of a very rigorous nature, but it might be a little less marginal than the review conducted at Strasbourg in relation to such activities since the doctrine of the margin of appreciation would not be invoked.

8.16   The future of privacy

Summary of Chapter 8

Privacy

No tort of invasion of privacy exists in the UK to control the activity of the media in publishing personal information. However, certain legal controls do exist, although they are not aimed directly at the invasion of privacy, and these are found in the laws of confidence, copyright, defamation and malicious falsehood. However, these controls are on the whole limited in scope and are aimed at the protection of other interests making them ill-suited to the protection of privacy. Further control of the press has traditionally been undertaken by self-regulation but proposals for further press regulation have been made which can be divided into three main areas: firstly, different methods of self-regulation or a statutory tribunal to regulate the press; secondly, proposals for a statutory tort of invasion of privacy; thirdly, proposals to remedy various kinds of intrusion made with the intent to obtain personal material for publication.

Control over personal information: freedom from interference

Duke of Argyll v Duchess of Argyll (1965)
Stephens v Avery (1988)
AG v Guardian Newspaper Ltd (1987)
Lion Laboratories v Evans (1985)
X v Y (1988)
Corelli v Wall (1906)
Kaye v Robertson and Another (1990)
Hellewell v Chief Constable of Derbyshire (1995)

Access to personal information has been achieved in certain areas. Under the Data Protection Act 1984 any person using a computerised system in order to store data relating to people must register with the Data Protection Registrar and the subject of the data must be allowed access to it unless it falls within an exempted area such as crime or national security.

Access to personal information

In the wake of the 1984 Act access rights to manual files were gradually extended. The Access to Personal Files Act 1987 allowed access to 'accessible information' held by certain local government departments and therefore provided for the rectification of errors. Access was broadened by the Access to Personal Files Regulations 1989, which provide that social services departments must give personal information to individuals unless the contributor of the information can be identified and he or she does not consent to the access. A further method of obtaining access to personal information arises under the Access to Medical Reports Act 1988 which provides for limited circumstances in which a person can obtain access to personal medical information; it was succeeded by the Access to Health Record Act 1990, which took the principle of access in this area much further by allowing general access to health records.

Gaskin case (1989)

R v Mid-Glamorgan Family Health Services and Another ex p Martin (1993)

Control over intrusions: bodily and sexual privacy

Bodily and sexual privacy encompass a negative right to be 'left alone' in a physical sense, which has been recognised in relation to corporal punishment. However, it is accepted under the Police and Criminal Evidence Act 1984 in relation to strip searches that this right has to give way to the interest in the prevention of crime, although only in limited and well defined circumstances. In sexual matters it also has to give way to the notion that moral standards may decline if greater freedom of choice as regards participation in various sexual acts is allowed by the criminal law. Bodily privacy may also encompass a positive claim on the state to ensure that personal autonomy in relation to disposal of the body is maintained. This might include disclosure of risks in medical treatment but the law has not so far afforded much recognition to this interest.

Lindley v Rutter (1980)

Campbell and Cosans v UK (1982)

Sidaway v Board of Governors of the Bethlem Royal Hospital (1985)

Dudgeon v UK (1981)

R v Donovan (1934)

Brown (1993)

Control over intrusions on private property

The term 'intrusion' is used here to denote any activity emanating from an external source which diminishes the privacy of property. Trespass and nuisance afford a remedy for certain intrusions on property but are of limited value in relation to activities such as bugging, electronic surveillance and snooping.

The police under the Police and Criminal Evidence Act 1984 and members of the Security Services under the Security Services Act 1989 and the Intelligence Services Act 1994 are authorised to enter property, and under the 1989 and 1994 Acts the controls over such entry are fairly meagre. Telephone tapping may be authorised under the Interception of Communications Act 1985 in a very wide range of circumstances. The issuance of intercept warrants under the 1985 Act and of 'burgling' warrants under the 1989 Act is expressed to be unreviewable in a court.

Hickman v Maisey (1900)

Bernstein v Skyviews (1978)

Khorasandijan v Bush (1993)

Malone v UK (1985)
R v Secretary of State for Home Affairs ex p Ruddock (1987)
R v Effick (1992)
R v Preston (1993)

Chapter 9

Freedom of the Person and Police Powers

The exercise of police powers such as arrest and detention represents an invasion of personal liberty which is tolerated in the interests of the prevention and detection of crime. However, in accepting the need to allow such invasion the interest in personal liberty requires that it should be strictly regulated. Thus, the rules governing the exercise of police powers are of crucial importance as providing safeguards for civil liberties. At present these rules are largely contained in the scheme created under the Police and Criminal Evidence Act 1984 (PACE) (as extended under the Criminal Justice and Public Order Act 1994), which is made up of rules deriving from the Act itself, from the Codes of Practice made under (as revised in 1991) it and the Notes for Guidance contained in the Codes. It is also influenced by Home Office Circulars. The difference in status between these four levels and the significance of adopting this four tiered approach is considered below. It will be found that one group of suspects – those suspected of crimes under the Prevention of Terrorism Act 1989 are covered by this scheme but that at many points they receive less protection than other suspects because they are perceived as representing such a serious danger.

Before the inception of PACE the police had no general and clear powers of arrest, stop and search or entry to premises. They wanted such powers put on a clear statutory basis so that they could exercise them where they felt it was their duty to do so without laying themselves open to the possibility of a civil action. PACE was introduced in order to provide such clear and general police powers but these were supposed to be balanced by greater safeguards for suspects. Such safeguards were in part adopted due to the need to ensure that miscarriages of justice such as that which occurred in the *Confait* case 1977, would not recur. The Royal Commission on Criminal Procedure, whose report influenced PACE, was set up largely in response to the inadequacies of safeguards for suspects which were exposed in the report on the *Confait* case. Ironically, a further spate of miscarriages of justice, some post-dating the introduction of PACE (such as *Silcott* (1991)), led in 1992 to the setting up of another Royal Commission in order to consider further measures which could be introduced to address the problem.

9.1   Introduction

In this chapter the powers of the police and the safeguards which affect the use of their powers are considered first and this is followed by consideration of the means of redress available if the police fail to comply with the rules. The powers are considered in the order in which they would be likely to arise in an investigation, beginning with stop and search powers and ending with the charge. At every stage the efficacy of the safeguards available is considered and is contrasted with those applicable to a person suspected of terrorist activity.

9.2   The sources of the rules

The student approaching the PACE scheme may be confused by the web of provisions deriving from its four different sources and may wonder whether a provision is affected by appearing as part of the Codes instead of in the statute itself. Therefore, before considering the substantive provisions, an attempt will be made to explain the methodology of this multi-levelled scheme.

9.2.1   PACE and the codes

There are at present five Codes of Practice: Code A covering stop and search procedures, Code B covering searching of premises, Code C covering interviewing and conditions of detention, Code D covering identification methods and Code E covering tape recording. Thus, each covers a particular area of PACE although not all areas are covered: arrest, for example, is governed only by statutory provisions. It may be asked why all of the stop and search rules, for example, were not merely made part of the Act. The answer may partly lie in the need for some flexibility in making changes: the Codes are quicker and less cumbersome to amend than statutory provisions. However, it is also possible that the government did not want to create rules which might give rise to liability on the part of the police if they were broken; rules which could operate at a lower level of visibility than statutory ones may have appeared more attractive.

PACE s 67(10) makes clear the intended distinction between Act and Codes in providing that no civil or criminal liability will arise from a breach of the Codes. This distinction is of significance in relation to the stop and search, arrest and detention provisions of PACE Parts I to IV as breach of such provisions may give rise to an action in trespass or false imprisonment. However, it does not seem to have any significance as far as the interviewing provisions of Part V are concerned. The most important statutory safeguard for interviewing, the entitlement to legal advice, has not been affected by the availability of tortious remedies. Thus statutory *and* Code provisions concerned with safeguards inside the police station are in an equally weak position in the sense that a clear remedy is not available if they are breached. The context in which breaches of the interviewing provisions has been considered is that of exclusion of evidence. This means that if the police have breached the rules (whether statutory or part of a Code) in order to obtain a piece of evidence a court may decide that it would be wrong to admit it; if so, the jury will never know of its existence. In that context the courts have not drawn a distinction between provisions of Act or Codes except to require that breach of a Code provision should be of a substantial and significant nature if exclusion of evidence is to be considered.

The Notes for Guidance are contained in the Codes but are not part of them. They were apparently intended, as their name suggests, merely to be used as interpretative provisions. However, as will be seen, they contain some very significant provisions although it is unclear what the consequences of breach of a Note are. Evidence tainted by breach of a Note for Guidance is unlikely to be excluded as, unlike Code provisions, s 67(11) of PACE does not require a court to take the Notes into account in determining any question. However, in *DPP v Blake* (1989) the Divisional Court impliedly accepted that a Note for Guidance will be considered in relation to exclusion of evidence if it can be argued that it merely amplifies a particular Code provision, and can therefore be of assistance in determining whether breach of such a provision has occurred. Moreover, certain Notes need not merely be considered in conjunction with the paragraph they derive from; the ruling in *DPP v Rouse* and *DPP v Davis* (1992) that they can sometimes be used as an aid to the interpretation of Code C as a whole extended their potential impact. Thus it may be said that the Notes are of a very uncertain status but that their importance is just beginning to be recognised in decisions as to admission of evidence.

9.2.2   Notes for Guidance

There are a large number of Home Office circulars dealing with disparate subjects relevant to the use of police powers; some of them are intended to work in tandem with a part of PACE and some operate in their own right. They are in an even more equivocal position than the Notes. Their legal significance derives from their relevance to the obligations arising from the relationship between police forces and the Home Office, and it is likely to be in that context rather than in relation to questions of admissibility that they will be considered. Clearly, argument that a court may be disinclined to consider a Note for Guidance applies *a fortiori* to the Circulars.

9.2.3   Home Office circulars

9.3   Stop and search powers

In a draconian society the police might be empowered to stop and strip search anybody within a radius of five miles around the scene of actual or suspected criminal activity, while in an extremely liberal or permissive society they might not be empowered to stop and search at all. The stop and search powers under PACE represent a middle ground between these two extremes; the powers are meant to maintain a balance between the interest of society, as represented by the police, in crime control and the interest of the citizen in personal liberty. The use of such powers may be a necessary part of effective policing and represents less of an infringement of liberty than an arrest, but on the other hand their exercise may create a sense of grievance and of violation of personal privacy. Such feelings may contribute to the alienation of the police from the community, leading to a breakdown in law and order expressed in its most extreme form in rioting, and otherwise in general lack of cooperation with the police.

There was no general power at common law to detain without the subject's consent in the absence of specific statutory authority. Instead there were a miscellany of such powers, the majority of which have been superseded.

Under s 1 of PACE, for the first time, a general power to stop and search persons or vehicles is conferred on the police if reasonable suspicion arises that stolen goods, offensive weapons or other prohibited articles may be found. It may be that the suspect appears to be in innocent possession of the goods or articles; this will not affect the power to stop although it would affect the power to arrest, and in this sense the power to stop is broader than the arrest power. Under s 1(6) if an article is found which appears to be stolen or prohibited the officer can seize it.

Section 1 does not allow an officer to enter a dwelling (that power arises under ss 17 and 18) but an officer can search a person outside a dwelling (assuming of course that the provisions of s 1 as to reasonable suspicion are fulfilled) if it appears that he or she does not have the permission of the owner to be there.

This general power to stop, search and seize is balanced in two ways. Firstly, the concept of reasonable suspicion allows it to be exercised only when quite a high level of suspicion exists. Secondly, under s 2 the police officer must provide the person to be searched with certain information.

9.3.1   'Reasonable grounds for suspicion'

The concept of reasonable suspicion as the basis for the exercise of stop and search powers is set out briefly in Code of Practice A on Stop and Search paras 1.6 and 1.7. It is not enough for a police officer to have a hunch that a person has committed or is about to commit an offence; there must be a concrete basis for this suspicion which relates to the particular person in question and could be evaluated by an objective observer. Such suspicion must not be based on racial or other stereotyping.

When Code A was revised in 1991 the requirement that the suspicion should be of the same level as that necessary to effect an arrest was omitted. The original intention behind including this provision was to stress the high level of suspicion required before a stop and search could take place; this change therefore tends to remove some of that emphasis and could be taken to imply that there are two levels of suspicion, the level required under Code A being the lower. This omission may convey such a message to police officers but may not make much significant difference to the way the police actually use stop and search powers; research in the area suggests that there is already a tendency to view reasonable suspicion as a flexible concept which may denote quite a low level of suspicion.

The procedural requirements of ss 2 and 3 and Code A must be met. The constable must give the suspect certain information before the search begins, including 'his name and the name of the police station to which he is attached; the object of the proposed search; the constable's grounds for proposing to make it'. Under s 3 the constable must make a record of the search, either on the spot if that is practicable, or as soon as it is practicable. The subject of the search can obtain a copy of the search record later on from the police station. Such record-keeping is intended to ensure that some officers do not over-use the stop and search power, partly because it means that the citizen can make a complaint, and partly because the police station will have a record of the number of stops being carried out. The guidance as to the conduct of the search contained in Code A para 3 is fairly general; it requires the officer to complete the search speedily, to minimise embarrassment and to seek co-operation.	9.3.2 Procedural requirements
Code A does not affect ordinary consensual contact between police officer and citizen; officers can ask members of the public to stop and can ask them to consent to a search without exerting any compulsion. This is a necessary part of policing. However, voluntary contacts can have a more sinister side: some people might 'consent' to a search in the sense of offering no resistance to it due to uncertainty as to the basis or extent of the police power in question. The search could then be classified as voluntary and subsequently it would be difficult if not impossible to determine whether such classification was justifiable. Once a search is so classified none of the statutory or Code A safeguards need be observed.	9.3.3 Voluntary searches

However, Notes for Guidance 1D(b) and 1E create certain restrictions on voluntary searches. Under Note 1E persons belonging to three of the vulnerable groups recognised throughout the Codes as requiring special treatment – juveniles, the mentally handicapped or mentally disordered – may not be subject to a voluntary search at all. The prohibition also applies to a range of other persons who do not appear capable of giving an informed consent to a search. This group may well include the hearing-impaired or persons not proficient in English who are also recognised in the Codes as belonging to vulnerable groups, but perhaps they should have been expressly included. Persons who do not fall within the above groups may be subject to a voluntary search under Note 1D(b) but the officer should 'always make it clear that he is seeking the co-operation of the person concerned'.

These provisions represent a welcome move towards dealing with this problem but it may be argued that they are deficient in a number of respects. Firstly, no specific form of words need be used under Note 1D(b); a requirement that an officer issue a caution in similar terms to that used in Code B para 4.2 in respect of searching of premises might have clarified matters: eg 'You do not have to consent to this search but anything that is found may be used in evidence against you'.

Secondly, it is unclear why the word 'co-operation' as opposed to 'consent' has been used in Note 1D(b). Paragraph 3.2 includes a new provision that the co-operation of the person to be searched should always be sought; this appears to mean that if an involuntary search is to be carried out – one reliant on the use of the stop and search power – the police should attempt to avoid the use of force, but the use of the word 'co-operation' at both points is needlessly confusing: the impression given is that co-operation is generally desirable during *any* search rather than that a clear consent to a voluntary search should be obtained beforehand.

9.3.4   Stop and search under the Criminal Justice and Public Order Act 1994 s 60

Section 60 of the 1994 Act provides police officers with a further stop and search power which does not depend on showing reasonable suspicion of particular wrongdoing on the part of an individual. An officer of at least the rank of superintendent can authorise the stop and search of any person within a particular locality if he or she reasonably believes that incidents involving 'serious violence' may take place in that area and that authorisation is expedient in order to prevent their occurrence. The authorisation may apply to a period not exceeding 24 hours. If such an authorisation is in force an officer may stop anyone within the specified locality in order to look for offensive weapons or dangerous instruments. This power is subject to the same procedural requirements under Code A as those relating to the powers under s 1 of PACE, apart from the Code A provisions relating to reasonable suspicion (Code A, para 1.5(b)).

Since these wide powers are not subject to limitation flowing from the concept of reasonable suspicion they represent a departure from the principle that only an individual who has given rise to such suspicion due to his or her actions should suffer the infringement of liberty represented by a stop and search. Such infringement appears to require a strong justification on crime control grounds, but research into past use of such blanket police powers suggests that they may tend to arouse resentment rather than lead to a clear reduction in crime.

The 1989 Act (PTA) provides a power to stop and search under s 15(3) which does not depend on the need to show reasonable suspicion that the suspect is carrying the items which may be searched for. However, the officer must have reasonable grounds for suspecting that the suspect is liable to arrest for certain offences under the 1989 Act. This power arises in addition to the general PACE power to stop and search in connection with all offences including, of course, those under the PTA. There is a further power to search a person who has arrived in or is seeking to leave Britain or Northern Ireland under para 4(2) of Schedule 5 to the 1989 Act, and again this power is not dependent on showing reasonable suspicion. Para 1.5 of Code A provides that this power of stop and search is covered by the Code.

9.3.5   Searches under the Prevention of Terrorism (Temporary Provisions) Act 1989

Section 81(1) of the Criminal Justice and Public Order Act 1994 amends the Prevention of Terrorism Act by inserting into it a new s 13A. Section 13A provides police officers with a further stop and search power which does not depend on showing reasonable suspicion of particular wrongdoing on the part of an individual. An officer of at least the rank of commander or assistant Chief Constable can authorise the stop and search of any person within a particular locality if he or she considers that it is expedient to do so to prevent acts of terrorism. The authorisation may apply to a period not exceeding twenty eight days and it is renewable. If such an authorisation is in force an officer may stop anyone within the specified locality in order to look for articles which could be used for the commission of acts of terrorism. This power is subject to the same procedural requirements under Code A as those relating to the powers under s 1 of PACE, apart from the Code A provisions relating to reasonable suspicion (Code A, para 1.5(c)). It should be pointed out that there is no requirement that the officer granting the authorisation should reasonably believe that it is necessary in order to prevent the commission of acts of terrorism. In respect of all these powers it is notable that one of the main safeguards arising in respect of the general stop and search powers is removed.

9.4   Powers of arrest and detention

Any arrest represents a serious curtailment of liberty; therefore use of the arrest power requires careful regulation. An arrest is seen as *prima facie* illegal necessitating justification under a specific legal power. If an arrest is effected where no arrest power arises a civil action for false imprisonment will lie. Despite the need for clarity and precision such powers were until relatively recently granted piecemeal, with the result that prior to PACE they were contained in a mass of common law and statutory provisions. No consistent rationale could be discerned and there were a number of gaps and anomalies. For example, the Criminal Law Act 1967 gave a power of arrest without warrant where the offence in question arose under statute and carried a sentence of five years. Thus no power of arrest arose in respect of common law offences carrying such a sentence. This situation was detrimental to civil liberties due to the uncertainty of the powers, but it was also detrimental to the maintenance of law and order as officers were sometimes deterred from effecting an arrest where one was necessary. The powers are now contained largely in PACE but common law powers remain, while some statutes create a specific power of arrest which may overlap with the PACE powers.

9.4.1   At common law — power to arrest for breach of peace

PACE has not affected the power to arrest which arises at common law to prevent a breach of the peace. Factors present in a situation in which breach of the peace occurs may also give rise to arrest powers under PACE, but may extend further than they do due to the wide definition of breach of the peace. The leading case is *Howell* (1982) in which it was found that breach of the peace will arise if violence to persons or property either actual or apprehended occurs. Threatening words are not in themselves a breach of the peace, but they may lead a police officer to apprehend that a breach will arise. A police officer or any other person may arrest if a breach of the peace is in being or apprehended but not when it has been terminated unless there is reason to believe that it may be renewed (see further Chapter 7 at 7.4 and 7.9).

9.4.2   Arrest without warrant under PACE: general

PACE contains two separate powers of arrest without warrant, one arising under s 24 and the other under s 25. In broad terms s 24 provides a power of arrest in respect of more serious offences while s 25 covers *all* offences however trivial (including, for example, dropping litter) *if* certain conditions are satisfied *apart from* suspicion that the offence in question has been committed. Thus s 25 operates to cover persons suspected of offences falling outside s 24. Obviously had s 25 not contained special conditions there would have been no need for s 24. The difference between s 24 and s 25 is quite important because once a person has been arrested under s 24 he or she is said to have been arrested for 'an arrestable offence' and this may have an effect on his or her treatment later on. An 'arrestable offence' is therefore one for which a person can be arrested if the necessary reasonable suspicion is present without the need to show any other ingredients in the situation at the time of arrest.

Section 24 applies:

9.4.3   Arrest under s 24

to offences for which the sentence is fixed by law;

to offences for which a person of 21 years of age or over (not previously convicted) may be sentenced to imprisonment for a term of five years (or might be so sentenced but for the restrictions imposed by s 33 of the Magistrates' Courts Act 1980); and

to the offences to which subs (2) applies, and in this Act 'arrestable offence' means any such offence.

A police officer can arrest for one of the offences covered by s 24 if he or she has reasonable grounds to suspect that the offence is about to be, is being or has been committed. An ordinary citizen can arrest under s 24 in the same way with the omission of the possibility of arresting where the offence is about to be committed.

Offences for which a person can be arrested under s 24 may also be classified as 'serious arrestable offences' under s 116. This does not affect the power of arrest but it does affect various safeguards and powers which may be exercised during detention. The s 24 offences which may also fall into this category fall into two groups – firstly, those which are so serious (such as murder, manslaughter, indecent assault which amounts to gross indecency) that they will always be serious arrestable offences, and secondly, those which will be so classified only if their commission has led to certain specified consequences, namely, serious harm to the security of the state or public order, serious interference with the administration of justice or investigation of offices, death or serious injury, substantial financial gain or serious financial loss. This last possibility may considerably widen the category of serious arrestable offences in that whether or not a loss may be serious may need to be judged in relation to the financial consequences to the person suffering it: a loss of a small amount of money might be serious to a poor person; someone suspected of its theft could therefore be classified as in detention for a serious arrestable offence.

9.4.4   Arrest under s 25

The police acquired the general power of arrest under s 25 which they had lacked previously. However, this power does not merely allow an officer to arrest for *any* offence so long as reasonable suspicion can be shown. Such a power would have been viewed as too draconian. It is balanced by what are known as the 'general arrest conditions' which must also be fulfilled. Therefore in order to arrest under s 25 *two* steps must be taken: first, there must be reasonable suspicion relating to the offence in question; second, one of the arrest conditions must be fulfilled. The need for the officer to have suspicion of the offence in question *and* the general arrest conditions was emphasised in *Edwards v DPP* (1993). A police constable (but not an ordinary citizen) can arrest if he or she has reasonable grounds to suspect the person of having committed or having attempted to commit the offence or of being in the course of committing or attempting to commit it.

The general arrest conditions divide into two groups: those in which there is or appears to be a failure to furnish a satisfactory name or address so that the service of a summons later on would be impracticable, and those which concern the immediate need to remove the suspect from the street in order to avert the harm he may cause which would make it inappropriate to serve a summons later. The harm in question includes harm to persons or property, an offence against public decency, or obstruction of the highway. The inclusion of these provisions implies that the infringement of civil liberties represented by an arrest should be resorted to only where it may be argued that no other alternative exists.

9.4.5   'Reasonable suspicion'

Sections 24 and 25 both depend on the concept of reasonable suspicion. The idea behind it is that an arrest should take place at quite a late stage in the investigation; this limits the number of arrests and makes it less likely that a person will be wrongfully arrested. It seems likely that it will be interpreted in accordance with the provisions as to reasonable suspicion under Code A although the courts have not relied on Code A in ruling on the lawfulness of arrests (see below). However, Annex B para 4 of original Code A stated that the level of suspicion for a stop would be 'no less' than that needed for arrest.

Although this provision is omitted from the revised Code A, it would seem that in principle the Code A provisions should be relevant to arrests if the Codes and statute are to be treated as a harmonious whole. Moreover, it would appear strange if a more rigorous test could be applied to the reasonable suspicion necessary to effect a stop than that necessary to effect an arrest. If this is correct it would seem that certain matters, such as an individual's racial group could *never* be factors which could support a finding of reasonable suspicion.

The objective nature of suspicion required under Code A is echoed in various decisions on the suspicion needed for an arrest. In *Dallison v Caffrey* (1965) Lord Diplock said the test was whether 'a reasonable man assumed to know the law and possessed of the information which in fact was possessed by the defendant would believe there were (reasonable grounds). Thus it is not enough for a police officer to have a hunch that a person has committed or is about to commit an offence; there must be a concrete basis for this suspicion which relates to the particular person in question and could be evaluated by an objective observer. If an officer only has a hunch – mere suspicion as opposed to reasonable suspicion – he or she might continue to observe the person in question but could not arrest until the suspicion had increased and could be termed 'reasonable suspicion'. It would seem that a future revision of the Codes might usefully state that the concept of reasonable suspicion in Code A applies to arrest as well; if so it would at least be clear that certain factors can *never* support reasonable suspicion.

However, this still leaves a great deal of leeway to officers to arrest where suspicion relating to the particular person is at a low level, but they want to further the investigation by gathering information. At present the courts seem prepared to allow police such leeway, and it should be noted that PACE endorses a reasonably low level of suspicion due to the distinction it maintains between belief and suspicion, suspicion probably being the lower standard.

In *Ward v Chief Constable of Somerset and Avon Constabulary* (1986) the grounds for suspicion were fairly flimsy and might have warranted further enquiries before arresting. Similarly, in *Castorina v Chief Constable of Surrey* (1988) the Court of Appeal appeared reluctant to take a rigorous approach to the question of reasonable suspicion. Detectives were investigating a burglary of a company's premises and on reasonable grounds came to the conclusion that it was an 'inside job'. The managing director told them that a certain employee had recently been dismissed and that the documents taken would be useful to someone with a grudge. However, she also said that she would not have expected the particular employee to commit a burglary. The detectives then arrested the employee, having found that she had no previous criminal record. She was detained for nearly four hours and then released without charge. She claimed damages for false imprisonment and was awarded £4,500. The judge considered that it was necessary to find that the detectives had had 'an honest belief founded on a reasonable suspicion leading an ordinary cautious man to the conclusion that the person arrested was guilty of the offence'.

However, the Court of Appeal overturned the award on the basis that the test applied by the judge had been too severe. It was held that the question of honest belief was irrelevant; the issue of reasonable suspicion had nothing to do with the officer's subjective state of mind. The question was whether there was reasonable cause to suspect the plaintiff of burglary. Given that certain factors could be identified, including inside knowledge of the Company's affairs and the motive of the plaintiff, it appeared that there was sufficient basis for the detectives to have reasonable grounds for suspicion.

Purchas J ruled that once reasonable suspicion arises officers have discretion as to whether to arrest or do something else, such as making further enquiries. This discretion can be attacked on *Wednesbury* principles: an arrest will be found to be unlawful if no reasonable person, looking at the circumstances, could have considered that an arrest should be effected, if the decision is based on irrelevant considerations and if it is not made in good faith and for a proper purpose. It was found that no breach of these principles had occurred and as reasonable grounds for making the arrest were found the first instance judge had erred in ruling that further enquiries should have been made before making it.

Thus, the need to make further enquiries would be relevant to the first stage – arriving at reasonable suspicion – but not to the second – determining whether to make an arrest. That it must be relevant to the first is axiomatic: an investigation passes through many stages, from the first in which a vague suspicion relating to a particular person arises up until the point when it is proved – if it is – that proof of that person's guilt can be shown beyond reasonable doubt. At some point in that process reasonable suspicion giving rise to a discretion as to whether to effect an arrest arises; thus, there must be a point in the early stages at which it is possible to say that more enquiries should have been made, more evidence gathered, before the arrest could lawfully take place. As the courts appear prepared to accept that arrest at quite an early stage in this process may be said to be based on reasonable grounds, and that the application of *Wednesbury* principle leaves little leeway for challenge to the decision to arrest, it may be said that the interest of the citizen in his or her personal liberty is not being accorded sufficient weight under the current tests.

Under s 24 it is not always necessary to show that reasonable suspicion exists. If an arrestable offence is *in fact* being committed, or has been committed, or is about to be committed, a constable can arrest even if he or she is just acting on an hunch which luckily turns out to be justified. Of course, if an officer arrests without reasonable suspicion he or she is taking a risk. These provisions were included because it might seem strange if a person could found an action for false imprisonment on the basis that although they were committing an offence they should not have been arrested for it. However, if it cannot be established that the offence was committed, or was about to be committed, it is not enough to show that reasonable grounds for suspicion did in fact exist although the officer did not know of them. In *Siddiqui v Swain* (1979) the Divisional Court held that the words 'reasonable grounds to suspect' used in s 8(5) of the Road Traffic Act 1972 include the requirement that the officer should actually suspect. This approach was also adopted in *Chapman v DPP* (1988).

The power of arrest with warrant does not arise under PACE. There are a large number of statutory provisions allowing an arrest warrant to be issued, of which the most significant is that arising under the Magistrates Court Act 1980 s 1. Under this power a warrant may be issued if a person aged at least 17 is suspected of an offence which is indictable or punishable with imprisonment, or where no satisfactory address is known allowing a summons to be served. This provision therefore limits the circumstances under which a warrant will be sought as opposed to using the non-warrant powers under PACE, and as the police now have such broad powers of arrest under ss 24 and 25 it seems that arrest in reliance on a warrant will be used even less under PACE than it was previously.	9.4.6 Power of arrest with warrant
If a statute creates an offence which is a serious offence falling within s 24 then obviously the arrest power under s 24 is applicable. If a statute creates a more minor offence then equally the arrest power under s 25 is applicable so long as one or more of the general arrest conditions are satisfied. Section 11 of the Public Order Act 1986 and s 51 of the Police Act 1964 provide examples of such offences. However, certain statutes expressly create specific powers of arrest which are not dependent on ss 24 or 25 such as ss 12 and 14 of the Public Order Act. In such cases the procedure under s 28 (below at para 9.4.9) will still apply.	9.4.7 Other statutory powers of arrest

| 9.4.8 | Arrest under the Prevention of Terrorism Act (PTA) 1989 | Almost all the indictable offences under the PTA carry a penalty of at least five years imprisonment and are therefore arrestable offences under s 24 PACE. There is also a power of arrest under s 14 of the PTA itself. This power has two limbs. The first (s 14(1)(a)) empowers a constable to arrest for certain specified offences under the PTA. As these offences are arrestable offences in any event this power would seem to overlap with that under s 24. However, if an arrest is effected under s 14 PTA as opposed to s 24 PACE this has an effect on the length of detention as will be seen below. |

The second limb of s 14 (s 14(2)(b)) provides a completely separate power from the PACE power; it allows arrest without needing to show suspicion relating to a particular offence. Instead the constable needs to have reasonable grounds for suspecting that a person is concerned in the preparation or instigation of acts of terrorism connected with the affairs of Northern Ireland or 'any other act of terrorism except those connected solely with the affairs of the UK or a part of the UK'. This arrest is not for an offence but in practice for investigation, questioning and general intelligence gathering. Thus, this power represents a clear departure from the principle that liberty should be curtailed only on clear and specific grounds which connect the actions of the suspect with a specific offence under criminal law.

| 9.4.9 | Procedural elements of a valid arrest | For an arrest to be made validly, not only must the power of arrest exist, whatever its source, but the procedural elements must be complied with. The fact that a power of arrest arises will not alone make the arrest lawful. These elements are of crucial importance due to the consequences which may flow from a lawful arrest which will not flow from an unlawful one. Such consequences include the right of the officer to use force in making an arrest if necessary and the loss of liberty inherent in an arrest. If an arrest has not occurred the citizen is free to go wherever she will and any attempt to prevent her doing so will be unlawful. |

It is therefore important to convey the fact of the arrest to the arrestee and to mark the point at which the arrest comes into being and general liberty ceases. At common law there had to be a physical detention or a touching of the arrestee to convey the fact of detention, unless he or she made this unnecessary by submitting to it; the fact of arrest had to be made clear and the reason for it had to be made known.

The common law safeguards have been modified and strengthened by s 28 PACE. Under s 28 both the fact of and the reason for the arrest must be made known at the time or as soon as is practicable afterwards. However, an ordinary citizen is not under this duty if the fact of the arrest and the reason for it are obvious. Conveying the fact of the arrest does not involve using a particular form of words but it may be that reasonable detail must be given so that the arrestee will be in a position to give a convincing denial and therefore be more speedily released from detention. Given the infringement of liberty represented by an arrest and the need therefore to restore liberty as soon as possible consistent with the needs of the investigation, it is unfortunate that s 28 did not make it clear that a reasonable degree of detail should be given.

However, the reason for the arrest need only be made known as soon as practicable. The meaning and implications of this provision were considered in *DPP v Hawkins* (1988). A police officer took hold of the defendant to arrest him but did not give the reason. The youth struggled and was therefore later charged with assaulting an officer in the execution of his duty. The question which arose was whether the officer was in the execution of his duty as he had failed to give the reason for the arrest. If the arrest was thereby rendered invalid he could not be in the execution of his duty as it could not include effecting an unlawful arrest.

It was determined in the Court of Appeal that the arrest became unlawful when the time came at which it was practicable to inform the defendant of the reason but he was not so informed. This occurred at the police station or perhaps in the police car, but did not occur earlier due to the defendant's behaviour. However, the arrest did not become retrospectively unlawful and therefore did not affect acts done before its unlawfulness came into being, which thus remained acts done in the execution of duty.

Thus the police have a certain leeway as to informing the arrestee; the arrest will not be affected and nor will other acts arising from it, until the time when it would be practicable to inform of the reason for it has come and gone. However, if no reason is given but there was nothing in the behaviour of the arrestee to make giving it impracticable then the arrest will be unlawful from its inception.

Following the decision in *Hawkins* what can be said as to the status of the suspect before the time came and passed at which the requisite words should have been spoken? Was he or was he or not under arrest at that time? In *Murray v Ministry of Defence* (1988) soldiers occupied a woman's house, thus clearly taking her into detention, but did not inform her of the fact of arrest for half an hour. The question arose whether she was falsely imprisoned during that half hour. The House of Lords found that delay in giving the requisite information was acceptable due to the alarm which the fact of arrest, if known, might have aroused in the particular circumstances – the unsettled situation in Northern Ireland.

Members of Mrs Murray's family applied to the European Commission on Human Rights, alleging a breach of Article 5 which guarantees liberty and security of the person and of Article 8 which protects the right to privacy. Article 5(1) requires *inter alia* that deprivation of liberty can occur only if arising from a lawful arrest founded on reasonable suspicion. The European Court of Human Rights found *(Murray v United Kingdom* (1994)) that no breach had occurred, even though the relevant legislation (s 14 of the Northern Ireland (Emergency Provisions) Act 1987) required only suspicion rather than reasonable suspicion, since there was some evidence which would provide a basis for the suspicion in question. No breach was found of Article 5(2) which provides that a person must be informed promptly of the reason for arrest. Mrs Murray was eventually informed during interrogation of the reason for the arrest and allowing an interval of a few hours between arrest and informing of the reason for it could still be termed prompt in the view of the court. The violation of privacy was found to fall within the exception under Article 8(2) in respect of the prevention of crime. No violation of the Convention was therefore found.

Thus it seems that under domestic law and under Article 5 an arrest which does not comply with all the procedural requirements will still be an arrest as far as all the consequences arising from it are concerned, for a period of time. It is therefore in a more precarious position than an arrest which from its inception complies with all the requirements, because it will cease to be an arrest at an uncertain point. Therefore, some departure has occurred from the principle that there should be a clear demarcation between the point at which the citizen is at liberty and the point at which her liberty is restrained.

Where the procedural elements are not complied with but no good reason for such failure arises, or if no power to arrest arose in the first place, the arrestee will have grounds for bringing an action for false imprisonment. Also, if a false arrest occurs and subsequently physical evidence is discovered or the defendant makes a confession, the defence may argue that the evidence should be excluded due to the false arrest. This is considered below.

9.4.10   Consensual detainment

Apart from situations in which reasonable suspicion relating to an offence arises, there is nothing to prevent a police officer asking any person to come to the police station to answer questions. There is no legal power to do so, but equally there is nothing to prevent such a request being made. The citizen is entitled to ask whether he or she is being arrested and if not to refuse. However, if he or she consents no action for false imprisonment can arise. This creates something of a grey area since the citizen may not realise that he or she does not need to comply with the request.

The government refused to include a provision in PACE requiring the police to inform citizens of the fact that they are not under arrest. However, certain provisions were included in Code of Practice C (see below) intended to ensure that volunteers were not disadvantaged in comparison with arrestees. Of course such provisions do not affect the fact that some 'volunteers' might not have gone to the police station at all had they realised that they had a choice.

The police may use reasonable force in making an arrest or using other powers so long as they are within the provisions under the PACE scheme. This was provided for under the Criminal Law Act 1967 s 3 and is now continued in PACE s 117. Force may include as a last resort the use of firearms; such use is governed by Home Office guidelines which provide that firearms should be issued only where there is reason to suppose that a person to be apprehended is so dangerous that he could not be safely restrained otherwise. An oral warning should normally be given unless impracticable before using a firearm.

9.4.11   Use of force

In America the Fourth Amendment to the Constitution guarantees freedom from unreasonable search and seizure, thus recognising the invasion of privacy which a search of premises represents. A search without a warrant will normally be unreasonable; therefore an independent check is usually available on the search power. In contrast, in Britain the ruling in *Ghani v Jones* (1970) allowed search and seizure on wide grounds, going beyond those authorised by statute. Thus, the common law did not provide full protection for the citizen and PACE goes some way to remedy this by placing powers of entry and seizure on a clearer basis and ensuring that the person whose premises are searched understands the basis of the search and can complain as to its conduct if necessary. Whether the new procedures actually do provide sufficient protection for the interests of the subject of the search is the question to be examined by this section.

9.5   Power to enter premises to search and seize goods: introduction

The power to enter premises conferred by ss 17 and 18 PACE is balanced in a manner similar to the method employed in

9.5.1   Under PACE: without warrant

respect of stop and search. The power can be exercised under s 17 where: an officer wants to arrest a person suspected of an arrestable offence; in order to arrest for certain offences under the Public Order Act 1936 or the Criminal Law Act 1977; to recapture someone unlawfully at large such as an escapee from a prison, court or mental hospital; to save life or limb or prevent serious damage to property, or to execute a warrant of arrest arising out of criminal proceedings. This last provision allows an entry to be made to search for someone wanted under a warrant for non-payment of a fine.

A further power of entry arises under s 18 if a person has been arrested for an arrestable offence and the intention is to search the person's premises immediately after arrest:

> a constable may enter and search any premises occupied or controlled by a person who is under arrest for an arrestable offence, if he has reasonable grounds for suspecting that there is on the premises evidence, other than items subject to legal privilege, that relates –
>
> (a) to that offence; or
>
> (b) to some other arrestable offence which is connected with or similar to that offence.

Thus, the power is subject to some significant limitations, in particular because it does not arise in respect of an arrest under s 25. If a search was considered necessary in respect of a s 25 arrest a search warrant would have to be obtained unless the provisions of s 32 applied. Section 32 allows a search of premises after arrest for *any* offence if the arrestee was arrested on those premises or was on them immediately before the arrest.

9.5.2   Search warrants

Searching of premises other than under ss 17 and 18 can only occur if a search warrant is issued under s 8 PACE by a magistrate. A warrant will only be issued if there are reasonable grounds for believing that a serious arrestable offence has been committed and where the material is likely to be of substantial value to the investigation of the offence. Further safeguards are set out in ss 15 and 16. The warrant must be produced to the occupier and identify the articles to be sought, although once the officer is on the premises other articles may be seized under s 19 if they appear to relate to any other offence. Further, the warrant authorises entry to premises on one occasion only.

These provisions provide a scheme which is reasonably sound in theory but which is dependent on magistrates observing its requirements. Research suggests that in practice some magistrates make little or no attempt to ascertain whether the information a warrant contains may be relied upon, while it seems possible that magistrates who do take a rigorous approach to the procedure and refuse to grant warrants are not approached again. A warrant authorising the police to search premises does not of itself authorise officers to search persons on the premises. The Home Office Circular on PACE states that such persons can be searched only if a specific power to do so arises under the warrant (eg warrants issued under the Misuse of Drugs Act 1971 s 23).

Under the PTA Schedule 7 there are certain special powers to search for evidence which relates to a terrorist investigation. No specific offence need be alleged: it is only necessary to show reasonable belief that the material is of substantial value to the investigation. Under para 7(1) a warrant order can be issued by a police superintendent if he reasonably believes that immediate action is in the interests of the state and the case is one of great emergency. Thus the intervention of a judge as a check on this power is prevented.

At common law a power to enter premises in order to prevent crime arises from the much criticised case of *Thomas v Sawkins* (1935). Lord Hewart CJ contemplated that a police officer would have the right to enter private premises when 'he has reasonable grounds for believing that an offence is imminent or is likely to be committed'. This judgment may receive some endorsement from s 17(5)(6) which provides that all common law powers on entry are abolished except to deal with or prevent a breach of the peace. However, this narrows down the power of entry as it does not arise in respect of *any* offence. *Thomas v Sawkins* arose in the context of a public meeting held on private premises, but common law powers do not seem to be confined to such circumstances; in *McGowan v Chief Constable of Kingston on Hull* (1968) it was found that police officers were entitled to enter and remain on private premises when they feared a breach of the peace arising from a private quarrel.

9.5.3   Common law: power to enter premises

Code B, which governs powers of entry, search and seizure, makes special provision for voluntary searches. Paragraph 4 of Code B provides that a search of premises can take place with the consent of the occupier but under para 4(2) she must be informed that she need not consent to the search. In requiring that the consent should be in writing para 4 recognises that there may sometimes be a doubt as to the reality of such consent and goes some way towards resolving that doubt. Sub-paragraph 4.3 provides that the search must cease if the consent is withdrawn during it, and also contains an express provision against using duress to obtain consent. However, these provisions are only of value in ensuring that use of

9.5.4   Voluntary searches

consensual search is not abused if it is made clear to occupiers that they can withhold consent.

9.5.5   Power of seizure

At common law prior to PACE a wide power of seizure had developed where a search was not under warrant. Articles could be seized so long they either implicated the owner or occupier in any offence, or implicated third parties in the offence for which the search was conducted. However, the power of seizure under PACE is even wider than this. Under s 8(2) a constable may seize and retain anything for which a search has been authorised. The power of seizure without warrant is governed by s 18(2) which provides that: 'A constable may seize and retain anything for which he may search under subsection (1) above.' This power is greatly widened, however, by the further power of seizure arising under s 19:

> 'The constable may seize anything which is on the premises if he has reasonable grounds for believing:
>
> (a)   that it has been obtained in consequence of the commission of an offence; and
>
> (b)   that it is necessary to seize it in order to prevent it being concealed, lost, damaged, altered or destroyed.
>
> (3)   The constable may seize anything which is on the premises if he has reasonable grounds for believing:
>
> (a)   that it is evidence in relation to an offence which he is investigating or any other offence; and
>
> (b)   that it is necessary to seize it in order to prevent the evidence being concealed, lost, altered or destroyed.'

It was made clear in *Chief Constable of Lancashire ex p Parker and McGrath* (1992) that the above provisions assume that the search itself is lawful; in other words, material seized during an unlawful search cannot be retained and if it is, an action for trespass to goods may arise. It was accepted in this instance that the search was unlawful (see below at para 9.5.9) but the Chief Constable contended that the material seized could nevertheless be retained. This argument was put forward under the provision of s 22(2)(a) which allows the retention of 'anything seized for the purposes of a criminal investigation'. The Chief Constable maintained that these words would be superfluous unless denoting a general power to retain unlawfully seized material. However, it was held that the subsection could not bear the weight sought to be placed upon it: it was merely intended to give examples of matters falling within the general provision of s 22(1). Therefore the police were not entitled to retain the material seized.

Under s 8 excluded or special procedure material or material covered by legal privilege cannot be seized during a search not under warrant and is exempt from the s 8 search warrant procedure. However, under s 9 the police may gain access to excluded or special procedure material by making an application to a circuit judge in accordance with Schedule 1. Access to excluded material may only be granted where it could have been obtained under the previous law relating to such material. Excluded material is defined under s 11 to consist of material held on a confidential basis, personal records, samples of human tissue or tissue fluid held in confidence and journalistic material held in confidence. Personal records include records held by schools, universities, probation officers and social workers.

'Special procedure material' as defined under s 14 operates as a catch-all category which is, it seems, frequently used to cover confidential material which does not qualify as personal records or journalistic material. It should be noted that under the PTA, Schedule 7 para 3 of the Act allows access to both special procedure and excluded material. The judge only needs to be satisfied that there is a terrorist investigation in being, that the material would substantially assist it, and it is in the public interest that it should be produced. It may well be that once the first two requirements are satisfied it will be rare to find that the third is not.

The ruling in *Guildhall Magistrates' Court ex p Primlacks Holdings Co (Panama) Ltd* (1989) made it clear that a magistrate must satisfy him or herself that there were reasonable grounds for believing that the items covered by the warrant did not include material subject to the special protection. The magistrates had issued search warrants authorising the search of two solicitors' firms. Judicial review of the magistrates' decision to issue a warrant was successfully sought; it was found that the magistrate had merely accepted the police officer's view that s 8 was satisfied rather than independently considering the matter.

Thus the strongest protection extends to items subject to legal privilege, which under s 10 will include communications between client and solicitor connected with giving advice or with legal proceedings. However, if items are held with the intention of furthering a criminal purpose they will not, under s 10(2) attract legal privilege. It seems that this will include the situation where the solicitor *unknowingly* furthers the criminal purpose of the client or a third party. In *Crown Court at Snaresbrook ex p DPP* (1988) it was found that only the *solicitor's* intentions regarding the criminal purpose were relevant but the

9.5.6   Excluded or special procedure material or material covered by legal privilege

House of Lords in *Central Criminal Court ex p Francis and Francis* (1989) rejected this interpretation, finding that the criminal purpose of a third party could bring s 10(2) into operation. This interpretation of s 10(2) was adopted on the basis that otherwise the efforts of the police in detecting crime might be hampered but it may be argued that it gives insufficient weight to the need to protect the special relationship between solicitor and client.

9.5.7   Safeguards under
          Code B

The power to search and seize is balanced by the need to convey certain information to the subject of the search in question, thereby rendering officers (at least theoretically) accountable for searches carried out. It may be said that the provisions are of a largely presentational nature: they ensure that a large amount of information is conveyed to the occupier and under para 2.5 make an attempt to ensure that community relations are not adversely affected by operation of the search power, but have little to say about the way the search should be conducted.

Broadly speaking, the regulation of the search power under Code B emphasises the provision of information to the owner of premises so that officers can be rendered accountable for searches made, rather than regulating circumstances relating to the nature of the search itself in order to minimise the invasion of privacy represented by such searches. In contrast, searches made in order to gain evidence relating to civil proceedings, under orders known as Anton Pillar orders, must observe a number of safeguards: they must be organised on weekdays in office hours so that legal advice can be obtained before the search begins; the defendant must be allowed to check the list of items to be seized before items can be removed, and it was found in *Universal Thermosensors Ltd v Hibben* (1992) that in some circumstances an independent solicitor experienced in the execution of such orders must be present, instructed and paid for by the plaintiff.

It may be argued that there is a greater public interest in the prevention of crime than in ensuring that evidence is obtained by a party to civil proceedings and therefore the police need at times to make an immediate search of premises, but the power to do so without judicial intervention should, it is submitted, be narrowed down to instances where the urgency of the search was demonstrable. Further, Code B should contain clearer safeguards applicable to all searches, allowing, for instance, for a legal advisor to be present during a non-urgent search and including a clear prohibition on non-urgent searches at night. At present searches should be conducted at 'a reasonable hour' and under Note for

Guidance 5A this is explained to mean at a time when the occupier or others are unlikely to be asleep. But, as discussed above at para 9.2, the Notes for Guidance are not part of the Codes and are of very uncertain legal status: a prohibition (subject to tightly drawn exceptions) on the entry and search of property at night by state agents – perhaps one of the most serious invasions of privacy possible – requires a more certain basis. No provision is made for giving warning to the occupier that the search is imminent so that he or she could seek legal advice if desired. Such a provision would no doubt have to be subject to exceptions in order to allow urgent searching but might well be indicated in many instances. The provision under para 5.11 that an occupier may ask a friend or neighbour to witness the search unless there are reasonable grounds for believing 'that this would seriously hinder the investigation' would usually be inadequate to allow the occupier to obtain legal advice or the presence of a solicitor.

Code B provides for an increase in the amount of information to be conveyed to owners of property to be searched by use of a new standard form, the Notice of Powers and Rights (para 5.7). It covers certain information including specification of the type of search in question, a summary of the powers of search and seizure arising under PACE and the rights of the subjects of searches. This notice must normally be given to the subject of the search before it begins, but under para 5.8 need not be if to do so would lead to frustration of the object of the search or danger to the police officers concerned or to others. These exceptions also apply under para 5.8 to leaving a copy of the warrant where the search is made under warrant. Under s 18(4) premises occupied or controlled by a person arrested for an arrestable offence may be searched after the arrest if an officer of the rank of inspector or above gives authority in writing. Under para 3.3 the authority should normally be given on the Notice of Powers and Rights. This clears up previous confusion as to the form the authority should take.

9.5.8   All searches: information to be conveyed

Under new paras 4 and 5, the subjects of all searches, regardless of the status of the search, must receive a copy of the Notice of Powers and Rights and, under new para 5.8 where a consensual search has taken place but the occupier is absent, the Notice should be endorsed with the name, number and station of the officer concerned. Oddly enough, it is not stated expressly that this information must be added to the Notice where the subject of a consensual search is *present*. Sub-para 5.5 provides that officers must identify themselves except in the case of enquiries linked to terrorism but this provision appears to apply only to non-consensual searches due to the heading of that section. It might be thought that a person who voluntarily allows police officers to come onto his or her premises does not need the information mentioned, but this is to ignore the possibility that such a person might wish to withdraw consent during the search but might feel too intimidated to do so.

| 9.5.9 | Providing a copy of the warrant | Under s 16 a copy of the warrant must be issued to the subject of the search. The importance of complying with this safeguard was reaffirmed in *Chief Constable of Lancashire ex p Parker and McGrath* (1992). Police officers conducted a search of the applicant's premises in the execution of a search warrant issued under s 8 of PACE. However, after the warrant had been signed by the judge the police detached part of it and reattached it to the other original documents. In purported compliance with s 16 of PACE the police produced all these documents to the applicants. Thus the police did not produce the whole of the original warrant and moreover did not supply one of the documents constituting the warrant. The applicants applied for judicial review of both the issue and the execution of the warrants. Firstly it was determined that s 16(5)(b) PACE had been breached in that the warrant produced to the applicants was not the original warrant as seen and approved by the judge. A declaration was granted to that effect. The police had admitted that there was a breach of the requirement under s 16(5)(c) that a copy of the warrant should be supplied to the occupier of the premises. Thus, this decision emphasised the need to observe all the safeguards if the search was to be lawful. |

| **9.6** | **Assault on or obstruction of a police constable in the execution of his duty** | Obstruction of a constable, which arises under s 51(3) of the Police Act 1964, creates an area of liability independent of any other substantive offence. In other words, it may criminalise activity which is otherwise lawful. Of course, this statement may appear superfluous: *all* offences criminalise otherwise lawful activity. However, criminal law in general concerns behaviour which has a general anti-social impact. In contrast this offence criminalises behaviour in relation to police officers which would not give rise to criminal liability if directed at any other group of persons. Thus, contact between police and citizens may result in the creation of liability where otherwise none would have existed. |

| 9.6.1 | Obstruction | Of course, society considers it desirable that the police should be able to make contact with citizens in order to make general enquiries without invoking any specific powers; on the other hand citizens do not need to reply to such enquiries. A police officer can ask a citizen to refrain from doing something but the citizen may refuse if the action is not in itself unlawful. If this |

was not the case there would be little need for other specific powers; an officer could, for example, merely ask a person to submit to a search and if he refused warn him that he could be charged with obstruction. However, the way this offence has been interpreted determines the border between legitimate and illegitimate disobedience to police instructions or requests.

Following *Rice v Connolly* (1966) three tests must be satisfied if liability for this offence is to be made out. Firstly it must be shown that the constable was in the execution of his or her duty. Actions outside the officer's duty would seem to include any action which is unlawful or contrary to Home Office Circulars or the Codes. However, some actions which may be termed unlawful may be found too trivial to take the officer outside the execution of his or her duty.

In *Bentley v Brudzinski* (1982) an officer laid a hand on the shoulder of the defendant in order to detain him so as to ask further questions. The court found that in trying to prevent the defendant from returning home the officer was acting outside the execution of his duty, but considered that not all instances in which an officer used some physical restraint would be treated in the same way. Reference was made to *Donelly v Jackman* (1970) in which on very similar facts it was found that an officer was not outside the execution of his duty.

All that can be said then is that all the circumstances of the case must be considered in determining whether an officer is within the execution of his duty, and that the more significant the restraint used, the more likely it is that the officer will be outside it. Does this mean then that any action of an officer which is not unlawful or contrary to official guidance will be within the execution of duty? It was found in *Coffin v Smith* (1980) that any action within the officer's duty as a 'keeper of the peace' would be within his or her duty. Thus an officer does not need to point to a specific requirement to perform a particular duty imposed by superiors, but equally some actions which are not unlawful would seem to fall outside an officer's duty.

Secondly, it must be shown that the defendant did an act which made it more difficult for the officer to carry out her or his duty. Physically attempting to prevent an arrest as in *Hills v Ellis* (1983) will satisfy this test. This is not to imply that a physical act must occur but that the police must actually be impeded in some way. In *Lewis v Cox* (1985) a persistent enquiry as to where an arrested friend was being taken was held to amount to obstruction. The defendant opened the door of the police van, clearly preventing it from driving off, in order to make the enquiry after being told to desist.

The ruling in *Ricketts v Cox* (1981) that a refusal to answer questions accompanied by abuse was obstruction may delineate the lowest level of behaviour which may be termed obstructive. According to *Rice v Connolly* (1966) a refusal to answer questions does not amount to obstruction; therefore the abuse alone must have constituted the obstruction. This decision, which has been widely criticised, is perhaps hard to reconcile with *Bentley v Brudzinski* and possibly interpreted the meaning of 'obstruction' too widely.

It must finally be shown, following *Lewis v Cox*, that the defendant behaved wilfully in the sense that he acted deliberately with the knowledge and intention that he would obstruct the police officer. A defendant may be 'wilful' even though his purpose is to pursue some private objective of his own rather than to obstruct the officer, so long as his act is deliberate and he realises that it will in fact impede the officer. This will be the case, according to *Hills v Ellis*, even if the purpose of the defendant is to help the officer.

9.6.2   Assault on a police constable

This offence arises under s 51(1) of the Police Act 1964 and may be fulfilled even though the defendant is unaware that the person he is assaulting is a police officer. However, if the defendant believes that unlawful force is being used against him he is not prevented from setting up a defence of self-defence, although according to *Albert v Lavin* (1982), the belief in the need to act in self-defence must be based on reasonable grounds. This limitation has however been disapproved of by the Court of Appeal in *Gladstone Williams* (1983): it was found that an honest belief would be sufficient. However, it appears that if the honest belief is arrived at due to intoxication the facts will be considered as an objective observer would have perceived them (*O'Connor* (1991)). Apart from the assault the other elements will be interpreted as for obstruction.

9.7   Detention in police custody

The position under the law prior to the 1984 Act with regard to detention before charge and committal before a magistrate was very vague. It was governed by the Magistrates Court Act 1980 s 43 which allowed the police to detain a person in custody until such time as it was 'practicable' to bring him before a magistrate, in the case of a 'serious' offence. Since a person would be charged before being brought before the magistrate this meant that the police had to move expeditiously in converting suspicion into evidence justifying a charge. However, the common law had developed to the point when it could be said that detention for the purpose of questioning was recognised. Thus, prior to PACE, the police had no clearly defined power to hold a person for questioning.

The new detention scheme governed by Part IV of PACE has now put such a power on a clear basis and it is made clear under s 37(2) that the purpose of the detention is to obtain a confession. Under s 41 the detention can be for up to 24 hours but in the case of a person in police custody for a serious arrestable offence (defined in s 116) it can extend to 96 hours. Part IV does not apply to detention under the PTA s 14 and Schedule 2 or 5 (see below at 9.7.2), or to detention by immigration officers.

Under s 42(1) a police officer of the rank of superintendent or above can sanction detention up to 36 hours if three conditions apply: he or she has reasonable grounds for believing that either the detention is necessary to secure or preserve evidence relating to an offence for which he is under arrest or to obtain such evidence by questioning him; an offence for which he is under arrest is a serious arrestable offence; and the investigation is being conducted diligently and expeditiously.

After 36 hours detention can no longer be authorised by the police alone. Under s 43(1) the application must be supported by information and brought before a magistrates' court who can authorise detention under s 44 for up to 96 hours if the conditions are met as set out above. Detention must be reviewed periodically and the detainee or his solicitor (if available) has the right to make written or oral representations. However, research suggests that these reviews are not treated as genuine investigations into the grounds for continuing the detention, but as formal procedures which must be gone through.

These are very significant new powers which are, however, supposed to embody the principle that a detained person should normally be charged within 24 hours and then either released or brought before a magistrate. They are supposed to be balanced by all the safeguards created by Part V of PACE and by Codes of Practice C and E.

If a person is arrested under the PTA s 14 as opposed to s 24 PACE, whether the arrest is for an offence or otherwise (see above at 9.4.8), the detention provisions under PACE do not apply. The arrestee may be detained for up to 48 hours following arrest (PTA s 14(4)) but this period can be extended by the Secretary of State to further periods not exceeding five days in all (PTA s 14(5)). Thus the whole detention can be for seven days and, in contrast to the general PACE provision, the courts are not involved in the authorising process; it occurs at a low level of visibility as an administrative decision.

The similar provision under the PTA 1984 was found to be in breach of the European Convention Article 5(3) in *Brogan v*

9.7.1   Time limits on detention after arrest

9.7.2   Detention under the Prevention of Terrorism Act (PTA)

UK (1989) on the ground that holding a person for longer than four days without judicial authorisation was a violation of the requirement that persons should be brought promptly before a judicial officer. The government made no move to comply with this requirement; instead it entered a derogation under Article 15 to Article 5(3) which was challenged unsuccessfully in *Brannigan and McBride v UK* (1993) as broader than it needed to be. The European Court of Human Rights found that the derogation was justified as the state of public emergency in Northern Ireland warranted exceptional measures.

As a result, at present, periods of up to six days detention will not breach Article 5. This might appear an unfortunate decision because the derogation was entered *after* the *Brogan* decision. On the other hand states should not be encouraged to enter derogations too readily on 'insurance' grounds in order to preempt claims; it might be said that although there was a state of emergency in 1989 the UK had *chosen* not to enter a derogation even though one would have been warranted. Whatever the merits of this argument in the particular situation, it is questionable whether the exigencies of the situation do require detentions of six days without recourse to independent review. It might be possible to arrange for such review without prejudicing the legitimate purpose of the investigation.

Schedule 5 of the PTA allows a person to be detained for 12 hours before examination at ports of entry into Britain or Northern Ireland, but the period may be extended to 24 hours if the person is suspected of involvement in the commission, preparation or instigation of acts of terrorism. This 24 hour period seems to create a largely illusory restriction as it is subject to the provisions of para 6 Schedule 5 which allow further detention on three different grounds. These are: 'pending conclusion of his examination', pending consideration of the Secretary of State whether to make an exclusion order, or pending the decision of the Attorney General whether to institute proceedings against the detainee. Such detention may be for 48 hours on the authority of the examining officer and for a further period, up to a maximum of seven days, on the authority of the Secretary of State. If exclusion of the detainee is to take place he or she may be further detained pending removal; there is no statutory limit on such detention.

At no stage during this detention scheme is there need for recourse to a court; the introduction under Schedule 3 to the PTA 1989 of the need for periodic review of detention placed such review in the hands of police officers. If the review officer does refuse to grant a further extension of detention the Secretary of State may still grant it (Schedule 3 para 3(1)(b)).

Detained persons may not automatically be searched but the power to search under s 32 is quite wide. It arises under s 32(1) if an officer has reasonable grounds to suspect that a detained person has anything on him which might be evidence relating to an offence or might be used to help him escape from custody or that the arrested person may present a danger to himself or others.

The much wider power arises under s 32(2) and allows search, again on reasonable grounds, for anything which might be evidence of an offence or could help to effect an escape from lawful custody. The nature of the search must relate to the article it is suspected may be found; if it is a large item the search may not involve more than removal of a coat. Such searching may occur routinely but it must be possible to point to objectively justified grounds in each case which must not go beyond those specified. A power of search also arises under s 54, as amended, allowing search to ascertain property the detainee has with him or her, which will apply if someone has been arrested at the police station or brought there after being arrested elsewhere.

This section does not concentrate only on treatment and questioning of suspects *inside* the police station because contact between police and suspect takes place a long time before the police station is reached, and this has been recognised in the provisions of and Code of Practice C which govern treatment of suspects and interviewing, but have some application outside as well as inside the police station. It should be noted that many of the key provisions relating to treatment and interviewing are contained in Code C rather than in PACE itself. The most crucial event during a person's contact with police will probably be the interview and therefore this section will concentrate on the safeguards available for the suspect intended to ensure that interviews are fair and are properly recorded. This section, however, begins by a brief consideration of some general features of the treatment of the suspect once he or she has arrived at the police station. The scheme as regards questioning and treatment is largely governed by Part V of PACE in conjunction with Code C. However provision relating to custody officers in Part IV is also relevant.

If police officers detain a person under the provisions of the PTA 1989 Code C will govern his or her treatment, although, as will be seen, at certain points there are differences in the treatment of such a detainee and an ordinary detainee. However if the detention under the PTA is by examining

9.7.3   Searches of detained persons

9.8   Questioning and treatment of suspects inside and outside the police station: introduction

officers who are not police officers Code C will not apply; the officers need only 'have regard' to its provisions (PACE s 67(9)).

9.8.1   General treatment inside the police station: custody officers

The general use of custody officers provided for under Part IV s 36 is a key feature of the questioning and treatment scheme. The Custody Officer's role is to underpin the other safeguards by ensuring that the suspect is treated in accordance with PACE and the Codes and by generally overseeing all aspects of his or her treatment.

The idea was that somebody separate from the investigating officer should keep a check on what was occurring. The scheme was not a new idea; in certain police stations an officer was already fulfilling this role, but PACE clarifies the duties of custody officers and ensures that most stations have one. Thus best practice is now placed on a statutory basis.

However, the efficacy of the Custody Officer scheme may be called into question on two grounds. Firstly, it may not always be in operation: a number of stations do not have one and those that do may not always have one on duty. The ruling in *Vince and Another v Chief Constable of Dorset* (1992) makes it clear that s 36 does not require that an officer must always be present. The plaintiffs (acting for members of the joint branch board of the Police Federation of England and Wales of the Dorset Police) sought a declaration that by virtue of s 36(1) of the Police and Criminal Evidence Act 1984 a Custody Officer should normally be available in a police station.

However, it was found that s 36(1) clearly provides that the Chief Constable has a duty to appoint one custody officer for each designated police station and a power to appoint more in his discretion which has to be reasonably exercised. It was found that there had been no breach by the Chief Constable, implying that a decision that a Custody Officer need not always be on duty is a reasonable one. It may be argued that this case exposes a weakness in one of the central safeguards provided under PACE. This was referred to by Lord Justice Steyn who commented that the 1992 Royal Commission on criminal procedure might wish to consider this loophole in the PACE provisions.

Secondly, the Custody Officer may not always be able to take a stance independent of that of the investigating officer. This weakness in the scheme arises from the lowly rank of the Custody Officer; under s 38(3) the officer need only be of the rank of sergeant; he or she may therefore be of a lower rank than the investigating officer and therefore may find it very difficult to take an independent line on the treatment of the suspect. If the two disagree the custody officer must refer up the line of authority (s 39(6)); there is no provision allowing the custody officer to overrule the investigating officer. Thus there is a danger that the custody officer will merely rubber-stamp the decisions of the investigating officer; whether this is so may depend on the attitude of the superior officers to the provisions of the PACE scheme.

When the detainee arrives at the police station he or she will be 'booked in'. This may be a crucial stage in the proceedings as discussed below (at para 9.11.2) in relation to legal advice. Under para 3 of Code C (paragraphs or Annexes mentioned in relation to questioning and treatment all refer to Code C) a person must be informed orally and by written notice of four rights on arrival at the police station after arrest: the right to have someone informed of his detention; the right to consult a solicitor and the fact that independent legal advice is available free of charge; the right to consult Code C and the other Codes of Practice, and the right to silence as embodied in the caution.

9.8.2 Caution and notification of rights

Until 1995 the caution was in the following terms: 'You do not have to say anything but what you say may be given in evidence' (para 10.4). In response to the provision of s 34 of the Criminal Justice and Public Order Act 1994 the caution will now be in the following terms: 'you do not have to say anything. But it may harm your defence if you do not mention when questioned something which you late rely on in court. Anything you do say may be given in evidence'. Minor deviations do not constitute a breach of this requirement provided that the sense of the caution is preserved. The caution must be repeated during the interview if there is any doubt as to whether the detainee realises that it still applies. If a juvenile or a person who is mentally disordered or mentally handicapped is cautioned in the absence of the appropriate adult, the caution must be repeated in the adult's presence under para 10.6.

Throughout Code C recognition is given to the special needs of certain vulnerable groups: juveniles, the mentally disordered or handicapped, those not proficient in English, the hearing impaired or the visually handicapped. In particular juveniles and the mentally handicapped or disordered should be attended by an 'appropriate adult'.

9.8.3 Vulnerable groups

Under para 1 the 'appropriate' adult in the case of a juvenile will be the parent or guardian, a social worker or another adult who is not a police officer. Under the revision of Code C in April 1991 the estranged parent of a juvenile can no longer be the appropriate adult (Note for Guidance 1C); previously this was possible and in such instances the parent was likely to collude with the police or generally show hostility to the juvenile rather than look after his or her interests. This change was probably prompted by the decision in *DPP v Blake* (1989) that a confession obtained from a juvenile in the presence of an estranged parent acting as the appropriate adult may be excluded from evidence. Compliance with the original Note 13C (now sub-para 11.16) which indicated the respects in which the appropriate adult should look after the interests of the juvenile could not be ensured if an estranged parent was present; now Note 1C may ensure that sub-para 11.16 can be given full effect.

Under Note 1F the solicitor should not be the appropriate adult; this was included because it was thought that the roles of legal adviser and appropriate adult differed; the same person should not therefore fulfil both. There is some evidence that the police have been treating the solicitor as the appropriate adult thereby producing a conflict of interests.

It should be noted that under Annex C, which deals with urgent interviews, the juvenile can be interviewed without the presence of an appropriate adult if an officer of the rank of superintendent or above considers that delay will involve an immediate risk of harm to persons or serious loss of, or serious damage to, property. At various points to be discussed the particular vulnerability of juveniles is recognised, but although this is to be welcomed, research completed in 1993 for the Royal Commission on Criminal Procedure suggests that the treatment of juveniles, particularly during interviews, is still at times unsatisfactory.

In the case of a mentally disordered or handicapped detainee the appropriate adult under para 1 will be a relative, guardian, other person responsible for his or her welfare, or an adult who is not a police officer. The custody officer must as soon as practicable inform the appropriate adult of the grounds for the person's detention and ask the adult to come to the police station to see him or her. The custody officer must also immediately call the police surgeon or, in urgent cases, send the person to hospital or call the nearest available medical practitioner (para 9.2). The notification of rights must be given in the presence of the adult which may mean repeating the notification, but if the suspect wants legal advice this should not be delayed until the adult arrives.

It will be found in discussion below of unreliable confessions that mentally handicapped or disordered persons are very likely to make an untrue or exaggerated confession, and therefore it is particularly important that all the safeguards available should be in place when such a person is interviewed. However, under para 11.14 and Annex C there is provision for urgent interviewing of such persons without the appropriate adult if an officer of the rank of superintendent or above considers that delay will involve an immediate risk of harm to persons or serious loss of or serious damage to property. The main defect in the provisions relating to such persons is that they rely on the ability of officers who will have had little or no training in the field to determine that a person *is* mentally disordered. It would seem essential that custody officers at least should have special training in this regard.

The appropriate adult who is present at an interview should be informed that he or she is not expected to act simply as an observer; and also that the purposes of being present are, first, to advise the person being interviewed and to observe whether or not the interview is being conducted properly and fairly, and, secondly, to facilitate communication with the person being interviewed (para 11.16). It may be noted that the Royal Commission Report 1993 recommended review of the role of appropriate adults with a view to considering their training and availability and the criteria employed by the police in order to determine when an adult was needed.

Various provisions are available for the protection of members of the other vulnerable groups mentioned. A blind or visually handicapped person must have independent help in reading documentation (para 3.14). A deaf or speech handicapped person or someone who has difficulty under-standing English must only be interviewed in the presence of an interpreter (para 13), but this may be waived in the case of urgent interviewing under Annex C.

Physical treatment is governed by para 8 and is intended to provide basic physical care. It does however allow more than one detainee to be placed in the same cell if it is impracticable to do otherwise and, although a juvenile must not be placed in a cell with an adult, does not make sufficiently clear provision for frequent checks on juveniles in police cells see (Note 8A). It is intended to ensure that cells are adequately heated, cleaned, lit and ventilated; and that meals should be offered in any 24 hour period. A juvenile will only be placed in a police cell if no other secure accommodation is available and the custody officer considers that it is not practicable to supervise him if he is not placed in a cell. The custody officer must immediately call the police surgeon (or, in urgent cases, send the person to hospital or call the nearest available medical practitioner) if a person appears to need treatment.

Persons detained should be visited every hour, but juveniles should be visited more frequently; those who are drunk should be visited every half hour. No additional restraints should be used within a locked cell unless absolutely

9.8.4 Physical treatment

necessary and then only suitable handcuffs. Reasonable force may be used if necessary but only to secure compliance with reasonable instructions and to prevent escape, injury, damage to property or the destruction of evidence.

9.8.5   Intimate searches

An intimate search under s 55 can only be ordered if an officer of the rank of superintendent or above has reasonable grounds for believing that an article which could cause physical injury to a detained person or others at the police station has been concealed; or that the person has concealed a Class A drug which he intends to supply to another or to export. Even if such suspicion arises the search should not be carried out unless there is no other means of removing the object.

An intimate search at a police station may only be carried out by a registered medical practitioner or registered nurse unless the authorising officer considers in the case of a concealed object which could cause injury that it is not practicable to wait, in which case a police officer of the same sex as the suspect can carry it out. An intimate search at a police station of a juvenile or a mentally disordered or mentally handicapped person must take place only in the presence of the appropriate adult of the same sex unless the person requests otherwise (see Annex A para 4).

9.9   **The interviewing scheme**

The most significant safeguards available *inside* the police station include contemporaneous recording under para 11.5 or tape recording under Code E para 3, the ability to read over, verify and sign the notes of the interview as a correct record under para 11.10, notification of legal advice under para 3.1, the right to have advice before questioning under para 6 and, where appropriate, the presence of an adult. One of the most important issues in relation to these safeguards, and reflected in the 1991 and 1995 revisions of Code C, is the question *when* they come into play. In other words, there may be a number of stages in a particular investigation beginning with first contact between police and suspect and perhaps ending with the charge. At various points the safeguards mentioned have to come into play and two factors can be identified which decide which safeguards should be in place at a particular time. Firstly, it must be asked whether an exchange between police and suspect can be called an interview and secondly whether it took place inside or outside the police station.

9.9.1   Interviews and non-interviews: the original scheme

The correct interpretation of the term 'interview' under the original Code C scheme was highly significant because the relevant safeguards were unavailable unless an exchange between police officer and suspect was designated an interview. The term therefore tended to be given a wide interpretation and eventually the definition given to it by the Court of Appeal in *Mathews* – 'any discussion or talk between suspect and police officer' – brought within its ambit many exchanges far removed from formal interviews. It also covered many interviewees as it spoke in terms of 'suspects' not arrestees. However, it was qualified by the ruling in *Scott* (1990) that unsolicited admissions cannot amount to 'interviews', and by the ruling in *Marsh* (1991) to the same effect as regards 'genuine requests' from the police for information. In *Marsh* police officers investigating a burglary suddenly came across wraps of papers and asked the appellant about them; the questions and answers were admissible although no caution had been given because until that point the officers had had no reason to suspect her of any drug-related offence.

The ruling in *Marsh* bears some resemblance to that in *Maguire* (1989) which pre-dated *Mathews*: it was determined that questioning an arrestee near the scene of the crime, apparently in order to elicit an innocent explanation, did not constitute an interview. Thus the original interpretation of an interview created some leeway – but not much – for gathering (or apparently gathering) admissions in informal situations before any safeguards were in place.

In one respect distinguishing between interviews and non-interviews will not be as crucial under the current Code C scheme as it was under the original scheme: under para 11.13 *any* comments relevant to the offence made by a suspected person outside the context of an interview must be accurately recorded and then verified and signed by the suspect. However, making such a distinction will still be highly significant because it remains the first step towards bringing the other safeguards into play.

9.9.2   Interviewing under the current scheme

A definition of the term 'interview' is now contained in para 11.1.A which reads:

> An interview is the questioning of a person regarding his involvement or suspected involvement in a criminal offence or offences which by virtue of para 10.1 of Code C is required to be carried out under caution.

Para 10.1 reads:

> A person whom there are grounds to suspect of an offence must be cautioned before any questions about it (or further questions if it is his answers to previous questions which provide the grounds for suspicion) are put to him regarding his involvement or suspected involvement in that offence if his answers or his silence (ie failure or refusal to answer a question or to answer satisfactorily) may be given in evidence to a court in a prosecution. He therefore need not be cautioned if questions are put to him

for other purposes, for example, solely to establish his identity or his ownership of any vehicle or to obtain any information in accordance with any relevant statutory requirement ... or in furtherance of the proper and effective conduct of a search ...

It may be noted that the list of examples of instances under para 10.1 in which no caution would be necessary is not exhaustive. No such definition appeared in the original Code but Note 12A read: 'The purpose of any interview is to obtain from the person concerned his explanation of the facts and not necessarily to obtain an admission.' The new definition under paras 11.1A and 10.1, taken together, obviously differs from this considerably and differs even more from the definition of an interview contained in *Mathews*.

The new definition echoes the rulings of the Court of Appeal in *Maguire* and *Marsh* in attempting to draw a distinction between questioning a person regarding suspected involvement in an offence and questioning for other purposes. The difficulty is that para 10.1 does not make it sufficiently clear that where questioning for other purposes has some bearing on suspected involvement in an offence, an interview will take place. Thus, para 10.1 may on occasion act as an invitation to police officers to play down the level of suspicion excited by the circumstances or to characterise the questioning as for 'other purposes' in order to demonstrate that no interview took place requiring contemporaneous recording. If this was accepted an accurate record made later on would be admissible in evidence.

The para 10.1 test may need to be qualified by the ruling of the Court of Appeal in *Weekes* (1992): once an exchange becomes an interview that fact will have a retrospective effect on earlier exchanges; if safeguards applicable to an interview were not available in respect of such exchanges they will be excluded from evidence. It will not be possible to sever them from the 'interview'. This ruling seems to be in conflict with *Marsh*; however, as the *Weekes* ruling concerned a juvenile it may be confined to such instances.

Where the level of suspicion clearly falls within paras 11.1A and 10.1 as, of course, it will do after arrest, the use of the term 'questioning' nevertheless impliedly excludes instances where nothing definable as questioning has taken place, such as chats or discussions between suspect and police officer or statements or commands which happen to elicit an incriminating response. This interpretation seems to lead to a clear conflict between these provisions and the ruling from *Mathews* which could perhaps be resolved by arguing that rulings of the Court of Appeal will prevail over a provision contained only in a

Code of Practice. This would be the more satisfactory result as more likely to curtail opportunities for 'verballing' (concocting admissions).

However, a possible response might be that the definition from *Mathews* is now enshrined in para 11.13 and is not therefore inconsistent with paras 11.1A and 10.1. In other words, the *Mathews* definition applies to most exchanges between suspect and police officer but these provisions apply to certain particularly important ones labelled 'interviews'. This interpretation is to an extent supported by the wording of para 11.13: 'a written record should be made of any comments made by a suspected person, including unsolicited comments which are outside the context of an interview but which might be relevant to the offence', thus implying that comments relevant to the offence other than unsolicited comments will not invariably be part of an interview.

This contention also receives some support from the ruling in *Williams* (1992) which seems to have accepted impliedly that 'social visits' by police to suspects in the cells, involving conversation relevant to the offence in question, do not constitute interviews although they are to be discouraged. This interpretation would mean that a number of exchanges which would previously have been interviews will no longer be so labelled, and is especially of concern due to the evidence that police officers favour the informal chat in the police station. The improvement in the position of some suspects should not be allowed to obscure the fact that certain safeguards may now be triggered off only in a confined group of situations.

Whether this will be the effect of para 11.1A and 10.1 is still unclear, but in *Cox* (1993) the Court of Appeal adopted what might be termed a 'purposive approach' to it in finding that the intention of the 1991 revision was to *increase* rather than decrease protection for suspects, and therefore Note 11A should be interpreted in the light of previous decisions such as *Mathews* which *broadened* the definition of an interview. This might also be said, although with less certainty, of the 1995 provision. It is fairly apparent that Code C does not provide a means of distinguishing clearly between interviews and non-interviews. This is an important point since 'interviews' must be recorded on the spot (para 11.5) while 'non-interviews' – which are however relevant to the offence – can be recorded later (para 11.13). Moreover, the 'non-interview' need not be recorded as fully as the interview. Also, if an exchange is an 'interview', para 11.1 will come into play.

9.9.3   Interviews inside and outside the police station

Once an exchange can be called an interview the safeguards applying to it differ depending on where it takes place. If the interview is in the street the suspect must be given the record of the interview to verify and sign under para 11 which is headed 'Interviews general', although this change is made less significant by the provisions of para 11.3. The verifying and signing rules have been supplemented by the requirement, imposed, however, only by the 1991 Home Office Circular, and now under Note for Guidance 11D, that the suspect should declare in his or her own hand on the interview record that it is correct. Such a provision clearly has more value than the requirement only to obtain a signature. Under para 11.5 the interview must be recorded contemporaneously wherever it takes place unless this would not be practicable.

However, the suspect interviewed outside the police station will be unaware of the right to legal advice and it is also at present unlikely that the interview would be tape recorded: Code E does not envisage tape recording taking place anywhere but inside the police station. Certain suspects will not, however, be disadvantaged by these differences due to the provisions of para 11.1 which read: 'Following a decision to arrest a suspect he must not be interviewed about the relevant offence except at a police station' (except in certain instances specified in 11.1 (a), (b) and (c) which call for urgent interviewing).

Paragraph 11.1 could have read: 'Once the level of suspicion would justify an arrest a suspect must not be interviewed about the relevant offence except at a police station ... etc'. Clearly, it was designed to allow *some* interviewing outside the police station due to its requirement of a higher level of suspicion than that denoted by para 10.1, but the question is – how high a level in comparison with that denoted by para 10.1? Para 11.1 implies that a police officer should categorise someone either as quite probably involved in an offence or as on the verge of arrest; so long as the first category is applicable questioning can continue. This category was presumably intended to include persons under caution.

However, it will be difficult to be certain in retrospect as to which category applied, although the police might find it difficult where there are very strong grounds for suspicion to support a claim that interviewing could continue because the decision to arrest had not been taken. It is clear that the problems associated with exchanges between suspect and officer still remain, but admissions or silences occurring outside the police station may now receive some form of corroboration due to their acceptance by the suspect on tape at the police station under para 11.2A. However, crucially, para

11.2A does not provide that admissions or silences made outside the police station will be inadmissible if not accepted on tape by the suspect at the police station. Therefore, presumably, if no breaches of Code C have occurred, they would be admissible even though uncorroborated.

Where the level of suspicion would obviously justify an arrest a police officer who wishes to keep a suspect out of the police station for the time being, might be able to invoke one of the exceptions allowing urgent interviewing in order to avert certain specified risks certain of the exceptions are particularly broadly worded. The first exception under para 11.1(a), allowing interviewing to take place at once where delay might lead to interference with evidence could be interpreted very broadly and could apply whenever there was some likelihood that evidence connected with any offence but not immediately obtainable was in existence. Even if there were no others involved in the offence who had not been apprehended it could be argued that the evidence was at risk from the moment of arrest because news of the arrest might become known to persons with a motive for concealing it. This argument could also apply to the exception under (c) allowing urgent interviewing if delay might hinder recovery of property obtained due to the offence, with the proviso that it will apply to a narrower range of offences. The exception under (b) relating to the danger that others who are involved may escape may also arise fairly frequently.

Once the suspect is inside the police station under arrest or under caution, any interview, apart from those with a person suspected of an offence triable only summarily (under para 3.1(a)), should be tape recorded unless he or she is suspected of involvement in terrorism or of espionage under s 1 of the Official Secrets Act 1989. This provision under Code E para 3.2 is clarified under Note for Guidance 3G of Code E; interviews with those suspected of terrorism solely connected with the affairs of the UK or any part of the UK other than Northern Ireland should be tape recorded.

A written contemporaneous record will still be made of interviews which fall within Code E para 3.2. This exemption was included because it was feared that the contents of tapes might become available to terrorist organisations. At present the Home Office has it under review, and it is suggested that two issues in particular deserve attention. First, what is the likelihood that tape-recording an interview or part of an interview, possibly with editing of the tape, would create more of a threat to national security than making contemporaneous notes available to the defence? The difficulty of editing the tape as compared to editing notes should be weighed against the advantages of tape recording which seem to be generally recognised.

Second, bearing in mind that persons apparently connected with the relevant terrorist offences may vary enormously in terms of their experience and ability to withstand pressure from the police, it must be questioned whether the imposition of a blanket ban on tape recording of all such interviews can be justified. At the least it is arguable that interviews with mentally disordered or handicapped terrorist suspects (Judith Ward comes to mind) might reasonably be exempted from the para 3.2 provision. It should be recognised that tape recording is to an extent irrelevant as a safeguard against miscarriages of justice while this exemption exists, especially as terrorist cases may be most likely to miscarry.

9.9.4	Varying levels of protection for exchanges

It is now possible to identify the points at which the safeguards will be brought to bear and it is apparent that there are four levels of protection available:

- Inside or outside the police station, if the exchange cannot be labelled an interview even though it may be relevant to the offence, it seems that the level of protection provided by para 11.13 only will apply. This will be the case even where the suspect is an arrestee or a volunteer under caution.

- If an interview takes place outside the police station but falls outside the para 11.1 prohibition the verifying and recording provisions under paras 11.10 and 11.5 will apply with the proviso that contemporaneous recording may be impracticable. (What is impracticable does not connote something that is extremely difficult but must involve more than mere inconvenience (*Parchment* (1989).) Where appropriate an adult must be present.

- Inside the police station, if the person in question is an arrestee or a volunteer under caution and the exchange is an interview, all the available safeguards including tape recording will apply.

- If the conditions under the third level are satisfied but the person is suspected of involvement in terrorism under para 3.2 (or falls within one of the other exemptions from tape recording) all the available safeguards *except* tape recording will apply.

Thus, wide but uncertain scope still remains for interviewing outside the police station and for gathering admissions outside the context of an interview. The main objection to this scheme, apart from its complexity, is that the degree of protection available is too dependent on factors irrelevant to the level of suspicion in question. It may be pure chance, or something more sinister, which dictates whether a volunteer under caution is interviewed inside or outside the police station, or whether or not an exchange with an arrestee can successfully be characterised or disguised as a non-interview. Bearing in mind that unreliable confessions may be most likely to emerge from informal exchanges, it is argued that the mechanisms triggering off the main safeguards – paras 10.1 and 11.1 – are deficient both in creating large areas of uncertainty as to the level of protection called for at various points and in allowing the minimal level of protection under para 11.13 to operate in too many contexts.

The Police and Criminal Evidence Act 1984 placed the right to legal advice on a statutory basis for the first time. With a view to ensuring that suspects actually receive legal advice, s 58 entitles a person to consult a solicitor privately and provides under s 59 for duty solicitors to attend suspects. A detainee is to be informed of this right under Code C para 3, given, if necessary, the name of the duty solicitor and permitted to have the solicitor present during questioning under C para 6.5. In cases involving 'serious arrestable offences' however, there are certain saving provisions under s 58 allowing delay in the obtaining of advice, and a further power to delay access arises under Code C para 6.3(b)(ii). Thus, Parliament drew back from making this right absolute; nevertheless the exceptions are narrowly drawn and so should not significantly undermine it.	**9.10** **The legal advice scheme**

However, the factor which previously motivated the police to delay (or refuse) access to legal advice remains unchanged: the suspect still has the right to remain silent and the legal advisor may advise him or her to exercise it. Even if the solicitor does not advise silence the police may think that they are more likely to obtain incriminating admissions from detainees in the absence of a solicitor and therefore at times may deny or subvert the access to one envisaged by s 58. As will be seen there are various means of undermining the scheme with the result that some suspects who need it do not receive advice.

The most direct method of denying legal advice involves invoking one of the three s 58(8) exceptions. The exceptions come into operation if the suspect is in police detention for a serious arrestable offence and the decision to invoke them must be taken by an officer of at least the rank of superintendent. If both these conditions are fulfilled, access to legal advice, if requested, can be denied if the officer believes on reasonable grounds that exercise of the right at the time when the person in police detention desires to	9.10.1 Avenues of escape from the scheme: denying access

exercise it *will* lead to the solicitor acting as a channel of communication between the detainee and others – alerting them or hindering the recovery of stolen property.

The leading case determining the scope of the s 58 exceptions is *Samuel* (1988). The appellant was arrested on suspicion of armed robbery and after questioning at the police station, asked to see a solicitor. The request was refused, apparently on the grounds that other suspects might be warned and that recovery of the outstanding stolen money might thereby be hindered; the appellant subsequently confessed to the robbery and was later convicted. On appeal the defence argued that the refusal of access was not justifiable under s 58(8) and that therefore the confession obtained should not have been admitted into evidence as it had been obtained due to impropriety. The Court of Appeal took into account the use of the word 'will' in s 58(8) which suggests that the police officer must be virtually certain that a solicitor, if contacted, will thereafter either commit a criminal offence or unwittingly pass on a coded message to criminals. It must be asked first whether the officer did believe this and secondly whether he believed it on reasonable grounds.

The court considered that only in the remote contingency that evidence could be produced as to the corruption of a particular solicitor would a police officer be able to assert a reasonable belief that a solicitor would commit a criminal offence. They went on to hold that showing a reasonable belief that a solicitor would inadvertently alert other criminals would also be a formidable task; it could only reasonably be held if the suspect in question was a particularly resourceful and sophisticated criminal, or if there was evidence that the solicitor sought to be consulted was particularly inexperienced or naive.

The court found that as no evidence as to the naivety or corruption of the solicitor in question had been advanced, it could not be accepted that the necessary reasonable belief had existed. The police had made no attempt to consider the real likelihood that the solicitor in question would be utilised in this way; in fact it was apparent that the true motive behind the denial of access was a desire to gain a further opportunity to break down the detainee's silence. It should be noted that Code C expressly disallows denial of access to a solicitor on the ground that he or she will advise the suspect to remain silent (Annex B para 3).

This interpretation of s 58(8) has greatly narrowed its scope as it means that the police will not be able to make a general, unsubstantiated assertion that it was thought that others might be alerted if a solicitor was contacted. The authorising officer will have to show, on very specific grounds, why this was thought to be the case. (The question of exclusion of the confession due to this impropriety is considered below.) This decision appears to have prevented mere refusals to allow access to advice in many instances. However, there are a number of loopholes in the legal advice scheme which may allow for less formal methods of evading its provisions and it may be that suspects who are thereby most disadvantaged are those most in need of legal advice.

Notification of the right to advice under para 3.1 of Code C is still reserved for arrival at the police station, thus disadvantaging certain suspects not already aware of it at the point when admissions may be made. It is probably fair to assume, firstly, that many suspects, including those who are criminally experienced, are aware of the right to legal advice, and, secondly, that the group who are not so aware would tend to include some of the more vulnerable members of society. It has already been noted above at 9.9.2 that there is leeway in the interviewing scheme to allow admissions to be made before notification of advice.

9.10.2   Subverting notification

At the point of notification the suspect not already aware of the right to advice is in a very vulnerable position as he is dependent for information on the very persons who have an interest in withholding it or misleading him. Research conducted by Sanders in 1989 demonstrated that notification could be subverted by various methods, most commonly by ensuring that suspects never really took in what was on offer.

When Code C was revised in 1991 this problem was recognised and an attempt was made to address it. The requirement of notification under para 3.1 is now backed up by a new para 6.3, requiring that police stations display a prominent poster advertising the right to have advice. However, it must be questioned whether the provision of posters will make much difference. The 'booking in' stage is likely to be one of the more traumatic points in the process especially for the suspect who is inexperienced or in some way vulnerable. Whether he is likely to notice and take in a message conveyed in this way which is not specifically directed at him is open to question. If he remains silent in the face of a rapid notification, his silence can be taken as a waiver of advice when in actuality it merely denotes incomprehension. Research conducted in 1993 for the Royal Commission found that a higher proportion of suspects were being informed of the right to legal advice after the 1991 revision of the Codes but that the information was given in a quarter of cases in an unclear or unduly rapid fashion.

| 9.10.3 | Encouragement to defer advice | If the suspect does take in what is being offered he may be encouraged not to exercise the right straight away. In fact, the Sanders research suggested that encouraging a suspect to defer the decision to have advice was quite popular. The 1991 revision of Code C did address this problem. Paragraph 3.1 now provides that it is a 'continuing right which may be exercised at any stage' and under para 11.2 a suspect must now be reminded of the right before each interview in the police station. Although this change is to be welcomed it should not obscure the value of having advice before any interviewing at all takes place and it is therefore unfortunate that new para 3.1 does not make this clear and could even be said to encourage the suspect to defer the decision. |

However, Note 3G seems designed to dissuade some suspects from deferring it by providing that a request for advice from a mentally disordered or handicapped person or a juvenile should be pursued straight away without waiting for the appropriate adult to arrive. It appears intended to prevent police officers playing off adult against suspect by telling the suspect to defer making a decision about advice until the adult arrives, and then giving the adult the impression that the juvenile has waived advice or does not need it. It appears that this provision has not had much impact, which might be because it is contained in a Note and not in the Code itself. Provision aimed at preventing this ploy could have been taken further by including a requirement that even where a suspect had waived advice suspect and adult should be left alone together for a few minutes after re-notification of the right.

| 9.10.4 | Encouragement to forego advice | Suspects who are thinking of asking for legal advice straight away may still be persuaded out of doing so by various methods; the Sanders research found that such methods – termed 'ploys' – were most successful against least experienced suspects. However, there has been some attempt to combat the use of such ploys. For example, suspects were supposed to be given a leaflet under original Note 3E explaining the arrangements for obtaining advice, including the fact that it was free, but in practice a number of suspects did not receive it or did not understand it, thereby enabling police officers to mislead them. Under para 3.1(ii) the suspect must be informed that advice is free (although the posters need not carry this information). Further, general discouragement of ploys is articulated in new para 6.4 which provides that no attempt should be made to dissuade the suspect from having advice. |

The requirement introduced in 1995 under para 6.5 that the suspect should be asked his reason for declining legal advice, and that this should be noted on the custody record, may go some way towards ensuring that suspects understand what is on offer, and may curb ploys, as may the requirement to point out that the suspect may speak on the telephone with a solicitor. Nevertheless, the possibility of manipulation of the custody record remains since the whole process of making the record remains in the hands of the custody officer. It has been suggested that a requirement of an own hand declaration of waiver of advice on the custody record would have represented an effective means of addressing the problem since it would have forced the Custody Officer to ensure that the suspect understood what was being offered and would have required positive action on the suspect's part to refuse it.

The detainee who has decided to have advice can nevertheless change his or her mind; this is provided for by Code C 6.3(d), providing that the consent is given in writing or on tape. However, there is some leeway allowing police officers to engineer a change of heart. No limitations were placed on the reasons for giving such consent, thus creating a serious flaw in the legal advice provisions. But if the consent is based on a police misrepresentation ought it to be treated as genuine? This question arises in part due to the lack of certainty as to the relationship between Code C 6.3(d) and (c); 6.3(c) provides that the detainee can be interviewed without legal advice if the nominated solicitor is unavailable, and notification of the duty solicitor scheme is given, but the duty solicitor is unavailable or not required; 6.3(c) and (d) appear to be expressed as alternatives, but the draughtsman's intention must surely be that the police cannot obtain the detainee's consent to be interviewed merely by failing to inform him or her of the scheme.

The ruling of the Court of Appeal in *Hughes* (1988), however, suggested that if the police misled the suspect without bad faith a resultant consent would be treated as genuine. The appellant, disappointed of obtaining advice from his own solicitor, enquired about the duty solicitor scheme but was informed, erroneously, (but in good faith) that no solicitor was available. Under this misapprehension he gave consent to be interviewed and the Court of Appeal took the view that his consent was not thereby vitiated. Code C 6.3(c) and (d) were treated as alternatives and the fact that the detainee was within (c) did not vitiate his consent under (d). Thus, no breach had occurred.

Generally, consent to forego a right should be treated with caution when the parties are on an unequal footing; and the possible unfairness is exacerbated when the party who will obtain an advantage from the consent gives false information in obtaining it. Had the Court of Appeal found itself able to hold that such consent is not true consent the onus would have been placed on the police to ensure that administrative practice in relation to the duty solicitor scheme was tightened up. As it is, moves towards obtaining consent in similar circumstances may become more marked and it is likely to be the more suggestible detainee who suffers.

After the 1991 revision, once the suspect has changed his mind about having advice, the interview can proceed subject to the need to obtain the permission of an officer of the rank of inspector or above. This is the only real change from the original Code and it is obviously not a full safeguard against the possibility of pressure from the police considered above. Inclusion of a provision that a consent based on erroneous information given by the police could not be treated as true consent might have avoided a recurrence of the *Hughes* type of situation. A provision included in the 1991 Home Office Circular requiring a note to be made in the custody record of the reason for the suspect's change of heart, may allow a court to determine whether the consent *was* based on misleading information and this Circular provision, in the form of a requirement to record the reason for the change of mind and repeat it on tape, became part of para 6.5 under the 1995 revision to Code C. This provision may allow a court to determine whether the consent *was* based on misleading information, but it leaves open the possibility of treating the consent as valid so long as such information was apparently given in good faith.

9.10.5   Debarring solicitors' clerks

Under Code C 6.12, if the solicitor who has been contacted decides to send a clerk, he or she should be admitted to the police station. However, since the decision of the Court of Appeal in *Chief Constable of Avon ex p Robinson* (1989), access to a clerk can be denied in a wide range of circumstances. The Chief Constable had issued instructions that the character and antecedents of certain unqualified clerks employed by the applicant – a solicitor – were such as to make their presence at police interviews with suspects undesirable. The Chief Constable left the final decision on access to the officer in question but gave his opinion that it would only rarely be appropriate to allow these particular clerks access to a suspect. The applicant sought judicial review of the instructions, contending that they were in breach of Code C 6.9 (now Code C 6.12).

The Court of Appeal considered the scope of the express exception to Code C 6.9: 'the clerk shall be admitted unless an officer of the rank of inspector or above considers that such a visit will hinder the investigation of crime'. It was held that the investigating officers had been entitled in each instance to invoke the exception because they had known of the criminal activities of the clerks. They had been informed of such activities by the Chief Constable but he had not imposed a blanket ban on the clerks; the discretion to debar the clerks had been left with the officers concerned; accordingly, there had been no breach of Code C 6.9. The police would be entitled to exclude a clerk if he appeared incapable of giving advice due to his age, appearance, mental capacity or known background.

The concern as to the results of employing these untrained clerks is understandable but the result of this decision is to confer a very wide power on the police to exclude clerks which may have unfortunate consequences. If the police take advantage of its width to exclude clerks rather too readily, some detainees may be likely to experience substantial delay in obtaining advice. The 1995 revision addresses this possibility to some extent: the proposed changes to para 6.12 will restrict the grounds for exclusion as far as clerks or other accredited representatives of solicitors are concerned since it defines such persons as 'solicitors'. This means that the trainee, clerk or legal executive is 'accredited in accordance with the Law Society's scheme for accreditation'. Therefore the more restrictive provisions relating to exclusion from the interview of solicitors, paras 6.9, 6.10 and 6.11 will apply. The broad discretion to exclude advisers from the police station under paras 6.12 and 6.13 will still, however, apply to non-accredited or probationary representatives so that it will be hard ever to challenge a decision to exclude such persons, leaving open the possibility that officers may at times exercise this power rather too readily. Once advice is delayed a detainee may succumb to pressure to forego it in order to speed matters up. However, the real answer to this difficulty seems to be that *solicitors* should provide advice; this is discussed below in relation to the *quality* of advice given.

There seem to be two main weaknesses in the scheme as it stands – the ease of evading its provisions, and the quality of advice given – which may mean that right to legal advice is little more valuable to the suspect than it was prior to PACE. If so, the balance between suspects' rights and police powers is not being maintained.

9.10.6   Improving the scheme

Various suggestions for reform of the legal advice scheme have already been made which could bring about significant improvement without necessitating a radical change. There are other possibilities: ploys could be discouraged and untrue allegations by suspects of lack of notification of advice precluded if, as proposed by the 1993 Royal Commission, the booking in stage were video or audio-taped. Such an innovation could be used in conjunction with the para 6.4 prohibition of attempts to dissuade the suspect to forego advice. Inadequate notification of advice could be characterised as an attempt at persuasion to forego it on the ground that it was intended to and did have that effect. Finally, and very importantly, notification of legal advice could take place on arrest or even on caution, thereby harmonising the position of all suspects. Clearly, such changes would not ensure that all suspects who needed it received advice; the process of delivering advice would still remain in the hands of a body which has an interest in withholding it, while many suspects would continue to need disinterested advice regarding the decision whether to have advice'.

Improvement in the quality of advice can be brought about only by an increase in funding for the scheme. It may be argued that only solicitors should offer advice but until sufficient funding is available solicitors will delegate this function. The Royal Commission proposed in 1993 that the performance of solicitors should be monitored, and that the police should receive training in the role solicitors are expected to play (proposals 64–69).

9.11 The right to silence: relationship with access to legal advice

It is generally thought that the provision of legal advice to the suspect in police custody is one of the most fundamental rights provided by PACE. This is partly due to the relationship between access to legal advice and the right to silence. This is a complex relationship but the available research seems to lend some support to the following propositions. The suspect will be fully aware of the need to remain silent at times and of the risks involved in so doing if he has had advice, especially if the legal advisor attends the interview. He or she may sometimes advise silence despite the risks involved and may help the suspect to maintain silence where advice alone might not be enough. It should be recognised, however, that the key question is not whether the presence of a legal advisor's means that the detainee remains silent but whether it means that he is unlikely to make an unreliable confession. Further, assuming for the moment an inverse correlation between a legal advisor's presence and an unreliable confession, what contribution to it, if any, is made by the curtailed right to silence? Obviously the detainee will not make such a confession if he remains silent but this is a rather crude and in any event ineffective way of tackling the risk of such confessions; the real concern here is with the question whether the legal advisor's will enable the detainee to maintain a selective silence or refuse to depart from his version of events at key points in the interview.

A study conducted in 1993 by Hodgson and McConville for the Royal Commission on Criminal Justice found, not surprisingly, that the relationship between legal advice and the right to silence was affected by the *quality* of the advice given. The research found that many 'legal advisors' are clerks, secretaries and former police officers with no legal education or training in the provision of custodial legal advice. Thus the mere fact that a person labelled a 'legal advisor' turns up at the police station and may be present in the interview may have little impact in terms of evening up the balance of power between suspect and police officer. Indeed, the presence of such a person may be to the *disadvantage* of the suspect as it may offer a reassurance which it does not warrant. This possibility was the subject of comment in *Glaves* (1993): it was noted that the legal advisor had done nothing but take notes during the interview of a juvenile in which oppressive tactics were used.

Thus, despite the general perception that legal advice reduces the likelihood that unreliable confessions will be made, it is only possible to suggest that the advisor may ensure that the client is aware of the curtailed right to silence and may sometimes advise that he exercises it, especially where the client does not seem able to cope with the interview. In this context it is worth bearing in mind that it tends to be a feature of cases in which a miscarriage of justice has occurred – such as that of the Birmingham Six and *Silcott* (1991) – that the confessions were uttered in the absence of a legal adviser. This has not been invariably the case; the confessions gained by oppression in the case of the Cardiff Three, *Miller* (1991), were obtained in the presence of a solicitor.

The presence of a solicitor can affect the likelihood that the confession will be reliable in other ways. The suspect may feel generally reassured due to the presence of a person independent of the police who is undaunted by the interview process. Moreover, his or her presence may sometimes be a potent factor discouraging use of improper tactics, and may help to alter the balance of power between interviewer and interviewee, thus tending to create a climate in which an unreliable confession is less likely to be uttered. Reassurance deriving from the presence of a solicitor is not merely valuable in terms of the reliability of the confession; it may serve to make the whole experience of police detention less traumatic and daunting. In theory the advisor will intervene if the interview is conducted in an intimidatory fashion or if other improper tactics are used.

In particular, curtailment of the right to silence may tend to affect the nature of custodial legal advice. It may change the role of the legal advisor in the police station; that role is already, it seems, interpreted in a variety of ways by advisors, but in circumstances where silence would previously have been advised by most of them it seems likely that in future it may not be. Possibly the difficulty of advising the client as to when to remain silent and when not to take the risk of so doing may mean that some advisors tend to adopt the role of referee or counsellor rather than that of legal advisor. The advisor's most obvious concern may in future be to check on adherence to the PACE scheme at various stages in the process and to offer reassurance and support to the client.

However, the availability of legal advice may not always have such effects. Sanders criticised the great variation in practice between solicitors, and considered that too many gave telephone advice only, thereby depriving the client of most of the benefits of legal advice. Research conducted in 1993 for the Royal Commission echoed these findings as to the quality of advice and suggested that solicitors were adopting a passive stance in interviews, failing to intervene where intervention was clearly called for. Professor McConville found that the presence of some advisors in interviews may have had a detrimental impact on suspects: 'Lacking any clear under-standing of their role in the process, some advisers simply become part of the machine which confronts the suspect.'

9.11.1   Curtailment of the right to silence: implications

It might appear that the right to silence would have a significant impact on the conduct of the interview and would ensure that a suspect had a bulwark against giving in to pressure to speak. In fact, few suspects refuse to answer questions and silence is not routinely advised by legal advisors. The main reason for retaining the right to silence is that the suspect may be under stress and unable to assess the situation clearly; he or she may have a number of reasons for reluctance to speak including fear of incriminating another, and uncertainty as to the significance of various facts. It is generally thought that pressure on the suspect in police interviews is already high and is not compensated for by other factors such as tape recording and access to legal advice; thus the large body of writing on the right to silence generally comes down on the side of its retention.

The Royal Commission Report 1993 favoured retention with some modification; it considered that once the prosecution case was fully disclosed defendants should be required to offer an answer to the charges made against them at the risk of adverse comment at trial on any new defence they then disclose. This proposal would deal with the 'ambush defence', often put forward as one of the reasons for abolishing the right to silence, while leaving the right itself intact in the investigation as a safeguard against undue police pressure to speak.

Sections 34–37 of the Criminal Justice and Public Order Act 1994 brought about curtailment of the right to silence in the police interview, and the caution under para 10 of Code of Practice C made under the Police and Criminal Evidence Act 1984 was accordingly revised. Curtailment of the right to silence rather than abolition is referred to since it is suggested that the common law right of silence which received recognition in Code C para 10.4 has only been curtailed by the provisions of ss 34–37 and that in so far as it has not been expressly abolished it will continue to exist.

The general caution under para 10.4 of revised Code C, which answers to the provisions of s 34 of the 1994 Act, provides in essence that a person may remain silent but if he or she holds back matters which are later used as a defence in court the defence may be harmed. Further special cautions have been adopted under para 10.5A of revised Code C which answer to the provisions of ss 36 and 37 of the 1994 Act. Paragraph 10.5A provides that adverse inferences may be drawn from a failure to account for possession of substances or objects, or presence at a particular place.

The Runciman Commission considered that abolition of the right to silence might create the risk that wrongful convictions would be obtained. Some suspects, in particular vulnerable and suggestible persons interviewed outside the police station, may be confused by the caution (usually the 10.4 caution since it can be used before arrest) and without the benefit of legal advice may be pressurised into making inaccurate and ill-considered admissions.

Persons interviewed outside the police station who remain silent in the face of the caution, perhaps confused by its contradictory message – you need not speak but on the other hand it may be dangerous not to – may find that adverse inferences are drawn at court although had they had legal advice they might not have made admissions. This may also be true of those who do not have legal advice in the police station either because they choose not to or because they were encouraged to forego it. However, in such circumstances the defence might be able to put forward a sound argument that it would not be proper for a court to draw adverse inferences from silence.

Inferences may only be drawn from silence if a sound explanation for silence is not put forward. In other words, it cannot be inferred that the reason for silence was the need to concoct a defence or a false explanation of incriminating factors if the real and innocent reason for silence is put forward. It might be argued that the defendant interviewed without legal advice (perhaps in breach of the legal advice scheme or in the street) had needed the presence of a legal advisor partly in order to provide support and partly to advise on his or her response to the new-style caution. The defendant might argue that lacking such support and advice he or she had stayed silent, uncertain under pressure what to say. Alternatively, a defendant might argue that he had stayed silent until aware of the prosecution case; a judge might accept that in the circumstances that was reasonable (since the question of what is reasonable in the circumstances can properly be taken into account under s 34) and would not allow the drawing of adverse inferences.

As a further alternative, a defendant unlawfully denied legal advice might argue under s 78 that the fact of silence should be excluded from evidence so that no adverse inferences could be drawn from it on the basis that had he had legal advice he would not have remained silent. Of course, it would be open to the prosecution to argue that the breach could make no difference to the situation since the drawing of adverse inferences could be no more damaging to the defendant than admissions would have been, but in turn this argument would appear to depend on the nature of the explanations or admissions which it is argued would have been made.

| 9.11.2 | Advising silence under the new regime |

It is not suggested that under the new regime created by ss 34, 36 and 37 of the 1994 Act silence would never be advised. Some advisors in the particular circumstances of the case may still consider that advice to remain silent at certain points in the interview is appropriate even in the face of the knowledge that such silence may be commented on adversely in court. For example, an inexperienced suspect may feel that he or she must make admissions in response to the new style caution, but an experienced advisor, weighing up the situation, may feel that in the particular circumstances the suspect will be more severely disadvantaged by speaking than by remaining silent. Also, if an innocent or apparently innocent suspect is disbelieved by police, an advisor may consider that the safest course for him to adopt is to remain silent. This might also be the case if a suspect was becoming emotional and confused. Although staying silent carries risks it is less risky than making ill-considered admissions.

Apart from these possibilities, the questioning, although still in some way relevant to the offence, may be directed to aspects of the situation which may appear to fall outside the provisions of ss 34, 36 or 37 of the 1994 Act. This would seem to be the case if is not intended to elicit either an explanation of the presence of a substance which has been discovered or of the suspect's presence in a particular place or a possible defence which might be put forward later.

Further, the advisor might consider that in certain circumstances adverse inferences would not be drawn later on at court from a failure to answer questions and therefore might consider it safe to advise the client to remain silent. Under s 34(1)(b) inferences may only be drawn from a failure to disclose facts which in the circumstances existing at the time the suspect could reasonably have been expected to mention. Under all three sections only 'proper' inferences may be drawn. If there was an uncertainty as to the case the prosecution might be likely to rely, on the advisor might argue that the suspect could not reasonably be expected to mention a defence in those circumstances. Alternatively he or she might consider that it would not be proper to draw inferences from a failure to mention a fact which he might wish subsequently to rely on since the only inference which could 'properly' be drawn was that the was uncertain as to the prosecution case. The right to silence may therefore still apply in relation to questioning falling within such unprovided for areas. Moreover, it probably still exists prior to the giving of the caution (this seems to be implied by s 34(1)(a) of the 1994 Act). In other words, the residual common law right to silence referred to above may still enjoy a narrow existence at certain points in the process and in some circumstances.

It is possible that curtailment of the right to silence under ss 34, 36 and 37 of the 1994 Act may breach Article 6 of the ECHR on the basis that it infringes the presumption of innocence under Article 6(2) and/or on the basis that it infringes the right to freedom from self incrimination which the court has found to be covered by the right to a fair hearing under Article 6(1) (*Funke v France* (1993)). In *Saunders v UK* (1994) the Commission found that the applicant's right to freedom from self-incrimination had been infringed in that he had been forced to answer questions put to him by Inspectors investigating a company takeover or risk the imposition of a criminal sanction. The ruling of the court is awaited. In *Murray (John) v UK* (1994), on the other hand, the Commission did not find that Article 6(1) had been breached where inferences had been drawn at trial from the applicant's refusal to give evidence.

9.11.3   The right to silence and Article 6 of the European Convention on Human Rights

9.11.4   The right to silence:
          serious fraud cases

In one group of cases – those involving serious fraud – the right to silence had already been eroded prior to the coming into force of ss 34, 36 and 37 of the 1994 Act. If, for example, enquiries are made into a failed business its owner may receive a 's 2 notice' from the Serious Fraud office issued under the Criminal Justice Act 1987 which means that he or she will commit a criminal offence if he or she does not attend for interview and answer questions. Also if the company is being investigated he or she may have to answer questions under s 432(2) of the Companies Act 1985 and it seems will again commit a criminal offence if he or she refuses to do so.

In *Director of the Serious Fraud Office ex p Smith* (1992) after Mr Smith had been charged with an offence under s 458 of the Companies Act 1985 the Director of the Serious Fraud Office (SFO) decided to investigate him, and served a notice on him under the Criminal Justice Act 1987 s 2(2) requiring him to attend for an interview. He was informed that he would not be cautioned but would be obliged to answer questions truthfully, and that his replies could be used in evidence against him if anything he said at his trial was inconsistent with them. He applied for judicial review and the House of Lords found that the powers under s 2 operated *even after* charge on the basis that Parliament had clearly intended to institute an inquisitorial regime. Thus, even though the prosecutor must have thought that there might well already be sufficient evidence to convict, questioning could continue. Did this mean it could continue up to and even during the court hearing? The House of Lords thought not, but nevertheless it was clear that it could do so up until *some* point at which the trial was obviously imminent. Obviously the answers given would be used at trial. Thus this decision eroded the right to silence not only in the police interview, but to an extent also at trial.

Saunders (1995) also concerned the existence of the right to silence in serious fraud investigations. Inspectors of the Department of Trade and Industry interviewed Saunders regarding allegations of fraud. They acted under s 437, Companies Act 1985 which provides for a sanction against the person being investigated if he or she refuses to answer questions. Thus Saunders lost his privilege against self-incrimination, which he argued was unfair and amounted to an abuse of process. He further argued that the transcript of answers given should have been found inadmissible under s 78 of the Police and Criminal Evidence Act 1984. It was found that Parliament had eroded the privilege against self-incrimination in relation to DTI interviews and therefore that ground alone could not provide a basis for finding that an abuse of process had occurred. In relation to exclusion of the interviews the House of Lords considered the relevance of Article 6 of the European Convention in Human Rights which provides *inter alia* that the presumption of innocence must not be eroded. However, domestic law was unambiguous and therefore must be applied regardless of Article 6. However, in exercising discretion under s 78 the judge could take into account the question whether the statutory regime in question had created unfairness. In the particular circumstances it was found that admission of the evidence did not render the trial unfair. The appeal was therefore dismissed.

This decision will clearly have no impact in terms of curbing the erosion of the privilege against self-incrimination which has been brought about under the particular statutory regime in question. That regime is to an extent in accord with the general regime now in place under ss 34, 36 and 37 of the Criminal Justice and Public Order Act 1994. As mentioned in the instant case, the *Saunders* case has been declared admissible by the European Commission on Human rights which has also given its opinion that the domestic law in question breached Article 6. The European Court of Human Rights is due to rule on the matter imminently. If it finds that the regime in question is in breach of Article 6, this might appear to call into question the provisions under the Criminal Justice and Public Order Act 1994. However, it is possible that the government response to any such ruling would relate only to the powers of DTI Inspectors and would leave the general regime curtailing the right to silence intact.

The recording of police interviews must be one of the most rapidly developing areas of policing. The recent introduction of tape recording replacing contemporaneous note-taking may soon be overtaken by video taping; if so the process will have gone as far as technology will presently allow it to go. Commentators have given video taped interviews a cautious welcome; criticism has largely been directed towards the difficulty of ensuring that they are not subverted by 'informal' contacts between police and suspect, rather than at the quality of the recordings. Arguably such difficulties are endemic in the interviewing scheme as currently conceived regardless of the recording technique used.

9.12   Conduct of the interview and recording methods

There seems to be a tendency in some quarters to see developments in recording techniques as going a long way towards solving the problem of unreliable confessions. However, it is important not to over-emphasise the value of recording techniques at the expense of provisions which may have a more direct effect on their reliability. Improvement in the recording provisions is not aimed directly at promoting the reliability of a confession but at allowing a court to consider an accurate record of it and to assess what occurred when it was made.

In contrast to the success of the scheme in this direction there has been little development in the area of provisions able to affect what occurred; PACE does not attempt to regulate the conduct of the interview except in so far as such regulation can be implied from the provision of s 76 that confessions obtained by oppression or in circumstances likely to render them unreliable will be inadmissible. Obviously the provisions governing detention and the physical comfort of the detainee have relevance in this context; they provide the setting for the interrogation and remove from the situation some of the reasons why a suspect might make an unreliable confession. But once their limits have been set they cannot influence what occurs next, and it seems that use of intimidation, haranguing, use of indirect threats is still quite common especially in interviews with juveniles.

The 1992 Royal Commission which reported in June 1993, put forward proposals which would affect the conduct of the interview with a view to ensuring that police officers would perceive its purpose to be the discovery of the truth rather than obtaining a confession. Such proposals were thought to be particularly relevant after the evidence of use of bullying techniques in interrogations which arose from the post PACE case of *Miller* (the Cardiff Three) 1991. It appears that some police forces have put on courses designed to improve interview techniques with a view to anticipating the Royal Commission findings.

9.13   Identification of suspects

The identification procedure is governed by the provisions of Code D which has as its overall aim the creation of safeguards against wrongful identification, bearing in mind that mistaken identification can be a very significant cause of wrongful convictions. It also contains provisions which are intended to safeguard vulnerable groups and to ensure that the invasion of privacy represented by some methods of identification is kept to a minimum consistent with the Code's overall aim. Many of the procedures will only take place with the suspect's consent, although if consent is not forthcoming this may be used in evidence against him or her. In the case of a mentally handicapped or disordered person consent given out of the presence of the 'appropriate adult' will not be treated as true consent, while the consent of a juvenile alone will not be treated as valid if the adult does not also consent (Code D para 1.11). Identification can take place by various means which include by witness, by fingerprints and by the taking of samples from the body of the suspect.

If identification is to be by witness the following methods of identification may be used: a parade; a group identification; a video film; or a confrontation. A group identification consists of allowing the witness an opportunity of seeing the suspect in a group of people and it should, if practicable, be held in a place other than a police station (for example, in an underground station or shopping centre). The suspect will be asked to consent to a group identification but where consent is refused the identification officer has the discretion to proceed with a group identification if practicable. Under para 2.13 if neither a parade nor a video identification nor a group identification procedure is arranged, the suspect may be confronted by the witness and such a confrontation does not require the suspect's consent, but it may not take place unless none of the other procedures are practicable.

9.13.1   Witness identification

A parade must be used if the defendant requests it and it is practicable. A parade may also be held if the officer in charge of the investigation considers that it would be useful, and the suspect consents. The aim is to use the best means of identification available; therefore if it is impracticable to use a parade the police may move on to a group identification; they cannot merely move straight to the last possible method – a confrontation. However, there is uncertainty as to when it could legitimately be said to be impracticable to hold an identification parade. In *Ladlow, Moss, Green and Jackson* (1989) 20 suspects had been arrested and the confrontation method of identification used as otherwise it would allegedly have been necessary to hold 221 separate parades. Despite this it was ruled that evidence derived from the confrontations would be excluded.

Under Code D para 3 a person may be identified by fingerprints if he or she consents or without consent under s 61 PACE which also allows the use of force. A person may also be identified by body samples, swabs and impressions. An intimate sample may only be taken if an officer of the rank of superintendent or above has reasonable grounds to believe that such an impression or sample will tend to confirm or disprove the suspect's involvement in a recordable offence and with the suspect's written consent (para 5).

9.13.2   Identification by fingerprints or bodily samples

However, the suspect will be warned that a refusal may be treated, in any proceedings against him, as corroborating relevant prosecution evidence (para 5.2 and Note 5A). He must also be reminded of his entitlement to have free legal advice and the reminder must be noted in the custody record. Under para 5 intimate samples can only be taken by a registered medical or dental practitioner whereas non-intimate samples may be taken by a police officer. They may be taken without consent if an officer of the rank of superintendent or above has reasonable grounds for believing that the sample will tend to confirm or disprove the suspect's involvement in a recordable offence (para 5.5). This paragraph takes account of the new provision to this effect under s 63 of PACE as amended by s 56 of the Criminal Justice and Public Order Act 1994. A juvenile has the right to have the appropriate adult present when such procedures are undergone unless he or she requests otherwise in the presence of the adult (para 1.14).

9.14   Redress for police impropriety: exclusion of evidence

This chapter has been concerned so far with the question of the balance to be struck between the exercise of powers by the police in conducting an investigation on the one hand, and safeguards for the suspect against abuse of power on the other. As we have seen, PACE sets out to maintain this balance by declaring certain standards for the conduct of criminal investigations. However, it may be that an investigation does not, at certain points, reach those standards. Obviously the police may sometimes feel hampered by all the provisions of Code C; they may feel that they are close to obtaining a confession from a detainee, but that in order to obtain it they need to bend the rules a little. In such circumstances, if the rules are broken, various methods of redress are available, of which the most significant is exclusion of evidence. An example may illustrate the effect of exclusion of evidence.

Assume that the police have arrested a man on suspicion of theft. They are certain that he is guilty and think that they have a good chance of getting him to confess. However, he asks for legal advice. The police think that a solicitor may advise him to remain silent or may at least help him to withstand aggressive questioning and so they tell him (untruthfully) that the duty solicitor is unavailable and that they might as well get on with the interrogation rather than prolong the process. They then question him for four hours without a break. Eventually, he succumbs to the pressure and makes a full confession to theft.

The police have breached Code C (paras 6.5 and 12.7) and the suspect does have a means of redress. He can make a complaint (see below), but whether he pursues this means of redress or not the flawed interrogation will continue to produce consequences for him; it will probably lead to a trial, a conviction and imprisonment. He may, of course, decide to plead guilty. But if he pleads not guilty his counsel may ask the judge at the trial not to admit the confession in evidence on the basis that the interrogation which produced it was conducted unfairly.

The trial judge could then ensure that the original abuse of power on the part of the police produced no more consequences for the detainee. It may not lead to a conviction and imprisonment if the judge refuses to admit the confession in evidence (depending on any other evidence against the defendant). The judge can hold a *voir dire* (a trial within a trial) by sending out the jury and then hearing defence and prosecution submissions on admitting the confession. If it is not admitted the jury will never know of its existence and will determine the case on the basis of any other available evidence. The judge is in a difficult position. On the one hand it is apparent that the police have abused their powers; the judge does not want to condone such behaviour by admitting evidence gained thereby. On the other, the prosecution case may collapse and a possibly guilty man walk free from the court if the confession is excluded.

If the defendant did commit the theft it might be said that the end in view – the conviction – justifies the means used to obtain it, but should the judge ignore the fact that the confession might not be before the court at all had the police complied with Code C? Should the judge merely consider the fate of one defendant in isolation? If the confession is admitted the judge is in effect making a public declaration that the courts will not use their powers to uphold standards for police investigations. The result may be that in future the PACE standards are not adhered to and that, occasionally, an innocent citizen is convicted after a false confession has been coerced from him. The multiplicity of issues raised by examples of this nature have provoked a long-running debate among academics and lawyers as to the purpose of excluding evidence which has been obtained improperly, and three main schools of thought have arisen.

The first such school advocates the 'reliability principle' and argues that evidence should be excluded only if it appears to be unreliable, ie in the case of a confession, untrue. Taken to its logical conclusion this would mean that if a true confession has been extracted by torture it should nevertheless be admitted. This is argued on the basis that the function of a criminal court is to determine the truth of the charges against the accused, not to enquire into alleged improprieties on the part of the police. It is not equipped to conduct such an enquiry; therefore if evidence is excluded on the basis that impropriety occurred in the investigation the reputation of the police officer in question is damaged after a less than full

9.14.1   The 'reliability principle'

investigation into his or her conduct. Also, even if impropriety did occur in the investigation, this should not allow an obviously guilty defendant to walk freely from the court. On this argument, the court in admitting evidence obtained by improper methods is not condoning them: it is acknowledging that it is not within its function to enquire into them.

9.14.2	The 'disciplinary principle'

The second group advocates the 'disciplinary principle' on the basis that a court cannot merely inquire into the truth of the charges against a defendant: it must also play a part in maintaining standards in criminal investigations. The court has one particular part to play in the processing of the defendant through the criminal justice system: it should not play its brief part and ignore what has gone before. If the courts are prepared to accept evidence obtained by any methods the police may be encouraged to abuse their powers to the detriment of the citizen. Advocates of this principle have argued for either a deterrent or a punitive role for exclusion of evidence.

9.14.3	A 'protective principle'

A further possibility has been canvassed in the shape of a 'protective principle'. This argument is that once a legal system has declared a certain standard for the conduct of investigations, the citizen obtains corresponding rights to be treated in a certain manner. If such rights are denied and evidence gained as a result the court can wipe out the disadvantage to the defendant flowing from the denial by rejecting the evidence in question. If, for example, the defendant has made a confession because the police have failed to caution him or her, the judge could recreate the situation for the jury's benefit as it would have been had the caution been given, by excluding the confession. In the eyes of the jury the position would be as if the right had never been denied; the judge would therefore have succeeded in protecting the defendant's right to silence in the interrogation.

9.14.4	The common law position pre-PACE

The common law went some way towards endorsing the reliability principle. Illegally obtained evidence other than 'involuntary' confessions was admissible in a criminal trial. Involuntary confessions were inadmissible on the ground that if a defendant was in some way induced to confess during a police interrogation his confession might be unreliable. A confession would be involuntary if it was obtained by oppression or 'by fear of prejudice or hope of advantage exercised or held out by a person in authority' (*Prager* (1972)). According to the Court of Appeal in *Isequilla* (1975) 'oppression' denoted some impropriety on the part of the police, but the House of Lords in *Ping Lin* (1976) doubted whether such impropriety was necessary if the real issue was the reliability of the confession. Uncertainty as to the need for impropriety on the part of the police, and as to the kind of impropriety which could amount to oppression, allowed cases such as the *Confait* case (1977) to slip through the net. In that case, three young boys, one of them mentally handicapped, confessed to involvement in a murder they could not have committed after they had been denied both legal advice and the presence of an adult during the police interrogation. The confessions were admitted in evidence and led to the conviction of all three. They were finally exonerated seven years later.

The concept of fear of prejudice or hope of advantage was at one time interpreted strictly against the police and very mild inducements were held to render a confession involuntary. In *Zaveckas* (1969), for example, the Court of Appeal held that a confession had been rendered involuntary because the defendant had asked the police officer whether he could have bail if he made a statement. However, in the case of *Rennie* (1982) Lord Lane held that a confession need not be excluded simply because it had been prompted *in part* by some hope of advantage. This case paved the way for the relaxation of this rule which can be found in the PACE scheme on exclusion of evidence.

Physical evidence discovered as a result of an inadmissible confession was admissible; the police witness would have to state at the trial that after interviewing the defendant the evidence in question was discovered – in the hope that the jury would see the connection. In general, illegally obtained physical evidence, such as fingerprints, was admissible at common law unless the evidence had been tricked out of the detainee in which case there would be a discretion to exclude it. However, this rule did not include instances where the police had acted as agents provocateurs, entrapping the defendant into a crime he would not otherwise have committed (*Sang* (1980)).

PACE contains four separate tests under ss 76, 78 and 82(3) which can be applied to a confession to determine whether it is admissible in evidence. In theory, all four tests could be applied to a particular confession, although in practice it may not be necessary to consider all of them. There is a large area of overlap between all four tests; the courts have gone some of the way towards creating a distinct role for each but not all the way. In some circumstances a confession will obviously fail one of the two tests under s 76 and there will be no need to consider the other three. In others it will be worth considering

9.14.5   The PACE tests: introduction

all four tests. The scheme in respect of non-confession evidence is less complex: only ss 78 and 82(3) need be considered. Thus, PACE preserves the common law distinction between confessions and other evidence, on the basis that physical evidence will always be reliable (unless it has been 'planted' on the detainee) while a confession may not be. This is not however true of all non-confession evidence such as identification evidence which nevertheless can be considered only under ss 78 and 82(3). Physical evidence, which is discovered as a result of an inadmissible confession, will be admissible under s 76(4)(a).

9.14.6   Section 76(2)(a): the 'oppression' test

Section 76(2)(a) provides that where 'it is represented to the court that the confession was or may have been obtained by oppression of the person who made it … the court shall not allow the confession to be given in evidence against him except in so far as the prosecution proves to the court beyond reasonable doubt that the confession (notwithstanding that it may be true) was not obtained as aforesaid'.

This test derives from the rule as it was at common law: if the prosecution cannot prove beyond reasonable doubt that the police did not behave oppressively the confession produced is inadmissible. The judge has no discretion in the matter. The idea behind this is that threats of violence or other oppressive behaviour are so abhorrent that no further question as to the reliability of a confession obtained by such methods should be asked. This rule appears to have the dual function of removing any incentive to the police to behave improperly and of protecting the detainee from the consequences of impropriety if it has occurred. Under this head, once the defence has advanced a reasonable argument (*Liverpool Juvenile Court ex p R* (1987)) that the confession was obtained by oppression it will not be admitted in evidence unless the prosecution can prove that it was not so obtained. The reliability of a confession obtained by oppression is irrelevant: it matters not whether the effect of the oppression is to frighten the detainee into telling the truth or alternatively into lying in order to get out of the situation.

The only evidence given in the Act as to the meaning of oppression is the non-exhaustive definition contained in s 76(8): 'In this section 'oppression' includes torture, inhuman or degrading treatment, and the use or threat of violence (whether or not amounting to torture)'. The word 'includes' ought to be given its literal meaning according to the Court of Appeal in *Fulling* (1987). Therefore the concept of oppression may be fairly wide as was suggested by the definition offered by the court: 'the exercise of authority or power in a burdensome, harsh or wrongful manner; unjust or cruel treatment of subjects.' It thought that oppression would almost invariably entail impropriety on the part of the interrogator. However, the terms 'wrongful' and 'improper' used in this test could cover any unlawful action on the part of the police. This would mean that any breach of the Act or Codes could constitute oppression. This wide possibility has been pursued at first instance in *Davison* (1988), but the Court of Appeal in *Hughes* (1988) held that a denial of legal advice due not to bad faith on the part of the police but to a misunderstanding could not amount to oppression. In *Alladice* (1988) the Court of Appeal also took this view in suggesting, *obiter*, that an improper denial of legal advice, if accompanied by bad faith on the part of the police would certainly amount to 'unfairness' under s 78 and probably also to oppression. In *Beales* (1991) rather heavy-handed questioning accompanied by misleading suggestions, although not on the face of it a very serious impropriety, was termed oppressive because it was obviously employed as a deliberate tactic. A similar conclusion was reached in *Glaves* (1993) in relation to such questioning of a juvenile; there had also been a breach of Code C in that the 'appropriate adult' was not present, and this exacerbated the situation.

The general view appears then to be that the disciplinary function of s 76(2)(a) should take precedence over its protective function: the emphasis should be placed on the question of bad faith rather than on considering the fundamentality of the right denied and the effect of the denial on the detainee. It is, however, arguable that the protective principle should dominate – the test for oppression should depend partly on the nature of the right denied and partly on the effect of the denial on the detainee: particular susceptibility could be taken into account. If, for example, the detainee had been deprived of sleep for a substantial length of time or had been unlawfully strip-searched, it appears that such action could not on the present interpretation of s 76(2)(a) amount to oppression if these breaches of Code C had come about through some kind of administrative mix-up. Such mistreatment might have a significant impact on some detainees but a court could not automatically exclude the confession; it would have to go on to consider the likelihood of its reliability under s 76(2)(b).

This interpretation can be criticised because from the point of view of the detainee it matters little if mistreatment occurs because of an administrative mix-up, an innocent misconstruction of powers, or malice. Looking to the state of mind of the victim rather than that of the oppressor would enable account to be taken of the very great difference in impact of certain conduct on a young, inexperienced suspect and on a hardened, sophisticated criminal. However, at present the courts have not shown any desire to import a subjective assessment of oppression into s 76(2)(a).

However, it cannot be said that the Court of Appeal has consistently invoked s 76(2)(a) rather than s 78 when the police *have* deliberately misused their powers in obtaining a confession. In *Mason* (1987), for example, a trick played deliberately on the appellant's solicitor led to exclusion of the confession under s 78. Thus, bad faith appears to be a necessary but not sufficient condition for the operation of s 76(2)(a), whereas it will probably automatically render a confession inadmissible under s 78. Improper treatment falling outside s 76(8) and unaccompanied by bad faith could fall within s 76(2)(b) if the confession is likely to have been rendered unreliable thereby. The emphasis on bad faith at least gives an indication as to when improper behaviour on the part of the police will lead to automatic exclusion of the confession under s 76(2)(a), and when it will merely suggest the likelihood of unreliability under s 76(2)(b).

The bad faith must be accompanied by impropriety of a certain level of seriousness. A trivial breach of Code C, carried out deliberately, would not amount to oppression. In *Paris, Abdullahi and Miller* (1992) (the case of the 'Cardiff 3') the Court of Appeal quashed the convictions of the appellants for murder on the basis that their confessions had been obtained by oppression. Miller was interviewed for 13 hours; he denied his involvement in the offence over 300 times but was bullied by the officers into confessing. Physical violence was not used but the officers shouted at him in an intimidating manner what they wanted him to say. The court called this a travesty of an interview. This behaviour was clearly improper but it is not possible to determine with certainty at present the borderline between improper behaviour capable of being termed oppressive and non-oppressive improper behaviour. The obviousness of the bad faith may be relevant in making such a determination.

9.14.7   Section 76(2)(b): the 'reliability' test

Section 76(2)(b) provides that where a confession was or may have been obtained 'in consequence of anything said or done which was likely in the circumstances existing at the time, to render unreliable any confession which might be made by him in consequence thereof, the court shall not allow the confession to be given in evidence against him except in so far as the prosecution proves to the court beyond reasonable doubt that the confession (notwithstanding that it may be true) was not obtained as aforesaid'.

The 'reliability' test derives from the rule as stated in *Prager* on inducements to confess. However, as will be seen, it represents a relaxation of that rule as it was applied in *Prager*. It also works certain changes in the emphasis of the test. The test does not adopt the strict reliability approach explained above that a confession extracted by torture but determined to be true should be admitted in evidence. Instead it is concerned with objective reliability: the judge must consider the situation at the time the confession was made and ask whether the confession would be *likely* to be unreliable, not whether it *is* unreliable.

It must be borne in mind that if an offer of some kind is made to the detainee in response to an enquiry from him this will not render the subsequent confession unreliable under Code C 11.3, thus explicitly rejecting the *Zaveckas* approach. It is not necessary to show that there has been any misconduct on the part of the police; in *Harvey* (1988) a mentally ill woman of low intelligence may have been induced to confess to murder by hearing her lover's confession. Her confession was excluded as being likely to be unreliable. In *Harvey* the 'something said or done' (the first limb of the test under s 76(2)(a)) was the confession of the lover, while the 'circumstances' (the second limb) were the defendant's emotional state, low intelligence and mental illness). The 'something said or done' cannot consist of the defendant's own mental or physical state according to *Goldberg* (1988). In that case the defendant was a heroin addict who confessed because he was desperate to leave the police station and obtain a 'fix'. The contention of the defence counsel that the defendant's decision to confess prompted by his addiction amounted to 'something said or done' was not accepted by the court.

In many instances the 'something said or done' will consist of some impropriety on the part of the police, and in such instances a court will go on to consider whether any circumstances existed which rendered the impropriety particularly significant. The 'circumstances' could include the particularly vulnerable state of the detainee. In *Mathias* (1989) the defendant was particularly vulnerable because he had not been afforded legal advice, although an offer of immunity from prosecution had been made to him. The Court of Appeal held that the offer had placed him in great difficulty and that this was a situation in which the police should have ensured that he had legal advice. From the judgment it appears that if an inducement to confess is offered to the detainee the police should ensure that he or she can discuss it with a solicitor, even if the police are entitled to deny access to legal advice because the detainee falls within s 58(8) (see above at 9.10.1). Thus the 'circumstances' will be the lack of legal advice and the 'something said or done', the inducement.

The vulnerability may relate to a physical or mental state. In *Trussler* (1988) the defendant, who was a drug addict, had been in custody 18 hours, had been denied legal advice and had not been afforded the rest period guaranteed by Code C para 12. His confession was excluded as likely to be unreliable. In *Delaney* (1989) the defendant was 17, had an IQ of 80 and, according to an educational psychologist, was subject to emotional arousal which would lead him to wish to bring a police interview to an end as quickly as possible. These were circumstances in which it was important to ensure that the interrogation was conducted with all propriety. In fact, the officers offered some inducement to the defendant to confess by playing down the gravity of the offence and by suggesting that if he confessed he would get the psychiatric help he needed. They also failed to make an accurate, contemporaneous record of the interview in breach of Code C para 11.3. Failing to make the proper record was of indirect relevance to the question of reliability as it meant that the court could not assess the full extent of the suggestions held out to the defendant. Thus, in the circumstances existing at the time (the mental state of the defendant), the police impropriety did have the special significance necessary under s 76(2)(b). *Marshall* (1992) was to similar effect although it did not identify a specific breach of Code C: the defendant was on the borderline of subnormality and therefore after an interview accompanied by his solicitor he should not have been re-interviewed unaccompanied about the same matters.

From the above it appears that the 'circumstances existing at the time' may be circumstances created by the police (as in *Mathias*) or may be inherent in the defendant (as in *Delaney*). In other words, impropriety on the part of the police could go to either limb of the test, but a state inherent in the detainee (such as mental illness) can go only to the second limb (the 'special circumstances'). Thus a single breach of the interviewing rules, such as a denial of legal advice in ordinary circumstances, would not appear to fulfil both limbs of the test. On the other hand, a doubtful breach or perhaps no breach, but rather, behaviour of doubtful propriety, may fulfil the first limb where special circumstances satisfying the second exist.

So far, the courts have considered instances where something is said or done, in particularly significant circumstances, which increases the likelihood that a confession will be unreliable. However, s 76 might exceptionally be applicable where something is said or done which might affect a subsequent confession, but the circumstances are normal. The example was given above of a detainee who was deprived of sleep as a result of an administrative mix-up. Deprivation of sleep would be likely to render a confession unreliable but which 'circumstances' could be pointed to as existing at the time – the second limb of s 76(2)(b)? The answer would probably be that the ordinary police methods of interrogation, applied to a detainee who had been deprived of sleep, would amount to 'circumstances' falling within s 76(2)(b). Thus this would be an impropriety which could go to both limbs of the test. Such instances of breaches of Code C could also fall within s 78 as will be seen below. However, defence counsel would always argue the point first under s 76(2)(b) as the prosecution would then have the onus of proving beyond reasonable doubt that the deprivation of sleep had not taken place.

It must now be apparent that s 76(2)(b) could be used to exclude all confessions obtained by oppression. It may then be wondered why s 76(2)(a) exists at all. The principle lying behind the two heads of s 76 appears to be that some types of impropriety on the part of the police are so unacceptable that it would be abhorrent in a court to go on to consider the reliability of a confession gained by such methods. In other words, s 76(2)(a) speeds up a process which could be carried out under s 76(2)(b).

The words of s 76(2): (if) 'it is represented to the court that the confession was or may have been obtained' (by oppression or something conducive to unreliability) appear to import a causal link between the police behaviour (the 'something said or done' or the oppression) and the confession. If the police threaten the suspect with violence *after* he has confessed this will be irrelevant to admission of the confession. However, it is likely that under s 76(2)(a) the causal link will not be much scrutinised so long as the oppression precedes the confession, on the ground that the court is concerned with the oppressive behaviour and not with its effect on the detainee. This receives some support from the ruling in *Alladice* (1988); the Court of Appeal determined that the improper denial of legal advice had had no effect on the detainee but still found that had it been made in bad faith exclusion of the confession under s 76 might have been undertaken. The general rule appears then to be that where the causal link in question could not possibly exist s 76(2)(a) cannot be invoked, but in all other instances the fact that the confession was made subsequent to the oppression may be sufficient.

The question of causation under s 76(2)(b) appears, on the face of it, complex. From the wording of the section it appears to be necessary to adopt a two-stage test, asking firstly whether something was said or done likely in the circumstances to render any confession made unreliable,

9.14.8   Causation and the two
          heads of s 76

an objective test, and secondly whether that something caused the detainee to confess, a subjective test. In other words, something has happened which has been held previously to be likely to render a confession unreliable or would be likely to be so held, but did it actually cause *this* defendant to confess? Was the defendant in fact unaffected by the 'something said or done' and for his own reasons decided to confess (a decision which he now regrets)? However, at present the courts are content to ask the first question only, leaving the causal link to be assumed. This was the course adopted in *Mathias* and *Trussler*. It avoids the difficulty of second-guessing the defendant's motive in confessing. As will be seen below, this difficulty has had to be overcome under s 78.

| 9.14.9 | Relationship between ss 76 and 78 |

The need to identify some special factor in the situation in order to invoke either head of s 76 means that breaches of the interviewing rules unaccompanied by any such factor are usually considered under s 78. For example, in *Canale* (1990) the police breached the recording provisions and allegedly played a trick on the appellant in order to obtain the confession. Ruling that the confession should have been excluded under s 78, the Court of Appeal took into account the fact that the appellant could not be said to be weak-minded; it was therefore thought inappropriate to invoke s 76(2)(b). Moreover, allegedly fabricated confessions cannot fall within s 76(2) due to its requirement that something has happened to the defendant which causes *him* to confess; its terms are not therefore fulfilled if the defence alleges that no confession made by the defendant exists. Thus s 78 operates as a catch-all section, bringing within its boundaries many confessions which pass the tests contained in either head of s 76. It must be remembered, however, that s 78 only confers an exclusionary *discretion* on a judge.

| 9.14.10 | Section 78: the 'fairness' test |

Section 78 provides:

> In any proceedings the court may refuse to allow evidence on which the prosecution proposes to rely to be given if it appears to the court that, having regard to all the circumstances, including the circumstances in which the evidence was obtained, the admission of the evidence would have such an adverse effect on the fairness of the proceedings that the court ought not to admit it.

Thus s 78 can be used to exclude evidence if admitting it would render the trial unfair. In other words, admission of improperly obtained evidence will not *automatically* render the trial unfair, but under some circumstances it may seem that it will do so in which case it should be excluded.

The tests evolved for exclusion of confession evidence after breaches of PACE have become more sophisticated and complex than those in relation to other forms of impropriety; therefore the s 78 tests in relation to other forms of impropriety will be considered separately below. It is possible to identify four questions which tend to be asked when defence counsel suggests that s 78 should be invoked in these circumstances. The first question is whether a breach of the rules has occurred at all and then secondly whether it is significant and substantial. Once such a breach is found the third question to be asked will be whether admission of the confession gained during the improperly conducted interview will render the trial unfair. Usually, the fourth question will not need to be asked if the third is answered in the affirmative. However certain special features of the proceedings may lead a judge to go on to consider whether fairness to the prosecution nevertheless requires that the confession be admitted.

9.14.11 Section 78 and confessions obtained in breach of the interviewing rules

Before considering these questions it should briefly be noted that if the police have acted *deliberately* in breaching the rules the exercise under s 78 will be far less complex. Lord Lane CJ in *Alladice* (1988) stated that he would not have hesitated to hold that the confession should have been excluded had it been demonstrated that the police had acted in bad faith in breaching s 58. This approach appears to involve asking only whether a breach was accompanied by bad faith. If so, that would appear to be the end of the matter: exclusion of the confession will follow almost automatically.

The PACE interviewing scheme may be infringed or undermined in a variety of ways. In the paradigm case there may be a clear failure to put in place one of the safeguards such as access to legal advice or tape recording. For example, as in *Samuel* (1988), the police may deny the detainee access to legal advice on insufficient grounds. However, it is not always possible to identify such a clear breach of the rules. The interviewing scheme lends itself to many methods of infringement, some of which may occur at a low level of visibility, but which may nevertheless be of significance. For example, there may be breach of a rule contained in a Note for Guidance as opposed to PACE itself or Code C; there may be evasion or bending of a rule as opposed to breaking it, and instances where the interviewing scheme itself leaves it unclear whether or not a particular safeguard should have been in place at a given stage in the process. As already discussed, Note 11A which determines whether an exchange can be called an 'interview', (in which case more safeguards will apply) is not free from ambiguity.

9.14.12 Identifying a breach

9.14.13	Is the infringement substantial and significant?

In *Keenan* (1989) the Court of Appeal ruled that once a breach of the rules can be identified it will be asked whether it is substantial or significant. It found that a combination of breaches of the recording provisions satisfied this test. In contrast a breach of para 10.2 requiring a police officer to inform a suspect that he is not under arrest, is free to go, and may obtain legal advice has been held to be insubstantial (*Rajakuruna* (1991)). This view of para 10.2 seems to have been implicit in the ruling of the Court of Appeal in *Joseph* (1993), although a breach of para 10.5 in contrast was clearly found to be substantial and significant in order to merit exclusion of the confession.

In *Walsh* (1989) the Court of Appeal held that what was significant and substantial would be determined by reference to the *nature* of the breach except in instances where the police had acted in bad faith: 'although bad faith may make substantial or significant that which might not otherwise be so, the contrary does not follow. Breaches which are themselves significant and substantial are not rendered otherwise by the good faith of the officers concerned.'

This test has so far been applied only to Code provisions. It seems likely that breach of rules contained in Notes for Guidance or Home Office Circulars might fail it – assuming that a court was prepared to consider such breaches at all. However, in *DPP v Blake* (1989) the Divisional Court impliedly accepted that a Note for Guidance will be considered if it can be argued that it amplifies a particular Code provision and can therefore be of assistance in determining whether breach of such a provision has occurred. The question arose whether an estranged parent could be the appropriate adult at the interview of a juvenile under Code C para 13.1 (now para 11.14 under the revised Code); that provision was interpreted in accordance with Note 13C which describes the adult's expected role, and it was then found that para 13.1 had been breached. A variation on this view of the Notes which nevertheless supports the argument that they are unlikely to be considered in their own right was expressed by the Court of Appeal in *Cox* (1993) in relation to one of the most significant Notes, Note 11A. It was taken into account on the basis that it could be seen as *part* of para 11.1 and could thereby acquire the status of a paragraph.

It should be noted that once a breach has been identified in one interview it may 'taint' a subsequent interview (*Ismail* (1990)) although this will not inevitably be the case (*Glaves* (1993)).

Once a court has identified a substantial breach of the interviewing rules the third stage will depend on the function of the rule in question. Broadly speaking, two functions can be identified. Rules governing access to legal advice and the right to silence provide rights which are valuable in themselves as placing the suspect on a more even footing with police during the interview and perhaps as making it less likely that unreliable admissions will be made. In contrast, the Code C recording provisions may be said to be concerned only with the evidential integrity of the evidence rather than with providing rights valuable in themselves. Before a judge or jury can consider the truth or otherwise of a confession they must be able to be sure that an accurate record of it is before them; if it is possible that the police have fabricated part of it the enquiry into its truth cannot begin. Thus in determining whether breach of a rule would lead to unfairness at trial, its function will be relevant.

9.14.14   The unfairness at trial: general

If breach of such a rule has occurred it will be asked not whether the confession is reliable but whether it would have been made at all had the breach not occurred. This may seem odd; it might be thought that a court confronted with a confession which was properly recorded will be concerned only with its truth. However, had the courts confined such enquiries to the question of reliability the police might have been encouraged to ill-treat the detainee in the hope of obtaining a true confession. Taken to its extreme this approach would have sanctioned torture if the confession obtained appeared to be true. Thus the causal relationship between the breach and the confession has been used as a sieve which may exclude true or untrue confessions. This approach accords with that under s 76(2)(b) which inquires into the causal relationship between the 'something said or done' and the confession but not into its truth.

9.14.15   Unfairness at trial: breach of rules providing rights

The argument runs on these lines: if the unfairness had not occurred the defendant would not have confessed and the prosecution would not have been able to use the admissions in question against him or her at the trial. The significant and substantial impropriety which took place during or before the interview must have *caused* the defendant to confess, but it may be difficult to determine whether the defendant confessed for other reasons. Cases to be considered in this context are all concerned with breaches of the legal advice scheme but in principle a failure to caution could be treated in the same way as probably could any other breach of Code C *capable* of being causally related to the confession.

In *Samuel* (1988) the Court of Appeal found that the confession should have been excluded under s 78 because it was causally linked to the police impropriety – a failure to allow the appellant access to legal advice. In order to establish this point the solicitor in question gave evidence that had he been present he would have advised his client to remain silent in the last interview, whereas in fact he made damaging admissions in that interview which formed the basis of the case against him. It could not be said with certainty that he would have confessed in any event: he was not, it was determined, a sophisticated criminal who was capable of judging for himself when to speak and when to remain silent. Thus – although this was not made explicit – the Court of Appeal was prepared to make the judgment that a trial *would* be rendered unfair if a court associated itself with a breach of the PACE interrogation procedure.

The Court of Appeal in *Alladice* (1988), also faced with a breach of s 58, accepted that the key factor in exercising discretion under s 78 after a breach of the interrogation procedure was the causal relationship between breach and confession, and, by implication, between breach and fairness at the trial. On the basis of this factor it was determined that the confession had been *rightly* admitted despite the breach of s 58 because no causal relationship between the two could be established. This finding was based partly on the defendant's evaluation of the situation (that he only wanted the solicitor to see fair play and did not require legal advice), and partly on the fact that he had exercised his right to silence at certain points. Therefore, it was determined that he would have made the incriminating admissions in any event – even with the benefit of legal advice. Possibly this was surprising in view of the fact that the appellant, as the court itself accepted, was an unsophisticated criminal who did in fact make admissions in the absence of a solicitor which formed the basis of the case against him.

At times there has been a tendency for judges to move rather rapidly from a finding that the police have breached Code C to a determination that s 78 should be invoked without explicitly considering whether a causal relationship between the breach and the confession exists. Such a tendency can be discerned in the case of *Absolam* (1988) in which the Court of Appeal in finding that 'the prosecution would not have been in receipt of these admissions if the appropriate procedures had been followed' seemed to consider that the causal relationship between the impropriety and the admissions did exist. The chain of causation would have been fairly long – had the detainee been informed of his right to legal advice he would have exercised it; had he exercised it he would not have made the incriminating admissions – but the Court of Appeal did not make much attempt to scrutinise its links. However in *Walsh* (1989) the Court of Appeal reaffirmed the need to identify the causal relationship between the breach in question and the confession.

Deciding that an impropriety is causally linked to the confession does not of itself explain why admission of the confession will render the trial unfair, although it is perhaps reasonable to conclude that admission of a confession which is not so linked will *not* render the trial unfair. The necessary unfairness must arise due to admission of the confession, in other words *after* its admission; the unfairness in the interrogation cannot therefore satisfy this requirement. It has to be said that at present the courts have not addressed this problem. In *Samuel*, for example, the Court of Appeal merely stated:

> ... the appellant was denied improperly one of the most important and fundamental rights of the citizen ... if (the trial judge had found a breach of s 58 he would have determined that admission of evidence as to the final interview would have 'such an adverse effect on the fairness of the proceedings' that he ought not to admit it.

If fairness is interpreted very broadly it could be argued that if the court refuses to take the opportunity afforded by s 78 to put right what has occurred earlier in the process this will give an appearance of unfairness to the trial. This argument is based on the 'protective principle': if admissions gained in consequences of denial of a right (in the broad sense of an entitlement) are excluded the particular right is being protected in the sense that the defendant is being placed at trial – as far as the jury is concerned – in the position he or she would have been in had the right not been denied. If s 78 is, at least in part, concerned with ensuring fairness to the defence it is arguable that the court should take the opportunity offered to it of upholding the standards of fairness declared by PACE. However, if the police unfairness has had no consequences for the defendant the court need not exclude the confession as to do so would place him in a *more* favourable position than he would have been in had the proper standard of fairness been observed.

An alternative but allied argument would be that admitting the confession causes the trial to appear unfair because the court thereby appears to condone or lend itself to the original unfairness. The imprimatur of the court is necessary in order to allow the impropriety to bear fruit. If the trial is viewed, not as a separate entity, but as the culmination of a process in which the court and the police both play their part as emanations of the state, it can be argued that the court should refuse to lend itself to the unfairness which has gone before in order to ensure that the state does not profit from its own wrong. It cannot wipe out the unfairness but it can wipe out its consequence. But it need concern itself with the police unfairness only if that unfairness did have consequences. If it concerned itself with an inconsequential breach the reputation of the criminal justice system would again suffer as the detriment caused to society in allowing someone who has perpetrated a serious crime to walk free from the court would be perceived as entirely outweighing the detriment to the defendant caused by the breach.

9.14.16   Unfairness at trial: breach of recording rules

In contrast, once a substantial breach of a recording provision has been identified, a court will be likely to react by excluding the confession on the basis that it is impossible to be sure of its reliability. In other words, a jury may place reliance on an inaccurate record which clearly has little evidential value. An obvious example of such a breach is a failure to make contemporaneous notes of the interview in breach of Code C 11.5. The defence may then challenge the interview record on the basis that the police have fabricated all or part of it, or may allege that something adverse to the detainee happened during the interview which has not been recorded. The court then has no means of knowing which version of what happened is true, precisely the situation which Code C was designed to prevent. In such a situation a judge may well exclude the confession on the basis that it would be unfair to allow evidence of doubtful reliability to go before the jury. If, however, as in *Dunn* (1990) the defence has an independent witness to what occurred – usually a legal advisor – the judge may admit the confession as the defence now has a proper basis from which to challenge the police evidence.

It is fairly clear that allowing a confession which may have been fabricated to go before the jury may render a trial unfair: on the one hand the jury may rely on a confession which may be entirely untrue, while on the other, if the defendant alleges that the police fabricated the confession the prosecution can then put his character in issue and the jury may then hear of his previous convictions. The jury may then tend to rely on his convictions in deciding that his guilt is established on this occasion. In both circumstances the defendant is placed at a clear disadvantage.

9.14.17   Balancing fairness to the defence and the prosecution

As noted above, this fourth stage may not be necessary because, although fairness to the prosecution will be of *general* relevance at the third stage, it will not normally need to receive special consideration. The courts have assumed that the types of unfairness referred to above may render a trial unfair, but even where one of these types of unfairness could be identified a judge might exceptionally admit the confession because some particular feature of the trial proceedings made it necessary to do so in order to maintain the balance of fairness between prosecution and defence. In other words, if it was clear that in some way the prosecution was at a disadvantage which could be seen as equal to that experienced by the defendant, the judge might allow the confession to be admitted (*Allen* (1992)).

Of course, the impropriety in question may not involve a breach of the expressed PACE standard and although it might be said generally to subvert the PACE scheme it might involve a technique of a completely different nature. In *Mason* (1987) the defendant had been tricked into confessing to damaging his neighbour's car by the police who had falsely informed him and his solicitor that his fingerprints had been found on incriminating evidence. The Court of Appeal held that the confession should have been excluded under s 78: the trial judge had erred in omitting to take into account the deception practised on D's solicitor. The court appeared to view the deliberate deception practised by the police as the most significant factor without making it clear why the trial would be rendered unfair by admission of the confession gained thereby.

9.14.18   Other forms of impropriety

In *Bailey* (1993), in contrast, investigating officers and the Custody Officer put on a charade intended to convince the suspects who had been charged that they did not wish to place them both in the same cell which was bugged. This fooled the suspects who made incriminating admissions. It was submitted that the admissions should not have been admissible as undermining the spirit of Code C and especially the right to silence as the men could not have been questioned by police at that point. However, the Court of Appeal rejected this argument on the basis that the evidence was reliable and that the conversation between the suspects could not be equated with a police interview.

Section 82(3) provides:

9.14.19   Section 82(3): the common law discretion

> Nothing in this part of the Act shall prejudice any power of a court to exclude evidence (whether by preventing questions from being put or otherwise) at its discretion.

This presumably preserves the whole of the common law discretion to exclude evidence due to inclusion in it of the words 'or otherwise'. In practice its role as regards exclusion of evidence is likely to be insignificant due to the width of s 78. However, in *Sat-Bhambra* (1988) it was held that ss 76 and 78 only operate before the evidence is led before the jury but that s 82(3) can be invoked *after* that point. Zander assumes that the common law discretion to exclude evidence is contained in s 78 and that s 82(3) has therefore a merely residual role to play in preserving the judicial function of the judge in protecting witnesses or asking the jury to disregard evidence. In *O'Leary* (1988) May CJ expressed the view that s 82(3) rather than s 78 preserves the common law discretion to exclude unreliable evidence (presumably in circumstances falling outside s 76(2)(b)). However, it is hard to see how to separate the questions of the admissibility of unreliable evidence and of unfairness at the trial. Admission of unreliable evidence will always affect the trial. In *Parris* (1989) evidence which may have been fabricated by the police was excluded under s 78, not s 82(3). It appears likely that s 78 will be used as a means of excluding unreliable evidence if s 76(2)(b) cannot be invoked although this leaves no role for s 82(3) other than that suggested by Michael Zander.

9.14.20	Mentally handicapped or ill defendants	The confession of such defendants must be treated with especial caution. Section 77 provides that if the confession of a mentally handicapped person was not made in the presence of an independent person and if the case depends largely on the confession, the jury must be warned to exercise particular caution before convicting. (This does not apply to the mentally *ill* but the Royal Commission in its 1993 Report recommended that it should be extended to cover all categories of mentally disordered suspects.) In some such instances s 77 need not be invoked because the judge should withdraw the case from the jury. The Court of Appeal found in *McKenzie* (1992) that where the prosecution case depends wholly on confessions, the defendant is significantly mentally handicapped, and the confessions are unconvincing, the judge should withdraw the case from the jury.
9.14.21	Exclusion of non-confession evidence	The argument above has concentrated on exclusion of confession evidence but it must be borne in mind that non-confession evidence can also be excluded under s 78 or s 82(3) but not s 76. Where non-confession evidence is concerned the tests considered above will be relevant. For example, identification evidence is seen as particularly vulnerable: if some doubt is raised as to the reliability of the identification due to delay as in *Quinn* (1990) or to a failure to hold an identification parade where one was practicable as in *Ladlow* (1989), the identification evidence is likely to be excluded.

Although there is as yet less case law on the point than in relation to confessions it would be possible to divide the rules relating to identification according to function as has been done here in relation to confessions. For example, if no reminder as to the availability of legal advice was given before an identification was arranged it could be argued that the form of the identification used prejudiced the position of the defendant who would have asked for a different form had he had advice. It could be argued that no identification would have been made had the other form been used and that therefore the failure to remind of the right to advice was causally linked to the identification evidence obtained.

If bad faith is shown in conducting the identification procedure *Finley* (1993) suggests that the courts will react to it as they would in relation to confessions. It will mean that no causal relationship between the breach and the evidence obtained need be shown and, presumably, that the breach need not be substantial and significant. It may be argued that there is a stronger case than that considered above in relation to confessions, for treating bad faith shown during the identification process with particular stringency due to the appearance of unfairness created to the defendant, who may think that there has been collusion between witnesses and the police.

Theoretically the above argument (at para 9.13.15) as to the causal relationship between an impropriety and a confession (where bad faith is not shown) could be applied to *physical* evidence such as a weapon or drugs found on the suspect or his premises; in practice it appears that it will not be. The first instance decision in *Edward Fennelly* (1989) in which a failure to give the reason for a stop and search led to exclusion of the search appear to be on the wrong track. Furthermore, even if the principles developed under s 78 with respect to confession evidence could properly be applied to other evidence *Edward Fennelly* would still be a doubtful decision as no causal relationship could exist between the impropriety in question and the evidence obtained. According to *Thomas* (1990) and *Effick* (1992) physical evidence will be excluded only if obtained with deliberate illegality; the pre-PACE ruling of the House of Lords in *Fox* (1986) would also lend support to this contention.

9.15   Tortious remedies

Tort damages will be available in respect of some breaches of PACE. For example, if a police officer arrests a citizen where no reasonable suspicion arises under ss 24 or 25 of PACE an action for false imprisonment will be available. Equally such a remedy would be available if the Part IV provisions governing time limits on detention were breached. Trespass to land or to goods will occur if the statutory provisions governing search of premises or seizure of goods are not followed. Malicious prosecution will be available where police have abused their powers in recommending prosecution to the Crown Prosecution Service. Actions for malicious prosecution are quite common but as the ruling in *Glinskie v McIver* (1962) made clear, the plaintiff carries quite a heavy burden due to the need to prove that there was no reasonable or probable cause for the prosecution. It may be that if the prosecution is brought on competent legal advice this action will fail, but this is unclear.

Tortious remedies are becoming extremely significant in such instances perhaps due to a lack of confidence in the police complaints procedure. However, they are inapplicable to the provisions of the Codes under s 67(10). Thus, the fact that a stop and search is carried out in breach of Code A will not give rise to a tortious remedy. Most significantly, this means that almost the whole of the interviewing scheme, which is contained almost entirely in Codes C and E rather than in PACE itself, will be unaffected by tortious remedies.

This lack of a remedy also extends to some *statutory* provisions, in particular the most significant statutory interviewing provision, the entitlement to legal advice under s 58. There is no tort of denial of access to legal advice: the only possible tortious action would be for breach of statutory duty. Whether such an action would lie is a question of policy in relation to any particular statutory provision. At present the application of this remedy must be purely conjectural.

Theoretically, an action for false imprisonment might lie in respect of breaches of the interviewing provisions; argument could be advanced that where gross breaches of the statutory questioning provisions had taken place, such as interviewing a person unlawfully held incommunicado, a detention in itself lawful might thereby be rendered unlawful. However, although the ruling in *Middleweek v Chief Constable of Merseyside* (1985) gave some encouragement to such argument it now seems to be ruled out due to the decision in *Weldon v Home Office* (1991) in the context of lawful detention in a prison. It seems likely therefore that access to legal advice, like the rest of the safeguards for interviewing, will continue to be unaffected by the availability of tortious remedies.

9.16   Police complaints

The police complaints mechanism covers any breaches of PACE including breaches of the Codes under s 67(8) but it is generally agreed that it is defective as a means of redress. It does not allow for compensation to the victim or for the victim to attend any disciplinary proceedings. In any event most complaints do not result in disciplinary proceedings: as many as 30% of complaints are dealt with by informal resolution and commentators have suggested that unreasonable pressure may be put on complainants to adopt the informal resolution process. It appears that no disciplinary proceedings have been brought in respect of breaches of the Codes. The suspect concerned might in many instances be unaware that a breach of the Codes had occurred, and while theoretically another officer could make a complaint leading to disciplinary proceedings for such a breach, in practice this appears to be highly unlikely. When civil actions are brought successfully they may not result in disciplinary actions against police officers. Bringing a complaint may affect the civil action detrimentally as statements made in relation to the complaint may not be disclosed in civil proceedings, while by bringing it the plaintiff will have to disclose part of his or her case to the police.

The fundamental defect in the complaints system, despite the involvement (albeit limited) of the Police Complaints Authority (PCA), is that it tends to be perceived as being administered by the police themselves. Under s 84 PACE a complaint will go in the first instance to the Chief Officer of Police of the force in question who must determine by reference to the section whether or not he is the appropriate person to deal with it. A complaint must be referred to the PCA if it concerns serious misconduct and in addition there is a discretionary power to refer complaints to the PCA. It does not carry out the investigation itself in such cases but supervises it and receives a report at the end of it. Thus its role in relation to complaints is limited.

The disciplinary hearing itself may be perceived as unduly favourable to the officer in question due to the burden of proof – the criminal standard – and the low success rate. Moreover very few complaints lead to a hearing. Therefore a great deal of criticism has been directed against the whole police disciplinary process including the hearings and this has led the Royal Commission to propose that the burden of proof in such hearings should no longer be the criminal standard; it has not however made more radical proposals which might address the fundamental problems associated with this process. The perception that the system is not independently administered may generate a lack of confidence in it and mean that many complaints are not brought.

The perceived defects of the present system led the government to issue a consultation paper in April 1993 which included various proposals such as abolishing the criminal standard of proof in discipline cases and the double jeopardy rule which means that criminal proceedings against officers are not followed by disciplinary proceedings. However, an independent disciplinary system was not proposed. In its briefing guide in 1984 the Home Office stated that an independent system would be ineffective as it would probably be unable to obtain the confidence of police officers; friction might develop and thus public confidence in the system would be lost. On the other hand, if the independent body tried to cooperate with the police it might be perceived as losing its independence and would equally lose the confidence of the public. These findings have lost some of their credibility due to the fact that there is in any event some evidence of friction between police forces and the PCA; the Police Federation passed a motion of no confidence in the PCA at its annual conference in 1989.

Freedom of the Person and Police Powers

Section 1 of PACE provides a general power to stop and search persons or vehicles if reasonable suspicion arises that stolen goods, offensive weapons or other prohibited articles may be found. Under s 1(6) if an article is found which appears to be stolen or prohibited the officer can seize it. A stop and search will be unlawful unless the procedural requirements of ss 2 and 3 and Code A are met. The constable must give the suspect certain information before the search begins including 'his name and the name of the police station to which he is attached; the object of the proposed search; the constable's grounds for proposing to make it'. Under s 3 the constable must make a record of the search either on the spot if that is practicable or as soon as it is practicable. The subject of the search can obtain a copy of the search record later on from the police station.

Stop and search under PACE and under the Criminal Justice and Public Order Act 1994, s 60

Section 60 of the 1994 Act provides police officers with a further stop and search power which does not depend on showing reasonable suspicion of particular wrongdoing on the part of an individual.

PACE contains two separate powers of arrest without warrant, one arising under s 24 and the other under s 25. Section 24 provides a power of arrest in respect of more serious offences. Both are dependent on the concept of 'reasonable suspicion.' A police officer can arrest for one of the offences covered by s 24 if he or she has reasonable grounds to suspect that the offence is about to be, is being or has been committed. Section 25 covers *all* offences *if* certain conditions, known as the general arrest conditions, are satisfied. Therefore in order to arrest under s 25 *two* steps must be taken: first, there must be reasonable suspicion relating to the offence in question; second, one of the arrest conditions must be fulfilled.

Arrest under the Police and Criminal Evidence Act 1984

Edwards v DPP (1993)
Dallison v Caffrey (1965)
Castorina v Chief Constable of Surrey (1988)

A power to arrest arises at common law for breach of the peace. Also certain statutes expressly create specific powers of arrest which are not dependent on ss 24 or 25 PACE. The power to arrest under warrant arises under the Magistrates Court Act 1980 s 1.

Powers of arrest other than under PACE

R v Howell (1981)

Procedural requirements

For an arrest to be made validly, not only must the power of arrest exist, whatever its source, but the procedural elements must be complied with. Under s 28 PACE both the fact of and the reason for the arrest must be made known at the time or as soon as practicable afterwards.

DPP v Hawkins (1988)
Murray v Ministry of Defence (1988)

Searching of premises and seizure of property

A police officer may enter premises under s 17 in order to effect an arrest or under s 18 immediately after arrest for an arrestable offence if he has reasonable grounds for suspecting that evidence other than items subject to legal privilege relating to that offence or a connected arrestable offence is on the premises. A magistrate can also issue a search warrant under s 8 PACE if there are reasonable grounds for believing that a serious arrestable offence has been committed and where the material is likely to be of substantial value to the investigation of the offence. Under s 8(2) a constable may seize and retain anything for which a search has been authorised. The power of seizure without warrant under ss 18 and 19 allows seizure of anything which is on the premises if he has reasonable grounds for believing that it has been obtained in consequence of the commission of an offence or that it is evidence relating to any offence; and it is necessary to seize it in order to prevent the evidence being concealed, lost, altered or destroyed. If a search is under warrant it must be produced to the occupier. The owners of any property to be searched must be provided with the Notice of Powers and Rights (para 5.7 Code B) and if the search is with consent the consent must be given on the Notice (para 4.1). The subjects of non-consensual searches must be informed of the purpose of the search and the grounds for undertaking it (para 5.5).

R v Chief Constable of Lancashire ex p Parker and Mc Grath (1992)
R v Guildhall Magistrates' Court ex p Primlacks Holdings Co (Panama) Ltd (1989)
R v Central Criminal Court ex p Francis and Francis (1989)

Obstruction of a constable

The offence of obstruction of a constable in the course of his duty arises under s 51(3) of the Police Act 1964. Three tests must be satisfied if liability for this offence is to be made out. Firstly it must be shown that the constable was in the execution of his or her duty and secondly that the defendant did an act which made it more difficult for the officer to carry out that duty. Thirdly it must be shown that the defendant behaved wilfully in the sense that he acted deliberately with the knowledge and intention that he would obstruct the police officer.

Bentley v Brudzinski (1982)

Donnelly v Jackman (1970)
Coffin v Smith (1980)
Lewis v Cox (1985)
Rice v Connolly (1966)

The scheme governed by Part IV of PACE put the power of detention on a clear basis and it is made clear under s 37(2) that the purpose of the detention is to obtain a confession. Under s 41 the detention can be for up to 24 hours but in the case of a person in police custody for a serious arrestable offence (defined in s 116) it can extend to 96 hours. Part IV of PACE does not apply to detention under the PTA 1989 s 14 and Schedule 2 or 5.

Detention in police custody

An interview inside the police station should only take place if all the safeguards for interviews are in place, of which the most significant are the caution, contemporaneous recording under para 11.5 or tape recording under Code E para 3, the ability to read over, verify and sign the notes of the interview as a correct record under para 11.10, notification of legal advice under para 3.1, the right to have advice before questioning under s 58 and para 6 and, where appropriate, the presence of an adult (para 11.14).

Interviews: safeguards

An interview as defined under Code C para 11.1A and 10.1 may only take place outside the police station if one of the exceptions under para 11.1 applies or the decision to arrest has not yet been made. In that case the suspect must be cautioned and it must be contemporaneously recorded under para 11.5, read over, verified and signed by the suspect under para 11.10.

If an exchange occurs which cannot be classified as an interview but is relevant to the offence it must be accurately recorded and offered to the suspect to read over, verify and sign under para 11.13.

Mathews (1990)
Marsh (1991)
Maguire (1989)
Cox (1993)

If the police have broken one or more of the PACE rules or behaved in some other way improperly any confession obtained during the investigation may be excluded under s 76(2)(a) which operates to exclude a confession obtained by oppression, s 76(2)(b) which operates to exclude a confession obtained in circumstances conducive of unreliability, or s 78 which confers on a judge a discretion to exclude a confession if admitting it might create unfairness at the trial. Only s 78 will be considered in respect of non-confession evidence and it

Redress for police impropriety: exclusion of evidence

seems that physical evidence will be excluded only if obtained with deliberate illegality.

Fulling (1987)
Mason (1987)
Paris (1992)
Delaney (1989)
Marshall (1992)
Canale (1990)
Ismail (1990)
Keenan (1988)
Walsh (1988)
Samuel (1988)
Alladice (1988)
Bailey (1993)
Ladlow (1989)
Finley (1993)
Thomas (1990)
Fox (1986)
Effick (1992)

Redress for police impropriety: damages

Damages for false imprisonment will be available in respect of some breaches of PACE such as breaches of the arrest or detention rules. Damages for assault and battery will also be available for the use of violence not in furtherance of a particular power or of an excessive nature. Trespass to land or to goods will occur if the statutory provisions governing search of premises or seizure of goods are not followed. Malicious prosecution will be available where police have abused their powers in recommending prosecution to the Crown Prosecution Service. However, tort damages will not be available for any breach of the Codes or, it seems, for breaches of the statutory interviewing rules including s 58.

Glinskie v McIver (1962)
Weldon v Home Office (1991)

Redress for police impropriety: police complaints

The police complaints mechanism covers any breaches of PACE including under s 67(8) breaches of the Codes but it is generally agreed that it is defective as a means of redress. Very few complaints result in disciplinary action and the system is not perceived as sufficiently independent. Under s 84 PACE a complaint will go in the first instance to the Chief Officer of Police of the force in question who must determine by reference to the section whether or not he is the appropriate person to deal with it. A complaint must be referred to the Police Complaints Authority who will supervise the investigation if it concerns serious misconduct.

Chapter 10

Freedom From Discrimination

Broadly speaking, UK anti-discrimination legislation embodies two methods of securing equality which may be termed: the 'individual method' and the 'administrative method'. Under the first, an individual who considers that he or she has been discriminated against can seek redress. In other words, specific instances of discrimination may be addressed only if the individual concerned is prepared to take on the burden of a legal action. Such an approach is clearly only capable of bringing about slow and piecemeal change, especially as the two parties concerned – usually employee and employer – will rarely be confronting each other on equal terms. The lack of legal aid exacerbates this situation. The second approach is intended to bring about *general* change by creating an administrative body which can investigate and address itself to institutionalised discrimination. The movements towards equality in racial and sexual terms have taken a similar legislative path as far as the administrative method is concerned but some differences of approach have affected the use of the individual method, and therefore in that respect sexual and racial equality will be considered separately.

10.1 Sexual discrimination: introduction

The view taken in the 1974 White Paper on Sex Discrimination preceding the 1975 Act was that women were being held back in employment and other fields because they were not being judged on their individual merits but on the basis of a general presumption of inferiority. It was apparent that the common law was not going to bring about change, partly because the judiciary saw the creation of a comprehensive anti-discrimination code as the province of Parliament, but also because even in the 1970s sympathy with discriminatory practices was evident among certain judges. In *Morris v Duke – Cohen* (1975), for example, a judge was prepared to find a solicitor negligent for taking advice from a wife when a husband was available, on the basis that a sensible wife would expect her husband to make the major decisions.

The legislation affords recognition to two competing views as to the most effective means of securing equality by the individual method: the so-called formal equality approach and the pluralist or substantive equality approach. The former, which is based on classic liberalism, and is the dominant approach, assumes that in a just society the sex of a person would carry no expectations with it; it would be as irrelevant as their eye colour. It takes the view that women and men are equal – that women are not under any particular disadvantage and that therefore if a man would have been treated in the same way as the woman has been treated no discrimination has occurred. Thus, once specific instances of differential treatment based on sex are prevented or addressed this approach assumes that legal intervention is no longer required.

The pluralist approach, on the other hand, which was imported from the USA, asks whether policies and practices which are neutral on their face actually have an adverse impact on women due to factors particularly affecting them which may have been the product of previous discrimination. It accepts that there may be differences between the situation of men and women but holds that no penalty should attach to the recognition of those differences. This approach derives from the Supreme Court decision in *Griggs v Duke Power Company* (1971); when the defendant company administered an aptitude test to all job applicants it was shown that significantly fewer blacks than whites passed the test, and that the skills examined by the test were not particularly relevant to the jobs applied for. In these circumstances, it was held that the test was discriminatory.

Sex discrimination law in the UK cannot be studied without taking into account European Community law which has been a highly significant influence (race discrimination provisions have also been influenced indirectly). Article 119 of the Treaty of Rome, which was signed by Britain in 1973, governs the principle of equal pay for equal work. This is amplified by the Equal Pay Directive 75/117, while the Equal Treatment Directive 76/207 governs other aspects of sexual discrimination. These provisions are far more valuable than the guarantee of freedom from discrimination under Article 14 of the European Convention on Human Rights, partly because they can have a direct influence in domestic courts, and partly because, as Chapter 2 shows, Article 14 only covers areas falling within the scope of the other Articles.

The 1975 Act only covers the non-contractual aspects of employment – the contractual aspects fall within the Equal Pay Act 1970. As will be seen this separation has created difficulties although the two statutes are intended to work together as a complete code. The Act does not make sexual discrimination generally illegal; it only outlaws discrimination in the contexts in which it operates: employment (s 6), education (s 22), and the provision of goods and services (s 29). Thus a two stage approach has been created; firstly discrimination must be shown and secondly that it falls within one of the contexts covered by the Act.

Discrimination on the grounds of marital status follows the same pattern but in this instance the comparison is between a single person and a married person of the same sex. Marital discrimination is more circumscribed as it is confined to the employment field only; discrimination on the grounds of divorce or of being unmarried is not covered.

The concept of direct discrimination on grounds of sex governed by s 1(1)(a) of the 1975 Act embodies the formal equality approach. It involves showing that the applicant has been less favourably treated than a comparable man has been or would be treated. There is little guidance in the Act as to what is meant by a comparable man; s 5(3) merely provides that there must be no material difference between the situations of the man and the woman. It should be noted that it is possible for the applicant to compare herself with a hypothetical man; the issue is not whether a man or a woman receives a benefit but whether the woman would have been better treated if she had been a man.

10.2   The individual method: direct discrimination

The test can be broken down into three stages. Firstly the woman must show that there has been differentiation in the treatment afforded to herself and a man (or a hypothetical man). Motive is irrelevant; the question at this stage is merely whether a woman has been treated one way and a man another. Secondly, she must show that her treatment has been less favourable, and thirdly, following the ruling of the House of Lords in *James v Eastleigh BC* (1989), that there is a causal relationship between her sex and the treatment; in other words that but for her sex she would have been treated in the same way as the man. Following *Birmingham County Council ex p EOC* (1989) it is not necessary to show that the less favourable treatment is accorded due to an intention to discriminate: motive is irrelevant.

The plaintiff bears the burden of showing that the differential treatment was on grounds of sex and not for some neutral reason. She is always likely to find difficulty in discharging this burden of proof as the ruling in *Saunders v Richmond upon Thames LBC* (1978) suggests. The applicant applied for a job as a golf professional and was asked questions at the interview which were *prima facie* discriminatory. She was asked, for example, whether she thought she would be able to control unruly male players and whether she considered the job unglamorous. She was not appointed although she was somewhat better qualified than the man who was. The Employment Appeal Tribunal (EAT) held that had her qualifications been substantially better than those of the appointee that would have raised a *prima facie* inference of discrimination which the employer would have had to rebut by giving a satisfactory explanation. It was found that the nature of the questions, taking all the circumstances into account, did not of themselves raise a sufficient inference.

In *Khanna v MOD* (1981) it was found that the evidential burden would shift only when the evidence was all on one side, but this was clarified by the finding in *Dornan v Belfast CC* (1990) that once the woman has raised a *prima facie* inference of discrimination, the burden will shift to the employer to show that the differentiation occurred on non-discriminatory grounds. In other words, although the plaintiff begins the case bearing the burden of proof it may shift to the defendant once a certain stage is reached. Thus the formal burden of proof remains on the plaintiff but once it appears that a minimum threshold of proof of discrimination is established the burden shifts to the defendant. This middle ground is arguably fairer than merely leaving the full burden with the employee or, alternatively, shifting it entirely to the employer.

| 10.2.1 | Pregnancy |

Dismissals and other detrimental action on the ground of pregnancy might appear to be discriminatory, but the wording of s 1(1) may not allow such action to fall readily within the scope of direct discrimination because in making the comparison between a woman and a man it is required that 'the relevant circumstances in the one case are the same, or not materially different, in the other' (s 5(3)). Under the Employment Protection (Consolidation) Act 1978 s 60 if a woman is dismissed because she is pregnant then the dismissal is automatically unfair. However, in order to rely on this an employee must have been employed for two years; where this is not the case the employee must seek to show that the 1975 Act applies.

This was the situation which arose in *Turley v Allders* (1980) because the applicant did not have the requisite period of continuous employment. The Employment Appeal Tribunal held that there was no male equivalent to a pregnant woman and therefore as no comparison could be made the action must fail. However, a method of making the comparison was found in a later EAT decision, *Hayes v Malleable WMC* (1985); it was made between a pregnant woman and a man with a long-term health problem. Thus it was determined that direct discrimination would occur if a woman was dismissed on grounds of pregnancy where a man needing the same period of absence due to illness would not have been dismissed.

This analogy has not been well received; commentators have found the comparison between a pregnant woman and a diseased man inherently distasteful. It is also highly disadvantageous to women, around 90% of whom may become pregnant at some time during their working life and in particular between the ages of 20 and 36 (the time when women are most likely to become pregnant) while the percentage of men likely to take around two or more months off work during those years due to an illness or accident is likely to be far lower.

The *Hayes* approach will no longer be followed after certain rulings of the European Court of Justice. It found in *Dekker v VJV Centrum* (1991) that a woman who was not appointed to a post because she was pregnant at the time of the interview, although she was considered to be the best candidate, was the victim of direct discrimination. *Webb v Emo Air Cargo (UK) Ltd* (1992) concerned the dismissal of the claimant after it was found that she was pregnant. She had been recruited to replace an employee going on maternity leave, but had then discovered herself to be pregnant, and therefore (it seemed) unavailable for duties in the period required. The question was whether her dismissal constituted direct discrimination within the terms of s 1(1)(a), Sex Discrimination Act 1975 in the light of Community law. When the Court of Appeal turned to this issue in *Webb*, it continued the *Hayes* approach in determining that if a man with a medical condition as nearly comparable as possible (with the same practical effect upon availability to do the job) with pregnancy would also have been dismissed then the dismissal of the woman was not sex discrimination. Thus, the plaintiff who was, due to pregnancy, unavailable for duties in the period required, could be dismissed without infringing the Sex Discrimination Act because a diseased man who was similarly unavailable at the relevant time would also have been dismissed. The argument was therefore rejected that since only a woman can be pregnant, it follows that a woman who is dismissed for any reason related to her pregnancy is dismissed due to her sex and thus discriminated against.

The House of Lords favoured the approach of the Court of Appeal, but since it considered that the relevant rulings of the Court of Justice did not indicate clearly whether the dismissal would be regarded as based on pregnancy or on unavailability at the relevant time, it referred the following question to the court:

Is it discrimination on grounds of sex contrary to the Equal Treatment Directive for an employer to dismiss a female employee:

(a) whom it engaged for the specific purpose of replacing another female employee during the latter's forthcoming maternity leave,

(b) when very shortly after appointment the employer discovers that the appellant herself will be absent on maternity leave during the maternity period of the other employee and the employer dismisses her because it needs the jobholder to be at work during that period, and

(c) had the employer known of the pregnancy of the appellant at the date of appointment she would not have been appointed, and

(d) the employer would similarly have dismissed a male employee engaged for this purpose who required leave of absence at the relevant time for medical or other reasons?

The court found that the plaintiff should not be compared with a man unavailable for work for medical or other reasons since pregnancy is not in any way comparable with pathological conditions. The court then found that, since the plaintiff had been employed permanently, her dismissal could not be justified on the ground of inability to fulfil a fundamental condition of her employment contract because her inability to perform the work was purely temporary. In other words, it could not be said that she had been taken on solely to cover a maternity leave. The court further found that the protection of Community law for pregnant women could not be dependent on the question whether the woman's presence at work during the maternity leave period is essential to the undertaking in which she is employed. Thus dismissal of the plaintiff clearly constituted sex discrimination, contrary to the Equal Treatment Directive.

Thus, in *Webb* the court consolidated its previous rulings on the rights of pregnant workers, in particular the ruling in *Dekker* that discrimination on the ground of pregnancy constitutes direct sex discrimination, contrary to the Equal Treatment Directive. However, a significant introduction in *Webb* is the court's reliance, in the particular case, on the fact that the employment contract in question was of a permanent and not fixed term nature. The decision of the court was based upon the mismatch between the period for which the employee would be unavailable and the period for which she had been employed (indefinitely). It seems then that the rights of pregnant women in EC law are based upon the nature of the employment contract concerned, rather than on any fundamental entitlement not to be adversely treated on grounds connected with pregnancy. This is a very significant development from the stark statement of principle in the *Dekker* case. It would, it is submitted, have been open for the court to exclude unavailability arising from pregnancy altogether as a possible justification for dismissal or other termination of the employment contract. Instead, the court, by implication, left the way open for acceptance of the distinction between unavailability and pregnancy which was emphasised by the House of Lords. Where the mismatch between the period of maternity leave and the period for which the employee has been employed is not present, it may be assumed that it is permissible to treat employees adversely on grounds of pregnancy.

Under the Trade Union Reform and Employment Rights Act 1993 ss 23–25 and Schedules 2 and 3 a woman is protected from dismissal on grounds of pregnancy and has an automatic right to 14 weeks maternity leave. (If she has two years continuous service she has a right to return to work within 29 weeks of the birth under the Employment Protection Consolidation Act 1978 s 39(1)(b)). However, detrimental action on grounds of pregnancy other than dismissal (such as demotion or failure to appoint) will fall within the *Webb* approach and arguably it is therefore unfortunate that the European Court of Justice failed to rule clearly that such action would be direct sex discrimination.

	10.2.2 Sexual harassment

Two issues have arisen in this context. It was made clear in *Porcelli v Strathclyde Regional Council* (1985) that if the employer subjects the applicant to a detriment in her employment arising from sexual harassment, such as a transfer from one establishment to another, this will be direct discrimination. Further, sexual harassment appears to be a detriment in itself even though it does not lead to *other* unfavourable action under s 6(6)(b) which speaks of 'or subjecting her to any other detriment'. The European Commission has defined sexual harassment as 'conduct of a sexual nature or other conduct based on sex affecting the dignity of men and women at work'. This clearly covers verbal or physical conduct. There seems to be some uncertainty as to whether 'detriment' should be interpreted subjectively or objectively (*Wileman v Minilec Engineering Ltd* (1988) and *Snowball v Gardner Merchant* (1987)).

Section 41(1) of the 1975 Act states that an act done by an employee in the course of employment shall be treated as done by the employer as well as by him or her, whether or not it was done with the employer's knowledge or approval. Thus a sexual harassment claim may be brought where the employer has made little or no effort to curb the harassment.

In 1992 the EC published a Code of Practice on sexual harassment giving guidance to employees and employers and stating that harassment 'pollutes the working environment and can have a devastating effect upon the health, confidence, morale and performance of those affected by it'. The

Commission has recommended that the Code should be adopted by Member States and that they should also take other action to address this problem, but the UK government has not yet shown any inclination to respond. However, in *Wadman v Carpenter Farrer Partnership* (1993) it was found that Industrial Tribunals faced with an allegation of sexual harassment as a form of direct discrimination should have regard to the guidance offered by the Code.

10.3   The individual method: indirect discrimination

The concept of indirect discrimination on grounds of sex or marital status was imported into the Act under ss 1(1)(b) and 3(1)(b) with a view to outlawing practices which while neutral on their face as between men and women have a disproportionately adverse impact on women. It was intended to outlaw not only isolated acts of discrimination but also institutionalised discrimination. This reflects the pluralist approach; it takes account for example of past discrimination against women. In asking not whether women can in theory comply with a condition, but whether they can do so in practice, it broadens the area of morally unjustifiable differentiation.

10.3.1   Steps in an indirect discrimination claim

There are four stages in operating this concept. Firstly, it must be shown that a condition has been applied to the applicant. It might be to be of a certain seniority, height or type of experience. It was found in *Perera v Civil Service Commission* (1983) that the condition must operate as an absolute bar. In other words, if it amounts to a practice as opposed to a condition and if it is sometimes waived, it cannot qualify as a condition for s 1(1)(b) purposes. This ruling has been much criticised since it creates a barrier to using the concept of indirect discrimination; it may be out of accord with the ruling of the European Court of Justice in *Enderby v Frenchay* (1991) which is discussed below. However, *Enderby* was an equal pay case and therefore is perhaps of limited application to an indirect discrimination claim. The *Perera* finding is very restrictive since non-absolute criteria could clearly be used and could have an adverse impact on an applicant. For example, an unjustifiable height bar might normally be operated but the employer might be prepared on occasion to consider people under it. Nevertheless, the bar could have a significantly adverse effect on women. Thus the development of indirect discrimination has been constrained and the EOC has therefore argued for reform of the meaning of 'condition'.

Secondly, it must be shown that the condition is one which will have a disproportionate impact on women; in other words considerably less women than men will be able to comply with it. The application of the phrase 'can comply' was considered in *Price v Civil Service Commission* (1978). The Civil Service had a rule that applicants had to be under 28 years of age. Mrs Price, who was 35, applied but was rejected and claimed sex discrimination. It was found that due to the prevailing social conditions more men than women could comply with the requirement because at the time there was an expectation that women would rear a family and so would be less likely to be available in the job market at that age than men. However, women could theoretically comply with a requirement to be 28 and available in the job market; they could choose not to have children. The words 'can comply' were interpreted to mean that *in practice* less women could comply with the condition.

The finding of disproportionate impact was considered in *Jones v Chief Adjudication Officer* (1990). It was found that this involves identifying a group comprising all those who satisfy the other criteria for selection and then dividing it into two groups representing those who satisfy the condition in question and those who do not. Then the actual male/female balances in the two groups is ascertained, and if women are found to be under-represented in the first group and over-represented in the second, it is proved that the criterion is *prima facie* discriminatory. For example, less women than men might have a certain type of experience due to a now outlawed system of keeping women at a certain level and thereby preventing them gaining the experience in question. The court in *Price* considered the means of identifying a group of men and women to be looked at in order to see whether less women could comply with the condition. It found that the group to be considered would be the pool of men and women with the relevant qualifications; it would not include the whole population. The applicant's case therefore passed all four tests and succeeded, with the result that the Civil Service altered the age bar. The ruling in *Jones v University of Manchester* (1993) reaffirmed this approach to the 'pool', finding that the applicant could not redefine its parameters which would be fixed by the relevant advertisement.

Thirdly, once the claimant has proved these two requirements, the burden of proof shifts to the employer to show that the condition is justifiable regardless of sex. For example, there are less women engineering graduates than men; therefore a requirement that applicants have a degree in engineering hits disproportionately at women. However, the employer will normally be able to show that a degree in engineering is genuinely needed for the job. The meaning of 'justifiable' has undergone considerable change since the ruling in *Ojutiku v Manpower Services Commission* (1982) in which, departing from the *Steel* interpretation, it was held to mean 'reasons which would appear sound to right-thinking people'. This obviously widened its meaning and would have allowed a great many practices to be justified, greatly undermining s 1(1)(b). However, in *Clarke v Eley (IMI) Kynoch Ltd* (1983) the meaning of justifiable was somewhat narrowed. The company had a policy of always selecting part time workers for redundancy first regardless of their length of service, although for full time workers a 'last in, first out' system was in operation. Therefore the requirement to work full time so as not to be made redundant hit disproportionately at women as more women than men worked part time. The employer argued that the practice could be justified because it was long-standing and the work force liked it, but it was found that this was not sufficient to render it 'justifiable', and the claimant therefore succeeded. This was clearly in accord with the policy of including indirect discrimination in the statutory scheme in order to outlaw longstanding discriminatory practices.

The test for the meaning of justifiable has now been more precisely defined by the European Court in *Bilka-Kaufhaus GmbH v Weber von Hartz* (1986). Under this test conditions creating disparate impact will be justifiable if they amount to a means chosen for achieving an objective which correspond to a real need on the part of the undertaking, are appropriate to that end and necessary to that end. So this test would be fulfilled if, for example, an undertaking had a real need to increase its scientific expertise in a certain area. The means used to do so would have to be appropriate, such as asking that applicants have a degree in a certain science. If other means of increasing its expertise were not available it would be seen as necessary to impose the condition that applicants have a science degree. This approach was taken in *Hampson v Department of Education and Science* (1989) and means that s 1(1)(b) has been brought into line with the 'material difference' defence under s 1(3) of the Equal Pay Act 1970 (see below).

Fourthly, if the employer cannot show that the requirement is genuinely needed for the job, the woman must show that it is to her detriment because she cannot comply with it. This requirement was included because it was thought necessary that the woman claimant should be the victim rather than allowing anyone to bring a claim in respect of a discriminatory practice operating at her place of employment.

The case of *Steel v The Post Office* (1977) illustrates the operation of the concept of indirect discrimination. The ruling concerned the allocation of postal walks to postmen or women. Certain walks were more in demand than others and the walks were allocated on the basis of the seniority of the employee. Ms Steel made a bid for a walk but lost it to a younger man. She had worked for the Post Office much longer than he had but she had only been accepted into the permanent grade in 1975 when the Sex Discrimination Act came into force. Before 1975 the Post Office had directly discriminated against women by refusing to allow them to enter the permanent grade. Ms Steel's seniority had been calculated from that point.

The practice in question was interpreted as a 'requirement', thereby widening the meaning of the term. It had a disparate impact on women because less of them could comply with it than men due to the past discrimination, and the requirement as to seniority could not otherwise be justified. 'Justified' was strictly interpreted as meaning 'necessary'. Finally, the requirement was clearly to her detriment as she could not comply with it.

Under s 4(1) less favourable treatment of someone because she has done a 'protected act' – brought an action or intends to do so, or has assisted in such action under the 1975 Act or the Equal Pay Act – amounts to victimisation. The usefulness of this provision has been diminished due to the need to show that the unfavourable treatment is due to the protected act and not for some other reason. This was the issue in *Aziz v TST* (1988) which is discussed below in relation to victimisation on grounds of race. It may often be hard to prove that this is the case, and this is particularly unfortunate due to evidence which is beginning to emerge in both race and sex discrimination cases that employers are becoming more likely to respond to a protected act by bringing disciplinary proceedings which might not otherwise have been undertaken. This occurred when Alison Halford brought discrimination proceedings in 1992 against *inter alia* Merseyside Police Authority and was probably a factor in her decision to settle the discrimination claim rather than pursue it to a conclusion.	**10.4 Discrimination on grounds of victimisation**
There are a large number of exclusions from the Act and therefore discrimination in such circumstances is lawful under domestic legislation. Certain occupations are excluded under s 19 which covers employment for the purpose of organised religion and s 21 which covers mine workers. The armed forces are also excluded under s 85(4). Acts safeguarding national security are exempted as are acts done under statutory authority. This is due to the status of the Act as not	**10.5 Defences and lawful discrimination**

prevailing over other statutes even though they were passed before it. Thus instruments intended to enshrine discrimination in their provisions such as tax, immigration or social security statutes are not affected by the 1975 Act.

A general exception to provisions against discrimination in the employment field also arises where sex can be said to be a genuine occupational qualification under one of the s 7 provisions. This arises in a number of contexts including those where the job appears to call for a man for reasons of physiology (excluding physical strength or stamina), or for reasons of authenticity in respect of plays or other entertainment, or to preserve decency or privacy, or where the job involves dealings with other countries where women are less likely to be able to carry them out effectively due to the customs of that other country. MacKinnon has argued that these exceptions are too broad as extending some way beyond biological differences and accepting differential treatment based solely on social categorisation, and it is therefore arguable that they are due to be overhauled and narrowed down, particularly the last – mentioned on the ground that the UK should not bow to discriminatory practices in other countries.

10.6   Equal pay

The Equal Pay Act governs contractual aspects of a woman's employment. It is anomalous in that it is separate from the Sex Discrimination Act; there is no good reason for having two separate instruments and it merely introduces further complexity and technicality into an already complex scheme. The Act received the royal assent in 1970 but it did not come into force until 1975; the idea was that employers would voluntarily remove sexual discrimination in pay. In fact, as the TUC warned the government would happen, employers moved women off the 'women's grade' on to the lowest grades with a view to minimising their statutory obligations and made sure that men and women were not working on comparable jobs.

10.6.1   Widening application of the equality clause

The aim of the 1970 Act is to prevent discrimination as regards terms and conditions of employment between men and women, and to this end it employs the device of an equality clause. If certain conditions are satisfied the terms of the woman's contract are deemed to include such a clause. Under the original provisions the equality clause only operated in two circumstances: that the woman was employed on like work with men in the same employment under s 1(2)(a) or on work rated by a job evaluation scheme as equivalent to that of a man in the same employment under s 1(2)(b). The latter provision was not of much value as it was voluntary and it was therefore left to the woman to persuade her employer to undertake such a scheme. In practice this meant that women were left with the like work provisions. Due to sexual segregation in the job market women were concentrated in certain occupations such as cleaning or cooking and were unable to point to a man doing like work even where he was in the same employment.

So the Act had little impact on women's lower pay as it could only be used against the most gross forms of pay discrimination. However, in 1982 the European Commission brought an action against the UK (*Commission of European Communities v UK* (1982)) on the basis that the UK was in breach of its obligations under the Equal Pay Directive due to the narrow application of the equality clause, and in response the UK government was forced to amend the Act in order to include the possibility of making an equal value claim. It did so very reluctantly and this was reflected in the response. The amendation was effected by Statutory Instrument, thereby curtailing debate on the new provisions, and the new regulations were intended to operate only as a last resort: the other two possibilities had to be tried first. Moreover, an attempt was made to widen the defences available to employers by using a different wording for equal value claims.

The first step under the Act in an equal value claim (the other two types of claim follow a similar but less complex route) is for the woman to choose a comparator. This might have caused difficulty where the woman was employed doing like work with a few men but wanted to compare herself with a man doing work of equal value; however the issue was resolved in favour of claimants by the House of Lords in *Pickstone v Freemans* (1988). Mrs Pickstone and other warehouse operatives were paid less than male warehouse checkers but a man was employed as an operative. The defendants therefore argued that the claim was barred due to the wording of s 1(2)(c): 'where a woman is employed on work which, *not being work to which (a) or (b) applied* is ... of equal value ... ' para (a) *did* apply because one man was employed doing the same work, and therefore it could be argued that a like work claim arose but not an equal value one.

The House of Lords considered that allowing this argument to succeed would mean that Parliament had failed once again to implement its obligations under Article 119 of the Treaty of Rome and it could not have intended such a failure. In the circumstances any interpretation should take into account the terms in which the amending regulations were presented to Parliament; in other words a purposive approach

10.6.2   Choice of comparator

should be adopted – an approach which would allow the purpose of the regulations to be fulfilled. Using this approach the defendants' argument could be rejected on the basis that the claimant should be able to choose her comparator, rather than allowing the employer to impose one on her. This ruling put an end to what has been termed the 'token man loophole': had the ruling gone the other way employers might have been encouraged to employ one man alongside a large number of women in order to bar equal value claims.

| 10.6.3 | 'Same' employment |

Once a claimant has chosen a comparator it must be shown that they are in the same employment. The meaning of this provision was considered by the House of Lords in *Leverton v Clwyd CC* (1987). A nursery nurse who wished to compare her pay with that of clerical staff was not employed in the same *establishment* as they were. The House of Lords had to determine what was meant by the 'same employment'. Under s 1(6) it is defined as meaning 'at the same establishment' *or* as by 'the same employer *and* the same conditions of employment are observed'. The claimant and comparators were employed by the same employer and, although there were some differences in the individual terms of employment, it was still possible to find, on a broad view of the agreement governing the terms of employment, of claimant and comparator, that they were sufficiently similar to satisfy the s 1(6) test.

| 10.6.4 | Determining equal value |

Assuming that a claimant can point to a comparator in the same employment the Industrial Tribunal will appoint an independent expert in order to determine whether the two jobs are of equal value under such heads as responsibility, skill, effort, qualifications and length of training. The expert's report is not conclusive of the issue but the tribunal is unlikely to reject it. If the jobs are of equal value then a term of the claimant's contract which is less favourable than a term of her comparator's will be compared.

| 10.6.5 | The 'term by term' approach |

It is now clear after the ruling of the House of Lords in *Hayward v Cammell Laird* (1988) that the term by term approach – as opposed to consideration of the contract as a whole – is correct. The defendants had resisted the plaintiff's claim on the ground that her contract and that of the male comparators must each be looked at as a whole, in which case her perks, such as free lunches and two additional days holiday, equalled the £25.00 per week extra which the men received. The House of Lords found that the word 'term' in s 1(2) was to be given its natural and ordinary meaning as a distinct part of a contract and therefore it was necessary to look at one term of the claimant's contract; if there was a similar provision in the comparator's contract which was found after they had been compared to be less favourable to the woman than the term in the comparator's, then the equality clause would operate to make that term equally favourable to her.

Obviously this ruling prevented employers claiming that fringe benefits equalled pay. Such a claim might be advantageous to an employer who might be able to provide a benefit at little real cost such as free meals for a cook. The employer might design a 'protective package' for female employees which included less pay but more time off or more sick benefits. All women, whether desirous of such a package or not, would then receive it whether or not they would have preferred to be paid more. Employers, however, feared that this ruling might lead to 'leap frogging': women would receive the male higher pay; men would then claim the women's old fringe benefits and all employees would 'level up', causing detriment to the company which would be faced with a great increase in costs. However, employers might be able to avoid this by gradually modifying practices on pay and fringe benefits. There would also be the possibility – mentioned only as *dicta* in *Hayward* – that certain fringe benefits might be used to found a *defence* to an equal value claim (see below).

Even if a woman is able to show that she is doing like work, work rated as equivalent, or work of equal value to that of her comparator the claim will fail if a s 1(3) defence operates:

10.7 Equal pay: defences

> An equality clause shall not operate in relation to a variation between the woman's contract and the man's contract if the employer proves that the variation is genuinely due to a material factor which is not the difference of sex and that factor –
>
> (a) in the case of an equality clause falling within subsection (2)(a) or (b) above, must be a material difference between the woman's case and the man's; and
>
> (b) in the case of an equality clause falling within subsection (2)(c) above, may be such a material difference.

This is known as the 'material factor defence'. The difference in wording as far as equal value claims were concerned was intended to mean that 'material factor' can be interpreted more widely in equal value claims. In fact, as will be seen, the width of the interpretation given to the defence in all three types of claim has meant that this possibility has been of less significance than was expected. The defence will operate if a material difference between the cases of the woman and man can be identified which is *not the difference of sex*.

10.7.1 Material factors: general

An example would be afforded by additional payment for the geographical difference in the location of two parts of the same concern. As the 1970 Act must be construed in harmony with the Sex Discrimination Act the factor must consist of a variation in pay which is genuinely due to the factor in question; otherwise it may be discriminatory. Thus in *Shields v E Coomes* (1978) the difference in pay was apparently due to the protective function exercised by the male employees in a betting shop. However, not all the men discharged such a function but all received the higher pay. Therefore, allowing the protective function to operate as a material factor would be directly discriminatory because a woman who exercised no protective function would not receive the higher pay while a man in the same position would.

In *Leverton v Clwyd County Council* (1987) the House of Lords found that different hours and holidays could amount to a material factor under s 1(3) if pay could be broken down into a notional hourly income. If, once this was done, the pay of claimant and comparator was found to be equal, the claim would fail on the basis that the difference in salaries was due to the difference in hours and not to the difference of sex. This point was touched on *obiter* in *Hayward* but in *Leverton* it was made clear that a s 1(3) defence might be available where a man and a woman had different contractual packages, so long as the packages did not contain any element of indirect discrimination.

10.7.2   Market forces as a material factor

The most far reaching and controversial argument under s 1(3) has been termed the 'market forces argument': it allows the employer to argue that because the market may favour some employees more than others they must be paid more and that to fail to do so would be to disrupt normal market forces. In other words, if a woman is willing to work for less than a man this provides a reason for paying her less.

The early cases rejected this argument; in *Jenkins v Kinsgate* (1981), for example, a part time worker was paid at a different hourly rate from the full time workers. The employer tried to use the s 1(3) defence in answer to her claim for equal hourly pay in arguing that part time workers have less bargaining power and therefore the market demanded that he should pay full time workers more. The argument was that this was a genuine difference between the two cases which was not sex-related; any part time worker, male or female, would have been paid less. However, the part timers were all female and so the practice had a disparate impact on women. Construing the Act in accordance with the Sex Discrimination Act, the EAT concluded that a practice which had a disparate impact on women could not sustain a s 1(3) defence as to allow it to do so would be indirectly discriminatory.

However, this approach was not followed in *Rainey v Greater Glasgow Health Board* (1987). The case concerned a comparison between female and male prosthetists working in the NHS. The men were receiving higher pay but the defendants argued that this was due to the need to attract them from the private sector in order to set up the prosthetist service. This argument entailed consideration not just of factors relating to the personal attributes of the claimant and comparator, such as length of experience, but also the difference in their individual positions in the market. In other words, it widened what could be considered as a material factor. The relevant circumstances were that those from the private sector must be paid above the normal rate to attract them.

However, the House of Lords held that although taking this into account as a material factor was acceptable it must be objectively justified – no element of discrimination must have crept into the circumstances. In order to ensure this the House of Lords used the same test as for justification under indirect discrimination – the *Bilka* test laid down by the European Court of Justice (see above at 10.3.4). Here the objective was setting up the NHS prosthetist service which entailed attracting sufficient experienced prosthetists. The means chosen involved attracting persons from the private sector which involved paying them more. It was accepted that this was both appropriate and necessary. So the material factor passed the *Bilka* test and further, because this was a like work case, the factor had to be a difference between comparator and claimant. The difference was that she was from the public while he was from the private sector.

Thus this ruling broadened what could be termed a material factor and allowed market forces to affect equal pay claims so long as no indirect discrimination was shown. Clearly, the danger of the market forces argument is that employers will often argue that business will suffer if a group of women are paid more. What are termed 'women's jobs' have traditionally been under-valued by the market; the equal value amendment was specifically aimed at breaking down traditional pay hierarchies. Thus, this argument, if allowed too wide a scope, could completely undermine equal value law. However, the *Rainey* ruling does appear to an extent to be trying to keep this in check in finding that only in objectively justified circumstances should more be paid to a certain group; this is not the same as allowing the market generally to set the rate.

The effect of this argument was further curbed in *Benveniste v University of Southampton* (1989); it was found that although particular constraints might affect pay and might lead to a pay differential between a man and a woman, they could do so only while the constraint was in operation. Once it had ceased to apply the lower pay should be raised to the level it would have been at had it not been affected by the constraint.

10.7.3   Separate bargaining processes as a material factor, and identification of a 'condition'

A variation on the market forces argument was put forward in *Enderby v Frenchay HA* (1992). Speech therapists wished to compare their pay with that of clinical psychologists and pharmacists who were paid at much higher rates. The employers denied that the work of the two groups was of equal value but argued that in any event a material factor justified the difference: it had emerged as a result of different pay negotiations and, moreover, the pharmacists were in demand in the private sector and this had influenced pay. The claimant, however, argued that the salaries of the therapists were low due to the fact that the profession was predominantly female.

The employers further argued that the speech therapists could not assert that the material factor was tainted by indirect discrimination without first showing that a condition had been applied to employees which had an adverse impact on women. The employer thus had two arguments: firstly, no condition could be identified which had been applied; secondly, if it had been it could be justified due to the factors mentioned: the separate pay processes or market forces. The claimants argued that whether a condition could be identified or not was immaterial: in practice one type of work was largely done by women and another largely by men, and although of equal value the men's work attracted a higher salary. These factors, it was claimed, gave rise to a presumption of discrimination which could not be objectively justified because the reason for the difference was that the profession in question was staffed by women. This argument if accepted would have distinguished the claim from that in *Rainey*.

The EAT found for the employers, ruling that the pay was the result of different bargaining processes which looked at separately were not indirectly discriminatory. Therefore, a material factor could be identified which was influenced by market forces. Further, even if the factor identified did not justify all of the difference in pay that did not matter because it was impossible to say how much was needed above normal rates to attract and retain certain staff. It was clear that the case raised difficult issues and so at the Court of Appeal stage three questions were referred to the European Court of Justice:

- if there is a difference in pay must it be objectively justified; in other words must all the steps needed to show indirect discrimination be taken, including identifying a particular barrier?

- Are separate bargaining processes a sufficient justification for a variation in pay if they are not internally discriminatory?

- If there is a need to pay men more to attract them, but only part of the difference in pay is for that purpose, then does that justify all the difference?

The first question relates to the determination of a *prima facie* case of indirect sex discrimination; is it necessary to be able to identify a 'barrier' or 'condition' which it is more difficult for women to meet than men (or *vice versa*) in order to show indirect discrimination? The second and third questions relate to justifications for indirect discrimination. First, is the use of separate sex neutral collective bargaining systems sufficient justification for indirect sex discrimination? Second, will the more favourable market position of certain employees justify unequal pay? In other words, can the overt operation of market forces justify indirect sex discrimination?

Assuming that the jobs compared were of equal value, the Court of Justice held, reiterating the well-established principle of reversal of the burden of proof in indirect sex discrimination cases (citing Case C-33/89 *Kowalska v Freie und Hansestadt Hamburg* (1990) and Case C-184/89 *Nimz v Freie und Hansestadt Hamburg* (1991) concerning measures distinguishing between employees on the basis of their hours of work, including equal pay cases) that, '... it is for the employer to prove that his practice in the matter of wages is not discriminatory, if a female worker establishes, in relation to a relatively large number of employees, that the average pay for women is less than that for men'. Applying these rulings by analogy to this equal value claim, the court concluded that there is a *prima facie* case of sex discrimination, where the pay of speech therapists is significantly lower than that of clinical psychologists and pharmacists, and speech therapists are almost exclusively women. The 'factual' considerations as to whether the jobs are indeed of equal value and whether the statistics adduced support the required disparities are questions for the national court. At this point, the burden of objective justification shifts to the employer.

The court replied in the negative to the question whether separate collective bargaining processes, which are each, in themselves, non-discriminatory, constitute sufficient objective justification for the differences in pay. The fact that the different wages are reached by separate processes of collective bargaining does not of itself justify the discrimination, since it is a merely descriptive explanation: it fails to explain why one process produced a more favourable result for the employees than the other. Moreover, allowing that justification would enable employers to circumvent the principle of equal pay very readily by using such separate processes.

In contrast to its answer to the second question, the court accepted 'the state of the employment market' in its answer to the third as a possible justification for indirect discrimination. The market forces concerned here were the shortage of candidates for the more highly paid job, and the consequent need to offer higher pay in that job in order to attract candidates. The court repeated that it is the duty of the national courts to decide 'questions of fact' such as this, and reiterated from its previous case law (Case 170/84 *Bilka* (1986), Case C-184/89 *Nimz v Freie und Hansestadt Hamburg* (1991) and Case 109/88 *Danfoss* (1989)) some forms of 'needs of the employer' which may constitute justification for indirect sex discrimination.

While the questions referred to the ECJ were unanswered, the second issue raised was resolved in *Barber and Others v NCR (Manufacturing) Ltd* (1993) using a completely different approach from that of the EAT in *Enderby*, and one which seems to be more in harmony with the policy of the Act. Indirect clerical workers, who were mainly women, wanted to compare their work with that of direct clerical workers who were mainly men. (The women's work was 'indirect' as not directly related to shop floor production.) The direct workers negotiated a new agreement regarding hours and moved to a shorter week. Thus the hourly rates of the two groups now differed although it had been the same.

The EAT considered whether the employer had established that because the difference arose from a different collective bargaining agreement untainted by discrimination this could found a s 1(3) defence. In putting forward this argument the employers had relied on *Enderby* where the EAT had held that this was possible. The EAT said that the correct question to be asked must first be identified. It might be asked whether the cause of the variation in pay was free from sex discrimination, or it might be asked whether the variation was itself genuinely due to a material factor other than the difference of sex. The second question was the right one because the cause – separate collective bargaining processes – might be free from discrimination but the *result* might not be. In this instance the evidence showed *why* the difference had been arrived at but did not show any objective factor which justified it. Thus, there was a pay difference which was not based on a material factor. The equality clause therefore operated, meaning that although the claimants did not get the *same* pay as the comparators due to the difference in hours, the hourly rates were equalised. The EAT considered that it did not need to refer to the ECJ or await the decision in *Enderby* as the proper result could be arrived at under domestic law.

The stance taken in *Enderby* by the ECJ is broadly in accord, it is suggested, with that taken in *Handels-og Kontorfunktionaerernes Forbund i Danmark v Dansk Arbejdsgiverforening* (the *Danfoss* case) (1989) which was a Danish reference to the court. The case also gives some general guidance as to the justifiability of using criteria which have an adverse impact on female employees. The Danfoss Company paid the same basic wage to all employees but also an individual supplement based on factors such as mobility and training. The result was that a somewhat lower average wage was paid to women. It was therefore claimed that the system was discriminatory.

The European Court determined that because the system lacked transparency, once a woman had shown that the average wage of women and men differed, the burden of proof would shift to the employer to prove that the wage practice was not discriminatory. It would have been unfair to expect the woman to *prove* that the system was discriminatory as she would not have been able to work out which factors had been taken into account. The court considered that even if the application of criteria, such as the need to be mobile, worked to the detriment of women the employer could still use them in relation to specific tasks entrusted to the employee so long as the *Bilka* test was satisfied. The court did not need to consider the question as to the relevance of two separate collective agreements, one for women, one for men, but when the Advocate General had addressed this point he had determined that the existence of such agreements would not exclude the operation of the Equal Pay Directive although it would not *inevitably* be unlawful to have two separate agreements; it would be the *manner* of the agreements which would be relevant.

This approach seemed to be endorsed in *Barber*, and should prevail, it is submitted, because merely to ask whether arriving at two levels of pay was due to the operation of two different bargaining processes might be to obscure the discriminatory nature of the result. As the ECJ pointed out in *Enderby*, t is necessary to look *behind* the bargaining processes and to ask why one was able to achieve a more favourable result. This might be because unions have traditionally been more effectual in obtaining better pay for men than for women, and in itself this may be due to the fact that mens' work has traditionally been valued more highly by the market than women's. Thus, to use different agreements as a material factor in themselves may be to cloak the discriminatory forces which lie behind them.

Similarly, asking an employee to identify a specific requirement or condition where it is alleged that a material factor is tainted by indirect discrimination appears misconceived. Sometimes it may be possible to identify a condition, such as a need to be mobile in order to attract higher pay. However, in many instances it may not be possible to identify any such condition with sufficient specificity. Instead, it may be argued that where two jobs are of equal value but that held by the woman attracts lower pay, the suggestion is that the market has allowed differentiation due to the traditional expectation that a woman would not be the breadwinner and would therefore work for less.

To require identification of some specific condition which the particular employer has imposed, is to misunderstand the nature of equal pay claims and the scheme of the Act, which is predicated on the assumption that it is not pure coincidence that some jobs done predominantly by women are paid less than those done predominantly by men. In other words, the 'condition' may be assumed as applying to a largely female profession; the question is whether the difference in pay can be justified, and it may be argued that where a particular occupation is staffed predominantly by women and is of equal value to one staffed predominantly by men, but there is a wide disparity in pay, it would be hard, if not impossible, to show that the difference arose from anything other than the mere fact that one occupation *was* female dominated.

10.7.4	The material factor defence: conclusions

The material factor defence could potentially be seen as operating at three different levels of generality. First, it might only arise where a difference in the 'personal equation' of the man and the woman, such as length of experience or qualifications, could be identified. This is the approach rejected in *Rainey*. Secondly, a factor might be identified going beyond the personal equation of the complainant although still amounting to a non sex-based difference between her and her comparator. At the present time this is the predominant approach. The most significant factor of this type and the one most likely to undermine the equal pay scheme is the 'market forces' factor which received some endorsement from the ECJ in *Enderby*. This factor is however subject to a rigorous application of the *Bilka* test; it does not mean that the laws of supply and demand can simply determine the rates of pay in question. Nevertheless, adoption of this second approach is likely to tend to retard the progress of the Act in removing pay discrimination.

Thirdly – and this defence would be available only in respect of equal *value* claims due to the wider wording applicable – there might be scope for a number of market-based arguments *not* founded on a difference between the man's and woman's case, such as using the leap-frogging argument from *Hayward* as being *in itself* a material factor, although arising only from the general operation of the concern in question. This possibility has not yet been put forward; it would, of course, be out of harmony with the policy of the Act and probably could not be termed an 'objectively justified reason' under the *Bilka* test.

As with sex discrimination it was apparent that the common law would not provide a sufficient remedy in this area. For example, in *Constantine v Imperial Hotels* (1944) only nominal damages were awarded in respect of clear racial discrimination although the applicant had claimed exemplary damages. There seemed to be a clear need for further measures and therefore the first Race Relations Act was passed in 1965; it was superseded by the 1968 Act and then by the 1976 Act. The 1976 Act is much more far-reaching than its predecessors; under the 1968 Act an individual had to complain to the Race Relations Board rather than take the complaint directly to court.

10.8 Racial discrimination: introduction

The 1976 Act was modelled on the Sex Discrimination Act; it makes discrimination a statutory tort, follows the same pattern as regards direct and indirect discrimination and sets up the Commission for Racial Equality with a similar role to the Equal Opportunities Commission (see below). It also operates in the same contexts and uses the same terms; therefore decisions under one of the two statutes affects the other. The Act provides a remedy for direct or indirect discrimination on racial grounds and the discrimination must occur within the areas covered by the Act: employment, education, housing, or the provision of goods and services.

However, there are some important differences between the two statutory schemes. The provisions under the Race Relations Act outlawing segregation and 'transferred discrimination' – discrimination on the grounds of another's race – have no counterparts under the Sex Discrimination Act. Employment covers 'pay', thus ensuring a less complex scheme than that in respect of sex discrimination claims.

The influence of the EC is less important, although rulings of the European Court of Justice and of the domestic courts taking EC provisions into account, may well affect concepts under the Race Relations Act. It should be noted that the EC has not ignored race discrimination, and has passed a number of resolutions and declarations giving guidance to Member States, but its influence in this area, although beginning to develop, is at a much earlier stage than its influence on sex discrimination. Aside from EC provisions, the UK is a party to a number of international declarations on race discrimination and xenophobia such as the International Convention on the Elimination of All Forms of Racial Discrimination, which although not part of UK law, may influence it.

10.9 The individual method: direct discrimination

Direct discrimination arises under s 1(1)(a), and the test to be applied mirrors that under the Sex Discrimination Act except that the unfavourable treatment in question must be on 'racial grounds'. This means that discrimination on the grounds of someone else's race is covered (transferred discrimination). For example, if, as in *Zarczynska v Levy* (1979), someone disobeyed an instruction to serve only whites and was dismissed for serving black customers that would be discrimination on racial grounds.

A decision made on racial grounds means that the alleged discriminator made a decision influenced by racial prejudice, but according to the ruling in *CRE ex p Westminster Council* (1984) this does not mean that the discriminator must have a racial motive. The council wanted to employ a black man as a refuse collector but withdrew the offer after pressure from the all-white work force. The CRE (Commission for Racial Equality) initiated a formal investigation and served a non-discrimination notice on the council. The council challenged the service of the notice by means of judicial review and sought *certiorari* on the basis that the CRE's findings were perverse – a finding that the CRE could not reasonably make. However, it was held that the decision *was* made on racial grounds, although it was found that the employer was not motivated by racial prejudice but by the desire to avoid industrial unrest. Nevertheless, that was irrelevant; the decision was *influenced* by racial prejudice although it was not the prejudice of the respondent.

10.9.1 Raising an inference of discrimination

Often the hardest task in a direct racial discrimination case will be proving that unfavourable treatment was on grounds of race. However, the decision in *Dornan* (1990) (mentioned above at para 10.2) will apply in race discrimination cases and will mean that once an inference has been raised that discrimination has occurred, the burden of proof will shift to the employer to prove that the decision in question was made on other grounds. Raising such an inference may involve obtaining statistical material from the employer.

In *West Midlands Passenger Transport Executive v Jaquant Singh* (1988) the applicant, who believed that he had been racially discriminated against as he had been refused promotion, wanted an order of discovery in respect of specific material held by his employers indicating the number of whites and non-whites appointed to senior posts. He claimed that if he was able to obtain access to the material he would be able to invite an inference of direct racial discrimination. The employers resisted discovery. The Court of Appeal held that discovery would be ordered only where it could be termed necessary, but that it could be so termed as the employee had to establish a discernible pattern of treatment towards his racial group, and there was no other way of raising the necessary inference.

Under s 1(2) of the Act it will be direct discrimination to maintain separate facilities for members of different races, even though they are equal in quality. However, if segregation grows up due to practices in the work force the employer will not come under an obligation to prevent it, according to the ruling in *Pel Ltd v Modgill* (1980), although this seems to be in conflict with s 32 of the Act which provides that an employer will be liable for acts done by employees in the course of employment unless he or she has taken reasonable steps to prevent such acts. It would seem that the employer should come under some obligation to prevent segregation even if he or she did not instigate it. Moreover, even if segregation in itself is not unlawful it may be that once a black/white divide in the work force is established, a practice of treating the black group differently may develop which will raise an irresistible inference of direct discrimination, even though such treatment might not raise such an inference if applied to an individual black worker.	10.9.2 Segregation
The tests to be applied under s 1(1)(b) are identical to those arising under the Sex Discrimination Act, apart from the need to show that a requirement or condition has been applied which hits disproportionately at persons of a particular racial group. Thus the first step in a case of indirect discrimination on racial grounds is for the applicant to define which racial group he or she belongs to. For example, an individual could be defined as non-British, non-white, Asian or a sub-group of Asian.	**10.10 The individual method: indirect discrimination**

The choice of group is important as discrimination affects racial groups differently. For example, a requirement to wear a skirt might be discriminatory against Muslim women but might not affect West Indian women. Therefore, if in such circumstances the applicant chose non-white as her group the claim would fail. However, if she chose Muslim and non-Muslim it would be more likely to succeed. The applicant should argue all possible groups in the alternative.

10.10.1   Racial group: interpretation

The applicant must show that the group falls within the definition of racial grounds in s 3(1) of the Act which covers 'colour, nationality, ethnic or national origins' and a racial group is defined by reference to the same. Employment of the concept of ethnic origins widens the meaning of racial group, and means that some religious groups may fall within it even though discrimination on the grounds of religion is not expressly covered. The leading case on the meaning of 'racial group' is *Mandla v Dowell Lee* (1983). The House of Lords had to consider whether Sikhs constituted an ethnic group, and defined the term 'ethnic group' as one having a long shared history and a cultural tradition of its own, often but not necessarily associated with religious observances. On that definition Sikhs were a racial group and fell within s 3(1).

This does not mean that a purely religious group will fall within s 3(1). Using this test it was found in *CRE v Dutton* (1989) that gypsies who have, it was noted, a shared history going back 700 years, may be termed a racial group. This definition of 'racial group' was considered further in *Dawkins v Dept. of Environment* (1993) in relation to the claim that Rastafarians constitute a racial group. It was found that the group in question must regard itself and be regarded by others as a distinct community by virtue of certain characteristics. The two essential characteristics were: a long shared history of which the group was conscious, and a cultural tradition of its own including family and social customs. Lord Fraser considered that there could be other relevant but not essential characteristics such as a common geographical origin, a common language, literature and religion.

It was found that Rastafarians did have a strong cultural tradition which included a distinctive form of music and a distinctive hair style. However, the shared history of Rastafarians as a separate group only went back 60 years; it was not enough for them to look back to a time when they in common with other Africans were taken to the Caribbean. That was not sufficient to mark them out as a separate group as it was an experience shared with other Afro-Caribbeans. It appears then that this first step is complex and, it might seem, not entirely free from ambiguity.

This next step according to *Perera v Civil Service Commission* (1983) is for the applicant to show that an absolute condition has been applied to him or her. In *Perera* this concerned a requirement that a candidate for the Civil Service had a good command of English. This requirement was sometimes waived; it was determined that it could not therefore amount to a 'requirement or condition' for indirect discrimination purposes. As noted above in relation to indirect sexual discrimination this decision has placed a brake on claims of indirect discrimination.

It was pointed out in *Meer v Tower Hamlets* (1988) by Balcombe LJ in the Court of Appeal that it allows discriminatory preferences free rein, as long as they are not expressed as absolute requirements. In that case a candidate who had previous experience working in the local authority was preferred although not absolutely required, and this had a tendency to debar non-British applicants. The CRE in its Second Review of the Race Relations Act 1994 recommended that this interpretation should be abandoned so that non-absolute criteria can be considered. It was found in *Orphanos v Queen Mary College* (1985) that if a condition can be identified the applicant must show that a 'considerably smaller proportion of his or her group can comply with it'.

Once the applicant has established a *prima facie* case of indirect discrimination the burden of proof shifts to the employer to show that the requirement or condition is justifiable. In *Ojutiku v Manpower Services Commission* (1982) two African students obtained places on a Polytechnic Management course but were refused grants by the MSC as they lacked industrial experience. They claimed that this requirement was indirectly discriminatory as it was more difficult for African applicants to show that they had previous management experience. However, the claim failed on the basis that the requirement could be justified. The test for justification was determined to be somewhat short of 'necessary', connoting a belief which would be justifiable if held on reasonable grounds, and this was reiterated in *Singh v British Railway Engineers* (1986). The applicant, who wore a turban in accordance with his religious beliefs, could not comply with a requirement to wear protective headgear and therefore had to take a less well paid job. It was found that while the requirement did have an adverse impact it was justifiable, partly because the other employees would resent exceptions being made.

However, the term 'justifiable' is now to be interpreted in accordance with the *Bilka* test which is applicable in sex discrimination cases (above at 10.3.4) and should therefore, by

10.10.2   The condition

10.10.3   Justifiability

extension, apply to the equivalent provision under the Race Relations Act according to *Hampson v DES* (1991). This accords with the ruling in *Rainey v Greater Glasgow Health Board* (1987) that the *Bilka-Kaufhaus* test would be applicable in sex discrimination and equal pay cases in respect of the grounds on which differential treatment could be justified. This is an important instance of the indirect influence of EC law on national provisions against racial discrimination.

10.10.4   Reform

The Commission for Racial Equality has criticised the interpretation of indirect discrimination and has proposed a new definition: any practice or policy which is continued or allowed should be unlawful if it has a 'significant adverse impact' on a particular racial group and is not necessary. It has further proposed that significant adverse impact should mean a 20% difference in impact between groups.

10.11   Discrimination by victimisation

Victimisation occurs when a discriminator treats a person less favourably for taking action under the Race Relations Act – for doing a 'protected act'. The provisions under the Act are almost identical to those under the Sex Discrimination Act and have the same aim – to deter employers and others from dismissing someone who undertakes a 'protected act'. Following *Aziz v Trinity St Taxis CA* (1988) there has to be a clear causal relationship between the action brought and the unfavourable treatment.

Aziz, a taxi driver and a member of TST, thought that TST were unfairly treating him and made a tape recording of a conversation to prove it. He took his claim to an industrial tribunal but it failed. He was then expelled from TST and claimed victimisation. The Court of Appeal considered the question of causation: had TST treated him less favourably by reason of what he had done in making the tapes with a view to bringing the case, or had it expelled him because of the breach of trust involved in making the tapes? It was found that the necessary causal relationship was not established; it was not apparent that TST were influenced in their decision to expel him by the fact that the tapes were made in order to bring a race relations case; they would have expelled him any way due to the breach of trust. This was a fine distinction to make and it is arguable that once a plaintiff has shown that unfavourable treatment has *some* causal relationship with a protected act, the burden of proof should shift to the employer to show that it was entirely unrelated to that act.

Like the Sex Discrimination Act the Race Relations Act cannot affect (a) discrimination which falls outside its scope or (b) discrimination enshrined in other statutes, even those which pre-date it (s 41(1)). In respect of (a) this includes racist behaviour falling outside the contexts covered by the Act (aside from that covered by the Public Order Act 1986: see above, Chapter 6) but also such behaviour occurring within those *contexts* but unable to find a legal niche within them due to the particular wording of the Act. For example, it was found in *De Souza v AA* (1986) that racial insults, as such, do not amount to 'unfavourable treatment' within employment.

The Act also employs the concept of a genuine occupational qualification but the GOQs are of much narrower scope. They come down to two. First, that for reasons of authenticity a person of a particular racial group must be employed. This might cover plays, and restaurants or clubs with a particular national theme. Second, the services being provided are aimed at persons of a specific racial group and can most effectively be provided by persons of that same racial group. In *Lambeth v CRE* (1990) it was determined that this requirement would be interpreted restrictively: a managerial position which involved little contact with the public would not fulfil it.

It is suggested that 'positive action' may take one of four forms: firstly reverse discrimination, which in its most absolute form would mean favourable treatment of a woman or a black merely due to gender or race; secondly, a presumption in favour of appointing a candidate from the disadvantaged group if his or her qualifications are roughly equal to those of a person from the non-disadvantaged group; thirdly, action to promote opportunities for members of the disadvantaged group in order to ensure that its members are in a strong position to compete for employment, or, fourthly, in its weakest form, adoption of equal opportunities policies particularly affecting advertising and recruiting.

The scope for positive action in the first two senses under the Sex Discrimination and Race Relations Acts is extremely limited. Acts done to meet the special needs of certain racial groups (such as by the provision of English language classes) in regard to education, welfare and training are permissible but such provision can only be made available where there were no or very few members of the group in question doing that work in the UK at the time. Also under s 37 employers can encourage applications from members of particular racial groups which are under-represented in the work force. Similarly, s 47(3) of the Sex Discrimination Act permits the restriction of access to training facilities to those 'in special

10.12   Lawful discrimination

10.13   Positive action

need of training by reason of the period for which they have been discharging domestic or family responsibilities'. It should be noted that employers and others are under no *duty* to make such provision.

But in general positive action is unlawful under the wording of s 1(1) of both statutes. Thus employers can pursue equal opportunities policies but it follows from *Riyat v London Borough of Brent* (1983) that in general they cannot appoint a less well qualified, or even equally well qualified, black or woman in order to address under-representation of black people or women caused by past discrimination. Except to a very limited extent positive action is also precluded under the Equal Treatment Directive following the decision in Case 450/93 *Kalanke v Freie Hansestadt Bremen* (1995). In the German public services an appointing procedure had been adopted whereby women with the same qualifications as men had to be given automatic priority in sectors in which they were under-represented. In evaluating qualifications family work, social commitment or unpaid activity could be taken into account if relevant to performance of the duties in question. Under-representation was deemed to exist when women did not make up at least half the staff in the individual pay brackets in the relevant personnel group or in the function levels provided for in the organisation chart. Mr Kalanke was not approved for promotion under this procedure and sought a ruling from the Bundesarbeitsgericht that the quota system was incompatible with the German basic law and the German civil code.

The Bundesarbeitsgericht considered that no such incompatibility arose since the system only favoured women where both sexes were equally qualified and, further, that once the quota system was interpreted in accordance with German basic law it meant that although in principle priority in promotions should be given to women exceptions must be made in appropriate cases. However, since the national court was uncertain that the system was in accord with the Equal Treatment Directive, it referred to the European Court of Justice questions relating to the scope of the derogations permitted to the principle of equal treatment under the Directive.

The court found that although there was a place for some positive action intended to combat past discrimination, national rules which guarantee women unconditional priority go beyond promoting equal opportunities and overstep the limits of the exception in Article 2(4). It drew a distinction between equality of opportunity and equality of outcome in finding that the quota system 'substitutes for equality of opportunity the result which is only to be arrived by providing such equality of opportunity'. Thus national rules of the present nature are precluded by Article 2(4). The court thus rejected the possibility, which it is suggested would have been open to it, of finding that the principle of proportionately had been sufficiently adhered to in instituting a quota system which was dependent on equality of qualifications and which, according to the national court would not be rigidly adhered to. It termed such a system 'unconditional', appearing to confuse positive action with reverse discrimination.

It may be argued that use of the quota system was warranted taking into account 'past inequalities', the traditional assignment of certain tasks to women and the concentration of women at the lower end of the scale'. The system appeared to be in accordance with substantive as opposed to formal equality in two respects; it sought to achieve an outcome which would counter past disadvantage and the system of assessing qualifications recognised the real and gendered situation in which women tend to take part in employment.

10.14   Remedies

The various remedies available, which are applicable in both race and sex discrimination cases, are generally perceived as inadequate as are the means of enforcing them. A tribunal can award a declaration which simply states the rights of the applicant and the respect in which the employer has breached the law. It can also award an action recommendation which will be intended to reduce the effect of the discrimination. However, the EAT in *British Gas plc v Sharma* (1991) held that this could not include a recommendation that the applicant be promoted to the next suitable vacancy as this would amount to positive discrimination. However, it might be argued that this would merely be putting the person in the position he or she should have been in rather than giving them a special preference due to race or sex.

It can also award compensation which will be determined on the same basis as in other tort cases. It will be awarded for financial loss and injury to feelings and substantial damages may be available under this head. Awards have tended to be low but they rose after the decision in *Noone* (1988) in which a consultant who was not appointed on grounds of race was awarded £3,000 for injury to feelings. In *Alexander v H O* (1988) it was held that awards for injury to feelings should not be minimal because this would tend to trivialise the public policy to which the Act gives effect. On the other hand they should be restrained and therefore should not be set at the same level as damages for defamation. £500 was awarded for injured feelings due to racial discrimination. The legislation placed an upper limit on awards which was equivalent to that payable under the compensatory award for unfair dismissal. However, the upper limit on damages in respect of sex discrimination was challenged before the European Court of Justice in *Marshall v Southampton and South-West Hampshire AHA (No 2)* (1993). The court found that the fixing of an upper limit of this nature was contrary to the principle underlying the Equal Treatment Directive since it was not consistent with the principle of ensuring real equality of opportunity. In response to this decision the upper limit for compensation under the Sex Discrimination Act was no longer lawful. The upper limit under the Race Relations Act was abolished under SI 1993/2798, Race Relations Remedies Act 1994.

No compensation is payable in respect of indirect discrimination unless there has been an intention to discriminate; this exclusion from the compensation scheme has been much criticised and may contravene European law. In the *Von Colson* case (1984) the European Court of Justice held that any sanction must have a real deterrent effect. Most significantly, it found in *Marshall v Southampton and SW Hampshire AHA* (1993) that the compensation should be capable of making good the loss in full. Thus it may be in accordance with this decision to pay compensation in respect of indirect discrimination even where there is no intention to discriminate.

It is fairly common for the defendant to fail to comply with the award. The applicant must then return to court in order to enforce it. If an action recommendation has not been complied with the tribunal will award compensation but only if compensation could have been awarded at the original hearing. As this is unlikely to be the case in an indirect discrimination claim there will be no remedy available except to apply to the CRE and the EOC alleging persistent discrimination.

10.15   Efficacy of the individual method

How successful has the individual method of bringing about change been? In 1976 there were 243 applications in respect of sex discrimination of which 40% were heard and 10% were successful, while in the same year there were 146 applications in respect of race discrimination of which 45% were heard and 3.4% were successful. In 1985 there were 26 applications in respect of sex discrimination of which 34% were heard and 19% were successful; there were 69 applications in respect of race discrimination of which 37% were heard and 11.6% were successful.

The number of applications began to decline from 1976 onwards although there is evidence that it is beginning, in the 1990s, to rise again. Possibly this is because the success rate is so low that applicants are deterred from ever bringing a claim in the first place. In other words, the number of applications may be self-limiting: only the very determined applicants will pursue cases all the way to a hearing. Of course, the decline in the rate of applications may be partly attributable to the initial rush to attack very blatant examples of sexism and racism which died away as employers and others began to ensure that policies enshrining such values were either abolished or made less overt.

Also, less than half of the applications are heard; there is obviously a strong tendency to give up a claim half way through. There may be a number of reasons why cases are not brought, why they are abandoned and why the success rate is so low. Obviously the applicant is in a very vulnerable position; the position of the parties is usually unequal especially if an applicant is bringing the claim against his or her employer. The applicant will be afraid of being labelled a troublemaker, perhaps of being sacked or of losing promotion prospects. There may be continual pressure not only on the applicant but on any work mates who have consented to act as witnesses in the claim, and they may withdraw their consent to act.

The weakness of the remedies is unlikely to encourage claims and the complexity and technicality of the substantive law may also act as a deterrent. It may do so in any event but coupled with the lack of legal aid the task facing the applicant may appear overwhelming. These two factors are exacerbated by and also contribute to the lack of experience tribunal members have of discrimination cases. The applicant may be aided by the EOC or the CRE but both have to refuse the majority of applications due to their lack of funds. This leads to a poor quality of decision-making and to the charge that the employers' lawyers may manipulate the members of the tribunal due to their lack of experience in the area. Thus a vicious circle is set up. The tribunals need more experience in these cases but do not receive it due to the factors mentioned here; when a tribunal does hear such a case it may deal with it badly, thereby having the effect of deterring future applicants and ensuring that tribunals do not gain more experience.

The CRE has proposed that there should be a discrimination decision of Industrial Tribunals dealing only with discrimination claims. Such tribunals would gather expertise in such cases and could be equipped with powers to order higher levels of compensation. Legal aid could be made available in this specialist division even though it remained unavailable in respect of other tribunal cases.

10.16   Administrative methods of combatting race and sex discrimination

Apart from the individual method of bringing about change there are also a number of 'administrative methods' which may be able to effect general change. The Race Relations and Sex Discrimination Acts contain an 'administrative method' which was included with the aim of relieving the burden on individual applicants. It may also represent a more coherent approach than the piecemeal method of bringing individual cases. The aim was to bring about general changes in discriminatory practices rather than waiting for an individual to take on the risk of bringing a case.

10.16.1   Investigative and remedial powers of the Commission for Racial Equality and the Equal Opportunities Commission

Both the CRE and the EOC have two main powers. They can assist claimants and they can issue a non-discrimination notice in respect of discriminatory practices where there may be no known victim who wants to bring a claim. This may be because the company or institution has effectively deterred certain people from coming forward with applications for a job. If indications of race discrimination appear – if, for example it appears that very few of a certain group are employed – then first a formal investigation will be conducted.

This decision might be taken if, for example, the workforce was only 1% black although the company was in a racially mixed area in which black people comprised about 20% of the population. It may be that the recruiting policy is indirectly discriminatory; for example it may largely be by word of mouth and therefore the existing workforce may tend to reproduce itself. Similarly, a formal investigation might be undertaken if a company employed a large number of women but very few above a certain level. However, the CRE (and by extension the EOC) has had the use of the power to issue a non-discrimination notice curbed by the House of Lords' decision in *CRE ex p Prestige Group* (1984). It was found that the CRE is not entitled to investigate a named person or company unless it already has a strong reason to believe that discrimination has occurred.

Thus the CRE and the EOC are now confined to a reactive approach; they can only react to very blatant forms of discrimination. They cannot investigate more subtle and insidious instances of discrimination which may be the more pernicious. After the *Prestige* decision the CRE had to abandon a number of investigations which it had already begun. There has therefore been a tendency for subtle institutionalised racism to continue unchecked, although more blatant racism such as the phrase 'no blacks', which used to appear in advertisements, has now disappeared.

Although the investigative powers of the EOC have been curbed it may be able to bring about general changes in discriminatory practices by seeking a direct change in domestic law in reliance on Community law. In *Secretary of State for Employment ex p EOC* (1994) it was found that the EOC can seek a declaration in judicial review proceedings to the effect that primary UK legislation is not in accord with EC equality legislation. Certain provisions of the Employment Protection (Consolidation) Act 1978 governed the right not to be unfairly dismissed, compensation for unfair dismissal and the right to statutory redundancy pay. These rights did not apply to workers who worked less than the specified number of hours a week. The Equal Opportunities Commission considered that since the majority of those working for less than the specified number of hours were women, the provisions operated to the disadvantage of women and were therefore discriminatory. The EOC accordingly wrote to the Secretary of State for Employment expressing this view and arguing that since the provisions in question were indirectly discriminatory they were in breach of EC law.

The Secretary of State replied by letter that the conditions excluding part-timers from the rights in question were justifiable and therefore not indirectly discriminatory. The EOC applied for judicial review of the Secretary of State's refusal to accept that the UK was in breach of its obligations under EC law. The application was amended to bring in an individual, Mrs Day, who worked part time and had been made redundant by her employers. It was found that Mrs Day's claim was a private law claim which could not be advanced against the Secretary of State who was not her employer and was not liable to meet the claim if it was successful.

The Secretary of State further argued that the EOC had no *locus standi* to bring the proceedings. However, the House of Lords found that since the EOC had a duty under s 53(1) of the Sex Discrimination Act to work for the elimination of discrimination, it was within its remit to try to secure a change in the provisions under consideration, and therefore the EOC had a sufficient interest to bring the proceedings and hence *locus standi*. The Secretary of State also argued that no decision or justiciable issue susceptible of judicial review existed. However, the House of Lords found that although the letter itself was not a decision, the provisions themselves could be challenged in judicial review proceedings. In other words, the real question was whether judicial review was available for the purpose of securing a declaration that certain UK primary legislation was incompatible with EC law, and, following

10.16.2   Direct challenge to UK law

Secretary of State for Transport ex p Factortame (1992) it appeared that judicial review was so available.

As regards the substantive issue – whether the provisions in question, while admittedly discriminatory, could be justified – the House of Lords thought that in certain special circumstances an employer might be justified in differentiating between full and part-time workers to the disadvantage of the latter, but that such differentiation, employed nationwide, could not be justified. Thus the EOC, but not an individual applicant, was entitled to bring judicial review proceedings in order to secure a declaration that UK law was incompatible with EC law. Declarations were made that the conditions set out in the provisions in question were indeed incompatible with EC law.

This was a very far-reaching decision: it means that where UK legislation is incompatible with EC law a declaration can be obtained to that effect more rapidly than if it was necessary to wait for an individual affected to bring a case against the particular person or body who was acting within the terms of the UK legislation in question. The decision may not directly have an effect on race discrimination but it opens the possibility that the EOC may challenge other provisions of UK law as out of accord with EC law, and where such provisions have an equivalent under the Race Relations Act they will also be affected.

10.16.3   The EOC and CRE: directions for reform

The CRE and the EOC have made a number of proposals for reform which would strengthen the administrative method and allow it to work more closely in harmony with the individual method. The CRE wants to try to narrow the gap between individual cases and what can be achieved by a formal investigation and has proposed that in order to do this it should be able to join in the individual's case as a party to the action so as to draw attention to the likelihood of further discrimination occurring. Thus, the individual would receive the remedy but the general effect of discrimination in the defendant company would be addressed by issuing a non-discrimination notice at the same time. This may be supported on the ground that if one individual brings a successful case against an employer it is probable that discrimination in that concern is quite widespread. Both the EOC and the CRE want legislation to reverse the *Prestige* decision. They want to be able to launch investigations into a named person or company even when there is no initial strong evidence of discrimination.

The EOC has recommended that equal pay and sex discrimination provisions should be combined in one statute and that the distinction between indirect and direct discrimination as regards compensation should be abolished. Thus, where a person had acted in an indirectly discriminatory fashion, although unmotivated by sexism, compensation would still be payable. This is desirable because there is evidence that some employers have deliberately failed to conduct a review of working practices so as to be able to put forward a convincing argument that they did not appreciate the discriminatory affect of certain practices.

10.16.4   Contract compliance

A particular type of positive action known as 'contract compliance' which had the potential to produce beneficial effects was largely outlawed under s 17 of the Local Government Act 1988. Under this method, organs of the state such as local authorities produced a 'check list' of equal opportunities policies and asked the companies with which it was thinking of dealing to show evidence of compliance with such policies. If the company could not show in response that certain procedures were in place intended to combat racism or sexism it lost business. However, Parliament left intact a limited power to vet potential contractors as regards their race relations record under s 18 of the 1988 Act.

Freedom from Discrimination

This concept is governed by s 1(1)(a) of the Sex Discrimination Act 1975. It involves showing that the applicant has been less favourably treated than a comparable man has been or would be treated. Firstly the woman must show that there has been differentiation in the treatment afforded to herself and a man (or a hypothetical man). Secondly she must show that her treatment has been less favourable, and thirdly that but for her sex she would have been treated in the same way as the man. The plaintiff bears the burden of showing that the differential treatment was on grounds of sex and not for some neutral reason. However, once the woman has raised a *prima facie* inference of discrimination, the burden will shift to the employer to show that the differentiation occurred on non-discriminatory grounds.

Direct discrimination on grounds of sex

James v Eastleigh BC (1989)
Dornan v Belfast CC (1990)
Webb v Emo (1994)

This concept was imported into the 1975 Act under ss 1(1)(b) and there are four stages in operating it. Firstly, it must be shown that a condition has been applied to the applicant. This must be a specific requirement which is never waived. Secondly, it must be shown that the condition is one which will have a disproportionate impact on women because in practice less women than men will be able to comply with it. Thirdly, the burden of proof shifts to the employer to show that there are grounds on which the condition is objectively justifiable regardless of sex. Fourthly, if the employer cannot show that the requirement is genuinely needed for the job the woman must show that it is to her detriment because she cannot comply with it.

Indirect discrimination on grounds of sex

Jones v Chief Adjudication Officer (1990)
Price v Civil Service Commission (1978)
Bilka-Kaufhaus GmbH v Weber von Hartz (1986)
Hampson v Department of Education and Science (1989)
Perera v Civil Service Commission (1983)

A woman who is doing like work, work rated as equivalent or work of equal value to that of a man in the same employment can claim equal pay with him under the Equal Pay 1970. Once

Equal pay

a claimant has chosen a comparator it must be shown that he (or they - more than one comparator may be chosen) is working in the same establishment or is employed by the same employer *and* that broadly speaking the same conditions of employment are observed. The Industrial Tribunal will then appoint an independent expert in order to determine whether the two jobs are equal; if they are a term governing pay in the claimant's contract will be compared with a similar term in the comparator's and unless the employer has a defence under s 1(3) an equality clause will equalise the two terms. The defence will operate if a material difference between the cases of the woman and man can be identified which is *not the difference of sex*. The defence may operate if market forces untainted by indirect discrimination have led to the difference in pay.

Pickstone v Freemans (1988)
Hayward v Cammell Laird (1988)
Leverton v Clwyd County Council (1989)
Rainey v Greater Glasgow Health Board (1986)
Enderby v Frenchay HA (1992)
Barber and Others v NCR (Manufacturing) Ltd (1993)
Handels-og Kontorfunk-tionaerernes Forbund i Danmark v Dansk Arbejdsgiverforening (the *Danfoss* case) (1989)

Direct discrimination on grounds of race

Direct discrimination arises under s 1(1)(a) of the Race Relations Act 1976 and the tests to be applied mirror those under the Sex Discrimination Act except that the unfavourable treatment in question must be on 'racial grounds' in the sense that it was influenced by racial prejudice.

R v CRE ex p Westminster Council (1984)
West Midlands Passenger Transport Executive v Jaquant Singh (1988)

Indirect discrimination on grounds of race

The tests to be applied are identical to those arising under the Sex Discrimination Act, apart from the need to show that a requirement or condition has been applied which hits proportionately at persons of a particular racial group. The applicant must show that the group falls within the definition of racial grounds in s 3(1) of the Act which covers 'colour, nationality, ethnic or national origins' and a racial group is defined by reference to the same. The two essential characteristics of a group with the same ethnic origins are: a long shared history of which the group was conscious, and a cultural tradition of its own including family and social customs.

Mandla v Dowell Lee (1983)

Orphanos v Queen Mary College (1985)
Singh v British Railway Engineers (1986)
Hampson v DES (1991)
Rainey v Greater Glasgow Health Board (1986)

The administrative method

Both the CRE and the EOC have two main powers. They can assist claimants and they can institute a formal investigation with a view to issuing a non-discrimination notice in respect of institutionalised discriminatory practices in a particular body. However, they cannot investigate a named person or company unless they already have a strong reason to believe that discrimination has occurred. The CRE and the EOC have made a number of proposals for reform which would strengthen the administrative method and allow it to work more closely in harmony with the individual method. In *R v Secretary of State for Employment ex p EOC* (1994) it was found that the EOC can seek a declaration in judicial review proceedings to the effect that primary UK legislation is not in accord with EC equality legislation.

R v CRE ex p Prestige Group (1984)
R v Secretary of State for Employment ex p EOC (1994)

Index